A New English Course

This ____ is designed to meet the needs of those s____ GCSE and similar first examinations in English Language. It can be used either in class or for private study. Students are reminded that different examining boards have different requirements. They are advised to study past papers or specimen papers actually set by the examining board for which they are sitting to ensure that they understand the form of the examination set by that particular examining board. A special Examination Handbook giving registration procedures is available free to students of the National Extension College from NEC, 18 Brooklands Avenue, Cambridge CB2 2HN (£3.00 to non-students).

The course was originally designed for GCE O Level, and the material is most suitable for students in the top half of the ability range taking GCSE. Much of the text remains unchanged, covering as it does guidance and practice in such fundamental skills as writing, comprehension, language work, vocabulary, spelling and response to literature. Appendices on multiple-choice comprehension, spoken English and course work have been added to bring the course into line with the requirements of the new GCSE examinations.

A New English Course

An Approach to GCSE English Language

for Individual Study or Class Use

Third Edition

with appendices on
Multiple Choice Comprehension
Spoken English and Course Work

by

Rhodri Jones

HEINEMANN
EDUCATIONAL

in conjunction with
THE NATIONAL EXTENSION COLLEGE
CAMBRIDGE

Heinemann Educational Books Ltd
Halley Court, Jordan Hill, Oxford OX2 8EJ

OXFORD   LONDON   EDINBURGH
MADRID   ATHENS   BOLOGNA   PARIS
MELBOURNE   SYDNEY   AUCKLAND   SINGAPORE   TOKYO
IBADAN   NAIROBI   HARARE   GABORONE
PORTSMOUTH NH (USA)

ISBN 0 435 10501 9

Printed and bound in Great Britain by
Thomson Litho Ltd, East Kilbride, Scotland

Contents

UNIT 1

THE AIMS OF THE COURSE

What you will learn from this course.

THE SCOPE OF THE COURSE

Explaining how each unit is divided into sections, what you will learn from each section, and how it all fits together.

HOW TO WORK

Advice on the best way to tackle the course. An important section that you will want to refer back to.

ASSIGNMENT A

A preliminary test, with some advice on how to tackle it, that will allow you and your teacher to see your current skills, and provide you with a starting point for getting down to work in Unit 2.

THE AIMS OF THE COURSE

This course aims to develop your skills in writing, reading and understanding English. We feel confident that if you are prepared to work conscientiously through the course you will have the satisfaction of knowing you are well able to tackle with a quiet mind most problems posed by communicating in English.

The course is designed to help you to help yourself. You will have a tutor/teacher to help you but the effort you put into your work and the satisfaction you gain from it will be all your own. It is not just a course to help you pass an examination—though, obviously, passing the examination is the desired end and everything possible is done to help you reach that end: the course is intended to be interesting in itself; it will deepen your understanding and appreciation of everything you read and will give you greater confidence in anything you may be called upon to write, be it a dutiful letter or a speech expressing your point of view at a meeting or a conference. In Arnold Wesker's play *Roots* one of the characters talks of words as being like bridges. Without words we cannot build bridges between ourselves and other people. The purpose of this course is to help you to build bridges more effectively, to communicate more meaningfully, and at a deeper level, with other people.

THE SCOPE OF THIS COURSE

This course will develop your ability to write, read and understand—and these are the skills that will be tested in the examination.

Writing; Reading and Understanding

After some preliminary advice on how to tackle an essay and a comprehension exercise, each unit will take a particular type of writing and examine it from the point of view of understanding a passage written in this style and then from the point of view of you yourself being asked to write in this style. The styles vary from descriptions to arguments, to factual accounts. In this way, it is hoped that you will become familiar with the various approaches that are possible and so will feel at ease when any kind of writing is presented to you in the examination.

Alongside this study of different types of writing, there will be sections concentrating on grammar and accuracy. You must get this question of accuracy into perspective. It is much more important to say or write something interesting, even if you sometimes make mistakes in spelling or punctuation, than to write accurately but say nothing of interest. In the final resort, content (the ideas

1

you have, the excitement you create in a reader, the vividness with which you present your ideas) is much more important than presentation (accurate spelling, correct paragraphing, neat sentence structure). Clearly, of course, you should try to achieve both, and the grammatical accuracy of your writing is not something to reject or despise. On the contrary, it is something that needs to be worked at and perfected, but this will come gradually with study. Consequently, there will be sections in each unit which are intended to help you towards this. The point I am making here is that you should not be too concerned at first if you mis-spell or forget to put in a full stop. The first step is to learn to write in a lively and interesting way.

The sections dealing with accuracy in the use of English fall into three sections: Vocabulary, Language and Spelling.

Vocabulary

In the first, an attempt will be made to encourage you to extend your knowledge of English words so that you can understand more easily a wider range of writing and can make the words your own and use them in your own writing.

Language

'Language' will deal with various aspects of the organization and presentation of words—the use of the full stop, figures of speech, the punctuation of speech, for example. In the 'Language' sections of this course much ground may be covered that is already well known to you, but in a course that hopes to be comprehensive, it will be necessary to go back to the first principles of writing and setting out material, even if this may seem at times obvious or elementary. Therefore, if you are confident that you know the points being discussed, bear with me and take this opportunity to refresh your memory about them. Other students may be meeting them for the first time. In any case, I hope the points made will be interesting in themselves and that they will help you in your own writing.

Spelling

The 'Spelling' sections will bring to your attention certain facts or rules about how words are spelled which should help you to be more accurate in this respect.

For a general book which discusses and explains points of grammar, usage, spelling, punctuation, prosody, etc. I should like to recommend my own book: *English Language Reference Book*, Rhodri Jones (Blackie). Many of the questions which will be raised in the Language and Spelling sections of this course—and many others—are itemized in this reference book, and you could find it a useful source of information when in doubt about points of grammar or expression.

Reading List

In addition, the units will provide brief lists of books. We would like you to read, or at least dip into, some of the books suggested here. Of course, the units themselves will provide you with a large variety of extracts from different books and other sources, but these in themselves will inevitably be rather short and there is not space to give a fully comprehensive and thorough range of reading. It is important, therefore, that you should try to do more reading on your own, to extend your horizons by exploring the printed word in as many guises as you can. First and foremost, this is for your own enjoyment. As far as the examination requirements are concerned, you don't have to read any books, but reading books is likely to increase your chances of passing by providing you with a wider background. And in any case, there is an element of studying under false pretences if you claim to be studying the English Language and the only pieces of English writing you actually read are contained in this course.

HOW TO WORK

1. Regular Working Sessions

It is important that you organize your work on a regular basis. Set aside regular sessions during the week which you will devote to work on the course. These sessions should be of reasonable length—at least an hour and a half and probably two hours.

2. Quick Reading and Close Study

There is a difference between quick reading and close study. It is often a good idea to read through your Unit, or a section of it, quickly the first time to get a general idea of the main drift of the lesson, but that is not enough. Later, you will have to go through the notes slowly and carefully, checking all the time that you have understood the points being made. You may have to study some sections several times before this is achieved.

3. Keeping Notes

One way of consolidating work and proving to yourself that you have understood the units is to make a summary of the important points. When you think you have understood a particular section, tabulate the main points in a notebook. These can be useful not only as a check that you have understood the points but also as a convenient source for revising work without reading the whole unit. We suggest that you keep a loose-leaf file, with dividers, labelled according to the sections of this course: not because these divisions are ultimately relevant to your understanding and skill in using the English Language— on the contrary, what you are learning is all part of the same thing—but because a systematic approach is an important aid to learning.

You would include in your notebook all your written work—your rough jottings and your written work for your tutor. This has two purposes:

(i) to encourage you to be critical of everything you write as you write;
(ii) to keep an honest record of everything you do. We hope you will look back through your notebook from time to time and use your increased experience to assess your earlier work. Self-criticism is an important part of this course and you will gradually learn to judge for yourself the quality of your own work.

Here are some suggestions for the sort of things you might include in your notebook:

Writing

Notes on the course material.
Your own essay outlines and essays.
The essays you write for your tutor.
Answers to questions in the 'Writing' sections of the course.
Topics you come across in, say, newspapers or TV that you feel you would find interesting to write about.
Extracts from newspapers or books you found particularly interesting.
Notes on unusual images you meet in your reading.

Reading and Understanding

Your answers to the exercises in the course.
Notes on the course material.
Extracts from newspapers.
Your comments on TV programmes, discussions you have witnessed, local issues discussed in the news.

Vocabulary

Notes and answers to exercises in the course material.
Unusual words you meet in your reading (don't just write them down with a dictionary meaning—try to use them in a sentence).

Language

Newspaper cuttings or book extracts that illustrate particularly well points you meet in the course.

Spelling

Notes on the course material—add to the lists you learn from the course.
Write out words you often get wrong.

Reading

Jot down your thoughts on the books you read. Does one character particularly interest you, and why?
Did one point of view presented strike you particularly?
You will find many more ideas as you work on.

4. Revision

There are two kinds of revision. The first is going over units or notes again to refresh your memory of the points made and to help you to remember them more firmly. This is important particularly before the examination itself, but also before doing a particular piece of work where relevant material has been discussed previously. Keep going back to previous units and make sure that you understand and remember the points made. Efficient notes of your own will be invaluable here.

The second kind of revision is checking over work carefully and making any alterations that you think will improve it. Some poets, like W. B. Yeats, are not satisfied with a poem they have written until they have made as many as fifty different versions, and even with the fiftieth they are not entirely convinced that this is the best possible version. You won't have time to write fifty different versions of an essay—and we don't expect you to! But don't rush at your work and hand in your first draft to be marked. You should be prepared to write two or three drafts to improve the detail and shape of what you write. The revision may involve changing a dull adjective to a more telling one or combining two short sentences into one longer one or changing the order of the paragraphs or omitting a paragraph altogether, but attention to detail can make all the difference. You must try to approach your work in this self-critical way, asking yourself all the time if this is the best possible word or the best possible order. The poet Coleridge defined poetry as 'the best words in the best order', and the same applies to prose in a less intense way. The best words in the best order don't choose themselves. They require thought and second thoughts and third thoughts. Only by constantly exposing your writing to this kind of scrutiny can you hope to improve its quality.

5. Extra Exercises

This course is designed as the minimum you should do if you hope to have a reasonable chance of passing GCSE English Language. Wherever possible, work out extra exercises you can do to consolidate the points being studied. It is not difficult to devise extra work of this kind. For instance, you can make notes for two essay subjects before deciding on the one you will finally write. You can look up the meaning of words in your current reading in a dictionary to add to your notebook. You can find further examples of words that obey a particular spelling rule. You can summarize the main points in a newspaper article or make a report of a speech. These are all ways in which the work of the course can be expanded and you can gain further practice in building up the necessary background ready to face the examination.

6. Odd Moments

In 1. I suggested that you should work in regular and reasonably long sessions, but some of the work could be effectively done in odd moments—while travelling to work or school, during a lunch break, while waiting to go out. The kinds of work suited to moments like these are learning spellings or going over a summary of relevant points in your mind or checking up meanings of words in a dictionary. No moment is so brief that it is useless.

7. Assignments

Throughout the course, you will be given assignments, twelve in all, which will consist of exercises to test that you have understood the points made in the units and that you are making satisfactory progress. These assignments will normally require about three hours' work if they are done conscientiously—perhaps longer to start with.

As well as these assignments you will be expected to do other work in the course of the units which will enable you to practise points discussed. This is for your own benefit and you should try to learn to criticize your own work as objectively as you can. The tutor or teacher is there to help you, but he can only do so much. The important point of this course is to help you to help yourself. It is mainly by learning to look at your own work in a critical and objective way that you will learn to improve and to distinguish between what is mediocre and what has quality. If you achieve this, then it will be something that will be with you for the rest of your life.

8. Regular Reading

I make no apology for repeating my belief in regular outside reading. Try to read something every day, even if it is only a newspaper or magazine. Try to set aside a regular daily period for reading, for example, after tea or before bed. Make notes about what you read, for example, the summary of an article in a newspaper that you have read and that may be of use if you were to write an essay on that subject, or an account of your reactions to a novel you have read (or a film you have seen). Writing about what you read enables you to remember what you read and helps you to be more critical as you read. If you are going to make a written evaluation of a novel, your critical faculties will be more alert as you read. Use a dictionary with your reading and note new words which you could introduce into your own vocabulary. You may not wish to interrupt the flow of your reading by looking up the word when you come across it, but try to go back on it to check the meaning when you have time. In Unit 2 we will give you advice on how to use a dictionary.

About Assignment A

It is necessary at the beginning of your course to have some idea of your current skills so that your tutor or teacher can have a clear impression of your strengths and weaknesses and can advise you accordingly. That is the purpose of this first assignment. It consists of two questions, an essay and a comprehension exercise. Don't worry if you find these assignments difficult. Give them your full concentration and answer them as well and as honestly as you can.

I do not intend to give much advice on how to set about writing an essay at this stage as it is likely to be the kind of task you will have attempted at some time during your previous education. You may, however, find the comprehension exercise more difficult to approach, and I am presenting you with a short specimen passage with suggested questions and answers which you can study before going on to the comprehension exercise in the Assignment itself. *Look back now at 'How to Study' section 2.*

The passage for study is taken from John Braine's novel Room at the Top. *Read it carefully two or three times and then study the questions and suggested answers below:*

The Leddersford Conservative Club was a large Italianate building in the centre of the city. The stone had been a light biscuit colour originally—sometimes I wonder if all nineteenth-century architects weren't a bit wrong in the head—and a hundred years of smoke had given it an unhealthy mottled appearance. The carpet inside the foyer was plum-coloured and ankle-deep, the furniture was heavy and dark and Victorian, and everything that could be polished, right down to the stair-rods, gave off a bright glow. It smelled of cigars and whisky and sirloin, and over it hung a brutally heavy quiet. There were a great many pictures of Conservative notabilities: they shared a sort of mean sagacity of expression, with watchful eyes and mouths like spring-traps, clamped hard on the thick juicy steak of success.

(JOHN BRAINE, *Room at the Top*)

Q. Using your own words as far as possible describe the exterior of the Leddersford Conservative Club.
A. The Leddersford Conservative Club was a large and ornate building in the Italian style. It had once been light brown in colour but was now discoloured by smoke and patchy in appearance.

Q. What does the narrator mean when he says, 'sometimes I wonder if all nineteenth-century architects weren't a bit wrong in the head,' and what does this remark tell us about his character and attitudes?

A. By this comment, the writer means that only someone who was lacking in intelligence would think of designing a building in this light-coloured stone in a smoky industrial city where it was certain to be turned black. He implies that all nineteenth-century architects are prone to this kind of mistake and lack of common sense.

The comment shows us that the narrator is realistic and down-to-earth, brooking no fancy artistic ideas. It implies that he has some knowledge of architecture, but the sweeping way in which he condemns *all* nineteenth-century architects suggests that he may be arrogant and self-opinionated.

Q. What impression does the author wish to give by saying the carpet was 'ankle-deep'?

A. By calling the carpet 'ankle-deep', the author implies that the carpet is so thick that you sink up to your ankles in the pile. He is exaggerating in order to create the impression that the carpet is luxuriously thick.

Q. What is significant about the way the Club smelled?

A. The author says the Club smelled of 'cigars and whisky and sirloin'. These are expensive items which suggest a life of ease made possible by money and success. They also suggest a very male world where women don't intrude.

Q. In your own words describe what the Conservative notabilities looked like.

A. The Conservative notabilities all had the same kind of appearance. They looked shrewd but tight-fisted. Their eyes were alert and their mouths tightly shut with a self-satisfied smugness.

Q. What is the narrator's attitude towards the building and its furnishings? Quote words or phrases that justify your answer.

A. The narrator is very hostile towards the Club and what it represents. The outward appearance is 'unhealthy'; the quiet in the Club is 'brutal' and 'heavy'; the portraits of the Conservative notabilities look 'mean' and they have mouths 'like spring-traps'. All of these words quoted have unpleasant associations and suggest dislike.

 ASSIGNMENT A

Take about an hour and a half over the planning and writing of Part I and try to write at least 500 words. Part II should take about an hour.

Look back now at *How to Study* section 4. When you have written your first draft of the essay go over it carefully, re-organizing and re-writing as you need. Try to limit yourself to an hour and a half as we suggest, spending about half an hour on preparation and about an hour on writing and revising your essay.

Part I Essay

Write an essay on *one* of the following. It could be a story, a description, an essay presenting a point of view, or a personal account of your own experience.

1. The Stranger
2. Travelling Abroad
3. The Younger Generation
4. Looking for a House
5. Bringing up a Family
6. The Wreck.

Part II Comprehension

Read the following passage carefully several times and answer the questions that are set below as fully as you can. The passage is a continuation of that used in the specimen comprehension exercise above.

I felt a cold excitement. This was the place where the money grew. A lot of rich people patronized expensive hotels and roadhouses and restaurants too; but you could never be really sure of their grade, because you only needed the price of a drink or a meal and a collar and tie to be admitted. The Leddersford Conservative Club, with its ten-guinea annual subscription plus incidentals ('Put me down for a hundred, Tom, if the Party doesn't get it the Inland Revenue will') was for rich men only. Here was the place where decisions were taken, deals made between soup and sweet. Here was the place where the right word or smile or gesture could transport one into a higher grade overnight. Here was the centre of the country I'd so long tried to conquer; here magic worked, here the smelly swineherd became the prince who wore a clean shirt every day.

I gave my name to the commissionaire. 'Mr Lampton? Yes, Sir, Mr Brown has a luncheon appointment with you. He's been unavoidably delayed, but he asked you to wait in the bar.' He looked at me a trifle doubtfully; not having had time to change I was wearing my light grey suit and brown shoes, my former Sunday best. The shoes were still good but much too heavy for the suit, and the suit was too tight and too short in the jacket. Third-rate tailors always make clothes too small. I saw, or fancied that I saw, a look of contempt in the commissionaire's eye, so I put back the shilling I was going to give him into my pocket. (It was fortunate that I did; afterwards I found out that you never tip club servants.)

The bar was crowded with business men slaving to help the export drive. An attempt had been made to modernize it; the carpet was a glaring zigzag of blue and green and yellow and the bar was topped with some kind of plastic and faced with what appeared to be black glass. There wasn't any sign that it was a stamping-ground reserved for the higher grades, unless you counted the picture of Churchill above the bar—a picture which you could find in most pubs anyway. And by no means all of them spoke Standard English. Leddersford's main manufacture is textiles and most of its ruling class receive their higher education at the Technical College where to some extent they're forced

to rub shoulders with the common people and consequently pick up traces of a Northern accent.

(JOHN BRAINE, *Room at the Top*)

1. What are the differences between the people who go to
   the expensive hotels or restaurants and those who go
   to the Leddersford Conservative Club?
2. What does the author imply by each of the following
   comments?

   (a) 'I felt a cold excitement.'
   (b) 'deals were made between soup and sweet.'
   (c) 'here the smelly swineherd became the prince who
       wore a clean shirt every day.'

3. Comment on the author's repetition of the word 'here'
   in the first paragraph and the following phrases.
   What effect is the author trying to create?
4. Why did the commissionaire look at Lampton 'a trifle
   doubtfully'?
5. 'I saw, *or fancied that I saw*, a look of contempt in
   the commissionaire's eye.' What does the phrase in
   italics tell us about how Lampton felt? What was his
   response towards this real or imagined contempt?
6. Explain the author's intentions behind his statement
   'the bar was crowded with business men slaving to
   help the export drive.'
7. What was Lampton surprised to find about the people
   in the bar?
8. How is it clear from the passage that Lampton has
   never been in a building like this before?

UNIT 2

 WRITING

Introduction I
Choosing an Essay title

 READING AND UNDERSTANDING

An Approach to Comprehension

 VOCABULARY

 LANGUAGE

 SPELLING

The Dictionary

 ASSIGNMENT B

You will learn to recognize which subjects are best suited to your own interests and skills, and discover the different ways you can write about a subject.

By understanding the different types of question that may be asked and how they relate to the passage you will be encouraged to write relevant answers. We also give you some basic advice on how to study passages and set about comprehension exercises.

The usefulness of a dictionary for all your work, with some exercises to give you some initial practice in its use.

 WRITING

Introduction I: Choosing an Essay Title

In Assignment A you were asked to write an essay. We gave you six titles to choose from. Some of you may have been able to choose without hesitation, while others may have found it difficult to choose between two or three subjects.

In this unit we are going to look at the question of choosing a subject to write on.

Before you go any further look back at those essay titles in Assignment A. What led you to make your choice? After writing the essay, do you think it was a wise choice? Was it a subject you could cope with well, or did you find it more difficult than you expected to organize your ideas?

In most of the assignments that accompany these units, you will be given lists of essay titles to choose from, and this will also be the case in the final written

examination itself when you will have from five to eight titles to choose from. It is therefore important to learn to make a good choice.

1. Choose a subject you know something about

Similarly, if you are writing an essay, you must have in your mind some knowledge, some facts, some opinions and relevant details about, and some acquaintance with, the subject you choose. If you don't have this personal background experience, then you are unlikely to produce an effective essay. So choosing the right subject for *you* is very important.

2. Distinguish between the different types of subjects that are listed

The kind of writing skills we will be developing are divided into two different categories: imaginative and practical.

7

Practical Writing

Some examples of practical writing:

1. A letter asking for information or setting out facts.
2. A report which arranges given facts in a logical and fluent order or requires you to give a factual account of something.
3. A newspaper or magazine article describing an incident, the details of which may be supplied to you.

The important factor here is the clarity with which you are able to describe the given incidents, the smoothness and naturalness with which you can write about these events, and the appropriateness of your expression of them. These are points that will be discussed in greater detail in later units.

Now look at the following examples of 'practical writing' assignments and see whether or not you understand the meaning of this term.

1. You have seen an advertisement in a weekly magazine offering a house in Paris during the holiday period in exchange for a house in Britain. The name of the advertiser is Latour, and the address is 71 rue de la Guerre. Answer the advertisement, asking for further details, and giving a description of your own house and an indication of the holiday pursuits and tourist interests in your own area.

2. A survey is being undertaken into people's television viewing, and you are asked to give an account of your viewing in any typical week. You should take into consideration the number of hours you watch, the types of programmes you watch, the different channels, the time of day you most frequently spend viewing.

3. Write a short article for the magazine *Homecare* on *one* of the following:

(a) how to decorate a ceiling
(b) gardening for lazy gardeners
(c) advice on spring cleaning.

Basically, 'practical writing' deals with facts and everyday situations and calls for little imagination or personal or creative response (though some ingenuity may be required). The important thing is the clarity and logic of your presentation of the facts.

Imaginative Writing

'Imaginative' essays cover a wider range and require more careful analysis. They call for some imaginative response, for original ways of looking at things, for stimulating ideas and persuasive arguments. They call for you to be able to put yourself imaginatively into the place of someone else or to be able to visualize a scene and recreate it in words.

Imaginative essays can be divided into the following categories:

1. **Characters.** You may be asked to describe a person, real or imaginary.

2. **Description.** You may be asked to write about a scene, e.g. a country scene or one set in a crowded urban situation. Or a few lines of poetry may suggest a picture to you which you could describe.

3. **Personal.** You may be asked to write about an event from your own experience, e.g. from your childhood days or at school or work.

4. **Argument.** You may be asked to give the case for or against a particular point of view, e.g. supporting or attacking capital punishment.

5. **Narrative.** This could be a story suggested by a simple title, e.g. *The Quarrel*. Or a situation may be presented to you which you would be asked to continue and develop. This situation could be in the form of a piece of poetry or a dramatic photograph.

6. **Critical.** You may be asked to write an account of a play or a film you have seen or a book you have read.

7. **Dialogue/Play/Diary/Letter/Report/Newspaper Article.** These are some of the other forms you may be asked to use when writing an imaginative essay.

All the kinds of imaginative essays described above could be written in one of these forms.

Look at the following suggestions for essays and decide into which of the above categories each falls. Note that a given title may be seen as belonging to, or as being adaptable to, more than one category. In other words, it could be tackled in a number of different ways. For example, the title 'The Stranger' could belong to 2. and 5. (and even to 3.). It could be treated as a character sketch and be developed as a description of a person who is a stranger; or it could be treated as the title for a dramatic situation or story involving a stranger.

1. By the River.
2. What are your views on abortion?
3. Looking for a House.
4. Write an eye-witness account of an accident, real or imagined.
5. The person who has influenced me most.
6. 'Advice to one about to be married: Don't!' What are your views?
7. Travelling Abroad.
8. The Younger Generation.
9. 'Spare the rod and spoil the child.' Do you agree?
10. Those who follow fashion are following convention.
11. Write about a book, a play or a film that has impressed you deeply and given you a new insight into life and people.
12. 'The straitjacket
    Of clock and calendar.'
13. Write a story ending with the words 'But when he opened the door, there was no one there'.
14. 'I would rather do without television than without radio.' Do you agree?
15. Out of this World.
16. Family Life.
17. Write a conversation between a fourteen-year-old teenager and his or her grandfather or grandmother discussing the attitudes and fashions of the young today.
18. My First Day at Work.
19. Bringing up a Family.

20. The Deserted House.

It is important that you learn to study lists of titles for a number of reasons.

1. Such study enables you to see whether you know anything about the subject.

2. It helps you to see the different possible ways in which a subject can be tackled.

The title 'The Wreck' may at first sight present no ideas, but if you ask, 'Could this be a description, a narrative?' then ideas and ways of approaching the subject may present themselves to you.

3. Through practice and experience, you will probably find that some types of essays appeal to you more than others and that you can achieve more success in one area than in another.

For instance, you may have plenty of knowledge and ideas about controversial matters and be able to organize facts and arguments well. You may find on the other hand that you can use words evocatively to create atmosphere and depict a scene in words. This evaluation of your own abilities and developing your powers of self-criticism so that you know where your strengths lie, is an important part of this course and an important step towards success in the examination.

Look again at the twenty titles above. See which subjects you feel you know something about. See which category of essay seems to appeal to you most at this stage. Jot down your response in your notebook; you will find it interesting to refer back to at a later stage to see how your idea of your abilities has changed. Time and practice may, of course, prove that your true strength lies in a different direction.

 **READING AND UNDERSTANDING**

An Approach to Comprehension

In Unit 1 we gave you a sample comprehension passage and we asked you to answer some questions on a passage in Assignment A. You have probably realized by now that everything you learn in this course is geared towards the end of writing and understanding English, and nothing is merely an exercise learnt for examination purposes. What we call 'comprehension exercises' are in fact a test of this understanding.

In this unit we will learn how to approach a passage set for comprehension. We will look at the kind of passage you will be studying, the kinds of questions you will be asked, and the kind of answers these questions require.

First of all, look back at the exercises in Assignment A. Which questions did you find particularly difficult to answer? What problems did you come across? Bear these in mind as you study the following section as it will help you overcome these difficulties in later exercises.

Types of passage

As with the essay, the pieces of writing we use will be of two varieties: imaginative and practical.

The 'imaginative' passage will be a piece of creative writing, an extract from a novel or a short story dealing with a fictional situation; it could alternatively be a poem.

(a) In answering the questions you will show that you can understand what the writer is talking about, not just on the surface, but also the subtleties and implications.

(b) You will also need to say something about *how* the writer is getting his points over, the effectiveness or otherwise of the way he uses words, images and sentences to create particular effects. In other words, some insight into matters of style and the appropriateness of style to content will be demanded.

The 'practical' passage will deal mainly with facts. It may be a report, an account of someone expressing his opinions on a particular matter, a series of instructions or a set of statistics which you will be asked to interpret. The emphasis here will be on making sure that you can understand the line of argument or the logical step-by-step statement of the facts. You may be asked to summarize the points made in the passage about a particular aspect of the matter being discussed.

Kinds of questions

The kinds of questions likely to be asked are as follows:

1. **Meaning.** You may be asked to explain the meaning of a word or phrase *as it is used in the passage*, e.g. when you see the word 'execute', you may immediately think of the meaning 'inflict capital punishment on'. But this would not be an appropriate meaning in a context like this: 'To execute the plan for redevelopment of the town will call for the support of all citizens.' Here 'execute' means 'carry into effect'.

2. **Facts.** You may be asked to answer questions about what the passage is actually saying to make sure that you understand it, e.g. if the piece of writing is about a character digging his allotment, you may be asked 'what is the character doing?'

3. **Reading between the lines.** Writers do not always state facts directly. They imply emotions and attitudes and suggest points of view, and they depend on the reader being perceptive enough to be able to form a total impression greater than the bare words on the page. For instance, an author may not state directly that he dislikes a particular character he is writing about, but the words he uses to describe that character and the situations he presents him in may convey the author's attitude towards the character, and that attitude is passed on to the perceptive reader. The words are not chosen accidentally but with a purpose, and you must be able to get beyond the surface meaning of the words and see what the implications of such words are. For example:

(a) the same soldiers could be called 'terrorists' or 'freedom-fighters', according to the writer's attitude towards them;

(b) in describing someone eating, a writer may use the words 'wolfed down', 'slobbered', 'guzzled'. If he is describing a baby eating, these words may be merely a statement of fact, but if they are about an adult, there may well be a suggestion of distaste towards the character.

9

4. Metaphorical language. You may be asked to explain what it is exactly that a writer has in mind when he makes a comparison or uses a metaphorical expression, e.g. in *The Story* by Dylan Thomas, the author says 'my uncle blew and bugled whenever he won' (at cards). The word 'blew' suggests a literal and factual way of expelling the breath from his mouth in a burst, but the word 'bugled' is being used in a metaphorical way. Thomas is making a comparison between the noise his uncle made and the sound of a bugle. He is trying to make more vivid to our imaginations the kind of noise his uncle made. The word 'bugled' suggests things like 'high-pitched', 'strident', 'sudden and loud', perhaps even 'triumphant'. These are ideas which this metaphorical used of the word conveys which a more literal word could not produce.

5. Style. Just as people are individual and different, so the way people write varies.

In addition, a particular writer may write in different ways depending on what effects he is trying to achieve, e.g. he may use very flowery language if he is trying to create an atmosphere; he may write very simply if he is concerned with getting important facts over; he may have his tongue in his cheek.

You may be asked to comment on the style of the passage you are studying and you may have to justify the appropriateness and effectiveness or otherwise of the style to the content—what the writer is saying. The kinds of points you would have to be aware of are the variety of sentences used, the kinds of words chosen, particular literary devices he uses, etc. These are very important aspects of understanding writing, and they will be discussed in greater detail in later units.

6. Summary. You may be asked to pick out certain facts in a passage relevant to a particular point, e.g. you may be asked 'what do we learn about X's physical appearance?' and you will have to search through the piece of writing to find all the details that the writer gives you about this.

7. Opinions. You may be asked to comment on the views expressed in the passage, to say whether you think they are convincing, or to give your own views on the topic, e.g. if the passage is about pornography, you may be asked, 'Do you think pornography is harmful?' Or you may be asked to develop or expand on an area of experience described in the passage, but this time treating it from a personal point of view. For example, the passage may be about working conditions, and you may be asked, 'Comment on the conditions under which you work, indicating the area in which you think improvements could be made.'

These are the main kinds of questions likely to be asked. There may be others, but if you become acquainted with these types and can understand them, you should be well prepared. One of the important aspects of this course is to make you familiar with the demands of the examination paper so that when you are actually faced with it, it doesn't come as a shock. Knowing the kind of question you will be asked will make you feel more secure and confident.

Refer to this section whenever you need. On page 11 we give you a comprehension exercise telling you which types the questions are.

Setting about comprehension exercises

1. Read the passage carefully several times. This seems very obvious, but it is surprising how many students think that a quick skim through the passage is sufficient to enable them to answer the questions set. Such an attitude is short-sighted and arrogant in the extreme. By all means read the passage through quickly first of all, to get a general idea of the theme, but then it is imperative that you read it through again slowly and carefully at least twice before going on to answer the questions. If you meet a word you don't know try to work out its meaning through the context. What sort of impression is the author trying to make? Why has he used that word? In the written examination itself you will not be permitted to use a dictionary, but there is no reason why you shouldn't use a dictionary in these practice exercises—after you have tried to work out the meanings of unknown words from their contexts. Look at the questions and work out mentally whereabouts in the passage the information required for the answer lies and what the answers are. Don't be in too much of a hurry to start writing. The really useful work is done in this preliminary time when you become familiar with the passage and the questions.

2. Make sure that you understand the questions being asked. Too often students glance at the questions and don't really digest their implications. Worry at the questions as a dog does a bone. Worm out the meaning. Ask yourself what information is really being asked for. Rephrase the question in simpler terms.

3. Make sure that your answer is relevant. Keep referring back to the question to ensure that the information you give is the information that is asked for. It is a good idea when you have answered the question to go back to the beginning mentally—to look at the question, read your answer and ask yourself, 'Have I answered the question?' Another danger here is that you will go on too long. Answer the point asked and then stop.

4. Use your own words unless asked to quote. The purpose of a comprehension exercise after all is to show that you have understood the passage. If you merely write out lines from the passage as your answer, then there is no evidence that you understand what those lines mean. Obviously it is not always possible to use completely different words when the words are simple or involve technical terms. Nevertheless, this is a rule that you should always bear in mind.

5. Keep to the facts given in the passage unless otherwise asked. The purpose of a comprehension exercise is to show that you understand the passage, not to show how much you know about the topic discussed in the passage. For instance, the passage may be about comprehensive education. You may disapprove of comprehensive education and may be in possession of facts which the passage doesn't mention. However, your personal views and information are irrelevant here. You must use only the facts in the passage. The only exception to this is the case of a question of type 7 (see above) when you are specifically asked to express your own view of the arguments presented or your own opinions.

6. Always answer in sentences—unless specifically told that you need not do so. You could sometimes present the necessary information a question requires in a simple word or phrase, but this is not the point of the exercise: you are learning to express yourself clearly in good English, and you should always prove that you can do so by answering fully.

We have made a lot of points in this unit and we don't expect you to remember all we've said all at once. As you work through the rest of this unit and the next units we advise you to look back at this introductory work and you will gradually become familiar with these points.

Meanwhile, here is another specimen comprehension

of our time and place, Kirk was beyond the pale. He even worked on Sundays.

Kirk lived with Baggie McLaughlin and his hairy old wife in the cottage at the foot of our hill. Baggie was a small wizened man who touched his forelock to everyone, even me aged eight, and always walked on the grass verge of the road. He called himself a pig-sticker. He went round the outlying crofts at Martinmas, killing off the pigs at a shilling a time, and this was the only work he ever admitted to. In fact, he was a beachcomber. Kirk used sometimes to say that he was a retired pirate, but I knew quite well that this was an exaggeration. Baggie would not have said boo to a gosling.

exercise with questions and suggested answers. Read the passage carefully and then study the questions, the notes indicating the type of question being asked and the suggested answers.

When I was a child I was dominated by a boy I shall call Kirk. I was brought up in a proud old town on the Moray Firth coast of Scotland, and I was brought up in the North Scottish Presbyterian way, that is, Very Properly Indeed. I have never really understood, therefore, why I was allowed to make a friend of Kirk, for Kirk was far from proper. He was a kind of Scotch Huckleberry Finn—a boy who went barefoot, wore orra[1] patched breeks, smoked a clay cutty, chewed plug tobacco, jeuked[2] the school. By all the standards

[1] *orra*: much, very   [2] *jeuked*: played truant from

His wife was very old. I suppose she must have been about the same age as Baggie, but she looked much older. She was crippled with arthritis, bent like a right angle, and heavily bearded. She rose late and retired early, and when she wanted to go to bed she would hobble to the cottage door and ring a big ship's bell that Baggie had picked up off the shore, and then Kirk had to run home and help get her into bed. He said it was a hell of a job getting her into bed, and I bet it was, for she was solid as teak and must have weighed close on sixteen stone.

(NEIL PATERSON, *Three Fingers are Plenty*)

Stop! Remember 1. on page 10. Read the passage through several times before going any further.

Q. What does the author imply by giving capital letters to the words 'Very Properly Indeed'? (This is a question that combines aspects of 3. 'Reading between the Lines' and 5. 'Style'. The use of capital letters implies a certain tone of voice on the part of the author, and it is up to you to catch this tone of voice and interpret it.)

A. By using capital letters for 'Very Properly Indeed', the author gives the words an emphasis that is in fact excessive. He is implying that his upbringing was a very serious and respectable matter, and by over-emphasizing it, he is poking fun at it to some extent and being ironic about it.

Q. What is the implication of the fact that Kirk 'even worked on Sundays'? (This is another question of type 3. 'Reading between the lines'.)

A. The fact that Kirk 'even worked on Sundays' was the final insult as far as the respectable people of the town were concerned. To these law-abiding Presbyterians working on Sunday was the worst sin of all and ought to have clinched the matter of whether Kirk was a suitable companion or not.

Q. What main point is the author making in this opening paragraph, and how does the use of language emphasize this point?

A. (This question involves aspects of 3 and 5.) The author is making a contrast between the respectable way of life that is the norm in this Presbyterian town and the wild carefree life led by Kirk. The language emphasizes this contrast by talking of the respectable life in very polite, even pompous terms, for example the author's repetition of the phrase 'I was brought up' and by his use of capital letters for the phrase 'Very Properly Indeed'; while when describing Kirk he uses Scottish dialect words like 'orra' and 'jeuked', a comparison with Huckleberry Finn and a series of racy details reaching a climax in the most dreadful crime of all—Kirk 'even worked on Sundays'.

(There are two points worth remembering here. (a) A passage may contain dialect words, but usually it is not necessary to know the precise meaning of these words as their function is often to add local colour to the writing. (b) More important, remember that effective comprehension questions are designed to deepen your understanding of the passage as a whole rather than to delve into irrelevant minor points. This question leads the reader into a deeper understanding of the author's intention in the opening paragraph of his story.)

Q. What do you understand by 'who touched his forelock to everyone'? (This question involves aspects of 1. 'Meaning' and 3. 'Reading between the Lines'.)

A. 'To touch your forelock' means literally to touch your forehead with your finger in a kind of salute as a sign of respect to a superior. The meaning here is that Baggie was servile in the extreme and kow-towed to everyone—even to the eight-year-old narrator—as though they were superior and he inferior.

Q. What impression do you get of Baggie's wife? (This is mainly a question of type 6. 'Summary' although

some aspects of 3. 'Reading between the Lines' may again come into it.)

A. Baggie's wife was old, probably as old as Baggie himself, although she looked even older. She was stricken with arthritis which bent her up, made her hobble and stay in bed late and retire early. She had a beard. She was very heavily built, probably weighing sixteen stone, and required assistance in getting into bed. She was probably rather demanding as when she wanted to go to bed she rang a bell and Kirk had to go running.

This passage is continued in Assignment B at the end of this unit.

VOCABULARY, LANGUAGE, SPELLING
The Dictionary

In future units, these aspects will be treated in detail as separate categories. In this introductory unit, I want to stress the importance to all of these aspects—and to writing, reading and understanding as well, of course—of learning to use a dictionary and using it constantly as your surest aid and support in need.

To start with, you must possess a good dictionary. *The Pocket Oxford Dictionary* is only just adequate; even better is one of the following: *The Concise Oxford Dictionary* (Oxford University Press); *The Penguin English Dictionary* (Penguin); *Chambers Twentieth Century Dictionary* (Chambers).

The usefulness of the Dictionary

No book has a more fascinating store of information.

1. It tells us how to pronounce words once we have taken the trouble to master the pronunciation key which most dictionaries possess.

Find out the correct pronunciation of 'harassed', 'trait' and 'medicine'.

2. It tells us how to spell words. Clearly, we must have a general idea of how a word is spelled before we can begin to search for the correct version, but at least a dictionary will tell us whether the 'i' comes before the 'e' in 'receive', whether 'grateful' has one or two 'l's', whether 'development' has an 'e' in the middle or not. You will be asked to find examples of words that conform to different patterns in the spelling sections of the course.

3. It can tell us what part of speech a word is, and this can also help us to spell correctly. For instance, if we know that 'advice' is a noun and 'advise' is a verb, we know the correct form in this sentence: 'His advice was disastrous.'

Look up the difference between 'practice' and 'practise'.

4. It can give us the variety of meanings that a word in English is capable of having and help us to distinguish between them. Thus 'board' as a noun can mean among other things 'a piece of timber', 'a table', 'daily meals

provided', 'a committee'; as a verb it can mean 'cover with boards', 'provide meals', 'force one's way on board (a ship)'. We can also distinguish the word from 'bored' which is pronouned the same way but which means 'wearied with dullness'.

Look up the different meanings of 'train'.

5. It can tell us the derivation of words and help us to understand the meanings of words through learning where the words come from and the roots, prefixes, and suffixes from which the words are made. For instance, 'Borstal' comes from the name of such an establishment in Kent; 'biology' comes from the Greek 'bios' = 'life' and 'ology' = 'study of'; 'scale' as used in music comes from the Latin 'scala' = 'ladder'.

Look up 'boycott', 'psychology' and 'erudite'.

6. Most good dictionaries give examples of the words in use or idiomatic expressions containing the word. For example: 'It is a *scandal* that such things should be possible; a grave *scandal* occurred; gave rise to *scandal*.' This makes it easier for us to understand the meaning of the word and how to use it correctly.

> Always keep a dictionary beside you and refer to it when in doubt. This is the kind of training that can be useful to you throughout life. No one can ever presume himself to be so erudite that he can do without a dictionary.

 # ASSIGNMENT B

Answer the following questions. Part I should take about an hour and a half over the preparation and writing and should be about 500 words in length. Part II should take about an hour and a quarter.

Part I: Essay

Write an essay on *one* of the following. Study each title carefully before choosing the one you will write on. Remember to consider each title for its possibilities of treatment—narrative, descriptive, argumentative, personal, etc. as indicated earlier in this unit.

(a) The Last Post.
(b) Memories of Christmas.
(c) Write a description of a room you know well (a bedroom, a living room, a kitchen, a bed-sitting room) as it is in reality, and as you would like it to be if you had unlimited resources to decorate and furnish it.
(d) Give arguments for and against living in a city as opposed to living in the country.
(e) Loneliness.

Part II: Comprehension

Read the following passage very carefully. It is a continuation of the one discussed earlier and you should bear the other passage in mind while answering the questions. Answer them as fully as you can. Remember to ask yourself mentally in each case what type of question is being asked and what type of information is being demanded as was indicated in the specimen comprehension exercise earlier. Read over again carefully the notes on how to answer a comprehension exercise after you have read the passage.

As far as anybody knew, Kirk had lived all his life with this old couple, but even I, who had no biological knowledge, knew that he did not belong to them. He was of different stock. He looked every man in the eye and touched his forelock to none. As I remember him he was tall for his age, straight as a mast, flat-backed, and uncommonly broad across the shoulders. His hair was red, and he wore it very long, except when Baggie put a bowl on top of it and cut round the rim, and then he was a sorry sight—but nobody ever laughed at him. At least, no boy did.

The most remarkable thing about him was his eyes. I never noticed the colour of anyone else's eyes until I grew up and started looking at girls, but I could not help noticing Kirk's. They were greenish-blue, the colour of blue-bottle flies in the sun, and they were full of devil. When Kirk flicked me with these blue-bottle eyes of his and said, 'What are we waiting for?' I just automatically said 'Let's go.' I always said it, and I always went. I guess I'd have gone anywhere at all with Kirk.

Kirk was a year and nine months older than me. When he was ten he built a boat out of three-ply wood and petrol-cans and we sailed this boat on the open sea. We were often afloat for the whole day, and sometimes we went so far out to sea that we lost sight of land. When it blew up we shipped a lot of water, and then I baled like fury with two Rowntree cocoa tins while Kirk sat cross-legged in the stern, keeping her bows up to the seas by judicious management of his oar (my sister's tennis racket with the gut out and a sheet of tin nailed in its place). He was never at a loss, never rattled—never afraid—and twenty years ago I had much the same degree of confidence in Kirk and his three-ply *Ruler of the Waves* as I now have in Captain Illingworth and the *Queen Mary*.

One day during an aquatic gala in the harbour of a small town nine or ten miles up the coast, Kirk paddled through the bottle-neck into the basin, and allowed himself to be captured by the judge's launch. When they asked where he had come from, he pointed out to sea and said 'Norge'.

The local folks made a great fuss of him, presented him to Lady somebody or other who was there for the prize-giving, fed him on chocolate and ice-cream, and billeted him with the Minister. The Minister had then three young daughters—one of whom is now my wife—and she has told me that Kirk made such a powerful impression, what with slapping his chest, emitting guttural growls, and declaiming, 'Ach so?' that she and her sisters were all slightly in love with him for weeks.

The imposture lasted less than a day, but it happened to be the day the weekly county paper went to press, and our normally reliable journal came out with a sober account of Kirk's adventure under the heading, 'YOUNG VIKING'S EXPLOIT'.

In due course Kirk and his boat were sent home in one of Alexander's big blue buses, the story was the talk of the town, and my father, discovering that I had sometimes gone to sea with Kirk, thrashed me judicially

and, with an axe over his shoulder, marched me down to Baggie's cottage, where he fulminated against Kirk and duly despatched the boat. It is characteristic of Kirk that while my father was telling Baggie exactly what he meant to do to *that boy* if ever he laid hands on him, that boy was grinning smugly down at us from a branch not six feet above my father's head.

Kirk was always one jump ahead of the other fellows. I am sure that was the secret of his leadership. When a gang of us went guddling,[1] Kirk would coax a whole frying of sizeable trout into his thick fingers while the rest of us puddled with a few miserable sticklebacks. If we went along the cliffs to rob gulls' nests, it was Kirk

[1] *guddling*: catching fish by hand.

14

who spotted the best colonies and only Kirk who would dare climb to them. It was Kirk who first showed me a bowline on the bight and Turk's head, who made fish-hooks for us out of horse-shoe nails, who taught us to lift and *cope* a ferret, who assembled the radio for our KU-KLUX clubroom. He was a born leader. He was always out in front, and whenever there was anything important to be done it was always Kirk who did it best.

(NEIL PATERSON, *Three Fingers are Plenty*)

1. How could the narrator tell that Kirk was not Baggie's son? (You may use material given in the opening paragraph of the story on p. 11.)
2. Why did no one ever laugh at Kirk?
3. What was remarkable about Kirk's eyes?
4. What were the narrator's feelings towards Kirk?
5. What do you understand by the phrase Kirk 'allowed himself to be captured by the judges' launch'?
6. Explain the meaning of 'fulminated' and 'despatched'. (You may use a dictionary to check your own first impressions.)
7. What do you understand by 'Kirk was always one jump ahead'?
8. Give an example of this from the passage.
9. What, in the narrator's view, are the qualities of a born leader?
10. What qualities do you consider a born leader should have?
11. Sum up the kind of person Kirk was as revealed in this passage and in the opening paragraph on page 11.

UNIT 3

WRITING

Introduction II
Gathering ideas
Organizing ideas
Beginning and ending

By the time you have worked through this unit you will be able to organize your ideas and give shape to your essay plan before you begin to write.

READING AND UNDERSTANDING

Characters

Most imaginative writing involves or is about people. We study the devices writers use to describe people and prepare you for writing about characters yourself in Unit 4.

READING LIST

The books chosen in this unit have particularly interesting descriptions of characters.

VOCABULARY

The words for vocabulary study are taken from one of the passages used in the section studying a character from Angus Wilson's *A Little Companion.*

LANGUAGE

Guidance on the use of paragraphs links very closely with the 'writing' section of this unit. Good essay planning and paragraphing are complementary.

SPELLING

The problems of spelling
'i' before 'e'

Some hints on how to improve your spelling.

One of the best-known spelling rules.

WRITING

Introduction II: Gathering Ideas

There are three important elements in writing a good essay: having ideas, organizing them logically and expressing them effectively. The first two of these will be dealt with in this unit.

Having chosen your title, the next step is to jot down any ideas that come to mind.

For instance, if you choose the subject 'By the River', you may make the following notes:

the colour of the water
anglers on the bank
figures reflected in the
water
people walking
children playing
boats on the water
trees
reeds
ducks

traffic on the bridges
crossing the river

the clouds and sunset
reflected
the changing colours in
the water
the ripples and waves as
boats pass
a swan gliding with cygnets
children swimming
houseboats moored

These points are jotted down haphazardly as they occur to you.

If ideas are slow to flow, it is often useful to ask a whole series of questions about the title to see if anything suggests itself: Where? When? Why? How? Who? What? Not all of these will necessarily be productive, but in the case of the title 'By the River' the following points could become clearer:

1. **Where?** Is it a river passing through a busy town which affords peaceful contrast to the bustle of the traffic and town life around it? This could be an important point to emphasize in the essay.

2. **When?** Are you going to describe one moment by the river or are you going to follow the changes from morning to evening? Again, asking the questions helps you to get your ideas in sharper focus.

3. **Why?** Consider why the various characters you have noted down—anglers, strollers, children, houseboat owners—are there.

4. **How?** This question is not very productive in this instance except as applied to the people. How are they behaving? How are they dressed? What are they doing?

floating in the water, the contrast of the brightly painted houseboats with the sombre grey of the water or the sky, the snow-white purity of the swan's plumage.

2. **The sense of hearing** may bring to mind the shouting of the children, the chugging of a tugboat, the roar of a motorboat, the regular lapping sound of oars, the quacking of the ducks.

3. **The idea of touch** may inspire you to try to describe more precisely the textures of the water—is it oily? smooth? flowing? cold? glittering? like glass? like a mirror?

4. **The sense of smell** may suggest pleasant or unpleasant associations. On the pleasant side could be the freshness of the atmosphere, the scent of flowers by the riverside, the clarity of the air and the absence of strong smells. On the unpleasant side could be the smell of rotting

5. **Who? What?** These questions have really already been answered. Who would be likely to be found by the river? What kind of activities go on there?

Another means of calling forth ideas, particularly for a descriptive essay, is to take each of the senses in turn and see whether it can be fruitful when applied to the subject. The senses are, of course, sight, hearing, touch, taste and smell.

1. **Sight** suggests most of the detail originally noted in the first rush of ideas, but it may also suggest more, such as the mosaic pattern of light on the surface of the water, the rainbow colours of a slick of oil, feathers and leaves

vegetation or waste in the river or the exhaust from boats lingering over sluggish water.

5. **Thinking of taste** may suggest how water tastes in a mountain stream—its coolness, its clearness, its freshness.

'By the River' is not perhaps a subject that immediately suggests being treated according to the senses. Titles like 'Food' or 'The Bonfire' or 'A Summer Evening' are more likely to respond to this kind of approach, but whatever the title, be on the look-out as applying the various senses can produce ideas.

Another way of helping to gather ideas is to think in

categories or areas of knowledge—political, religious, personal, physical, historical, geographical, social, economic, artistic, sexual, moral, creative, psychological. This is particularly useful with a title that involves an argument. Again, they may not all be productive, but applying these various categories may help ideas to flow. For instance, if the title chosen is 'What are your views on abortion?' the following may be useful lines of inquiry:

1. **Religious**—people with strong religious views, perhaps Roman Catholics, may disapprove strongly of abortion.

2. **Personal**—you may consider the view that each individual has the right to choose. And what about the right of the unborn child?

3. **Physical**—your final view on the question may be influenced by concern for the physical well-being of the mother-to-be.

4. **Historical**—attitudes towards the question in the past may be relevant here.

5. **Social**—different societies in the world may have different attitudes.

6. **Economic**—the question of increasing the world population may have a bearing on your final view.

7. **Sexual**—you may feel that too-easy abortion is an inducement to promiscuity and lax morality.

8. **Psychological**—you may wish to consider the psychological effect on a woman of having an abortion.

These are points which may not at first thought have occurred to you, but which arise through a consideration of the various areas of knowledge that may be appropriate.

Organizing Ideas

Having jotted down some ideas, the next step is to organize these ideas into a convincing and fluent whole. It is no use starting with one idea and then moving on to another and hoping that your essay will hang together. You must have a plan. What you are aiming at ultimately is such a sure control of the ideas at hand that you are able to impose a logical pattern on them and you are able, as it were, to survey your material as from a great height so that you can see the beginning, the course your essay will take, and how it will end. You may find that some of your ideas don't fit into the framework you will eventually choose and in that case you will have to discard them. The following suggestions should give you some idea of the kind of pattern, shape or plan that can be imposed on material. In each of them you may well use the same material, the only difference being the kind of framework that seems to you most appropriate.

Let us return to the title 'By the River'. These are some of the ways this subject could be treated:

1. **Twenty-Four Hours.** You could use a time-span as the unifying factor in your essay. You could begin your account at dawn with the river shrouded in mist, dank and chill, with the sound of the city's traffic on the bridge above momentarily stilled. Your description would then follow the changing scene throughout the day, ending with nightfall, the river again hidden in darkness apart from the gleaming reflection of the bridge's lights in the water and the lamps of passing boats.

2. **People.** You could concentrate on the people 'by the river', describing each in turn—the patient angler, the frolicking children, the woman hanging out washing on a houseboat, the boatman stowing his gear.

3. **Activities.** This could be rather similar to 2. but this time you would concentrate on all the different activities 'by the river'—fishing, boating, strolling, playing games.

4. **Panorama.** Imagine you are taking a panoramic photograph of the scene. Begin with the bridge, sweep your camera round slowly to end with the water and describe in detail and in order all the things which come into your view.

5. **Contrast.** You could treat the subject from a more impressionistic standpoint. The river scene is full of contrasts—the pensive angler, the noisy traffic; the busy tugboat, the graceful dinghies; the quacking ducks, the smooth-flowing swans; the turbulent water churned up by a passing motorboat, the glass-like surface when the ripples have ceased. The framework of contrast could be the guide-line you use to organize your material.

All of these methods treat the title 'By the River' as a descriptive essay. It could, of course, also be regarded as the title for a story or a play or some other imaginative approach. Always bear this in mind as you consider the various titles.

With a title that involves an argument like 'What are your views on abortion?', the obvious way to organize your material is under pros and cons, points for and against the argument. Although you are asked what *your* views on the subject are, your case generally won't be convincing unless you contrast the two sides of the argument.

Pro:

1. Every individual has the right to choose whether or not to have children.

2. If an embryo is unwanted, it would be fairer to it for it to be aborted rather than to allow it to be brought up in an unhappy atmosphere.

3. World population is growing at such a rate that abortion is necessary to reduce the birth-rate.

4. If it is a question of saving the mother or the child then it should be the mother, as the embryo is not yet an individual personality.

Con:

1. Even an embryo has a soul and therefore it is immoral to destroy it.

2. People should exercise sexual restraint; abortion freely available would lead to sexual promiscuity.

3. The psychological effect on a woman who has an abortion could be considerable and unfortunate.

4. If it is a question of saving the mother or the child, then it should be the child as, to put it brutally, the mother is the past, and the child is the future.

This is the first stage. You still have to decide whether this is the best order for the various points, which side of the argument you favour yourself, how best to counter the points put forward on the other side and what kind of conclusion you will arrive at. In this case your essay will usually end with your *own* view, the one you have been leading up to in your presentation of the argument.

Choose one title that can be treated in a descriptive way and one that can be treated as an argument from those given from 1–20 in Unit 2, jot down the ideas that come to you using the methods suggested earlier in this unit and work out paragraph plans for essays.

Beginning and Ending

This brings us to the two most important aspects of any essay: how to begin and how to finish. If you don't begin in an interesting way, a reader will hardly be encouraged to go on reading. If you end weakly, your essay will peter out and any power you have achieved or interest you have aroused in the body of your essay will be dissipated.

The opening sentence

It is difficult to give advice on the opening sentence of an essay, but here are some points to consider.

1. The opening sentence must attract and hold the reader's attention. This can be done by the content of the sentence (its unexpectedness, perhaps) and by the way it is phrased (the neatness of expression).

Here are some examples of opening sentences, actual and invented, for you to consider. How effective are they in arresting your attention? Do they make their effect by the idea or the expression of the idea or both? Write down your views about each of these sentences.

1. It is a truth universally acknowledged that a single man in possession of a good fortune, must be in want of a wife. (The opening sentence of Jane Austen's *Pride and Prejudice*.)

2. 'Hole!' said Mr Polly, and then for a change, and with greatly increased emphasis: ''Ole!' (The opening sentence of H. G. Wells' *The History of Mr Polly*.)

3. 'How did that alligator get in the bath?' demanded my father one morning at breakfast. (The opening of a short story called 'My Pet'.)

4. All criminals should be hanged. (The opening of an essay on 'Crime and Punishment'.)

5. 'In married life three is company and two is none,' said Oscar Wilde. (The opening of an essay on 'What makes a happy marriage?')

6. The night before young Larsen left to take up his new appointment in Egypt he went to the clairvoyante. (The opening of a short story by Algernon Blackwood called 'By Water'.)

7. There are two types of selfishness: doing what you want to do, and making others do what you want. (The opening of a book review by Michael Holroyd in *New Statesman*.)

8. The house shook, the windows rattled, a framed photograph slipped off the mantel-shelf and fell into the hearth. (The opening of John Wyndham's short story 'Meteor'.)

9. A wild, glassy morning—all winds and glitter ... the sun glared low between the chimneys, through black winter branches, blinding you at a slant, dazzling white and bright straight in the eyes—it made a splintering dance of everything, it made for squints and sniggering ... (The opening of William Sansom's short story 'Cat up a Tree'.)

10. Is it true that all Australians are called Bruce? (The opening of an article on Australia by James Cameron in the *Daily Telegraph Magazine*.)

Some guide-lines emerge from these examples:

1. Try the surprise attack or shock tactics.
2. Use a quotation to introduce your argument.
3. Try to use words to create an atmosphere.
4. Begin with a wittily-phrased summing-up of an idea.
5. Begin with a question.
6. Begin with a 'cliff-hanger' so that the reader asks why? or what happens next? or what's it all about?

Study the examples of opening sentences again and see which of these methods is being used in each.

Bad beginnings

One kind of opening sentence to avoid is the flat and pedestrian statement of the obvious. This is the kind of thing I mean:

Water has many uses. (The opening of an essay entitled 'Water'.)

As with most questions, there are two sides to the argument. (The opening of an essay on 'Capital Punishment'.)

It was a hot summer's day. (The opening of an essay entitled 'A Hot Summer's Day.)

None of these opening sentences would encourage any reader to continue further!

2. Get to the subject-matter straight away. For example, if the title is *The Flood*, the flood itself must have started by at least the second paragraph, if not the first. To spend the first paragraph describing the heavy oppressive weather, the next paragraph describing the first rain, the third describing people taking shelter, the fourth the storm breaking, and the fifth how the river burst its banks, is a waste of time. If the title is 'The Flood', 'The Storm', 'The Stranger', 'My First Day at School', 'Capital Punishment', then you must get the flood, the storm, the stranger, your first day at school, capital punishment in right at the very beginning and stick to it till the end.

Endings

'Begin at the beginning,' said Lewis Carroll's King of Hearts, 'and go on till you come to the end; then stop.' On one level, this is good advice. When you have said what you have to say, then stop; don't go rambling on repeating yourself. But it is not as simple as that; you also need to learn *how* to stop. How you finish an essay is as important in creating a favourable impression in a reader's mind as how you begin.

1. At all costs avoid beginning your final paragraph with a sentence like this:

Summing up then ...
In conclusion ...
So it can be seen that ...

In the first place, an ending like this is almost certain to be boring and obvious, and in the second place, you are very likely to be in danger of repeating what you have already said.

2. Try to leave the reader with a surprise, a new angle, an original point of view which leaves him thinking. It must be relevant to the subject and to what you have already written but should give a new insight into the subject. Above all, end strongly and firmly. Don't just fade away.

It is difficult in isolation to give examples of effective endings, but study the following extracts and consider how effective the endings are and what methods the authors use to make them effective—shock? surprise? firm conclusion? inevitability? fresh angle? a climax? an intentional anti-climax?

1. All day long, whilst the women were praying ten miles away, the lines of the dauntless English infantry were receiving and repelling the furious charge of the French horsemen. Guns which were heard at Brussels were ploughing up their ranks, and comrades falling, and the resolute survivors closing in. Towards evening, the attack of the French, repeated and resisted so bravely, slackened in its fury. They had other foes beside the British to engage, or were preparing for the final onset. It came at last; the columns of the Imperial Guard marching up the hill of St Jean, at length and at once to sweep the English from the height which they had maintained all day and spite of all: unscared by the thunder of the artillery, which hurled death from the English Line—the dark rolling column pressed on and up the hill. It seemed almost to crest the eminence, when it began to wave and falter. Then it stopped, still facing the shot. Then at last the English troops rushed from the post from which no enemy had been able to dislodge them, and the Guard turned and fled.

No more firing was heard at Brussels—the pursuit rolled miles away. Darkness came down on the field and city: and Amelia was praying for George, who was lying on his face, dead, with a bullet through his heart.

(W. M. THACKERAY, *Vanity Fair*)

2. I embraced the royal mast and shinned up. The wind blew my hair over my nose and made me want to sneeze. I stretched out my arm and grasped the round hardwood cap 198 feet above the keel and was surprised to find it was not loose or full of chocolate creams as a prize. Now the bloody man below me was telling me to sit on it, but I ignored him. I could think of no emergency that would make it necessary. So I slid down to the royal halliard and to the yard again.

'You can come down now,' shouted the Mate.

I did. It was worse than going up and more agonizing as I was barefoot, with my shoes stuffed inside my shirt.

'You were a fool to take your shoes off,' said the Mate when I reached the deck. 'Now you can learn to clean the lavatories.'

Since that day I have been aloft in high rigging many hundreds of times and in every kind of weather but I still get that cold feeling in the pit of the stomach when I think of the first morning out on the royal yard with the sheds of the York Deck below.

(ERIC NEWBY, *The Last Grain Race*)

Invent an opening or a closing sentence for each of the following essay titles and justify in writing the effectiveness of each of your suggestions:

1. The Funfair.
2. Spare the Rod and Spoil the Child.
3. Television—curse or blessing?
4. Hero-worship.
5. Gambling.
6. The Last Train.
7. The Wild West.
8. City Lights.
9. The Pleasures of Gardening.
10. Alone.

 # READING AND UNDERSTANDING

Characters

Almost every example of imaginative writing has to do with people in some way or other. We are going to look at some of the ways in which a writer is able to translate his vision of the people he is writing about to the reader by means of words. In some ways, a painter or photographer has an easier task in that he is able to present his ideas directly to us in visual terms—though, of course, interpretation is necessary here too. How then does an author achieve the same effect using only words?

1. In Action. One of the ways a writer does this is by showing the character performing some action which is typical of him or performing an action in a particular way that reveals the kind of person he is. The passage from Neil Paterson's *Three Fingers are Plenty* used for comprehension in Unit 2 is an example of this. The way in which Kirk paddled the make-shift boat with a tennis racket, the way he made his way into the midst of the aquatic gala and pretended to be Norwegian, the way he evaded the narrator's father, all tell us about the kind of person he is. These actions build up a picture of him in our minds.

Here is another example, a description of Pip's sister, Mrs Gargery, from Charles Dickens's *Great Expectations*.

My sister had a trenchant way of cutting our bread-and-butter for us, that never varied. First, with her left hand she jammed the loaf hard and fast against her bib—where it sometimes got a pin into it, and sometimes a needle, which we afterwards got into our mouths. Then she took some butter (not too much) on a knife and spread it on the loaf, in an apothecary kind of way, as if she were making a plaister—using both sides of the knife with a slapping dexterity, and trimming and moulding the butter off round the crust. Then, she gave the knife a final smart wipe on the edge of the plaister, and then sawed a very thick round off the loaf; which she finally, before separating from the loaf, hewed into two halves, of which Joe got one, and I the other.

(CHARLES DICKENS, *Great Expectations*)

What does this account of Mrs Gargery cutting bread tell us about her?

What impression does the use of words like 'trenchant', 'jammed', 'slapping dexterity', 'a final smart wipe', 'sawed' and 'hewed' build up?

Write your answers to these and the following questions in your notebook: it is good practice.

2. In Speech. Another way in which writers can indicate character is through the words they put into their characters' mouths. This is, of course, an important—possibly the most important—element of the dramatist's art, to reveal his characters through their speech, but other writers employ the device as well.

Study the following passage from P. G. Wodehouse's 'Thank You, Jeeves'.

'Jeeves', I said, 'do you know what?'
'No, sir.'
'Do you know whom I saw last night?'
'No, sir.'
'J. Washburn Stoker and his daughter, Pauline.'
'Indeed, sir?'
'They must be over here.'
'It would seem so, sir.'
'Awkward, what?'
'I can conceive that after what occurred in New York it might be distressing for you to encounter Miss Stokes, sir. But I fancy the contingency need scarcely arise.'
I weighed this.

BBC Copyright Photograph

'When you start talking about contingencies arising, Jeeves, the brain seems to flicker and I rather miss the gist. Do you mean that I ought to be able to keep out of her way?'

'Yes, sir.'

'Avoid her?'

'Yes, sir.'

(P. G. WODEHOUSE, *Thank You, Jeeves*)

Look at Jeeves's answers. Apart from one speech, they are very economical. What can we deduce about the kind of person Jeeves is and his attitude towards his master from this economy of speech, from what Jeeves actually says and from what is implied?

3. By Direct Statement. Some writers tell us about their characters directly instead of showing them and allowing us to draw our own conclusions. They build detail on detail until we have a clear picture of their appearance, their habits, their opinions, their life history.

Here is an account of a character called Miss Arkwright.

She was in no way a remarkable person. Her appearance was not particularly distinguished and yet she was without any feature that could actively displease. She had enough personal eccentricities to fit into the pattern of English village life, but none so absurd or anti-social that they could embarrass or even arouse gossip beyond what was pleasant to her neighbours. She accepted her position as an old maid with that cheerful good humour and occasional irony which are essential to English spinsters since the deification of Jane Austen, or more sacredly Miss Austen, by the upper middle classes, and she attempted to counteract the inadequacy of the unmarried state by quiet, sensible and tolerant social work in the local community. She was liked by nearly everyone, though she was not afraid of making enemies where she knew that her broad but deeply felt religious principles were being opposed. Any socially pretentious or undesirably extravagant conduct, too, was liable to call forth from her an unexpectedly caustic and well-aimed snub. She was invited everywhere and always accepted the invitations. You could see her at every tea or cocktail party, occasionally drinking a third gin, but never more. Quietly but well dressed, with one or two very fine old pieces of jewellery that had come down to her from her grandmothers, she would pass from one group to another, laughing or serious as the occasion demanded. She smoked continuously her own rather expensive brand of cigarettes—'My one vice' she used to say 'the only thing that stands between me and secret drinking.' She listened with patience, but with a slight twinkle in her eye, to Mr Hodgson's endless stories of life in Dar-es-Salaam or Myra Hope's breathless accounts of her latest system of diet. John Hobday in his somewhat ostentatiously gentleman-farmer attire would describe his next novel about East Anglian life to her before even his beloved daughter had heard of it. Richard Trelawney, just down from Oxford, found that she had read and really knew Donne's sermons, yet she could swop detective stories with Colonel Wright by the hour, and was his main source for quotations when *The Times* cross-

word was in question. She it was who incorporated little Mrs Grantham into village life, when that underbred, suburban woman came there as Colonel Grantham's second wife, checking her vulgar remarks about 'the lower classes' with kindly humour, but defending her against the formidable battery of Lady Vernon's antagonism. Yet she it was also who was first at Lady Vernon's when Sir Robert had his stroke and her unobtrusive kindliness and real services gained her a singular position behind the grim reserve of the Vernon family. She could always banter the vicar away from his hobby horse of the Greek rite when at parish meetings the agenda seemed to have been buried for ever beneath a welter of Euchologia and Menaia. She checked Sir Robert's anti-bolshevik phobia from victimizing the County Librarian for her Fabianism but was fierce in her attack on the local council when she thought that class prejudice had prevented Commander Osborne's widow from getting a council house. She led in fact an active and useful existence, yet when anyone praised her she would only laugh—'My dear,' she would say 'hard work's the only excuse old maids like me have got for existing at all, and even then I don't know that they oughtn't to lethalize the lot of us.' As the danger of war grew nearer in the thirties her favourite remark was 'Well, if they've got any sense this time they'll keep the young fellows at home and put us useless old maids in the trenches,' and she said it with real conviction.

(ANGUS WILSON, *A Little Companion*)

Sum up in a few sentences the main points of Miss Arkwright's character.

In what way are the reported comments that Miss Arkwright makes typical of her?

4. By Comparisons and Associations. Sometimes writers tell us about their characters by comparing them to something else which calls up an image in our minds or by associating them with some idea or object that is related or which is significant. Here is a description of Miss Murdstone.

It was Miss Murdstone who was arrived, and a gloomy-looking lady she was; dark, like her brother, whom she greatly resembled in face and voice; and with very heavy eyebrows, nearly meeting over her large nose, as if, being disabled by the wrongs of her sex from wearing whiskers, she had carried them to that account. She brought with her two uncompromising hard black boxes, with her initials on the lids in hard brass nails. When she paid the coachman she took the money from a hard steel purse, and she kept the purse in a very jail of a bag which hung upon her arm by a heavy chain, and shut up like a bite. I had never, at that time, seen such a metallic lady altogether as Miss Murdstone was.

(CHARLES DICKENS, *David Copperfield*)

Pick out the words or objects that directly suggest metal. Which words in the description of Miss Murdstone suggest characteristics of metal? How is this association with metal appropriate?

5. By associating the character with one particular point of view or action by which they can be easily and quickly identified. Who can ever forget, for instance, Uriah Heep in Charles Dickens's *David Copperfield* being 'ever so humble' and rubbing his hands together, words and an action that are forever associated with him?

It was no fancy of mine about his hands, I observed; for he frequently ground the palms against each other as if to squeeze them dry and warm, besides often wiping them, in a stealthy way, on his pocket handkerchief.

Here is a lesser known character from *Hard Times*:

Thomas Gradgrind, sir. A man of realities. A man of facts and calculations. A man who proceeds upon the principle that two and two are four, and nothing over, and who is not to be talked into allowing for anything over. Thomas Gradgrind, sir—peremptorily Thomas—Thomas Gradgrind. With a rule and a pair of scales, and the multiplication table always in his pocket, sir, ready to weight and measure any parcel of human nature, and tell you exactly what it comes to. It is a mere question of figures, a case of simple arithmetic. You might hope to get some other nonsensical belief into the head of George Gradgrind, or Augustus Gradgrind, or John Gradgrind, or Joseph Gradgrind (all suppositious, non-existent persons), but into the head of Thomas Gradgrind—no sir!

(CHARLES DICKENS, *Hard Times*)

HARD TIMES.

Underline the words that reinforce the idea that Thomas Gradgrind is a man of facts and calculations. What does the use of the word 'sir' add to the passage?

6. By choice of words and picking out a particular feature or detail that calls the character vividly to mind. Here are some examples taken from Edward Blishen's *A Cackhanded War*:

'He was a tiny fellow, with a leathery white face under black hair, and tied to the case he'd brought were the most enormous gumboots I'd ever seen.'

'Mrs Goss was a widow, a neat little woman of over seventy: and witchlike.'

'He was a deeply depressed man, this farmer, who always wore a white coat and cloth cap, and was always peppered with a white-and-black bristle.'

'He was a tall, silent, dark man, very gentle, who would tut over his machine as if it were some moody woman.'

'On the strawstack was a boy: a short, stout boy with a kind of naked pertness about his eyes and a very runny nose.'

Describe five varied characters, using one sentence for each, and try to make them alive by the way you use words or by giving to each a particular descriptive detail that defines him or her clearly and individually—as Edward Blishen has done.

At the end of assignment A you were asked to sum up the kind of person Kirk was as revealed in the passages. Look back at your answer. Would you add anything now, bearing in mind what you have learnt in this lesson? In your notebook, write a fuller description of Kirk in your own words, analysing the passage again and picking up the details you missed first time round.

 READING LIST

In Unit 1 we suggested you should read as much as you can manage. We have chosen books which, we hope, will give you pleasure; but as well as this they will help improve your understanding of writing and what a writer is trying to do. This first reading list is of books which contain a gallery of vivid and vividly described characters. You don't have to read any of these books though we hope you will read one or two, or at least dip into some. You should be able to borrow any of them from your public library.

Charles Dickens: *David Copperfield, Great Expectations.* These are long, but even reading a few chapters would give you an insight into how language can be used richly to portray character.

Leon Garfield: *Smith, Black Jack.*
These are similar in their richness to Dickens's novels, but they are much shorter and more easily approached; published as 'books for young readers', anyone would find their vivid evocations of eighteenth-century characters exciting and stimulating.
Dylan Thomas: *Under Milk Wood, Miscellany One.*
A play and short stories about racy Welsh characters.
Laurie Lee: *Cider with Rosie.*
Edward Blishen: *A Cackhanded War.*
Vivid evocations of the authors' younger selves.
Mayhew's London, London's Underworld, edited by Peter Quennell.
Records of interviews with some of the poor and strange characters of nineteenth-century London.
See also the short stories of the following writers which are full of interesting and interestingly described characters: Katherine Mansfield, Somerset Maugham, O. Henry, Saki, Angus Wilson.

 VOCABULARY

Words are obviously very important to a writer, and they should be very important to you as a writer in training. We each have our own stock of words which we use, and we should always be eager to increase this stock through our reading so that we are able to use a wider range of words and express our ideas more fully and more precisely. Many of the writers we read have a much greater command over a larger number of words than we possess, and a study of these writers can help us to extend our own store of words and use them more effectively.

We should also try to become increasingly aware that writers use different kinds of words and use them in different ways. The kind of people they are and the intention behind their writing affect the type of words they use. Angus Wilson, for instance, is in many ways a very literate writer. He writes for the well-read and intelligent reader and therefore he uses a large number of fairly difficult and sophisticated words. The following exercises should help you to become aware of this and should help you to increase your own vocabulary. Remember that there is not much use in learning these words in isolation; you must be able to know what they mean and be able to use them in a context. Try to make them your own. Try to use them in your own writing when suitable occasion arises.

1. Read the passage on page 23 from Angus Wilson's short story *A Little Companion* again and try to work out the meanings of the following words as used in the passage: distinguished, eccentricities, anti-social, irony, deification, pretentious, caustic, snub, ostentatious(ly), formidable, antagonism, unobtrusive, banter, agenda, welter, phobia, conviction.

2. Look these words up in a dictionary and check them against your first impressions. Write the words and their meanings in your notebook.

3. Put each of these words into a sentence of your own. Try to write interesting sentences which show the meaning of the words clearly. For instance, 'He was distinguished' tells us nothing about the word 'distinguished'—it could mean anything. The following sentence gives a much clearer indication of the meaning: 'It was obvious that he had had a distinguished military career from the great respect with which he was treated when he visited his old brigade as guest of honour.'

> Read through the extracts so far in this lesson. Pick out any words you are not sure of. Add them to your vocabulary list, look them up and put them into sentences in the same way as the words we have picked out.

LANGUAGE
Paragraphs

Almost any piece of writing is divided into paragraphs—a glance at this course book, at any newspaper or magazine, will show this. A paragraph is a sub-section into which the material of the article, essay or story falls. It begins on a new line and the opening is indented. The subject-matter of any reasonably long piece of writing can be divided into various sections, each of which can be dealt with in separate paragraphs. Within a particular paragraph, there should be a unity of material; in other words, all the information given in one paragraph should deal with one specific aspect of the subject. The purpose behind dividing writing into paragraphs is to help the reader. When he comes to the end of one paragraph and begins the next, he knows that he is moving on to another facet of the subject being written about. Paragraphs help to provide order for thought and understanding. In a well-constructed piece of writing, you ought to be able to sum up the idea of each paragraph in a short phrase, and everything in the paragraph should be relevant to that idea or phrase.

Topic sentences

Often, a paragraph has what is known as a topic sentence. This is a sentence which tells you what that particular paragraph is about. In many cases, it is the first sentence of the paragraph. It shows that the writer has moved on to another point in his argument and gives you a clue as to what the paragraph is dealing with.

Here is an editorial from The Guardian. *Read it carefully and study the analysis that follows.*

Nature Destroys, Man Destroys
The destruction of Managua by an earthquake and of Hanoi by bombing shows that the United States is good

at flying planes. In one case, the US is doing everything to relieve the effects of the appalling natural disaster which has levelled much of Nicaragua's capital. Here, their response has been worthy of Christmas. By contrast, the vicious bombing of Hanoi and the brief seasonal halt, followed by resumed bombing, is the cynical prosecution of a man-made disaster. This bombing is inhumanly pointless. It dwarfs benevolence to Nicaragua and will make a negotiated settlement to the end of the war in Vietnam more distant. It is hard to

In one sense, the UNDRO has been lucky that the earthquake occurred where it did. The US is the only country with the airlift capacity to cope swiftly with requirements on such a large scale. Florida, from where most of the US contributions were flown, is considerably closer to Managua that to Santiago or Calcutta.

The official British response by comparison has been weak. In dispatching camp beds, drugs and plasma in one aircraft with one crew (which must rest for several hours during such a long haul), it appears to be ignoring

Homeless victims of the Bangladesh disaster

believe that the same man, President Nixon, has ordered both actions.

From the misery of Managua it is possible to extract some slight encouragement. The United Nations Disaster Relief Organization (UNDRO) has functioned creditably in its first operation and under difficult circumstances. The organization has been an agonizing long time coming into existence. The cyclone disaster of East Pakistan (now Bangladesh) of November, 1970, showed how acutely was needed a body to assess the kind of aid required and to channel it to the right spots. Even so, the UN voted for its creation only earlier this year.

the need for haste. In dispatching only one aircraft Britain appears mean. Spain, which has to send its aircraft a comparably long distance, has sent three aircraft.

The Janus-faced actions of the US have shown once again that the UN can be effective only at the whims of its chief members. Because the US, a Security Council member, has chosen to play generous in the case of Managua, UNDRO has been able to do its job. By contrast, the UN has done little but protest verbally to the US about its Vietnamese policies. The UN unfortunately knows that it is immediately deprived of power when a Security Council member finds it politically expedient to act independently. The American decision to save Nicaraguan lives can in no way cover up for its brutal decision to kill Vietnamese.

(*The Guardian*, 27 December 1972)

Paragraph 1 deals with the then recent United States flying activity—taking aid to Nicaragua and bombing Hanoi. The opening sentence with its phrase 'good at flying planes' takes on by the end of the paragraph an ironic tinge.

Paragraph 2 leads on to 'some slight encouragement' by discussing the development of the United Nations Disaster Relief Organization. Note how the words 'some slight encouragement' in the opening sentence prepare the reader for the argument in this paragraph.

Similarly, the opening sentence of **paragraph 3** prepares the reader for a contrast—'The official British response by comparison has been weak.' This alleged weakness is then described in the rest of the paragraph.

The last paragraph returns to a consideration of the US attitude and the effect of a strong US on a weak UN. Again, the expression 'Janus-faced' (two-faced) in the first sentence prepares us for the final sentence stating clearly the US's ambivalent attitude. The opening sentence also sums up the material in the paragraph.

Here is another editorial from The Guardian. *Analyse it in the same way as the passage above. Sum up each paragraph in a short phrase or sentence. State how the opening sentence in each paragraph gives you clues as to what the paragraph is about.*

United in the Doghouse

The misfortunes of Manchester United are like Candide's—always appalling but never humdrum. The Munich air crash was tragic. The eccentricities of George Best were bizarre. Saturday's last-minute goal by Clarke of Leeds United was as unexpected as it was brilliant. Yesterday, Derby County beat Manchester United by three goals to one and pushed them to the bottom of the First Division. Having pirouetted so long on the pinnacles, United are now back near the bottom of the hill.

It remains to be seen what Tommy Docherty can do to remake a lost reputation. He is the General George S. Patton among football managers, the man who can lead a brilliant campaign as long as it is a continuous advance. This one has started less than brilliantly with one disappointment and one defeat. The question now is whether he can inspire United as he has inspired other teams and whether he can do this with mighty Matthew Busby brooding in the background. In football as in politics older statesmen cast long shadows.

The Docherty campaign will be the harder because United has for long believed in collecting stars and letting them perform. It has usually been more of a constellation than a team. Neither of Mr Docherty's predecessors managed to change this. The McGuinness-O'Farrell era left United no less galactic than it had been before, except for the departure (or extinction) of George Best. It was and is a team that might win brilliantly or lose disastrously often according to nothing more incurable than the way the players felt on the day.

Manchester United can be a maddening group of people but they have always been open to inspiration. The Docherty era may not last long but he ought to be able to inspire them while he is there. Like Patton's Third Army their instinct is to attack and to attack in unexpected ways. Almost everything could still happen to United except mediocrity. Their fate is unpredictable but will surely involve a blaze of glory—of one sort or the other.

(*The Guardian*, 27 December 1972)

Many of the more popular newspapers use very short paragraphs, often consisting of only one sentence. The effect may be racy, but it is also disjointed, and there is little logical necessity from the point of view of good style for dividing articles into so many paragraphs—if the term 'paragraphs' can be used correctly in this context.

Read the following news item. Ask yourself whether the 'paragraphs' are fully developed, whether there is any necessity for new paragraphs at each stage, what the general effect of the short paragraphs is.

Where murder is a way of life

THEY CALL IT MURDER CITY, U.S.A.—Detroit, Michigan. The homicide rate last year was 690, and this year so far it's 686, making it the highest of any American city with a million-plus population.

Why? The answer lies in the ghettoes of Detroit, the centre of the nation's car industry.

For those crowded, tumbling, mostly black areas which spawned the Motown Sound is where 9 out of 10 of the murders occur.

'It's kind of a by-product of ghetto life. If you never achieve what you think you are capable of achieving you have a tendency to get angry quick.

'I think there's a lot of self-hate involved, too,' said one veteran city social worker.

The experts agree that living in a frustrated stress-inducing environment like a ghetto every day of your life makes many people walking sticks of dynamite.

Most of the reasons for murder are remarkably trivial, one recently involving an old man who stabbed another over a can of vegetable soup.

(*Scottish Daily Express*, 27 December 1972)

Logical progression

When reading newspapers and magazines, books and this course, it is important that you make yourself conscious of how the writing is constructed and ask yourself what effect the paragraphing has—whether it is skilfully done, whether it helps the reader to follow the argument, whether the effect is jerky or jumbled or logical and ordered. Only by becoming aware of the effectiveness or otherwise of what you read will you be able to become critical and be able to apply your critical faculties to your own writing.

The style of the last extract quoted above, jerking from one fact to another without proper development, is one to be avoided in your own essays.

Sometimes a paragraph consisting of a single short sentence can be effective. As you read the following extract from a short story by Ray Bradbury, ask yourself what effect the three short one-sentence paragraphs have and why they are effective. The story is about the arrival of a white man on an all-black planet.

Across the sky, very high and beautiful, a rocket burned one sweep of orange fire. It circled and came down, causing all to gasp. It landed, setting the meadow afire here and there; the fire burned out, the rocket lay a moment in quiet, and then, as the silent crowd watched, a great door in the side of the vessel whispered out a breath of oxygen, the door slid back and an old man stepped out.

'A white man, a white man, a white man'. . . . The words travelled back in the expectant crowd, the children speaking in each other's ears, whispering, butting each other, the words moving in ripples to where the crowd stopped and the streetcars stood in the windy sunlight, the smell of paint coming out of their opened windows. The whispering wore itself away and it was gone.

No one moved.

The white man was tall and straight, but a deep weariness was in his face. He had not shaved this day, and his eyes were as old as the eyes of a man can be and still be alive. His eyes were colourless; almost white and sightless with things he had seen in the passing years. He was thin as a winter bush. His hands trembled and he had to lean against the portway of the ship as he looked out over the crowd.

He put out a hand and half smiled, but drew his hand back.

No one moved.

He looked down into their faces, and perhaps he saw but did not see the guns and the ropes, and perhaps he smelled the paint. No one ever asked him. He began to talk. He started very quietly and slowly, expecting no interruptions, and receiving none, and his voice was very tired and old and pale.

(RAY BRADBURY, *The Other Foot*)

Contrasts

One of the reasons the short paragraphs are effective is because of the contrast with the longer paragraphs. This gives a variety of pace. After a long paragraph, the short paragraph brings us up with a jolt which is appropriate to what is being stated in the short paragraphs. This kind of effect is not always suitable, but varying the length of your paragraphs—particularly when writing a story or a description involving dramatic events—is certainly something to bear in mind when you come to your own writing. Essays involving discussion or opinions usually require a more regular kind of paragraph construction as in the two editorials from *The Guardian* quoted earlier.

Write three or four paragraphs on one of the following subjects. Make a plan first stating which aspect of the subject you are going to deal with in each paragraph. Make sure that the paragraphs are arranged in the most interesting and logical order. Write the paragraphs. Make sure that all the material discussed in each paragraph is relevant to the aspect of the subject stated in your plan.

The subjects suggested are:

1. Women's Lib.
2. Strikes.
3. Leisure.
4. Decorating.
5. Mothers going out to work.

The plan need only be very simple. For instance, if one of the subjects were 'Comprehensive Education', the plan might be like this:

Paragraph 1: an explanation of what comprehensive education is.
Paragraph 2: points people make in favour.
Paragraph 3: points people make against.
Paragraph 4: where I stand personally.

 # SPELLING

Spelling is important. If you have difficulty with your spelling, you must try to combat this weakness. There is, unfortunately, no golden way of doing this. It requires perpetual vigilance on your part and hard grind. Use a dictionary constantly to check up on the words you are unsure of. Become aware of the words you spell incorrectly. Write them in your notebook correctly spelled and refer to your notebook every time these words crop up. Most of the words mis-spelled are common words, and most of the words you mis-spell are the ones you always spell wrongly. Try to associate the words you get wrong with other words so that you have a foolproof and personal way of remembering. For instance, many people spell 'medicine' with an 'e' in the middle, but if you associate the work with 'medical' which has an 'i' in the middle, you will remember that 'medicine' is spelled with an 'i'. If you confuse the spelling of the two words 'stationery' and 'stationary', remember that 'stationery' is sold in a stationer's which is difficult to spell any other way. Make sure you look at words and know them, and then tricks like these will help you to remember the words you get wrong, and ensure that you spell them correctly.

The 'spelling' sections in these units will provide some rules and guidance, together with exercises to help you remember them. But finally, learning to spell depends on you.

Let's take a simple and well-known rule to start with:

'i' before 'e' except after 'c'
when the sound is 'ee'

This is true of most words. Here are some examples:

belief	shriek	deceive
chief	thief, etc.	perceive
grief	ceiling	receipt
mischief	conceit	receive, etc.
retrieve	conceive	

Find further examples that obey this rule and make a list of them in your notebook.

There are, however, some important exceptions, viz:

seize (and seizure)
weir
weird
and neither }
either   } (which can be pronounced 'ee')

Perhaps a sentence like this would help you to remember these exceptions:

The weird sisters seized the weir.

Note also the following words with 'ei' spellings which are not pronounced 'ee'

feint	leisure	surfeit
foreign	reign	veil, etc.
forfeit	skein	

Learn this rule and these examples. The next time you read a newspaper, stop at every word with 'ei' or 'ie' and see whether it conforms to the rule.

UNIT 4

 WRITING

Characters

 READING AND UNDERSTANDING

Descriptions

 READING LIST

 VOCABULARY

 LANGUAGE

Punctuation Marks I:
the Full Stop

 SPELLING

 ASSIGNMENT C

Following on from the 'Reading and Understanding' section in Unit 3 we give you more help in learning to write about people yourself. You will be asked to describe a character in Assignment C.

This time we study descriptions of places and objects, and compare the writing techniques with those used to describe people.

Books which contain much descriptive material.

A look at some of the words in the extract from H. G. Wells' *A History of Mr Polly* used in the 'characters' section.

We start a study of punctuation marks with a section on the full stop, and we stress the importance of writing complete sentences. The hints and the exercises will help you overcome any problems you have.

A section explaining the spelling of the suffix 'ful' and some words often confused.

 WRITING

Characters

In 'Reading and Understanding' in Unit 3, we studied some of the ways in which writers describe people and help us to visualize the characters they are writing about. They give us facts about them. They show them in action, doing things in such a way as to tell us what kind of people they are. They use words to colour our view of the people they are describing. They select particular details to build up a particular impression.

Look again at the passages discussed there and the notes you made as a preparation to writing about people yourself.

When faced with writing a description of 'an old man' or 'a friend', you may at first be daunted, but it is not as difficult a task as it may at first appear. There are three

ways in which you can help yourself to be more prepared for such an assignment.

1. Try to improve your powers of observation. Much of the time we go through life with our eyes shut. If we were asked what the person sitting next to us on the bus this morning looked like, we would probably not be able to say a thing about him.

Try it! See how accurate a description you can give of a bus conductor or shop assistant you 'met' today. Or perhaps you noticed an interesting character—a tramp, say—in the street. Can you actually describe him?

Note unusual faces, try to describe what they look like to yourself, compare their appearance to other things, try to imagine what their family backgrounds are, what work they do, what they are thinking. Listen to the things they say. See how they are dressed. If you sharpen your perceptions in this way by actually looking at people, you are more likely to have something interesting to say when asked to write about people.

2. When faced with writing a character sketch of a person, remember to ask yourself questions in order to help gather material. What does he look like? His physical appearance. His dress. What does he do for a living? What are his social and family circumstances? What are his opinions? What kind of life has he led? What kind of things is he interested in? What kind of things would he talk about and what would he say? What do other people feel about him? Can you show him doing something that is typical of him and his character?

3. See how other writers describe people. We have already studied some example of this (in Unit 3). Here are two more for you to examine. The first is a description of Mr Polly.

Mr Polly's age was exactly thirty-seven years and a half. He was a short, compact figure, and a little inclined to a localized embonpoint. His face was not unpleasing; the features fine, but a trifle too large about the lower half of his face, and a trifle too pointed about the nose to be classically perfect. The corners of his sensitive mouth were depressed. His eyes were ruddy brown and troubled, and the left one was round with more of wonder in it than its fellow. His complexion was dull and yellowish. That, as I have explained, on account of those civil disturbances. He was, in the technical sense of the word, clean shaved, with a small fallow patch under the right ear, and a cut on the chin. His brow had the little puckerings of a thoroughly discontented man, little wrinklings and lumps, particularly over his right eye, and he sat, with his hands in his pockets, a little askew on the stile, and swung one leg.

'Hole!' he repeated presently.

He broke into a quavering song: 'Roöötten Beëëastly Silly Hole!'

His voice thickened with rage, and the rest of his discourse was marred by an unfortunate choice of epithets.

He was dressed in a shabby black morning coat and vest; the braid that bound these garments was a little loose in places. His collar was chosen from stock, and with projecting corners, technically a 'wing-pole'; that and his tie, which was new and loose and rich in colouring, had been selected to encourage and stimulate customers—for he dealt in gentlemen's outfitting. His golf cap, which was also from stock and aslant over his eye, gave his misery a desperate touch. He wore brown leather boots—because he hated the smell of blacking.

Perhaps after all it was not simply indigestion that troubled him.

Behind the superficialities of Mr Polly's being moved a larger and vaguer distress. The elementary education he had acquired had left him with the impression that arithmetic was a fluky science and best avoided in practical affairs, but even the absence of book-keeping, and a total inability to distinguish between capital and interest, could not blind him forever to the fact that the little shop in the High Street was not paying. An absence of returns, a constriction of credit, a depleted till—the most valiant resolves to keep smiling could not prevail forever against these insistent phenomena. One might bustle about in the morning before dinner and in the afternoon after tea and forget that huge dark cloud of insolvency that gathered and spread in the background, but it was part of the desolation of these afternoon periods, those gray spaces of time after meals when all one's courage had descended to the unseen battles of the pit that life seemed stripped to the bone, and one saw with a hopeless clearness.

(H. G. WELLS, *The History of Mr Polly*)

Read the passage again and consider these questions:
What are we told about Mr Polly's physical appearance?

What do we learn about his way of life at that particular moment?

What do we learn about Mr Polly from what he says himself?

What is the effect of having Mr Polly speak between the long paragraphs of description?

Looking at the description as a whole, how does Wells build up a picture of Mr Polly?

This is a fairly formal account and concentrates very much on a detailed description of Mr Polly's face and shape, his dress and a brief summary of his way of life at this particular moment. The description is prevented from becoming too heavy by having Mr Polly speak in characteristic style, thus dramatizing the situation and breaking the description in two. The character sketch makes its effect mainly by its accumulation of detail on detail.

Now look at the following account of Margaret Powell's parents from *Below Stairs*. This is much more rambling and informal, the intention being as much to give a picture of the author's childhood as of the author's parents.

I was born fifty-eight years ago in Hove, the second child of a family of seven. My earliest recollection is that other children seemed to be better off than we were. But our parents cared so much for us. One particular thing that I always remember was that every Sunday morning my father used to bring us a comic and a bag of sweets. You used to be able to get a comic for a halfpenny plain and a penny coloured. Sometimes now when I look back at it, I wonder how he managed to do it when he was out of work and there was no money at all coming in.

My father was a painter and decorator. Sort of general odd-job man. He could do almost anything: repair roofs, or do a bit of plastering; but painting and paper-hanging were his main work. Yet in the neighbourhood where we lived, there was hardly any work in the winter. People didn't want their houses done up then; they couldn't be painted outside and they didn't want the bother of having it done up inside. So the winters were the hardest times.

My mother used to go out charring from about eight in the morning till six in the evening for two shillings a day. Sometimes she used to bring home little treasures: a basin of dripping, half a loaf of bread, a little bit of butter or a bowl of soup. She used to hate accepting anything. She hated charity. But we were so glad of them that, when she came home and we saw that she was carrying something, we used to make a dive to see what she'd got.

It seems funny today, I suppose, that there was this hatred of charity, but when my parents brought us up there was no unemployment money. Anything you got was charity.

I remember my mother, when we only had one pair of shoes and they all needed mending, she went down to the council to try to get more for us. She had to answer every question under the sun and she was made to feel that there was something distasteful about her because she hadn't got enough money to live on.

It was very different getting somewhere to live in those days. You just walked through the streets, and there were notices up, 'Rooms to let'.

When we were extra hard up, we only had one room or two rooms in somebody else's house. But when Dad was working, we would go around looking for half a house. We never had a house to ourselves. Not many people could afford a house in those days, not to themselves. As for buying a house, why, such things were never even dreamed of!

I know I used to wonder why, when things were so hard, Mum kept having babies, and I remember how angry she used to get when a couple of elderly spinsters at a house where she worked kept telling her not to have any more children, that she couldn't afford to keep them. I remember saying to my mother, 'Why do you have so many children? Is it hard to have children?' And she said, 'Oh, no. It's easy as falling off a log.'

(MARGARET POWELL, *Below Stairs*)

Consider these questions carefully before reading the commentary that follows:

What are we told about how Margaret Powell's parents made a living?

What is the children's attitude towards their parents?

What concrete details are given and what effect do they have?

What do we learn about Margaret Powell's mother from her attitude towards other people?

What can we deduce about her from what she is quoted as saying?

What effect is made by contrasting the way of life then with that of today?

What do we learn about the physical appearance of Margaret Powell's parents?

We are told what Margaret Powell's parents do for a living, how they care for their children, their attitude towards charity, where they lived and how. The family is clearly very happy, with the children eagerly looking forward to father's treat on Sundays and to mother bringing home little tit-bits from work, and Margaret was able to discuss personal matters with her mother. The concrete details given—'a basin of dripping, half a loaf of bread, a little bit of butter or a bowl of soup'—help to give truth to the situation and make it much easier for a reader to visualize the way of life being described. The comparison between life then and life now is emphasized so that we are made to realize the hardships the parents had to undergo in order to try to give their children a decent life: these indicate their concern and love. We are informed very clearly that it wasn't easy.

We are told that Margaret Powell's mother 'hated charity'. She was independent and didn't want to be beholden to anyone. The suggestion that she had too many children was received with indignation. She is also very down-to-earth and is able to view the difficult situation with wry humour as can be seen from her comment about having children. We are not told anything about her physical appearance or about that of her husband, and yet the facts of their life, the concrete details of their attitudes and background and beliefs, and the scraps of reported comment, enable us to call up a picture of them in our minds: the lack of physical detail is no drawback in this respect.

Look at the passages again and jot down what we are told about the people. Organize these facts into various headings, such as physical appearance, work, style of dress, family background, opinions, attitudes.

READING AND UNDERSTANDING

Descriptions

When describing a scene or an inanimate object, authors use many of the same kinds of methods they employ when describing people. They use selected detail to build up a composite picture. They use concrete detail to build up a sense of reality. They use comparisons to make the details more vivid and easy to imagine. They use words in such a way as to appeal to our senses so that we see, hear or feel the object more precisely. They use words (particularly verbs and adjectives) and images to bring the objects more suddenly and surprisingly to our view.

Read the following description of a deserted house left to decay and become overrun.

The house was left; the house was deserted. It was left like a shell on a sandhill to fill with dry salt grains now that life had left it. The long night seemed to have set in; the trifling airs, nibbling, the clammy breaths, fumbling, seemed to have triumphed. The saucepan had rusted and the mat decayed. Toads had nosed their way in. Idly, aimlessly, the swaying shawl swung to and fro. A thistle thrust itself between the tiles in the larder. The swallows nested in the drawing-room; the floor was strewn with straw; the plaster fell in shovelfuls; rafters were laid bare; rats carried off this and that to gnaw behind the wainscots. Tortoise-shell butterflies burst from the chrysalis and pattered their life out on the window-pane. Poppies sowed themselves among the dahlias; the lawn waved with long grass; giant artichokes towered among the roses; a fringed carnation flowered among the cabbages; while the gentle tapping of a weed at the window had become, on winters' nights, a drumming from sturdy trees and thorned briars which made the whole room green in summer.

(VIRGINIA WOOLF, *To the Lighthouse*)

Try to answer these questions before reading the notes that follow.

What do we learn about the physical appearance of the house, its size and shape?

What does the author compare the house to?

Pick out the references to growing things and creatures.

Pick out the words and details that appeal to the senses.

Say what you think the author means when she uses the words 'nosed', 'thrust', 'pattered' and 'fringed'.

The following notes give some indication of the ways in which Virginia Woolf uses her skill as a writer to transfer her impression of the deserted house to the reader.

1. Selected detail. The author doesn't tell us the dimensions of the house or how old it is because these are not essential to her purpose which is to create an atmosphere of decay and to indicate how nature has taken over.

2. Concrete detail. The author mentions things like 'the swaying shawl', 'the tiles in the larder', 'rafters laid bare', 'the saucepan had rusted', and a whole series of creatures and plants—toads, swallows, rats, butterflies, thistles, poppies, long grass, giant artichokes, carnations, cabbages, briars. The description of the plaster fallen 'in shovelfuls' gives a sense of actuality. It is as though someone had actually measured the amount of plaster by trying to shovel it away. References to objects like these convince us that the author has seen this house, has visited it.

3. Comparisons. The house is 'like a shell on a sandhill' left 'to fill with dry salt grains'. The comparison between the shattered house and a shell forced open from which the mollusc has escaped is apt as both are now open to the elements and the original inhabitants have departed. The shell in the midst of the sand emphasizes too the transience of life.

4. The senses. The following words used by the author suggest sounds: 'pattered', 'tapping', 'drumming'. The sense of sight is stimulated by the colours and the movement: 'the swaying shawl', 'the lawn waved with long grass', 'the poppies and the dahlias', 'the artichokes and the roses', 'the whole room green in summer'. The verbs emphasize touch and movement: 'the clammy breaths, fumbling', 'a thistle thrust', the rats 'gnaw', butterflies 'burst' from the chrysalis. A picture is built up not just in words but in sense-perceptions which the words call forth.

5. The use of vivid words. Among the many examples that could be chosen, consider the use of the verb 'nosed' to describe the movement of toads, making their way forward and leading with their noses; the verb 'thrust' emphasizing the vigorousness and toughness of the thistle's growth; the verb 'pattered' describing the light repetitive sound of the butterflies' wings against the glass; the adjective 'fringed' to describe the feathery tasselled effect of the carnation.

6. Imagery. This will be discussed in greater detail in a later unit. But at this stage, it can be seen how examples of growth, colour and beauty—butterflies, poppies, carnations—are piled on top of each other to culminate in the final idea of the whole room being green in summer with vegetation. What had started as a description of something desolate and decayed ends up exultantly as a description of vitality and growth. This is the picture that is built up and that we are left with, and it is achieved largely through Virginia Woolf's control of imagery.

There are many more points that could be made about this description, but these should be sufficient to indicate how important words are in creating effects—not just any words that happen to come to mind, but particular words chosen because they call forth a specific response.

The description of the deserted house is very rich in effect. The way the words are used and the rhythmic pattern of the words give the impression of poetry. A description doesn't have to be 'poetic', however, in order to be effective.

Read the following description of a gun which the boy, Bob Starrett, has found:

What puzzled me most, though, was something it took me nearly two weeks to appreciate. And yet it was the most striking thing of all. Shane carried no gun.

In those days guns were as familiar all through the Territory as boots and saddles. They were not used much in the valley except for occasional hunting. But they were always in evidence. Most men did not feel fully dressed without one.

We homesteaders went in mostly for rifles and shotguns when we had any shooting to do. A pistol slapping on the hip was a nuisance for a farmer. Still every man had his cartridge belt and holstered Colt to be worn when he was not working or loafing around the house. Father buckled his on whenever he rode off on any trip, even just into town, as much out of habit, I guess, as anything else.

But this Shane never carried a gun. And that was a peculiar thing because he had a gun.

I saw it once. I saw it when I was alone in the barn one day and I spotted his saddle-roll lying on his bunk. Usually he kept it carefully put away underneath. He must have forgotten it this time, for it was there in the open by the pillow. I reached to sort of feel it—and I felt the gun inside. No one was near, so I unfastened the straps and unrolled the blankets. There it was, the most beautiful-looking weapon I ever saw. Beautiful and deadly-looking.

The holster and filled cartridge belt were of the same soft black leather as the boots tucked under the bunk, tooled in the same intricate design. I knew enough to know that the gun was a single-action Colt, the same model as the Regular Army issue that was the favourite of all men in those days, and that oldtimers used to say was the finest pistol ever made.

This was the same model. But this was no army gun. It was black, almost blue-black, with the darkness not in any enamel but in the metal itself. The grip was clear on the outer curve, shaped to the fingers on the inner curve, and two ivory plates were set into it with exquisite skill, one on each side.

The smooth invitation of it tempted your grasp. I took hold and pulled the gun out of its holster. It came so easily that I could hardly believe it was there in my hand. Heavy like father's, it was somehow much easier to handle. You held it up to aiming level and it seemed to balance itself into your hand.

It was clean and polished and oiled. The empty cylinder, when I released the catch and flicked it, spun swiftly and noiselessly. I was surprised to see that the front sight was gone, the barrel smooth right down to the end, and that the hammer had been filed to a sharp point.

Why should a man do that to a gun? Why should a man with a gun like that refuse to wear it and show it off? And then, staring at that dark and deadly efficiency, I was again suddenly chilled, and I quickly put everything back exactly as before and hurried into the sun.

(JACK SHAEFER, *Shane*)

1. Pick out all the words and phrases that actually describe the gun. What impression of the gun do you get when you take all these words and phrases together?

2. In what way is it suggested that the gun has a life of its own, that it is almost alive? ('The smooth invitation of it …')

3. The senses of touch and sight are appealed to here. Pick out the details which support this.

4. Why does the author spend so much time describing the general attitude towards guns in the Territory before describing Shane's gun?

5. The passage isn't just a description of the gun; it also tells us something about the narrator, Bob, and about Shane. The gun is used as a means by which the reader is able to deduce more about these two characters. What do we learn about them from this passage?

 # READING LIST

Description is an important element of any novelist's tools of the trade, whether it involves description of place, people or atmosphere. Here are some books in which description plays a large part. As we suggested in the last unit, try to read one or two at least.

Longer books by nineteenth-century authors (you may find these difficult, but they are rewarding):
George Eliot: *Silas Marner, The Mill on the Floss.*
Thomas Hardy: *The Mayor of Casterbridge, Far from the Madding Crowd.*
W. M. Thackeray: *Vanity Fair.*
Charlotte Brontë: *Jane Eyre, Villette.*

Much lesser works, but racy and enjoyable:
Margaret Powell: *Below Stairs, Above Stairs.*

Evocations of childhood:
Maxim Gorki: *My Childhood.*
Clifford Dyment: *The Railway Game.*
Richard Church: *Over the Bridge.*
James Kirkup: *The Only Child.*
Arthur Barton: *Two Lamps in our Street.*

Factual accounts of places and ways of life:
J. B. Priestley: *English Journey.*
George Orwell: *The Road to Wigan Pier, Down and Out in Paris and London.*
Clancy Sigal: *Weekend in Dinlock.*
Rosemary Millington: *A Nation of Trees.*
Doris Lessing: *In Pursuit of the English.*

 # VOCABULARY

H. G. Wells, although a twentieth-century writer, often writes in a style that seems old-fashioned, having more in common with Dickens than with more modern novelists. His style is also sometimes rather stilted, and this effect is produced largely by his use of rather literary and artificial words. Re-read the extract from *The History of Mr Polly* and see if you agree.

Try to work out the meanings of the following words as used there:

localized, embonpoint, discourse, epithets, superficiality, constriction, insistent, phenomenon, insolvency.

34

Look these words up in a dictionary and check with your definitions.

Put each of these words into a sentence of your own. Try to make your sentence interesting as was suggested in Unit 3.

> Read once more through the extracts in this unit. Pick out any words you are not sure of. Add them to your vocabulary list. Look them up and put them in sentences in the same way as the words we have picked out.

 # LANGUAGE
Punctuation Marks: The Full Stop

The full stop is a punctuation mark (.) which indicates the end of a sentence or a complete statement. A sentence which follows must begin with a capital letter. Thus:

The traffic lights turned green. The car started off.

There are two common incidences of failure to use the full stop. The first is to put commas where full stops are needed, e.g.

The policeman is coming, you had better run.

These are two separate statements and should be written as two separate sentences, thus:

The policeman is coming. You had better run.

The second common fault is to omit full stops and punctuation marks altogether as in the following incorrectly punctuated example:

There was a knock at the door when I answered it there was no one there for several minutes I waited to see if anyone would appear

The lack of full stops makes reading and understanding the passage difficult. At first reading the sense which emerges is 'There was a knock at the door when I answered it' and 'There was no one there for several minutes.' Obviously, on reconsideration, these statements are not logical. Full stops are needed as follows to make sense of the lines:

There was a knock at the door. When I answered it there was no one there. For several minutes I waited to see if anyone would appear.

There is no easy rule for knowing where full stops should go, but these four points may help:

1. Remember that full stops come after complete statements. The following are complete statements:

Since he was feeling ill, he went to bed early.

Help me.

The car came down the hill, turned the corner and stopped outside the garage.

2. Read anything you write carefully to yourself (or out loud if possible) pausing in an exaggerated way at the full stops, and ask yourself after every full stop if you have in fact made a complete statement, in other words that it makes complete sense on its own.

For practice, find the paragraphs you wrote for the 'Language' section in Unit 3. Read them out loud and judge for yourself whether the full stops are in the right places.

3. Put the full stops in as you go along. Don't add them later as though they are an ornament. If you try to do this, you are almost certain to get them wrong. Full stops are not ornaments: they are an organic part of prose.

4. Pay particular attention to punctuation when you are reading books, newspapers and these units. Punctuation is intended as a guide to reading and understanding, and if you study how it works in what you read, you should be able to apply it correctly to your own writing.

For practice, insert the correct punctuation in the following passage:

July 23rd 1840

My dear Milnes

If you have really any intention of paying me a visit I must describe the *locale* we live six miles from Taunton on the Minehead Road an inn at Taunton is the London Inn I shall be at home from the end of July to the end of October or rather the 20th of October you must give me good notice and wait my answer for we are often full and often sick it is but fair to add that nothing can be more melancholy than Combe Florey that we have no other neighbours than the parsonism of the country and that in the country I hibernise and live by licking my paws having stated these distressing truths and assuring you that as you like to lay out your life to the best advantage it is not worth your while to come I have only to add that we shall be very glad to see you

Yours very truly

Sydney Smith

A secondary use of the full stop is to indicate that a word has been abbreviated, e.g. 'a.m.' for 'ante meridiem', 'B.Sc.' for 'Bachelor of Science', 'Jan.' for 'January'. There is a tendency now to use the full stop only when the final portion of the word has been omitted as in the examples above. Where letters are dropped from the middle of a word, but the first and last letters are retained, it is common practice to omit the full stop, e.g. 'Mr' for 'Mister', 'St' for 'Street' or 'Saint', 'Dr' for 'Doctor'. This is not, however, a universal practice.

Another tendency is for what might be termed 'initial-words'—words like ITV, BEA, UNO—to omit the full stops. The official term for these is 'acronyms'.

Where shortened words have become widely accepted into common usage—e.g. 'ad' for 'advertisement', 'gym' for 'gymnasium', 'vet' for 'veterinary surgeon'—the full stop is omitted.

Find other examples of each of these categories.

 # SPELLING

A simple spelling error which a lot of students make and which is easily corrected is the spelling of the suffix '-ful' when added to a word. There is never a double 'l' when '-ful' comes at the end of a word, e.g.

bashful	frightful	sinful
beautiful	graceful	spoonful
bountiful	hopeful	thoughtful
careful	pitiful	wakeful
dutiful	pocketful	watchful, etc.

Find ten further examples of words like these and add them to your notebook.

When the suffix '-ly' is added to words ending in '-ful' there are always two 'll's', thus:

beautifully	helpfully
carefully	hopefully
gracefully	spitefully, etc.

Find ten further examples of words like these and add them to your notebook.

A further point about '-ful' words is worth commenting on here. For instance, what is the difference in meaning between the following pairs of sentences?

A bucketful of water should be enough.

The bucket full of water was easily knocked over.

He jingled a pocketful of coins.

The pocket full of pebbles would soon give way.

In the first sentence in each pair we are concerned with a particular measure or quantity; in the second we are concerned with the object—a bucket or a pocket—that happens to be full of something.

Note the plural forms: basketfuls, spoonfuls, bucketfuls, etc., baskets full, spoons full, buckets full, etc.

See how many further examples of words like this you can add to your notebook.

Here is an exercise to test that you have fully grasped the points made.

Complete the words in the following sentences which contain examples of the words discussed.

1. *What a dread— noise!*
2. *He brought out a hand— of change.*
3. *She looked after her mother most duti—.*
4. *The recipe requires 3 cup— of flour.*
5. *He made himself help—.*
6. *I am ful— aware that.*
7. *Throw in a hand— of raisins.*
8. *Give me a spoon— of syrup.*
9. *The three cupboard— of newspapers need to be cleared.*
10. *Three cupboard— of newspapers is a lot of newspaper.*

11. *His ankle was very pain—.*
12. *His voice rang out power—.*
13. *She looked at him wist—.*
14. *The postman brought some cheer— news.*
15. *She chattered on cheer—.*

 # ASSIGNMENT C

Part I should take about an hour and a half to prepare and write, and should be about 500 words in length.

Part II should take about an hour and a quarter.

Part I: Essay

Write a description of a person you know well. Consider the following headings: physical appearance, style of dress, job, family background, interests, opinions. What concrete details can you introduce? What comparisons can you make to help a reader to visualize your character? What pieces of conversation can you use to make your portrait more immediate? Can you show your character in some suitable action? Can you devise a framework into which your character can be introduced? You may not need to use all these suggestions.

Part II: Comprehension

Read the following passage and answer the questions set as fully as possible and in your own words. The extract describes conscientious objectors doing agricultural work during the Second World War.

Of all of us, still not really at home in the rural scene, Pringle was least at ease. He had never truly ceased to be a bank clerk. He lived in a respectable suburb, from which he thought it impossible to depart in the morning dressed in labourer's clothes: so he carried his overalls in a brief case, and changed behind the stack on arrival: still somehow contriving to look as if his day's work lay behind a bank counter. But to this unsuitable decency of appearance he added a flow of words on monetary matters, very difficult to staunch. He would soliloquize gravely about finance even on the top of a cornstack, with the dust flowing and the threshing tackle shrieking and munching a few feet away. And this, in the end, was to bring about his dispatch to the ditches.

It might not have done so alone: but Pringle also managed deeply to irritate Jimbo, usually during our lunch breaks. Partly the trouble lay in the formality with which he addressed the old man. Accustomed to being called 'old 'un' or ''chiner', Jimbo did not respond happily to Pringle's cry of: 'Oh *driver*...!' Pringle meant no harm: it was part of his general dry precision. 'Oh driver—I must draw your attention to an error that seems to have crept into my timesheet!' Jimbo's eyes would bulge: the meanest farmer in the county had never dared to 'draw his attention' to anything whatever. 'Oh, Matey. Is that so?' 'I'm sure you're as anxious as we are to keep the books straight, driver.' It was a

fair guess that this was, in fact, an anxiety as remote from Jimbo's mind as one could get. The books, in so far as they existed, were inside his sooty head, helped out now and then by chalk marks made on the wall of his cab. 'Oh. That's how it is, eh?' he'd reply, vague and dangerous at once; and bend to his meal, with brooding ferocity.

I found that meal difficult to contemplate, during those first weeks. We'd sit round an old tin of flame, and Jimbo would toast his sandwiches on the point of a penknife. Pressed to the black holes in the brazier, they'd emit a broad fatty stink. His hands, black and oily, would seize a fragment of meat: the knife would scrape at a bone. Bread would fall to the ground but Jimbo would pick it up, rub off the dust and chaff with a screwing motion of the palm of his hand, and introduce it into his mouth according to a principle, not of mastication, but of continuous stuffing and gulping. His tea he made in a can of the profoundest blackness, and he would inject condensed milk into it as a long white worm blown through a hole in the top of the tin. The meal was plainly two parts of soot, dust and engine grease to one part of meat, bread or tea, and my queasy suburban stomach was turned.

Pringle—and this made things worse between him and Jimbo—would sit slightly apart and eat a meal that seemed a rebuke addressed to the machiner's. Mrs Pringle would have wrapped everything in greaseproof paper, and each heap of sandwiches in paper serviettes of the sort used at parties. His tea came out of a very fat, expensive thermos flask. I'd catch Jimbo staring at him, sometimes, under those eyelids thick with dust, across some bone from which accidents of dust and grease were being approximately wiped. He'd be paying special attention to Pringle's hands which, since he always worked in gloves, were spotlessly white. It was plain that trouble was brewing.

It was a bruising winter: Pringle was finding it fairly intolerable. To him, bad weather was a kind of uncouthness. We were held up for several days by snow—had to sit in a barn, waiting for the enchantment to go away. Dreadful coarseness welled up in us all, in that long frozen idleness: Pringle sat apart from us, rather, stiffly uneasy, reading a book on banking, trying not to frown at the loose banter that occupied us. He did mean to be worldly, to demonstrate that this curious mix of high churchiness and nonconformity that had driven him to be a conchie was capable of the common touch. But here was more commonness than he could bear.

(EDWARD BLISHEN, *A Cackhanded War*)

1. Describe two things that Pringle did that showed that he still thinks of himself as a bank clerk.

2. Why did Jimbo 'not respond happily to Pringle's cry of "Oh *driver*...!"'?

3. In which ways is the following speech typical of Pringle: 'I must draw your attention to an error that seems to have crept into my timesheet!'?

4. What is the effect of this speech on Jimbo?

5. What does the author mean when he says that Jimbo bent over his meal 'with brooding ferocity'?

6. Comment on the difference in eating habits between Pringle and Jimbo.

7. In what way are these typical of each?

8. What is the effect of the comparison 'as a long white worm'?

9. Explain what you understand by the expressions: 'a kind of uncouthness', 'the loose banter' and 'the common touch'.

10. Comment on the author's final sentence.

UNIT 5

 WRITING

Descriptions

Following our reading of descriptions in Unit 4 we show you how to set about writing a description yourself, and ask you to write a descriptive essay.

 READING AND UNDERSTANDING

Arguments

We look at some of the methods writers use when they present an argument.

 READING LIST

Some books on controversial matters.

 VOCABULARY

Some words from the satirical article by Michael Frayn studied earlier in the unit.

 LANGUAGE

Sentence Structure

An account of what constitutes a sentence which will help you write correct sentences. A study, which also includes passages of description, showing how varying the sentence structure can vary the effect.

 SPELLING

Adding a suffix to words ending in 'y'. When does the 'y' change to 'i'?

 WRITING

Descriptions

Making the point of view consistent

One of the most important things to try to achieve when writing a descriptive essay is a consistent point of view. By this I mean that you must try to pass on to the reader your view and interpretation of and attitude towards the place or object being described. You may want to describe it objectively, adding no feelings of your own, or you may dislike it or you may find it stimulating and exciting, peaceful and restful, boring and dull. You may be ambivalent and have a whole series of different reactions to it. You may be overwhelmed by being presented with a large number of contrasting and conflicting attitudes. Whatever your reactions, you must get clear in your mind the effect you want to create in the reader's mind and keep this strictly in view all the time you are writing.

For instance, you may be describing a fairground. You may find this pleasant and exciting and therefore all the details you give and the way you describe it should be directed to producing the same sensation in the mind of the reader. You may think a fairground noisy and squalid, and therefore you would describe it in a different way. You may well use the same details but the words you use and the way you describe them will be directed to creating a different impression in the reader. You may find some things about a fairground attractive and others unattractive. You would therefore make it your business to present both sides of the scene to the reader. You will use your material accordingly.

For practice, jot down some ideas for describing a fairground, and arrange them under the headings 'pleasant and exciting' and 'noisy and squalid'. Imagine how you could present them in an essay.

You must decide on your point of view at the beginning and stick to it.

38

The following description of an industrial town, Coketown, shows a consistent point of view on the part of the author.

It was a town of red brick, or of brick that would have been red if the smoke and ashes had allowed it; but as matters stood it was a town of unnatural red and black like the painted face of a savage.

It was a town of machinery and tall chimneys, out of which interminable serpents of smoke trailed themselves for ever and ever, and never got uncoiled.

It had a black canal in it, and a river that ran purple with ill-smelling dye, and vast piles of building full of windows where there was a rattling and a trembling all day long, and where the piston of the steam-engine worked monotonously up and down, like the head of an elephant in a state of melancholy madness. It contained several large streets all very like one another, and many small streets still more like one another, inhabited by people equally like one another, who all went in and out at the same hours, with the same sound upon the same pavements, to do the same work, and to whom every day was the same as yesterday and tomorrow, and every year the counterpart of the last and the next ...

You saw nothing in Coketown but what was severely workful. If the members of a religious persuasion built a chapel there—as the members of eighteen religious persuasions had done—they made it a pious warehouse of red brick, with sometimes (but this is only in highly ornamented examples) a bell in a birdcage on the top of it. The solitary exception was the New Church; a stuccoed edifice with a square steeple over the door, terminating in four short pinnacles like florid wooden legs. All the public inscriptions in the town were painted alike, in severe characters of black and white. The jail might have been the infirmary, the infirmary might have been the jail, for anything that appeared to the contrary in the graces of their construction. Fact, fact, fact, everywhere in the material aspect of the town; fact, fact, fact, everywhere in the immaterial. The M'Choakumchild school was all fact, and the school of design was all fact, and the relations between master and man were all fact, and everything was fact between the lying-in hospital and the cemetery, and what you couldn't state in figures, or show to be purchasable in the cheapest market and salable in the dearest, was not, and never should be, world without end, Amen.

(CHARLES DICKENS, *Hard Times*)

How does Dickens feel about Coketown? How can you tell?

What is the effect of the comparisons in the first three paragraphs—'like the painted face of a savage', 'interminable serpents of smoke' and 'like the head of an elephant in a state of melancholy madness'?

What is Dickens trying to say in the last sentence of the third paragraph? How does he make this effective?

Show that 'You saw nothing in Coketown but what was severely workful' is the topic sentence of the last paragraph.

Dickens disapproves of the industrial scene, and the conformity and drabness that it brought to men's lives.

He is criticizing the town of Coketown, not so much the people who have to live there, but the people who caused the town to come into existence. Every detail he gives and every word he uses is a condemnation. His point of view is consistent.

Building up and using ideas

But it is not enough to have a consistent point of view if you are asked to write a descriptive essay and know nothing about the subject. As stated in Unit 2, you must have some ideas, information, impressions, concrete details from which you can build your description. Some ideas for gathering material were given at the beginning of Unit 3. Some points about how writers make their effects in descriptive writing were made in Unit 4. Have a look at these again to remind yourself of what they were. I shall be repeating some of them here but I shall be applying them specifically to the writing of a descriptive essay and I shall be suggesting other avenues of thought for approaching this type of writing.

1. **The general and the particular.** Sometimes you may wish to describe the scene in general terms. For example, part of your description of an industrial town might include this sentence: 'The streets were long dreary successions of grimy back-to-back houses.' At other times, you may wish to concentrate more on an individual part of the scene to emphasize a particular effect, thus: 'The paint on the door of the house at the bottom of the hill was old and peeling. Children had picked away at the flaky paint until the bare wood showed through.' The picking out of a particular detail like this in a general description can provide detail and variety. The same kind of distinction between the general and the particular can be made in describing people. For example, 'The crowd roared their disapproval of their Trades Union representatives. A fiery young man with a boxer's face near the front yelled, "Get off the platform!".'

2. **Pick out individual details.** It is usually more effective to pick out individual concrete details instead of talking in vague generalities.

3. **The senses.** In any description, appealing to the senses is very important. It is through the senses that we gain most of our impressions of the world. If these can be stimulated by a suggestion on the writer's part, then the reader's imagination will do the rest. But the senses have to be aroused by the writer first. Dickens in his description of Coketown writes about 'the vast piles of building full of windows where there was a rattling and a trembling all day long'. A descriptive essay should not just appeal to the sight. Use words and details that call the other senses into play and help to create a more fully rounded impression.

4. **The use of words.** The way words are used can enhance a description. The rhythmic pattern of the final sentence of the third paragraph of the extract from *Hard Times* is one way in which the words chosen and the arrangement of the words can have an effect. Look at the way in which the final sentence of the passage from *Hard Times* builds up momentum from phrase to phrase

to end in a tremendous climax of condemnation, all the more effective for being ironically stated.

5. Comparisons. Nothing is likely to make a particular visual effect or emotional attitude more vivid than a comparison. Some examples have already been indicated. Look also at the effect of the comparison 'terminated in short pinnacles like florid wooden legs' from *Hard Times*. A comparison like this can bring in a new dimension in a descriptive essay. It can relate the subject-matter of the essay to the world we know and can enable the reader to connect it with the real world.

Now read the following description of an Australian town. Study it carefully before attempting the questions which follow.

I walk into the pale palm-tree town under the waving green hills of the range. I've arrived in Cairns. A woman talks as if her mouth is full of leaping frogs and follows with her eyes a spinster who walks as if she had marbles between her legs.

Down where the waterside workers live the houses are unpainted, peeling, in yards where nothing grows.

From their verandahs the oriental pinnacles and turrets of the white buildings in the centre of town can be seen. And looking the other way, there are the piles of petrol-storage tanks and derricks and ships' cranes above the shouts and bouts of the boys expending life

in the streets and area, close to death and thoughtless procreation. The sight of hills and trees over the stinking waters of the estuary is as remote as the unobserved sky in their world. Which is real? The men drink away their lives and their women scold and the youth are bold with nubile girls. They give with one hand and take away with the other, living in a state of numbness and fierceness to survive the prison of their poverty.

A small boy drinks a glass of lemonade in the doorway of the topers and close-contact men, who work together and drink together, having his dirty-yellow head ruffled as they pass in and out. His sun-warmed head, down to the bone then the warmth of his blood where he thinks and knows and imagines his small life away. Trains grate heavily across the road at the end of the street, with goods and the back views of the islanders and their brown elbows poking out of the open windows for air, and their brown eyes reflecting inscrutably whatever it is these other people think about. And the waterside workers and stevedores, who know about things that are wonder-worlds to small boys, things that have to be accepted on a pure cor-blimey faith, for the time it takes to tell a story they are men again. And far and away in the centre of town are halls with polished parquet floors and pictures of the Queen on the walls, where outside the sea sighs and the palmtrees rustle like rain in the wind. The heat throbs in a higher key, tighter,

drawing up the tension before the wet and the up-coming monsoon that waits, and waits, and never unloads its burden on the violent town with its proud, high birth-rate and beer-rate and capitas per car. The rites of springless seasons burst among the people instead of rain. They kill time in semitones up the scale to the highest pitch of heat, and the suspense of withheld murder and frenzy adds up and up into the final madness. Till thoughts have bodies. Then anti-climax topples into collapse and capitulation, inertia and *mañana*, and the never-never of lazy bones and dreams. The dark-green avocado pear of town, the thick, lush, yellow substance of tropics. I eat the pear with relish. This is not my town; I don't have to live here—or in Darwin, or Mount Isa . . .

(ROSEMARY MILLINGTON, *A Nation of Trees*)

In some ways this is a more difficult passage to understand and interpret than the previous one, partly because it is more rambling, more vague and more impressionistic. Answer the following questions fully and then read the passage again and see if it is clearer.

1. What is the author's attitude towards the town of Cairns? Does she like it and its inhabitants? How can you tell?

2. Pick out the hard facts (as opposed to the opinions or impressions or generalizations) given about Cairns. Write a paragraph about it giving only facts.

3. Pick out four examples where the author makes generalizations about the inhabitants of Cairns.

4. Pick out three examples where she describes specific individuals.

5. Pick out four instances where the author gives concrete details.

6. Pick out details that appeal to the senses of hearing and taste.

7. Pick out three comparisons and bring out their effectiveness.

Now write an essay about a town you know well. You may wish to put it into a fictional framework, imagining, for example, that you are someone else visiting it for the first time, but it is important that it should be a town you know so that you have some basic facts to start from. Decide on the attitude towards the town and inhabitants that you want the reader to have from your essay. Organize your facts and material. Consider whether any of the points made here can help you to find some material or ways of using your facts. Now write a 500 word description. Remember to have an interesting opening and ending. Take about an hour and a half over the preparation and writing of this essay.

READING AND UNDERSTANDING

Arguments

Facts and opinions

Probably most of the reading you do will be concerned with opinions, points of view and the presentation of arguments for and against these views and opinions. Newspapers, through the editorial column and feature articles, present their attitude towards the news. Headlines and the way in which news is presented can also indicate the view of the newspaper and the way the editor or the owners wish us to react to the news.

For instance, an account of student unrest in Cairo received the following headline in the Daily Telegraph: *'Students go on rampage'. The* Guardian *reported it as 'Cairo students again protest'. What difference in attitude do these two headlines suggest on the part of these two newspapers?*

What is omitted or played down is almost as important an indication of attitudes as what is stressed and sensationalized. While a reader is usually aware of the political feelings held by the newspaper he reads, one of the dangers of modern journalism is the blurring of the distinction between fact and opinion. It is important to be able to differentiate between the two.

Nor are newspapers the only pressures trying to persuade us to their particular point of view. The whole world of advertising is geared towards making us accept claims that are made and arguments for buying the particular goods that are put forward. The political world too tries to win our approval and support. The statements and speeches of politicians, party pamphlets and manifestoes, the banners and leaflets of pressure groups have to be scrutinized and evaluated to see what is true and what is false, what is fact and what is opinion or assertion.

Read the following article bearing in mind particularly what is fact and what is opinion.

There is an interesting reference to 'the spirit of bravado' among teenagers in the cautionary memorandum just issued by the Howard League of Penal Reform. The league fears that this bold, juvenile spirit would provoke an even higher rate of crime than has already been reached if those who are filled with it were submitted to the painful indignity of a whipping. Arguments for and against the birch have gone on so long that many people are bored with them and some are sceptical as to whether it would make much difference, in the long run, if the supporters or the opponents of the Howard League case were victorious. On one point we must all agree. The spirit of bravado, or whatever it may be called, has led to a wave of senselessly destructive hooliganism that shows no signs whatever of dying down. Harsh disciplinary sanctions in the past failed; kindly and unsparing efforts to reform the little thugs by kindness have, beyond question, been equally ineffective.

Railways, as any passenger will know, have lately been the main sufferers. It was estimated the other day that in twelve weeks the Southern Region alone had suffered losses of more than £11,000 and 14,000 hours of skilled labour. Seats are ripped open, luggage racks torn down, and lights and windows smashed. This is not the worst of it. Signals set at 'safe' have been altered, no doubt, in a spirit of bravado. A short circuit, leading to a general hold-up, has been caused by cushions hurled out of windows. Some of the damage, it has been noted, could be done only by a very sharp blade such as a razor. The old-fashioned schoolboy's pocket knife is

scorned in the best bravado circles. Towns, especially those at the seaside, are victims of gangs of impudent youngsters with enough money in their pockets to equip themselves with motor scooters for mobility or choppers for attack when they reach their objective. The country-side is not immune. Villages have sad tales to tell of the expense incurred in repairing the ravages due to the spirit of bravado.

The need to put a stop to these goings-on is obvious both to protect life and property and to teach the culprits that they must not hope to get away without sanctions that they will really hate. Unfortunately, there is no question but that, as matters stand, they laugh, often openly, at attempts to control them. Their boldness in execution is matched by whining when they are caught and resentment if they are even lightly punished. This is a sombre picture. It is one of photographic accuracy as a reflection of what is happening daily in consequence of the unchecked spirit of bravado in a society full as never before of comparatively rich young people—not all of them teenagers—with unprecedented leisure on their hands and no fear of retribution from God or man in their hearts.

(*The Times Educational Supplement*)

What hard facts are actually stated?

The only facts that I can extract are: the Howard League for Penal Reform has published a memorandum; details of damage on the Southern Region of British Rail and the cost of these.

The rest is opinion or generalization:

The Howard League fears that the introduction of birching would increase the crime rate. (This may be true, but it is merely conjecture.)

The wave of hooliganism shows no signs of dying down. (This is opinion—the writer's interpretation of the situation.)

Harsh disciplinary sanctions in the past have failed. (Evidence for this statement?)

Kinder efforts at reform have failed (Evidence?)

Towns are victims of gangs. (A wild generalization. How many towns? Two? Fifty? Five thousand?)

These gangs have plenty of money to buy scooters and choppers. (Did they *all* have axes? Isn't this an exaggeration?)

Villages are also attacked. (Again, how many?)

The hooligans laugh at attempts to control them, whine when caught and resent being punished. (Another generalization. Is this true of *all* of them? What is the emotive power of the word 'whine', and what does it and the qualification 'even lightly' punished tell us about the writer's attitude?)

This sombre picture is a photographically accurate reflection of what is happening daily. (Evidence? Isn't this simply the writer's assertion?)

This state of affairs is the result of young people having too much money, too much leisure, and no fear of being punished. (Is this a logical statement? Is the one necessarily the result of the other? Are there other possible causes which the writer is unaware of or which he deliberately ignores?)

The writer of this article is right to find the behaviour of *some* young people deplorable, and it would be difficult to defend people who slash railway train seats or create a disturbance in a peaceful town. But part of the trouble with the article is that it is totally condemnatory and there is no shred of sympathy or understanding for the young people concerned. The article almost implies that *all* young people are like this and neglects to mention factors like the attitudes of society (commercial pressures, the emphasis on the profit motive, the glorification of violence on TV and films, the current validity given to ideas that the important thing is to enjoy yourself at all costs, and that work and craftsmanship are boring and square) and the lack of proper facilities for young people which could lead them into exploits like these. While a passionate attack like this can steam-roller the reader into accepting the point of view of the writer, it can also have the oppo-site effect. When the case against these young people is presented as blackly as this, it can lead the reader to ask: 'Well, are they as bad as this article suggests? Isn't the writer being a bit one-sided? Isn't there another point of view that needs to be stated?' The writer here is not weighing up the evidence, looking at both sides and try-ing to be fair to them, and then drawing his conclusions. His mind is clearly made up before he starts and he in-tends you to end up thinking the same way as he does. These are fair enough tactics when presenting an argu-ment, but you must be aware of what he is doing.

So far, we have seen that a writer may use facts, opinions, assertions, examples, generalizations and ex-aggerations to present his case—make sure you know what the difference is between these various means. What you must do is to learn to distinguish between them.

Which side is the writer on?

The second important factor you must deduce from a piece of writing presenting an argument is the writer's point of view. Is he impartial? Is he strongly committed to one side? Is he playing fair with the reader or trying to blind him with rhetoric or emotion, by a powerful flow of words or by an appeal to his sentiments? Are his methods prejudiced because of his own feelings? In the passage above, the hooligans are painted in a totally black light (perhaps justifiably) but to my mind the reaction towards them comes over too strongly. There is a kind of vindictive gloating over them. The hooligans 'laugh' at attempts to control them; they 'whine' when caught. There is a positive sadistic pleasure over the thought that they must receive sanctions 'that they will really hate' and of the 'retribution from God or man' that ought to come to them. The writer is trying to stir up in the reader hatred and disgust for these young people. The way the hooligans scorn the 'old-fashioned schoolboy's pocket knife' makes their use of sharp blades (which *may* be razors, we don't know) all the more evil. The way in which it is not just a few isolated towns and villages where this trouble occurs but town*s* and village*s* (all over the country and thousands and thousands of them is the implication) again blackens this small minority.

The sentence structure too helps to emphasize the writer's attitudes. The sentence 'Their boldness . . .' has a shape and a balance which seems to show the writer's relish at having a chance to attack these people. The final sentence builds up a powerful steam of emotion. The attitude expressed is similar to a comment Lord Arran made in the *Evening News*: 'For them I say the birch and the birch and the birch again. I cannot abide savagery, and those who indulge in it should pay the full price.' (*Comment on the logic of this statement.*)

Forceful assertion is not the only method of presenting a point of view. A lighter touch can sometimes be more effective. Read the following article by Michael Frayn which, while being comic, has a very serious intention behind it.

In this satirical article he is attacking the producers of one kind of poisonous article (which is sometimes claimed to be comparatively harmless) by substituting for it another poisonous article (which no one would claim was harmless). *What does 'methylated spirits' really stand for?*

Let's look at the facts, Mike, that's all I ask (*said Rollo Swavely, the well-known public relations consultant*). There are people who drink methylated spirits, and there are people who go blind. Some of the people who go blind also happen to drink methylated spirits. Those are the *facts*. And that's all the evidence there is for this half-baked nonsense about methylated spirits causing blindness!

What hurts me about this blindness scare, Mike, is that meths-bottling firms like the one I have the account for (who bottle under the famous 'Johnny Friendly' label), are giving genuine pleasure to a lot of ordinary people. For a great many folk, particularly the less wealthy ones who perhaps haven't been too successful in life—old folks, often enough—drinking meths is one of the few pleasures they can afford. Are we going to snatch it away from them with irresponsible haste, just because of some unsubstantiated hypothesis which has only been put forward in the last hundred years? After all, Mike, this is a democratic country. Correct me if I'm wrong. But I take that to mean that we have a duty to give the people what they want.

All the same, I shouldn't like you to run away with the idea that we're not doing our level best to get to the bottom of this matter in a proper scientific way. My clients have spent a great deal of money over the past few years financing research to prove that the sort of people who drink meths simply have a predisposition to blindness anyway. We are also running an alternative research programme to prove a hypothesis we have that any overfall of the blindness rate among methylated spirits drinkers as compared with the rest of the community is the result of their so often meeting on bombed sites, where there's a great deal of dust blowing about and getting in their eyes. Anyway, off the record, I think people make just a bit too much of this blindness business. I mean, if it wasn't blindness, it'd be something else, wouldn't it?

But that's not all. Our doctors have also discovered that methylated spirits have a great many definitely beneficial pharmacological properties. I've got a list of them back at the office, Mike, and I can assure you it's as long as your arm. I don't want to be too specific

without having the dossier to hand, but they range from reducing the tensions of competitive modern living to providing an effective alternative to overindulgence in sweets.

Still, we agree that school-children ought not to be encouraged to take up meths-drinking, in spite of its health-giving qualities. My clients are prepared to offer financial backing—I can't say exactly how much, but I can tell you they're thinking of going up to three figures —to a nationwide Government campaign in the schools, provided the theme is reasonably objective. The sort of slogans we should be prepared to approve would be ones like 'Not for Children—Meths Is a Real Man's Drink!' or 'X for Meths—the Sexciting, Sexsational Thrill for Over-16s Only!' Something in that line, we feel, would best serve the interests of all concerned.

In return, of course, we should expect the Government not to interfere with our traditional freedom to put the other side of the question through the various advertising media. To say, as some ill-informed critics have been doing recently, that the purpose of our advertising is to increase the total sales of meths is nonsense. We are simply trying to increase the sales of our particular brand. And what could be more wholesome and acceptable than the ads we've been running showing a couple of young lovers enjoying the pastoral pleasures of the countryside—sitting by a waterfall in high summer, or wandering through the russet autumn woods—and sharing a bottle of methylated spirits through straws as they look into one another's eyes? I think they've brought a touch of poetry into all our lives.

Anyway, we like them, and we intend to increase our advertising budget by about £2 millions. It's not just the selling effect we're thinking of. It seems to us that the more money we're paying out to newspapers and television companies for advertising space, the more objectively they're likely to treat the whole question.

(MICHAEL FRAYN in the *Guardian*)

Answer the following questions.
1. Make a list of the arguments Rollo Swavely makes to support the view that people should be allowed to drink methylated spirits if they want to.
2. Take each in turn and say how convincing you think each is when applied to smoking.
3. Comment on Rollo Swavely's interpretation of the word 'facts'; his definition of what makes 'a democratic country'; the examples he gives of the beneficial effects of methylated spirits; the effect the slogans given are likely to have; his explanation of the purpose behind their advertising; his description of the advertisements as bringing 'a touch of poetry into all our lives'.
4. What point is implied in the final paragraph?
5. How can we tell that Michael Frayn intends Rollo Swavely to appear ridiculous? For instance, are there examples of him being two-faced or illogical?

It should be clear from these passages that *how* writers present arguments is as important as *what* they say. People say that statistics can mean anything, that the figures can be twisted and interpreted to fit any point of view desired. The same is true to some extent of facts. Facts can be manipulated and coloured to fit almost any argument. When reading an argumentative article, the reader must distinguish between fact and opinion, truth and prejudice, reality and emotional appeal. He must study how a writer is saying something, what tone of voice he is employing, whether he is being serious or satirical, overflowing with uncritical anger or making a cool appraisal of the situation. The reader must not allow the writer to fool him with false arguments or blind him with powerful emotion. He must try to get behind the façade of the writer's words to the truth and so be in a position to make up his own mind.

READING LIST

Obviously, newspapers and magazines can be a valuable source of reading material dealing with controversial matters. Read them regularly and critically. Don't just accept what they say at face value. Question and analyse what you read.

A valuable series worth looking at which discusses important subjects about which there are arguments is the Connexions series published by Penguin Books. The titles available so far include:

Charlie Gillett: *All in the Game*—about sport.
Edith Rudinger and Vic Kelly: *Break for Commercials*—about advertising.
Sheila Tidmarsh: *Disaster*.
Kenneth Allsop: *Fit to Live In?*—about pollution of the countryside.
Jacky Gillott: *For Better, For Worse*—about marriage and the family.
Jennifer Rogers: *Foreign Places, Foreign Faces*—about other ways of life.
Joy Groombridge: *His and Hers*—about masculinity and femininity.
Fred Hooper: *The Language of Prejudice*—how we talk about people who don't fit.
Ray Jenkins: *The Lawbreakers*—about crime and punishment.
Nigel Calder: *Living Tomorrow*.
Peter Newmark: *Out of your Mind?*—about drugs.
John Barr: *Standards of Living*.
Colin Ward: *Violence*.

VOCABULARY

Michael Frayn is a satirist. In his article about 'meths drinking', he wants to make fun of Rollo Swavely. The words he puts into his character's mouth are a mixture of colloquial and pompous, down-to-earth and pseudo-official, as befits his position as a public relations officer. The following words chosen from the passage indicate these two aspects. Look at them carefully and see if you agree. Find them in their context and try to work out their meaning.

half-baked, irresponsible, unsubstantiated, hypothesis, democratic, predestination, beneficial, specific, over-indulgence, pastoral, objectively.

Look these words up in a dictionary and check with your

first impressions. Put each of these words into an interesting sentence of your own. Copy them in your notebook.

> Read through the extracts in this lesson again and pick out any words you are not sure of. Add them to your vocabulary list, look them up and put them in sentences of your own.

LANGUAGE
Sentence Structure

We don't want to go into grammatical technicalities in any detail in this course as they are unnecessary for your study, but we are going to introduce a few items here to help you grasp the idea of a sentence.

Sentence:
The grammatical name given to a group of words which can stand by themselves and make sense. The first word of a sentence begins with a capital letter, and the last word is followed by a full stop.

Subject:
The name given to a pronoun or noun about which a statement is being made in a sentence, e.g.
Ann is an air-hostess.
'Ann' is the subject.
'Ann' is a name or noun.
She has flown to many countries.
'She' is the subject.
'She' is a pronoun or word standing for a noun.
A sentence always has a subject. The rest of the sentence tells you more about the subject.

Predicate:
The name given to the part of the sentence which tells you about the subject, e.g.
Ann *is an air-hostess*.
'is an air-hostess' tells you about Ann.

Finite Verb:
To make it complete, each sentence must have a finite verb. A finite verb is a part of the verb that
(a) can have a subject
(b) can form a tense (present, past, future, etc.) e.g.
Ann *is* an air-hostess.
She *has flown* to many countries.
'is' and 'has flown' both have subjects.
'is' is present tense—what is happening now.
'has flown' is past—what she has done.

Non-finite forms of the verb:
Some forms of the verb cannot stand by themselves and make sense.
  (i) The infinitive: e.g. to come, to buy.
  (ii) The present participle: e.g. going, spending.
  (iii) The past participle: e.g. given, lost.
  (iv) The gerund or verbal noun: e.g. waiting, arriving.

45

Standing alone
To come here
Spending only two pounds
Given me five pence
Walking in the hills.

Do these make sense? Test them by saying them to yourself. You need to *add* something so that each sentence contains a subject and a finite verb.

She asked me to come here.
Spending only two pounds she was able to buy enough material.
His father had given me five pence.
Walking in the hills is pleasant in springtime.

Here are the sentences we have used as examples put into a simple table. Rule out your own table on a sheet of paper using the example as your model. Take the five sentences provided below: find the subject, verb and predicate and write them in the correct column.

Make up ten more sentences of your own and check that they are complete by writing them in on your table.

The house stood on top of the hill.
It rained all night.
Bob hit the foreman in the works this morning.
Painting the Forth Bridge is an endless task.
The children have gone home.

Subject		Predicate	
noun	pronoun	finite verb	
Ann		is	an air-hostess
	She	has flown	to many countries
	She	asked	me to come here
	She	was able	spending only two pounds to buy enough material
His father		had given	me five pence
Walking in the hills		is	pleasant in the springtime

Remember to ask yourself when you write sentences whether they make sense on their own, whether they are complete statements in themselves. If the statement leaves you hanging in the air, not knowing what on earth is being talked about, like the examples 'to come here' and 'given me five pence', then it is not a complete statement and is not a correct sentence. Almost without exception, essays and comprehension answers should be written in the form of complete statements and correct sentences.

At the risk of confusing you, it should be mentioned that sometimes seemingly incomplete statements can make complete sense.
Consider the following:
No Parking
Any left?
See you tomorrow.
Next, please.
Yes.
Hello.

These statements make sense because other words are understood or supplied mentally to complete the statements; or the words in a particular context or situation are completely understandable; or they are permissable in colloquial language or casual conversation. For instance 'No Parking' can be seen as a shortened official version of 'No parking is allowed here' or some such expression.

Expand the other phrases to show what words are understood or show how in a particular context they make sense.

Sometimes, particularly in descriptive writing, students are carried away in their enthusiasm to write passages like the following:

The scene after the snowstorm was breathtaking. Drifts of snow everywhere. Soft and pure white. Flakes still cascading. Flurries of feathery flakes. Melting on the window pane. Sweeping across the frozen surface of the lake. Swirling in the air when caught by a current of wind.

How many of these 'sentences' are complete statements containing a subject and a finite verb?

This impressionistic kind of writing can be effective but can also be dangerous. It may suggest to an examiner that you can't write conventional standard English.

Nor is it enough simply to write correct sentences. You must also become aware of the different effects of different kinds and different lengths of sentence. If a short paragraph consisting of a single sentence can be effective in contrast to a longer paragraph, the same is true of sentences. If all the sentences in your essay are short, the effect can become very monotonous. If all your sentences are very long, the effect can be heavy and pedantic. Variety is important. A short sentence following several long ones, for example, can have a dramatic effect that could be appropriate to what you are writing. Try to develop a self-critical attitude towards this aspect of writing. The kind of sentence you use should be related to what you are writing about just as much as the kind of words you use. Sometimes long sentences will be appropriate (for instance, if you are outlining an argument); sometimes short sentences will be more suitable (for instance, if you are describing an exciting piece of action in a story); sometimes contrasting one type of sentence with another will be what is required (for instance, long sentences outlining an argument followed by a short one which sums up the point in a terse way may be effective).

Consider the sentence structure in the following passages: what is the sentence pattern in each? Are the sentences long or short or varied? What is the subject

1. I came to in the midst of wild movement. All about me was the same movement. I had been caught up in a monstrous flood that was sweeping me I knew not whither. Fresh air was on my cheek and biting sweetly in my lungs. Faint and dizzy, I was vaguely aware of a strong arm around my body under the arms, and half-lifting me and dragging me along. Feebly my own limbs were helping me. In front of me I could see the moving back of a man's coat. It had been slit from top to bottom along the centre seam, and it pulsed rhythmically, the slit opening and closing regularly with every leap of the wearer. This phenomenon fascinated me for a time, while my senses were coming back to me. Next I became aware of stinging cheeks and nose, and could feel blood dripping on my face. My hat was gone. My hair was down and flying, and from the stinging of the scalp I managed to recollect a hand in the press of the entrance that had torn at my hair. My chest and arms were bruised and aching in a score of places.

    My brain grew clearer, and I turned as I ran and looked at the man who was holding me up. He it was who had dragged me out and saved me. He noticed my movement.

    'It's all right!' he shouted hoarsely. 'I knew you on the instant.'

    (JACK LONDON, *The Iron Heel*)

2. We were surprisingly healthy. As the routine of regular meals, clothes that could now be dried, and the more and more frequent warmth of the stove took charge of us, we grew stronger; even my foot-rot was checked. Bounded by the four sides of the raft, secure within its cabin from the rain, we felt life take on a kind of normality again. Only Wesley Otterdale did not lose his haunted hollow look, and Muriel, lying apart from him at night with the rest of the women, worried and pined for him.

    Then the tempest came.

    (JOHN BOWEN, *After the Rain*)

3. Many times Mrs Transome went to the doorsteps, watching and listening in vain. Each time she returned to the same room: it was a moderate-sized comfortable room, with low ebony bookshelves round it, and it formed an anteroom to a large library, of which a glimpse could be seen through an open doorway, partly obstructed by a heavy tapestry curtain drawn on one side. There was a great deal of tarnished gilding and dinginess on the walls and furniture of this smaller room, but the pictures above the bookcases were all of a cheerful kind: portraits in

pastel of pearly-skinned ladies with hair-powder, blue ribbons, and low bodice; a splendid portrait in oils of a Transome in the gorgeous dress of the Restoration; another of a Transome in his boyhood, with his hand on the neck of a small pony; and a large Flemish battle-piece, where war seemed only a picturesque blue-and-red accident in a vast sunny expanse of plain and sky. Probably such pictures had been chosen because this was Mrs Transome's usual sitting-room: it was certainly for this reason that, near the chair in which she seated herself each time she re-entered, there hung a picture of a youthful face which bore a strong resemblance to her own: a beardless but masculine face, with rich brown hair hanging low on the forehead, and undulating beside each cheek down to the loose white cravat. Near this same chair were her writing-table, with vellum-covered account-books on it, the cabinet in which she kept her neatly-arranged drugs, her basket for her embroidery, a folio volume of architectural engravings from which she took her embroidery patterns, a number of the *North Loamshire Herald*, and the cushion for her fat Blenheim, which was too old and sleepy to notice its mistress's restlessness. For, just now, Mrs Transome could not abridge the sunny tedium of the day by the feeble interest of her usual indoor occupations. Her consciousness was absorbed by memories and prospects, and except when she walked to the entrance-door to look out, she sat motionless with folded arms, involuntarily from time to time turning towards the portrait close by her, and as often, when its young brown eyes met hers, turning away again with self-checking resolution.

(GEORGE ELIOT, *Felix Holt*)

Note the fact that semicolons (;) and colons (:) are used in the first part of this passage to keep the sentences going. We will discuss these in Unit 7.

 SPELLING

Adding suffixes to words ending in 'y'

When adding a suffix or a plural ending to a word ending in 'y', the 'y' remains unchanged if the preceding letter is a vowel. If the preceding letter is a consonant, the 'y' is changed to 'i'. (Suffixes are endings joined to the root of a word to change its form, e.g. '-ly', '-ment', '-ful', '-ness'.)

Consider the following words where the 'y' is preceded by a vowel:

boy, boys
grey, greyness

enjoy, enjoyment
play, playful
employ, employee
play, played
monkey, monkeys
buy, buyer

Consider the following words where the 'y' is preceded by a consonant:

pretty, prettily
lady, ladies
lonely, loneliness
merry, merriment
pity, pitiful
marry, married

Find other words which follow these rules.

It is important to remember the following points:

1. Before the ending '-ing', the 'y' is retained, e.g. 'marrying', 'carrying', 'hurrying', 'tidying'. This is to prevent two 'i's' coming together. Similarly, note the spelling of words like 'babyish', 'dryish'.

2. Note the following words which do not entirely conform to the rules:

'Dry' has the forms 'drier', 'driest', 'drily' (or 'dryly'), 'dryish', 'dryness'
'Gay' has the forms 'gayer', 'gayest', 'gaily', 'gaiety'
'Shy' has the forms 'shyer', 'shyest', 'shyly', 'shyness'
'Sly' has the forms 'slyer', 'slyest', 'slyly', 'slyness'
'Wry' has the forms 'wryer' (or 'wrier'), 'wryly', 'wryness'

3. The word 'busy' has the forms 'business' (= 'job'), 'busily'; but the spelling 'busyness' is used when the meaning is 'the state of being busy'. Note also the spelling of 'busybody'.

There are no other exceptions.

Here is an exercise to test whether you have learned the spelling points illustrated above. Complete the words in the following sentences with forms in 'y' or 'i':

1. Looking after two bab— is a full time job.
2. Let's move to a dr—er part of the beach.
3. I enjoy watching the monk— at the zoo.
4. Vall— and hills give variety to a landscape.
5. She occupied herself bus— about the office.
6. Funn— enough, I was thinking that myself.
7. His emplo— gave him the sack.
8. Lad— and gentlemen, please be seated.
9. The sculpture embod— many hours of work.
10. She sang merr— about the house.
11. He is carr— a precious parcel.
12. The goods were conve— by train.
13. The ga—ty at the party increased.
14. The man killed in the accident was bur— yesterday.
15. He was hurr— to catch the post when he was run over.

UNIT 6

 WRITING

Arguments

Advice on planning and writing an argumentative essay, with exercises that lead you towards the essay you will be asked to write in Assignment D.

 READING AND UNDERSTANDING

Dialogue

An analysis of how writers use dialogue to distinguish characters, give information and tell a story.

 READING LIST

Some books in which dialogue is important.

 VOCABULARY

Some words from a passage from Jane Austen's *Emma* used as an example in the section of this unit on dialogue.

 LANGUAGE

Punctuation Marks II
The Punctuation of Speech

Advice on the correct punctuation to use when writing dialogue using the passages in the 'Reading and Understanding' section as models.

 SPELLING

A look at some words where double 'l' and single 'l' are confused.

 ASSIGNMENT D

 WRITING

Arguments

There are two main types of argumentative essay. One asks for the pros and cons of a particular subject; the other asks you to concentrate on one side only, either presenting a case for a particular point of view or condemning a particular point of view.

Whichever type of essay you are going to attempt, the first procedure is the same: find out whether you have enough facts and ideas on which to build an argument.

The second stage is to mull over the facts and ideas you have, and to start to organize them into some kind of plan. Through a consideration of the material at your command, your own point of view should become clearer, and this will help you in the organization of your material. Your point of view may be divided, and so you may wish to present a fair and impartial account of the evidence on both sides leaving the reader to make up his own mind. You may decide that one side of the argument is stronger and gains your support, and you will therefore emphasize the merits of this view and give it your blessing in your conclusions. Clearly, as with the descriptive essay, a consistent point of view is essential. You must know where you stand personally before you start writing the essay. There is nothing worse than starting an argumentative essay supporting one side and then finding when you are half-way through that you have changed your mind.

The following points should be kept in sight when you are writing an argumentative essay:

1. The line of your argument must be clear. This depends very much on how well you plan your essay and on how well you organize your paragraph construction. (Revise the section on paragraphs in 'Language' Unit 3 and study again the examples of editorials from *The Guardian* given there.) Really, the framework of your essay should be reducible to very simple, almost

49

mathematical proportions. For instance, if the subject is 'Give the case for and against space exploration', your plan might look something like this:

Paragraph 1. An account of the present situation and achievements of space exploration.

Paragraph 2. Valuable because
(a) increases our knowledge in the abstract;

Paragraph 3.
(b) in practical terms it could provide a solution to the growing pollution and using up of the resources of the earth;

Paragraph 4.
(c) it provides a better alternative for national rivalry than war;

Paragraph 5.
(d) it provides new worlds to explore and therefore it provides an outlet for man's sense of adventure.

Paragraph 6. But
(a) it is costly. Do the rewards justify the expense?

Paragraph 7.
(b) Wouldn't it be better to try to improve things on earth (e.g. poverty, starvation, over-population) before spending money on exploring other worlds?

Paragraph 8.
(c) The possibility of conflict over territories in space could lead to war on earth.

Paragraph 9.
Personal conclusion: better to improve the world we live in than to hanker after fairy-lands in the sky.

or The adventure of space exploration provides ideals in a world that has lost its idealism.

or Space exploration can be seen as a way in which distance shrinks and man comes closer to man.

The construction is very simple, but the line of the argument can be seen clearly and holds the thought together. The reader is able to move confidently from one point to another, from one paragraph to another, and to know whereabouts he is in the argument. First comes the introduction, then the points in favour of space research; then the pivotal 'but' which leads to the points against space research; and finally the conclusion which stresses the view the writer has come to after weighing the evidence presented. The pivotal 'but' is important here. Words like 'but', 'however', 'nevertheless', 'on the other hand', are useful in providing sign-posts for a reader in following an argument. They help to keep him on the right lines and to show him in which direction the argument is moving.

2. Clarity. This is obviously important if a reader is to be expected to follow your point of view. State your arguments simply and clearly. Sometimes students are afraid that what they think is too obvious to need saying, and they therefore leave out essential steps in their argument. Remember that short sentences are often useful, particularly at the beginning of a paragraph, to establish a point which can then be elaborated in greater detail and with illustrative examples later in the paragraph.

3. Try to be persuasive. The whole point of an argumentative essay is to win the reader over to your point of view, and therefore you must present your point of view as persuasively as possible. If there are arguments that count against your point of view, don't just ignore them; treat them objectively and balance them against your own points which you consider have more weight. For instance, in your essay on space research, you might say 'space research is expensive and many people think the money might be better spent in improving conditions in our own world. However, money spent on gaining knowledge of the universe is an investment in the future well-being of the earth, and it is the sort of investment well worth risking.'

4. Examples. One way of being persuasive is to give plenty of examples to support your point of view. Just as concrete realistic detail in a descriptive essay gives the impression that you know and have seen what you are describing, so details and examples of the area you are writing about in an argumentative essay can convince a reader that you know what you are talking about.

Don't generalize; be specific in your references. For instance, in the essay on space research, don't just say that exploration of space provides man with new areas for adventure; relate it to the past. For example 'Livingstone and his fellow explorers have long ago searched out the darkest parts of Africa, Antarctica is no longer a mystery, and even Everest was climbed over twenty years ago'. Specific references and examples like these give vitality to an argumentative essay.

5. Quotations and references. Another way of giving vitality to an argumentative essay is to refer to what other people have said or feel about the matter, quoting actual words where these are known, are relevant, and are expressed in a pithy arresting manner. For the essay on space research, an obvious quotation would be the words of the American astronaut on first walking on the surface of the moon: 'A small step for man, a giant step for mankind.' Quotations are particularly useful for beginning and ending an argumentative essay. They can give a lift to what might otherwise be pedestrian and flat, and they show that you have some acquaintance with the subject you are writing about.

6. Beginning and ending. As in all essays, these are very important. Using quotations was suggested above as one way of making an effective opening or ending, but this, of course, depends upon your knowing a quotation that is apt or that can be adapted. Remember that the purpose of an opening sentence and paragraph is to arrest the attention of the reader and to make him want to read on. Openings like 'There has been much space research in recent years', or 'The Russians and the Americans have both been very active in space research' are unlikely to evoke much response. Openings like 'Children used to think the moon was made of cheese', or 'The dark side of the moon has revealed its secrets' may.

The same is true of the concluding paragraph. Don't begin, 'In conclusion, I should like to say ...' or 'To sum up, my point of view is ...'. These are almost certain to be boring and repetitive. Don't say in your final paragraph something that you have already said. Try to move on to some new ground—still relevant, of course—but leaving the reader with a new angle on what has been said in the rest of the essay, summing up what has already been discussed but also leaving the reader with a new idea to think about, perhaps even leaving him with a question. For instance, 'Can anyone who has seen pictures of the squalor in Calcutta or of the Peruvian Indians really believe that the American astronauts are exploring anything but a Cloud-Cuckoo-Land? It is time we had our feet on the ground.' Or, 'Who knows what the next adventure may lead to. We may find life on Mars or explore the arid wastes of Saturn. Perhaps the science-fiction writers with their tales of bug-eyed monsters will be proved right after all!'

It can be useful practice to work out paragraph plans for argumentative essays, even if you don't actually write the essays themselves. Work out such paragraph plans on the lines of the one given earlier on space research for one or more of the following subjects:

1. Give the arguments for and against the use of corporal punishment.

2. Give the arguments for and against the compulsory carrying of identity cards.

3. Give the arguments for and against advertising.

4. Give the arguments for and against the Public School system.

5. Give the arguments for and against supermarkets.

Good talk can also be a useful preliminary to good argumentative writing. Expressing our thoughts in words can often help us to clarify them. When they take on the flesh of words, they can also reveal more readily their convincingness or fatuity.

Look at the following statements. Are they true or false, convincing or unconvincing? If possible, argue about them with friends—or at least think about them.

1. Woman's place is in the home.
2. Without tourists, bull-fighting in Spain would have died out long ago.
3. There's no place like home.
4. It's better to be Red than dead.
5. Once a thief, always a thief.
6. Fashion—ridiculous modes, invented by ignorance, and adopted by folly (Smollett).
7. Patriotism is not enough.
8. Nowadays, Christmas has no meaning.
9. History is bunk (Ford).
10. Next to the very young, I suppose the very old are the most selfish (Thackeray).
11. All the world's a stage (Shakespeare).
12. Nothing is politically right which is morally wrong (Daniel O'Connell).
13. A friend to everybody is a friend to nobody (Spanish proverb).
14. He that is not jealous is not in love (St Augustine).
15. A bird in a cage is not half a bird.
16. Children should be seen and not heard.
17. All men are equal.
18. No man flatters the woman he truly loves.
19. Travel is fatal to prejudice (Mark Twain).
20. If a thing is worth doing, it is worth doing badly (Chesterton).

READING AND UNDERSTANDING

Dialogue

One of the obvious purposes of using dialogue in a story is to break up the print on the page so that the eye—and the mind—is given variety and prevented from becoming satiated by long stretches of description and comment. As Alice said in *Alice in Wonderland*, 'What is the use of a book without pictures or conversations?' Just as the break of a new paragraph can give the mind a chance to catch its breath, as it were, so a piece of dialogue can give a variation in pace to a story for the refreshment of the reader.

Look back at Unit 4, p. 30. The description of Mr Polly with its brief quotation of his actual words is an example of this.

More important from the point of view of understanding the craft of the writer is a consideration of why writers use dialogue within the particular context in which they are writing. As in a play, it is important that the words a writer puts into the mouth of a particular character should be convincing and representative of that person. If in a play, the speeches of one character could be transferred to another character without anyone being aware of something strange or inconsistent, then this would suggest that the speeches are not particularly characterful and not distinctive or recognizable enough as being appropriate only to the original speaker: in other words, it is carelessly written dialogue. The same is true of dialogue in a story or a novel or an essay—the spoken words must be appropriate to the speaker and to the situation.

From this, it follows that when a writer puts words into the mouth of a speaker, he is concerned with *how* his character says something and *what* he says. A simple way of making a speaker's words individual is to give him a phrase which he uses frequently and which makes him instantly identifiable. Hanna Glawari in *The Merry Widow* uses the phrase 'and that's a fact' to emphasize the points she makes. Boniface, the old innkeeper in *The Beaux' Stratagem*, fills out his speeches with the tag 'as the saying is'. The frequent repetition of phrases like these is associated with the particular character so that we are led to anticipate their repetition and laugh when the expected happens.

Another method of making the speech of a character instantly recognizable is by having him speak in an idiosyncratic way entirely his own. A familiar example is the character of Mr Jingle in Charles Dickens's *The Pickwick Papers* with his telegraphic style. He is 'the loquacious stranger' in the following extract:

'Heads, heads—take care of your heads!' cried the loquacious stranger, as they came out under the low archway, which in those days formed the entrance to the coach-yard. 'Terrible place—dangerous work—other day—five children—mother—tall lady, eating sandwiches—forgot the arch—crash—knock—children look round—mother's head off—sandwich in her hand—no mouth to put it in—head of a family off—shocking, shocking!'

A more subtle example of a character speaking in a way specific to herself is Miss Bates in Jane Austen's *Emma*. Read the following extract and consider what kind of person Miss Bates is and how *the way she speaks* helps to tell us about her and the kind of person she is.

'Jane caught a bad cold, poor thing! so long ago as the 7th of November (as I am going to read to you), and has never been well since. A long time, is not it, for a cold to hang upon her? She never mentioned it before, because she would not alarm us. Just like her! so considerate! But, however, she is so far from well, that her kind friends the Campbells think she had better come home, and try an air that always agrees with her: and they have no doubt that three or four months at Highbury will entirely cure her; and it is certainly a great deal better that she should come here than go to Ireland, if she is unwell. Nobody could nurse her as we should do.'

'It appears to me the most desirable arrangement in the world.'

'And so she is to come to us next Friday or Saturday, and the Campbells leave town in their way to Holyhead the Monday following, as you will find from Jane's letter. So sudden! You may guess, dear Miss Woodhouse, what flurry it has thrown me in. If it were not for the drawback of her illness—but I am afraid we must expect to see her grown thin, and looking very poorly. I must tell you what an unlucky thing happened to me as to that. I always make a point of reading Jane's letters through to myself first, before I read them aloud to my mother, you know, for fear of there being anything in them to distress her. Jane desired me to do it, so I always do! and so I began to-day with my usual caution: but no sooner did I come to the mention of her being unwell, than I burst out, quite frightened, with "Bless me! poor Jane is ill!" which my mother, being on the watch, heard distinctly, and was sadly alarmed at. However, when I read on, I found it was not near so bad as I had fancied at first; and I make so light of it now to her that she does not think much about it: but I cannot imagine how I could be so off my guard. If Jane does not get well soon, we will call in Mr Perry. The expense shall not be thought of; and though he is so liberal and so fond of Jane, that I dare say he would not mean to charge anything for attendance, we could not suffer it to be so, you know. He has a wife and a family to maintain, and is not to be giving away his time. Well, now I have just given you a hint of what Jane writes about, we will turn to her letter, and I am sure she tells her own story a great deal better than I can tell it for her.'

'I am afraid we must be running away,' said Emma, glancing at Harriet, and beginning to rise, 'my father will be expecting us. I had no intention, I thought I had no power, of staying more than five minutes, when I first entered the house. I merely called because I would not pass the door without inquiring after Mrs Bates; but I have been so pleasantly detained. Now, however, we must wish you and Mrs Bates good morning.'

And not all that could be urged to detain her succeeded. She regained the street, happy in this, that though much had been forced on her against her will; though she had, in fact, heard the whole substance of Jane Fairfax's letter, she had been able to escape the letter itself.

(JANE AUSTEN, *Emma*)

Another extract from *Emma* shows the consistency with which Jane Austen makes the words her characters

say appropriate to the kind of people they are. *What Mr Woodhouse says in the following passage is always consistent with his view of life.*

What is his view of life? What kind of person is Mr Woodhouse?

Highbury, the large and populous village almost amounting to a town, to which Hartfield, in spite of its separate lawn, and shrubberies, and name, did really belong, afforded her no equals. The Woodhouses were first in consequence there. All looked up to them. She had many acquaintances in the place, for her father was universally civil, but not one among them who could be accepted in lieu of Miss Taylor for even half a day. It was a melancholy change; and Emma could not but sigh over it, and wish for impossible things, till her father awoke, and made it necessary to be cheerful. His spirits required support. He was a nervous man, easily depressed; fond of everybody that he was used to, and hating to part with them; hating change of every kind. Matrimony, as the origin of change, was always disagreeable; and he was by no means yet reconciled to his own daughter's marrying, nor could ever speak of her but with compassion, though it had been entirely a match of affection, when he was now obliged to part with Miss Taylor too; and from his habits of gentle selfishness, and of being never able to suppose that other people could feel differently from himself, he was very much disposed to think Miss Taylor had done as sad a thing for herself as for them, and would have been a great deal happier if she had spent all the rest of her life at Hartfield. Emma smiled and chatted as cheerfully as she could, to keep him from such thoughts; but when tea came, it was impossible for him not to say exactly as he had said at dinner:

'Poor Miss Taylor! I wish she were here again. What a pity it is that Mr Weston ever thought of her!'

'I cannot agree with you, papa; you know I cannot. Mr Weston is such a good-humoured, pleasant excellent man, that he thoroughly deserves a good wife; and you would not have had Miss Taylor live with us for ever, and bear all my odd humours, when she might have a house of her own?'

'A house of her own! but where is the advantage of a house of her own? This is three times as large; and you have never any odd humours, my dear.'

'How often we shall be going to see them, and they coming to see us! We shall be always meeting! *We* must begin; we must go and pay our wedding-visit very soon!'

'My dear, how am I to get so far? Randalls is such a distance. I could not walk half so far.'

'No, papa; nobody thought of your walking. We must go in the carriage, to be sure.'

'The carriage! But James will not like to put the horses to for such a little way; and where are the poor horses to be while we are paying our visit?'

(JANE AUSTEN, *Emma*)

These two last extracts indicate two further uses which writers make of dialogue: to pass on information to the reader in an amusing and palatable way, and to reinforce an author's comments so that we get a stronger impression of what he means. Miss Bates prattles on in an amusing and characteristic manner. We get an impression of her scatter-brained manner and her inconsequential way of moving from point to point with her exclamations and her confidences. But *what* she says is also important for the reader. As well as creating comedy of character out of Miss Bates's chattering, Jane Austen provides us with information that Emma wants to know and that we as readers need to know if we are to understand the full implications of the plot. The comedy of the situation and the fact that the necessary information has nevertheless been divulged—through dialogue—are clinched in the final sentence: 'though she had, in fact, heard the whole substance of Jane Fairfax's letter, she had been able to escape the letter itself.'

The second extract, concerning Mr Woodhouse, shows how dialogue can reinforce an author's comment. Jane Austen talks of Mr Woodhouse's 'habits of gentle selfishness' and the dialogue between Emma and her father shows him revealing this through his concern for poor Miss Taylor who has married Mr Weston and moved away from Hartfield to live in a house of her own. Mr Woodhouse fears that she will not be happy. What he really means is that he doesn't like change and is feeling sorry for himself at having lost her company. The dialogue makes stronger in our minds the picture of Mr Woodhouse suggested by Jane Austen as narrator. When she says Mr Woodhouse is a little self-centred, we as readers may not believe her, but when we hear Mr Woodhouse himself speaking in terms that reveal his 'gentle selfishness' we must be convinced. What Jane Austen is doing is dramatizing the situation. Not content with just telling us what Mr Woodhouse is like, she *shows* us as well.

Clearly, dialogue is a very important device in helping the reader to get a clear impression of the characters the author is creating. This has been indicated in Unit 4 and is also implicit in what we have said in this section.

 READING LIST

This unit's reading list consists of some books containing a great deal of dialogue. Browse through some of the books until you find something that takes your fancy.

One of the most subtle exponents of the use of dialogue is Ivy Compton-Burnett, and it is worth while at least savouring one of her novels though they are an acquired taste, and some may find them too cynical and doom-laden. They deal with closely-knit family and servant circles full of neurotic tensions in late Victorian–Edwardian England, and are written in almost continuous dialogue. Try *Manservant and Maidservant*, *A Family and a Fortune*, or *Pastors and Masters*.

Three present-day women writers use dialogue consistently well to explore emotional relationships: Edna O'Brien (*The Country Girls*, *Girl with Green Eyes*); Muriel Spark (*Memento Mori*, *The Prime of Miss Jean Brodie*); Iris Murdoch (*A Severed Head*, *The Sandcastle*).

As you can see from the passages from *Emma* quoted

in the previous section, Jane Austen is another mistress of dialogue. Try to read more of *Emma* or try *Pride and Prejudice*.

The short stories of writers like D. H. Lawrence (the stories in the volume *England, My England*), Saki (*The Chronicles of Clovis*), Christopher Isherwood (*Mr Norris Changes Trains*), Katherine Mansfield (*Bliss*), Ray Bradbury (*The Day it Rained Forever*) use dialogue to lively effect.

Dialogue also plays an important part in the following novels:

Graham Greene: *Our Man in Havana, Travels with my Aunt*.
Keith Waterhouse: *Billy Liar*.
Evelyn Waugh: *Decline and Fall, Vile Bodies, A Handful of Dust*.
P. G. Wodehouse: *Carry on, Jeeves, The Inimitable Jeeves, Thank you, Jeeves*.
John Braine: *Room at the Top, Life at the Top*.
John Steinbeck: *Of Mice and Men, Cannery Row*.

 VOCABULARY

Jane Austen uses words with great precision and elegance. Read the second extract from *Emma* again and note how carefully she balances her sentences and weighs her words. Try to work out the meaning of the following words as used there:

populous, afforded, consequences, universally, civil, in lieu of, reconciled, compassion, disposed, humours.

Look these words up in a dictionary and check with your first opinions.

Put each of the words into a sentence of your own. Try to make your sentences interesting.

> Make sure you understand the words in the other extracts in this unit. Check up on those you are not sure of and put them in sentences of your own.

 LANGUAGE
Punctuation Marks II: The Punctuation of Speech

If you are to use speech as part of a story or a descriptive essay, it is important that you know how to punctuate it correctly. The best way to learn how to write good dialogue and how to punctuate it correctly is to keep alert when you are reading and to note how speech is punctuated on the printed page in newspaper reports and novels. However, the following points will give you a guide to the main rules to observe.

1. Actual words spoken are enclosed by quotation marks. Quotation marks (or inverted commas as they are also called) can be single or double. It doesn't matter which you use, but be consistent.

'Why are you late?' Yvonne asked.

"Why are you late?" Yvonne asked.

'Why are you late?' are the actual words Yvonne spoke, and they are therefore enclosed in quotation marks.

2. The first spoken word has a capital letter, even if it comes in the middle of a sentence, e.g.

Stanley replied, 'My car broke down.'

Note that when a spoken sentence is interrupted by a verb of saying, the continuation of the sentence does not begin with a capital letter, e.g.

'You should have phoned me,' she cried, 'if you knew you were going to be late.'

Compare:

'I didn't know the car would break down,' he said, 'or I would have phoned.'

'That's no excuse,' she retorted. 'Your dinner is ruined.'
Why does 'or' have a small 'o' and 'Your' a capital 'Y'?

3. A comma is needed before quoted words if these begin in the middle of a sentence and at the end of quoted words if no other punctuation is already used. Look at the instances where the comma is used in the examples given in 2. above.

4. Punctuation marks are placed inside the quotation marks, e.g.

'I can't help that!' exclaimed Stanley.

'You should at least say sorry,' said Yvonne, 'for spoiling my evening.'

'Why should I?' demanded her husband. 'It's not my fault if you choose to sit here all evening moping and have no interests of your own.'

Note that when an exclamation mark or a question mark is used as part of the quoted words, the word of saying if it follows has a small letter, not a capital letter. See the examples above.

5. It is usual to begin a new paragraph every time there is a new speaker, as in the example given in 2.

6. If words are quoted within the spoken words, these are enclosed in double quotation marks if single ones are normally used, or in single quotation marks if double ones are normally used, e.g.

'Did you say, "Why should I?"' she asked. *or*

"Did you say, 'Why should I?'" she asked.

7. If a quoted speech continues for more than one paragraph, quotation marks appear at the beginning of each paragraph but not at the end except for the final one, e.g.

'Yes, I did,' said Stanley, 'and why shouldn't I say it? You lead your life and I'll lead mine. Stop nagging.

'Now, what about having a drink and starting again?'

It is worth mentioning at this point that quotation marks are also used in writing for quotations, for titles and for words used in a special sense or particularly referred to, and for foreign words which are not in general English usage, e.g.

'To be or not to be' is one of Shakespeare's best known lines.

'Twelfth Night' is one of Shakespeare's happiest comedies.

'Whisky' came into the English language from Gaelic.

He signalled to the 'garçon' to bring the bill.

(In printed books, titles are usually put into italics—this is something to avoid in writing.)

Note that students sometimes put slang words into quotation marks in the belief that this makes them respectable, e.g.

At Christmas time everyone buys a lot of 'booze'.

This belief is unjustified. Slang is always slang and should be avoided except where it adds colour to the speech of a character or a style.

Read some of the passages given earlier in these units which contain a lot of dialogue. Study the punctuation.

Get a friend to read out part of one of the passages to you and see if you can write down the punctuation correctly. If you can't manage this, copy a section leaving out the punctuation and insert it from memory. Check against the printed passage and make a mental note of the points you get wrong and need to watch out for.

 SPELLING

When to put a single 'l' or a double 'l' often presents problems. Study the following notes:

1. When a word that normally has a double 'l' is joined to another word to form a compound, the double 'l' becomes a single 'l'. Consider the following:

all + mighty = almighty
all + most = almost
all + ready = already
all + though = although
all + together = altogether
all + ways = always
full + fill = fulfil
joy + full = joyful
skill + full = skilful
un + till = until
well + come = welcome
will + full = wilful

2. Be careful to distinguish between the following:

all ready	and	already
all together	and	altogether
all ways	and	always

'All ready' means 'everyone or everything prepared'; 'already' refers to time and means 'beforehand', 'by this time', etc., e.g.

The children were all ready to start at one o'clock.

The train was already an hour late.

'All together' means 'all in one piece', 'joined as a whole'; 'altogether' means 'entirely', 'on the whole', etc., e.g.

Let's sing the chorus once more all together.

My view is altogether different.

'All ways' means 'every possible method'; 'always' means 'forever', 'every time', etc., e.g.

I have tried to fit the wheel in all ways, but it still won't fit.

Clare always complains.

Write further sentences showing the difference between these pairs of words.

3. Note the spelling 'all right' (two separate words). This is the most acceptable form, though the spelling 'alright' frequently appears.

4. For the difference between words like 'spoonful'

and 'spoon full' and 'pocketful' and 'pocket full', see 'Spelling' Unit 4.

Here is an exercise covering the points made in this section. Complete the words or choose one of the words in the pairs in the following sentences:

1. *He is very skil— with his hands.*
2. *The present he received yesterday ful— his every dream.*
3. *The car was (all ready/already) to be collected.*
4. *They went to the party (all together/altogether).*
5. *'(All together/Altogether) now', said the chorus master.*
6. *Having your cake and eating it is wish— thinking.*
7. *There was an —mighty crash.*
8. *'Are you —right?' she asked.*
9. *Wait un— the lights are red.*
10. *The paint splashed (all ways/always) over the floor.*
11. *You are (all ways/always) late.*
12. *He had his pocket— of pebbles.*
13. *For that throat you should take a spoon— of honey.*
14. *It is (all ready/already) one o'clock.*
15. *I was —most late for my appointment.*

ASSIGNMENT D

You should spend about an hour and a half on the preparation and writing of Part I and about an hour and a quarter on Part II.

Part I: Essay

Write an argumentative essay on *one* of the following:

1. You have been asked to speak in a debate supporting the motion: 'This House has no confidence in the future'. Write your speech.
2. Do you agree that the younger generation is conventional?
3. Write an essay in support of the pleasures of solitude.
4. Should we arm the police?
5. The motor car—a blessing or a curse?
6. Do you believe that a woman's role is to provide a comfortable home for her husband and family?

Part II: Comprehension

Read the following passage carefully and answer the questions set, using as far as possible your own words.

Pros and Cons of 'Ads'

'Whether we like it or not we have got it, and we are likely to go on having it.' Thus Mr Walter Taplin in a book which has just been published entitled *Advertising: a new approach*. Mr Taplin was formerly the editor of one of our distinguished and irreverent contemporaries: now he bears the striking title of Research Fellow in Advertising and Promotional Activity at the London School of Economics. Whether or not his approach is new, his post is unique: and his attitude to his subject is, on the whole, approving. Not that he is unaware that the art of advertising has from time to time met with a certain amount of criticism. For example, in a recent number of *The Listener* Mr Furneaux Jordan, reviewing recent guidebooks, made some rather gratuitous and perhaps insufficiently considered remarks about advertising to the effect that 'a fool and his money are soon parted' and so on. It is not our habit to censor our contributors' opinions, but naturally those who practise the profession of advertising were offended when they got round to reading this. After all, like all people who take their own business seriously, advertisers are extremely sensitive men and women. If one has not met them in real life, one has surely seen them in films, struggling with that just word or gem-like phrase that makes all the difference between tasty copy and mere copy-tasting. They are well aware that their work is often maligned. Mr Taplin quotes a sentence from a book on economics by Professor K. E. Boulding: 'There is a strong presumption that most competitive advertising is a social waste'.

In Mr Taplin, however, the profession has found a careful apologist. He brings his fire down on the critics of advertising from many different angles and levels. He reminds us, in a forthright way, that the newspaper industry would be 'decimated' and 'whole industries collapse, and a general depression be set off' if there were no such things as advertisements. But Mr Taplin is no mere pragmatist. He is not afraid of philosophical argument. 'The public discussion of advertising is shot through with moral arguments,' he says, 'not to say shot to pieces by them ... moral questions will keep breaking in ...' But Mr Taplin reminds us that the art of persuasion is an old and noble one; people like being persuaded: indeed they like paying to be persuaded. Also he emphasizes that the profession itself has its own code.

It might perhaps be said, on the other side, that in these days of consumers' councils and their like, which exist both in this country and in the United States of America, the claims put forward by advertisers are liable to be carefully scrutinized and can, if they are unjustified, to some extent be publicly exposed. Mr Taplin is breezy about consumers' councils (it is difficult to locate them in his index) and rather critical of Mr Priestley's 'Admass' and Professor Galbraith's *Affluent Society*. And he tells us, in effect, that if people like to pay more for their soaps and aspirins when they are presented to them with siren's songs, well, they get a good deal of pleasure out of it, don't they? But whichever way one looks at advertising, as he says, 'we have got it, and we are likely to go on having it.' And whatever the pros and cons may be, those of us who are journalists at least have reason to be grateful for it.

(The Listener)

1. What seems to you striking about the title of Mr Taplin's new post?
2. Why were advertisers offended by Mr Furneaux Jordan's comment?
3. How does the writer describe advertisers in the first

paragraph? What is his attitude towards them? What is his tone of voice when he writes about them?

4. Explain the meaning of 'There is a strong presumption that most competitive advertising is a social waste.'

5. Explain what you understand by the expression 'a careful apologist'.

6. Summarize the points in favour of advertising that Mr Taplin makes as quoted in the second paragraph.

7. How is the public safe-guarded against advertisers' false claims.

8. What do you understand by 'Mr Taplin is breezy about consumers' councils'?

9. Which word sums up the writer's attitude towards advertising—hostile, indifferent, friendly, resigned, cynical?

10. What is the significance of the final sentence?

11. From the passage as a whole, deduce the bad points about advertising.

UNIT 7

WRITING
Dialogue

Advice on writing an essay or part of an essay in the form of a dialogue.

READING AND UNDERSTANDING
A Play

Plays naturally follow after a study of dialogue. We look at some of the devices a writer uses when he writes a play.

READING LIST

Some plays you may enjoy.

VOCABULARY

Some words from the passage studied for dialogue from William Gerhardi's *The Polyglots*.

LANGUAGE
Punctuation Marks III

How to use the comma, semicolon and colon.

SPELLING

Where to use capital letters. Revision.

WRITING

Dialogue

In the last unit we looked at some examples of dialogue. We would now like you to gain some practice in writing a dialogue between two people representing different points of view. The subjects you could write on in this way could be something like this: 'Write a conversation about fox-hunting between a fox hunter and a supporter of the cause to abolish blood sports,' or 'In the form of a dialogue between a supporter and an opponent consider the case for and against capital punishment.' Ways of gathering ideas and organizing them for an argumentative essay have been suggested in Unit 6. Look at these again. In this unit, hints on how to present these ideas in the form of an interesting dialogue will be considered.

In many ways, an assignment like this is difficult. There is a great danger that the conversation will become stilted and unnatural, and there is a great temptation simply to put quotation marks around long paragraphs representing first one view and then the other. Try to remember the following points:

1. Try to create a natural and convincing background. Possibilities would be over a meal, at the pub, or at a meeting. Give brief details of the setting to help create an appropriate atmosphere, and use the setting to emphasize points in the argument. For example, 'He was so surprised by what John said that he laid down his knife and fork.' Or, 'He was about to drink his beer, but John's remark made him put the tankard down on the bar with a thump.'

2. Try to make your characters interesting. Remember what was said in Unit 4 about describing people. If your two characters have contrasting views, it is not unreasonable to expect that they are different types of people, and therefore they will look, react and speak in different ways. One could be very cool and collected; the other fiery and easily losing his temper.

3. Use examples to enliven your argument. Flat assertions and generalizations are not usually convincing in arguments. If one of your characters can say, 'I remember once ...' and then go on and give a personal example to support his case, this will be much more interesting and convincing.

4. Try to get some 'cut and thrust' into your dialogue. Too many long speeches, first one character and then the

57

other, become boring. Don't produce the kind of response Gladstone had from Queen Victoria when she complained that he addressed her as though she were a public meeting. Make your characters react to each other. Make them interrupt each other.

5. Remember that your essay needs an effective opening and ending. A final crushing comment from one of the characters or something firm and definite or surprising is needed to round off an essay like this.

Study the following extract. The characters are talking about the First World War.

'The war is over,' said my aunt, 'and yet there will be men, I know, who will regret it. The other day I talked to an English Captain who had been through the thick of the Gallipoli campaign, and he assured me positively that he liked fighting—and simply carried me off my feet. And I don't know whether he isn't right. He liked fighting the Turks because, he said, they are such splendid fellows. Mind you! he had nothing at all against them; on the contrary, he thought they were gentlemen and sportsmen—almost his equals. But he said he'd fight a Turk any day, with pleasure. Because they fought cleanly. After all,' my aunt continued, 'there's something splendid, say what you like—a zest of life!—in his account of fighting the Turks. The Turks rush out of the wood with glittering bayonets, chanting: "Allah! Allah! Allah!" as they advance into battle. Because, you see, they think they are already at the gates of Heaven, only waiting to be admitted. So they rush gravely and steadily into battle, chanting: "Allah! Allah! Allah!" I don't know—but it must be, as he says, exhilarating!'

'And then,' I said, continuing the picture, 'some sportsman sends a cold bayonet blade into the vulnerable parts of the man. You understand what happens?' I became cool, calculatingly suave. 'The intestines are a delicate tissue; when, for example, you eat a lump of something that your stomach cannot digest, you are conscious of pain. Now picture what happens in that human stomach at the advent of a sharp cold blade. It isn't merely that it cuts the guts; it lets them out. Picture it. And you will understand the peculiar intonation of his last "Allah!"'

'Oh, you are disgusting!' [said Sylvia, Aunt Teresa's daughter.]

'This is cruel! cruel!' said my aunt.

'Yes, to you, who would like your wars "respectable", conducted in good taste, outside in the yard, but please not on the drawing-room carpet! While my own feelings are that in a war soldiers should begin at home with the civilian population, particularly with the old ladies.'

'That is enough,' she said.

'No, I won't have you run away with a partial picture. Allah, indeed. What of your son in Flanders?'

'Oh, he is all right. Besides, it is all over now.'

'M-m ... wait a few days.' I was excited. But I knew that to give the full effect to your sermon you must be calm, let your passion sift through your sentences. When I am righteously angry I let my righteous anger gather, and then put the brake on it, and give vent to it in cool, biting, seemingly dispassionate tones. I harness my anger to do the work of indictment. Turning ever so gently towards her, I fix an evangelic look upon my aunt.

'What is the terrible thing in a war? In the war men's nerves gave way, and then they were court martialled for their nerves having given way—deserted them—and were shot at dawn—as deserters, for cowardice. And the sole judges of them were their superior officers who dared not know any better.

'And why is it,' I continued, avoiding momentarily the look which crept into Aunt Teresa's eyes, 'that stay-at-homes, particularly women, and more particularly old women, are the worst offenders as regards this stupid business of glorifying war? Why is it that they are more mischievous in mind, less generous in outlook than their youngsters in the trenches?'

Aunt Teresa closed her eyes with a faint sigh, as if to indicate that it was a strain on her delicate system to listen to my unending flow.

While, 'I remember,' I continued, 'an hotel in Brighton where I stayed two weeks before joining up in the so-called Great War. The inevitable old ladies with their pussy cats were by far the worst of all. They talked in terms of blood. They demanded the extermination of the whole of the German race; nothing less, they said, would satisfy them. They longed to behead all German babies with their own hands, for the genuine pleasure, they said, that this would give them. They were not human babies, they argued, but vermin. It was a service they desired to render to their country and the human race at large. They had a right to demonstrate their patriotism. I was not a little shocked, I must confess, at this tardy display of Herodism in old, decaying women. I told them as much, politely, and they called me a pro-German. They discovered unpleasant possibilities in my name that had slipped their attention heretofore—a serious oversight. A danger to the Realm. Diabologh—but in heaven what a name to be sure! One of them went as far as to say that there was—there seemed to be—a distinct suggestion of something—well—diabolical about it that should be watched. They talked of cement grounds prepared by German spies at various vulnerable points in England to serve the purpose of future German heavy guns, ingeniously disguised as tennis courts, and of me in the same breath. "Why don't you," said one of the old ladies, a particularly antiquated specimen of her sex, "rather than make that impossible noise on the piano, go and fight for your country?" "Die?" I said, "that you may live? The thought's enough to make anyone a funk."

'Throughout the countries which had participated in the war,' (I continued, because my aunt, breathless at my imputations, had nothing ready with which to interrupt my flow) 'there is still a tendency among many bereaved ones to assuage themselves by the thought that their dead have fallen for something at once noble and worth while which overtowers somehow the tragedy of their death—almost excusing it. Mischievous delusion! Their dead are victims—neither more nor less—of the folly of adults who having blundered the world into a ludicrous war, now build memorials—to square it all up with. If I were the Unknown Soldier, my ghost would refuse to lie down under that heavy piece of marble; I would arise, I would say to them: Keep your blasted memorials and learn sense! Christ died 1918 years back, and you're as incredibly foolish as ever you were.'

I subsided suddenly. There was a pause.

'Thank you. We are much obliged to you for your lecture,' said Aunt Teresa.

'Welcome,' I said, 'welcome.'

(WILLIAM GERHARDI, *The Polyglots*)

State briefly the difference in attitude between Aunt Teresa and George Diabologh, the narrator, towards the war.

What is the difference in character between these two?

Pick out the personal examples given by both characters. What points are being made by introducing these examples?

Which character, in your view, has the more convincing arguments?

Justify your view.

Comment on Aunt Teresa's reactions to George's arguments as indicated by her interruptions 'This is cruel! cruel!', 'That is enough', and 'Besides, it is all over now.'

Comment on the ending. Is it effective?

In what ways are the final remarks of the two characters representative of them?

This is, of course, an extract from a novel, and this discussion about war is only part of the general context of the novel. Gerhardi is not concerned with giving the complete arguments for both sides. But the extract does indicate how dialogue can be used to represent points of view and how it can be made lively and interesting. In an essay of the type suggested at the beginning of the unit, you would be expected to give a more balanced view of the two sides of the subject under discussion and to stick more closely to the subject.

Dialogue can be a useful part of almost any essay, not just confined to the rather specialized kind of essay topic that demands a dialogue form. A piece of dialogue in a descriptive essay or an essay describing a character can often have an enlivening effect. A story can be made more realistic and convincing through dialogue. An argumentative essay is less likely to require dialogue, though even there the odd bit of quoted speech can give variety and can make it more personal.

For examples, look back at and read again the extracts from Angus Wilson's A Little Companion *on page 22; The Scottish Daily Express on page 26, Ray Bradbury's* The Other Foot *on page 27, and H. G. Wells'* The History of Mr Polly *on page 30.*

When writing dialogue, you may find the following points useful:

1. Make sure that the spoken words you use are appropriate to the speaker. If the character in your story is a coward, you mustn't make him say, 'I'll knock your head off', unless your intention is ironic and you want to show that his words are all bluster and that underneath he is afraid.

2. Make sure that the dialogue is appropriate to the situation. If you are describing a mining disaster it is unlikely that one miner would say to another, 'There seems to have been a slight hitch'.

3. Avoid using unnecessary dialogue. Sometimes students are carried away and use dialogue all the time whether it is appropriate or not. Revise the points made about dialogue in 'Reading and Understanding' Unit 6. If you use dialogue, it must have a definite purpose, e.g. it gives variety, it reveals character, it gives information in a lively way, it advances the plot, it adds a touch of realism. The following is the kind of thing to avoid:

There was a knock at the door.

'Is that a knock at the door?' asked Mrs Waterhouse.

'Yes, it's a knock at the door,' replied Mr Waterhouse.

'Are you going to answer it?'

'All right, I'll answer it.'

Mr Waterhouse opened the door.

Dialogue like this, stating the obvious, gets the story nowhere.

4. Avoid, too, the use of dialect if this is possible. Students are often inclined to try to make their stories interesting by including in them characters with North Country or Cockney accents, or characters from 'low life' who say, 'ain't' and drop their haitches. The occasional grammatical lapse to create character is possible, but attempts to present a character who consistently makes mistakes or attempts to reproduce dialects in phonetic spelling are not likely to be very successful.

Writers who do use dialect or colloquialisms in dialogues are always very familiar with the forms. Often the skill at writing in dialect comes from years of close association with the group of people who speak it. For example, D. H. Lawrence was brought up in Nottinghamshire and was so familiar with local dialect that when he uses it in his stories and novels it reads quite naturally.

5. Remember that there are more words for introducing spoken words than 'said'. Consider the following: 'asked', 'replied', 'retorted', 'answered', 'returned', 'riposted', 'called', 'shouted', 'blurted', 'gasped', etc. Clearly, words like 'said', 'replied', 'asked' are the most common and are the obvious ones to use, but the occasional use of one of the others to give a more exact indication of the manner in which words are said can give variety. Don't overdo the less common words though, as the effect of constantly ringing the changes on the word of saying could be grotesque, e.g.

'Come here,' Charles wheedled.

'I don't want to,' Jane simpered.

'Come here,' he coaxed.

'Why should I?' she cooed.

'Come here,' he begged.

'All right,' she whispered.

Write a dialogue between one of the following pairs, each representing a different point of view.

1. A general and a conscientious objector.
2. A grandparent and a teenager.
3. A Company Director and a striker.
4. A policeman and a criminal.
5. A conservative and a socialist.
6. A career woman and a housewife.

Remember the following points: try to establish a convincing background; make your characters distinctive; give plenty of specific examples to enliven the argument; vary the lengths of the speeches; try to have an interesting opening and an effective ending.

READING AND UNDERSTANDING

A Play

Having looked at how writers use dialogue to enliven or help to dramatize their stories, it is natural to move on to plays where the writer has only the actual words spoken by his characters through which to tell his story and make his effects. Of course, in the theatre, the dramatist receives a great deal of help from other sources—the physical presence and skill of the actors, the interpretative insight of the producer, and contributory factors like costume, scenery, lighting, movement and music. The fact remains, though, that with most plays, the starting point is the words, and without them there would be nothing to build on. The basis for character development, interplay between characters, the creation of atmosphere and suspense must be in the words from the start.

We look first at the opening scene from Shakespeare's *Macbeth*. It is comparatively simple, very short, and indicates in a small space some of the factors that make Shakespeare a great playwright.

Enter three Witches
1 Witch: When shall we three meet again?
　In thunder, lightning, or in rain?
2 Witch: When the hurlyburly's done,
　When the battle's lost and won.
3 Witch: That will be ere the set of sun.
1 Witch: Where the place?
2 Witch: Upon the heath.
3 Witch: There to meet with Macbeth.
1 Witch: I come, Graymalkin.
2 Witch: Paddock calls.
3 Witch: Anon!
All: Fair is foul, and foul is fair:
　Hover through the fog and filthy air.

　　　　　　　　　　　(*Witches vanish.*)

What are we told about the general atmosphere of the scene?

What information is given?

Are there any indications of action that is to follow?

Are there any indications of the moral attitude of the witches?

Are the witches differentiated in any way? Could speeches be transferred from one witch to another?

Try to answer these questions before going on to read the following commentary.

The general atmosphere is established by the first speech. The line 'In thunder, lightning, or in rain' suggests a wild scene, and at the end of the scene there is a description of the murky foggy air. The fact that the characters are witches gives an unnatural eerie impression. We are told by the Second Witch that there is a battle taking place which will be settled before nightfall. We are led to expect a meeting between the three witches and Macbeth before the day is out. This will take place on the heath. We are therefore prepared for a scene soon

to follow. The second last line 'Fair is foul, and foul is fair' suggests that the witches' moral values are inverted. What is normally considered good is bad to them and vice versa.

There is little differentiation between the speeches of the three witches. A speech could be transferred from one character to another with little change in effect. Why is this? When talking about dialogue (Unit 6), I suggested that what a character said should be appropriate to him alone and if the speech could be put into someone else's mouth without being noticed, then it was bad dialogue. In this scene from *Macbeth*, we have to take into consideration the dramatist's intentions. Shakespeare is not here concerned with creating individual characters. What he wants to establish at the beginning of the play is the general atmosphere and the general feeling of malignity. It doesn't matter which witch says which line because they each represent the same kind of evil.

In this opening scene then, Shakespeare has created an atmosphere and a setting. He has given some information about events happening at that moment. He has given an indication of the form the action is going to take in the future. He has shown the kind of moral attitude the witches represent. All of this he has achieved in sixty or so words, using only the words spoken by the characters. Part of the power and effectiveness of the scene comes from this economy and compression.

In the following scene from Arnold Wesker's Roots, *we can see more easily the interplay between characters, how they are individualized, how the attitude of one conflicts with the attitude of another, how the opinions they express tell us about the kind of people they are. Read the extract carefully, paying particular attention to the kind of impression you get of Beatie and Mrs Bryant from their attitudes, how they react to the situation, and what they say.*

FRANK (*reading the paper*): I see that boy what assaulted the ole woman in London got six years.

MRS BRYANT: Blust! He need to! I'd've given him six years and a bit more. Bloody ole hooligans. Do you give me a chance to pass sentence and I'd soon clear the street of crime, that I would. Yes, that I would.

BEATIE (*springing into activity*): All right Mother—we'll give you a chance. (*Grabs Jimmy's hat and umbrella. Places hat on mother's head and umbrella in her arms.*) There you are, you're the judge. Now sum up and pass judgment.

MRS BRYANT: I'd put him in prison for life.

FRANK: You gotta sum up though. Blust, you can't just stick a man in prison and say nothing.

MRS BRYANT: Good-bye, I'd say.

BEATIE: Come on Mother, speak up. You sit there and you say you'd clear the streets o' crime an' I hear you pass judgment all the time, now you do it in a proper way. Anybody can say 'go to prison', but you want to be a judge. Well, you show a judge's understanding. Talk!

MRS BRYANT: Well I—I—yes I—well I—Oh don't be so soft.

FRANK: The mighty head is silent.

BEATIE: Well yes, she would be wouldn't she?

MRS BRYANT: What do you mean, I would be? You

60

don't expect me to know what they say in courts do you? I aren't no judge.

BEATIE: Then why do you say what you do? Suddenly —out of the blue—a judgment! You don't think about it. If someone do something wrong you don't stop and think why, you just sit and pass easy judgment. No discussin', no questions, just off with his head. Look Mother, when something go wrong in the family, do you ever sit and discuss it? I mean look at Father getting less money. I don't see the family sittin' together and discussin' it. It's a problem! But which of you said it concerns you?

MRS BRYANT: Nor don't it concern them. I aren't havin' people mix in my matters.

BEATIE: But they aren't just people—they're your family for hell's sake!

MRS BRYANT: No matters, I aren't havin' it!

BEATIE: But Mother I—

MRS BRYANT: Now shut you up Beatie Bryant and leave it alone. I shall talk when I hev to and I never shall do, so there!

(ARNOLD WESKER, *Roots*)

Mrs Bryant represents in many ways blind prejudice and a refusal to think or justify an opinion. On hearing that the boy who assaulted an old woman received a six-year prison sentence, her immediate reaction is 'Serve him right, he should have been put in prison for life.' But when asked by Beatie to support her reaction, she is at first speechless. Then she objects that this play-acting is 'soft'. She then pleads ignorance of the procedure of the courts and that she is no judge (after having passed a judgment). When Beattie says, 'If you won't talk about this, then let's talk about something that does concern us,' namely Mr Bryant being given a poorer job, Mrs Bryant closes up completely: she doesn't want to talk about what she considers her private affairs, even with the rest of her family. To have to think and talk about the problem is too painful or too much effort for her: she would rather let resentment grow in silence. All her reactions are abrupt statements or evasions. Beatie, on the other hand, wants things in the open. She wants to try to educate her mother, to show that we can't just make automatic reactions, that we must justify the comments we make; we must not keep things bottled up inside, but must try to confide in other people and get their sympathy and assistance. Her speeches are full of vitality and inventiveness, and she argues her case carefully.

This scene from *Roots*, then, shows how a dramatist can tell us about his characters from the opinions they express, from how they express them, and how they react to a particular situation. It also shows how a dramatist can communicate his own ideas. We are clearly meant to find Mrs Bryant unsympathetic because of her refusal to face the facts and because of her prejudice and automatic reactions, whereas we are meant to find Beatie's willingness to talk and think things out and her searching for the truth as admirable and praiseworthy. Most writers—and this applies to dramatists as well as to novelists—are not just telling stories or creating characters: they are also indicating attitudes to life which they feel are right and which they want us to share.

Some playwrights like G. B. Shaw and James Barrie add a great number of stage directions when their plays are published as books so as to help the reader to appreciate the play as a kind of novel, and so as to indicate the kind of intonations particular speeches require. For instance, a few random pages from Shaw's *John Bull's Other Island* produce the following suggestions as to how particular speeches are spoken: 'with Irish peevishness', 'disposing of the idea at once', 'in the highest feather', 'astonished', 'aghast', 'indignantly', 'buoyantly', 'naively', 'nervously relapsing into his most Irish manner', 'amazed', 'with curt sincerity', 'flaming up', 'with conviction'.

Look at the scene from Roots *again. What indications would you add to each speech to help a reader to read it correctly and with effect? For instance, Frank's first speech might be 'with interest'; Mrs Bryant's 'with indignation'.*

READING LIST

Some people find reading plays to themselves more difficult than reading a novel or a short story. More is demanded of the reader in terms of imaginative reconstruction. He has to try to visualize the setting and the characters and more or less produce the play in his own head as he goes along. The important thing to remember is that you must try to read the speeches as though they are being acted. You need to supply the appropriate dramatic intonations.

You may find one or other of the following plays worth reading:

Harold Brighouse: *Hobson's Choice.*
Shelagh Delaney: *A Taste of Honey.*
Arnold Wesker: *Roots.*
John Osborne: *Look Back in Anger.*
Willis Hall: *The Long and the Short and the Tall.*
Dylan Thomas: *Under Milk Wood.*
J. B. Priestley: *When we are Married.*
J. B. Priestley: *An Inspector Calls.*
Harold Pinter: *The Caretaker.*
Bertolt Brecht: *The Caucasian Chalk Circle.*
Arthur Miller: *The Crucible.*

Of course there is plenty of opportunity to see plays too—in your local theatre as well as on television. Try to get into the habit of writing down your reactions to plays and characters in them. If you can, it is a good idea to get a copy of a play from the Library after you have seen it: you can check up your idea of what the playwright is aiming to do and make your own notes with the text to help you.

VOCABULARY

William Gerhardi is a writer of the 1920s and 1930s who is rather neglected today. His tone is dry, ironic and satirical in flavour, and the vocabulary he uses tends to be precise and carefully chosen. In both these respects he resembles Angus Wilson, an extract from whose short story 'A Little Companion' appeared in Unit 3. Re-read the extract by Angus Wilson and the extract from William Gerhardi's *The Polyglots* used in this lesson and see whether you agree with this statement.

Try to work out the meanings of the following words as used in the passage from *The Polyglots*:

vulnerable, partial, dispassionate, indictment, momentarily, inevitable, extermination, demonstrate, ingeniously, antiquated, participated, assuage, delusion, subsided.

Look these words up in a dictionary and check with your definitions.

Put each of these words into an interesting sentence of your own.

LANGUAGE

Punctuation Marks III

The purpose of punctuation marks is to help to make the meaning of what you write clearer to a reader and to prevent the possibility of ambiguity. For instance, look at the following sentence:

The fifty odd spectators began to grow restless.

As it stands, the sentence means that the fifty strange-looking spectators began to grow restless. Perhaps this is what the writer intended, but it is more likely that he meant the spectators who were about fifty or more in number began to grow restless. The writer has omitted the hyphen between 'fifty' and 'odd' ('fifty-odd') which makes all the difference in meaning.

Here is another example:

Alan saw the three sisters last night at the National Theatre.

This could mean that Alan met three sisters whom he knew while attending a play at the National Theatre. What is more likely is that he saw a play by Chekhov entitled 'The Three Sisters', but if this latter meaning is intended, then the title of the play needs to have capital initial letters and be in quotation marks if the sense is to be clear.

Some punctuation marks have already been discussed —the full stop in Unit 4 and quotation marks in Unit 6. The other punctuation marks are the apostrophe, brackets, colons, commas, dashes, exclamation marks, hyphens, question marks and semicolons. The apostrophe and the hyphen will be dealt with later. This lesson will explain the comma, the semicolon and the colon. Unit 8 will comment on the exclamation mark, the question mark, brackets and dashes.

The Comma

The comma (,) is a punctuation mark used to indicate a slight division between different parts of a sentence or to indicate a small break in the sense of continuity within a sentence. It indicates a break that is less definite than that shown by a full stop or a semicolon. The comma is used in the following circumstances:

		BUT
1.	To separate the items of a list, e.g. He packed his socks, shirts, underwear.	No comma is needed before the final item in a list if a conjunction or linking word such as 'and' is used. E.g. He packed his socks, shirts and underwear.
2.	Between two clauses when the subjects of the clauses are different. E.g. Jim bought a tie, and Hilary bought a scarf.	If the subject is the same, no comma is needed. E.g. Hilary left home early and reached the station in time.
3.	After a subordinate clause or a participial phrase when it is followed by a main clause. E.g. When the train arrived, it was ten minutes late. Having run all the way to the station, Jim found he had plenty of time.	If the main clause comes first, no comma is required. The train was ten minutes late when it arrived.
4.	To cut off exclamations, parentheses, etc. from the rest of the sentence. E.g. Oh, what a pity you didn't catch him! Naturally, he wanted to see you. He didn't like, or didn't seem to like, the film.	

Incorrect uses of the comma

Look at these examples of correct and incorrect uses of the comma.

1.	The question of whether he is innocent or guilty, is still to be decided. × Jim, however, did not know this. √ The accused, standing with head bowed, waited for the verdict. √	A comma does not separate subject and verb unless there is an intervening phrase in parentheses (i.e. a phrase which could be left out without altering the grammatical structure of the sentence). In this case *two* commas are needed.
2.	He went outside, it was snowing hard. × He went outside. It was snowing hard. √ He went outside; it was snowing hard. √	A comma is not as strong as a full-stop or semicolon and cannot be used to divide separate statements.

Grammatical Note

Main clause: the main statement of a sentence, that can stand by itself and make sense.

Participial Phrase: a group of words introduced by the part of the verb called a participle and not containing a finite verb.

Subordinate Clause: gives additional information about the main clause, contains a finite verb, but cannot stand by itself and make sense.

The Semicolon

The semicolon is a punctuation mark (;) halfway between a comma and a full stop.

1. It is used in a sentence to divide statements which are separate but which are still very closely connected. Sometimes the statements could be written as separate sentences; sometimes they could be combined by a linking word like 'and', preceded by a comma. Compare:

The first present she opened was a box of handkerchiefs; the second was a box of chocolates.
The first present she opened was a box of handkerchiefs. The second was a box of chocolates.
The first present she opened was a box of handkerchiefs, and the second was a box of chocolates.

The first version is the most economical, and the semicolon emphasizes the connection between the statements. If the next sentence began, 'The third present was ...', then the second version above may be preferred, but if only two presents are mentioned, the first version using a semicolon provides a better unified sentence.

2. The semicolon is also used to separate items in a list when these are phrases rather than single words, e.g.
The weather was showing its most wintry face: dark storm clouds that rode fiercely across the sky; gusts of violent wind that rattled the window panes; the touch of ice in the air that made the flesh shiver.

The Colon

1. One use of the colon (:) is indicated in the example at the foot of p. 63, namely to introduce a list of items. Here is another example:

For this recipe, you will need the following ingredients: eggs, flour, sugar and butter.

The colon is often combined with the dash (:-) when used to introduce lists.

2. The colon is also used to introduce an example, a quotation or a phrase that sums up the point of the sentence. It can often take the place of an expression like 'namely' or 'viz.' as in the opening sentence of the previous paragraph, e.g.

One use of the colon is indicated in the example above: to introduce a list of items.

Here is another example from *Bleak House*:

The raw afternoon is rawest, and the dense fog is densest, and the muddy streets are muddiest, near that leaden-headed old obstruction, appropriate ornament for the threshold of a leaden-headed old corporation: Temple Bar.

3. A third use of the colon is to indicate the balancing of one phrase or one idea against another, e.g.

Man proposes: God disposes.

Look back at the descriptive passage in Unit 5 of Mrs Transome's house. Note the use of commas, semicolons and colons.

Write sentences of your own to illustrate the different uses of the punctuation marks discussed here.

Here is an exercise to test whether you have grasped the use of the punctuation marks discussed in this section. Replace / with the appropriate punctuation marks.

1. The cost / no matter what you may say / is excessive.
2. Red sky at dawning / sailors' warning / Red sky at night / sailors' delight.
3. The main problems are these / too much lawn to cut / too many beds to weed / too much clay in the soil / too many hedges to prune.
4. I look for the following on holiday / sea / sun / sand / wine and food.
5. Dame Maggie Tate said on receiving her honour / 'Too little too late'.
6. The house was old and dilapidated / it had stood empty for five years.
7. The director ignored the cost of his high-powered job / the break-up of his family / an ulcer / sleepless nights.
8. However / the financial rewards are considerable.
9. He could not / however / be expected to carry on at this rate for long.
10. Solving this problem is easy / find the woman.
11. After you have emptied the bins / please scrub the floor.
12. John was very pleased with his purchase / but Mary was less happy.
13. The boy / full of dinner / did not feel much like working.
14. The gardens were extensive / there were broad lawns and wide flower beds.
15. The solution was obvious / get out.

(Note that alternative punctuation is possible in some of these examples.)

 SPELLING

Capital Letters

Capital letters are often used when they are not needed or omitted at the beginning of words that require them. In the eighteenth century, writers frequently used capital letters for any important word that took their fancy, but nowadays there are certain conventions we generally conform to.

Capital letters are used in the following instances:

1. Proper names, e.g. Joan, Walter, Gabriel, Rover.
2. Titles, e.g. The Duke of Norfolk, Mr Smith, The Times, the Paper Industries Training Board.
3. The beginning of a sentence, e.g. It is winter. There is snow on the ground.
4. The first word in direct speech, e.g. She asked, 'Will you be staying long?'
5. The important words in titles of novels, plays, films, etc. e.g. *This Gun for Hire*; *The Prime of Miss Jean Brodie*; *A Passage to India*.

Note the following points which sometimes cause confusion:

1. Days of the week and months begin with capital letters, but seasons and points of the compass do not, e.g. Tuesday, January; summer, north.

Note, however, that when the points of the compass refer to geographical location, that is a particular part of a country, a capital letter is used. Compare:

The road runs due east.
The weather in the North is much more severe than in the South.

2. Titles such as prime minister, chairman, duke, headmaster, etc. have capital letters when used to refer to one definite individual (i.e. when the title can be replaced by an actual proper name), and small letters when used generally. Compare:

The Prime Minister made an important statement.
A prime minister carries heavy responsibilities.

3. Names of streets, rivers, mountains, etc. which consist of two or more words should have capital letters for each element of the name, e.g. Great North Road, the River Thames, the Southern Uplands.

4. A number of words which usually require a capital letter take a small letter when used in the name of a common object, e.g. french windows, venetian blinds, brussels sprouts. Some words retain the capital letter, e.g. Davy lamp, Bath chair, Bunsen burner.

5. In foreign names, capitals should not be used for

'de', 'du', 'di', 'von', etc., e.g. Achille de Rosalba, Erich von Stroheim. Capitals are sometimes used when the family name has become anglicized, e.g. William De Morgan.
Find further examples of all of these.

Here is an exercise for you to test whether you have learned and can apply the points about capital letters made in this section. Rewrite the word or words with the necessary capital or small letter. Then check against the rules above or in a dictionary.

1. eastwards
2. the president of U.S.A.
3. french chalk.
4. thursday.
5. christmas
6. the bishop of Norwich
7. Leicester square
8. bath buns
9. the north of Scotland
10. the river Severn
11. 'A midsummer night's Dream'
12. a headmaster
13. a centigrade thermometer
14. my dog blackie
15. shrove Tuesday
16. the roman ruins
17. borstal
18. 'After the Ball is over'
19. spring flowers
20. the Globe theatre

Revision

(a) *Carefully read through all the spelling sections in the course so far.*

(b) *Go through all your written work that has been corrected by your tutor/teacher and write out correctly in a list all the words that you mis-spelt.*
Learn them.

(c) *Here is an exercise to test that you have grasped the points made in the spelling sections so far. The figure after each sentence indicates the number of mistakes to be corrected.*
Warning: check this exercise very carefully to make sure that the incorrect spellings printed here do not stick!

1. The west of Ireland recieves much more rain than the east. (3)
2. The gayty at the Party fulfiled my highest expectations. (3)
3. Looking after babys leaves you very little time for liesure. (2)
4. Monkies and donkies are delightfull creatures. (3)
5. Niether of my demands has been fuly met. (2)
6. I all ways wellcome you to my house. (2)
7. Don't deceive yourself: he is all together a rogue. (1)
8. Counterfiet money is alright to look at but is totaly worthless. (3)
9. He is ful of the joys of Spring. (2)
10. His foriegn travels include west Africa, southern Asia and Tibet. (3)
11. What a beautifull day! It must be Summer. (2)
12. He employs twenty men at pityful rates of pay. (1)
13. The headmaster carrys a heavy responsibility. (2)
14. A spoon full of honey is always soothing. (1)
15. The cheif tried to sieze power. (2)

UNIT 8

WRITING

A Play

Having looked at how dramatists work in the previous unit, you are now given advice on how to set about wrting an essay in dramatic form.

READING AND UNDERSTANDING

Stories

A look at the skills that writers bring to the form of the short story and analysis of a short story.

READING LIST

Some writers of short stories that you may enjoy.

VOCABULARY

A revision of the vocabulary studied in previous units.

LANGUAGE

Punctuation Marks IV

How to use the exclamation mark, the question mark, brackets and dashes.

SPELLING

When to keep or drop a silent 'e' in a compound word.

ASSIGNMENT E

WRITING

A Play

Moving on from writing a dialogue the next stage is to try writing a short play or dramatized scene. For instance, suppose you were given the title 'The Quarrel' and were asked to develop this as a story or a play. You could be given some characters (e.g. two people who have not seen each other for ten years, or a girl who has announced to her parents that she is leaving home) and be asked to put them into a dramatized situation.

Many of the points made about dialogue ('Writing' Unit 7) would apply here. You should make sure that you have an interesting and appropriate background. You should try to make your characters alive and differentiate them one from another by the way they speak and by the opinions they express. You should try to vary the lengths of your speeches so that there is variety. You should make sure that your play opens and closes effec-

tively. Particularly, you should see that the words you give to a character are appropriate to him, that the dialogue is relevant to the situation, and that there is no padding—all the speeches are necessary. If you find one of your characters talking about the weather or asking after the health of his companion's wife, then it is likely that you are just filling in space.

The following points are particularly relevant to writing a play or a dramatized scene. Someone once said that the whole basis of drama is conflict, not necessarily violent hand-to-hand fighting, but the bringing together of people of different temperaments or views and seeing the resultant battle of wits or words, or placing a character in a situation with which he is unable to cope. These are the kinds of conflicts you should be looking for when considering writing a play. These will determine especially your choice of characters and plot or situation.

1. Characters. If you have any choice in the matter, stick to only two or three characters. Within a normal essay length (500 or 600 words) you are unlikely to be able to cope with more. To be able to provide some kind of individuality to your characters you need to give them space to expand, and 500 words would be spread too thinly if you chose to describe a whole range of people.

Your two or three characters should be sharply differentiated. If this is appropriate, they should be of different ages and represent different backgrounds, they should have different outlooks and attitudes to life (like Beatie and Mrs Bryant in *Roots*). In other words, there should be some conflict, or some possibility of conflict between your characters.

2. Plot or situation. Your play should have a definite shape. You must choose an incident which is capable of being developed and of coming to some definite conclusion. For instance, if you were asked to write a play called 'The Quarrel', you have to find a situation where a quarrel could occur naturally. It might be the case of a girl waiting outside a cinema for her boyfriend who is late. You now have to decide what kind of characters or reactions the girl and her boyfriend should have so that you can develop this situation effectively. You might make the girl angry, impatient, remembering other occasions when she has had to wait, wondering whether the boy is worth it. You could then make the boyfriend conciliatory, trying to calm her down, full of good reasons why he is late. Eventually, you reach a situation where things are calmer and they are on friendlier terms, so you make the boy casually remember some occasion when the girl was late and he had to wait. This has a disastrous effect. The girl flares up again and walks off. Or the boy cuts in before she has a chance to get going and says, 'Come on, the big picture's started. Anything for a quiet life!' Or, after flaring up, the girl suddenly realizes that she is being unreasonable and starts being nice to him—and they discover that the Box Office is closed, and the row starts all over again! These are some ways in which a particular situation can be developed.

Given a situation, choose characters who will react differently to it and produce conflict.

Find ways in which an idea or word will change the situation so that things move in another direction.

Find an ending giving a sense of finality, an interesting twist, *or* some indication of what is going to happen next.

One final point about the kind of plot you choose. Keep it as simple as possible. In 500 or 600 words, it is not possible to give the whole life histories of your characters. Keep to one scene and one basic idea. This is true too of stories and will be discussed in greater detail in a later unit.

3. Dialogue. Revise the points made on dialogue in 'Writing' Unit 7. It is often necessary in a play to pass on information about the background of a character or a situation to the reader or the audience. If you need to do this, take care that you don't produce unnatural or undramatic dialogue. In the suggested play 'The Quarrel' it would be natural for the characters to recall previous occasions when either one or other of them had been late: this is one of the weapons they use in their conflict of words, and it is helpful for the reader to know this so that he can understand the exasperation of the girl at having to wait yet again. But if the characters are a

mother and son, it would be very strange for the son to say 'You remember I was born in Cairo twenty years ago.' Or if the characters are a husband and wife, the wife would hardly tell her husband 'We have three children called Mary, Louise and Elizabeth.' If this is information which the reader has to have, then it must be passed on in a more natural and convincing way.

Note how dialogue is set out in a play. Look at the extract from Roots *in 'Reading and Understanding' Unit 7 again. The name of the speaker is followed by a colon. No quotation marks are needed.*

4. Stage Directions. These should be kept to a minimum. Set the scene briefly. For instance, 'The Quarrel' might begin like this:

The scene is outside a cinema. A girl is waiting. She is about eighteen and has clearly taken trouble with her dress and make-up. She looks impatiently at her watch from time to time. A boy of about eighteen hurries in, obviously out of breath with running.

From then on, only use stage directions to describe movements or actions which it is essential for the reader to know about but which are not deduceable from the spoken words. Avoid over-using indications of speech such as 'brightly', 'angrily', 'patiently' and so on. It is better to use too few rather than too many of these. After all, if your dialogue is good, it should be clear how the words are to be spoken.

Read the following scene. It is a revue sketch by Harold Pinter and is complete in itself. The scene leaves a lot to the imagination of the reader, and if you are to understand it, you must try to get inside the mind of the Woman and interpret correctly how *she would say particular speeches. Note the frequent pauses. Give them proper value as you read the sketch.*

Request Stop

A queue at a Request Bus Stop. A WOMAN *at the head, with a* SMALL MAN *in a raincoat next to her, two other* WOMEN *and a* MAN.

WOMAN (*to* SMALL MAN): I beg your pardon, what did you say?

Pause.

All I asked you was if I could get a bus from here to Shepherds Bush.

Pause.

Nobody asked you to start making insinuations.

Pause.

Who do you think you are?

Pause.

Huh. I know your sort, I know your type. Don't worry, I know all about people like you.

Pause.

We can all tell where you come from. They're putting your sort inside every day of the week.

Pause.

All I've to do, is report you, and you'd be standing in the dock in next to no time. One of my best friends is a plain clothes detective.

Pause.

I know all about it. Standing there as if butter

wouldn't melt in your mouth. Meet you in a dark alley it'd be ... another story. (*To the others, who stare into space.*) You heard what this man said to me. All I asked him was if I could get a bus from here to Shepherds Bush. (*To him.*) I've got witnesses, don't you worry about that.

Pause.

Impertinence.

Pause.

Ask a man a civil question he treats you like a three-penny bit. (*To him.*) I've got better things to do, my lad, I can assure you. I'm not going to stand here and be insulted on a public highway. Anyone can tell you're a foreigner. I was born just around the corner. Anyone can tell you're just up from the country for a bit of a lark. I know your sort.

Pause.

She goes to a LADY.

Excuse me lady. I'm thinking of taking this man up to the magistrate's court, you heard him make that crack, would you like to be a witness?

The LADY *steps into the road.*

LADY: Taxi ...

She disappears.

WOMAN: We know what sort she is. (*Back to position.*) I was the first in this queue.

Pause.

Born just round the corner. Born and bred. These people from the country haven't the faintest idea of how to behave. Peruvians. You're bloody lucky I don't put you on a charge. You ask a straightfor-ward question—

The others suddenly thrust out their arms at a passing bus. They run off left after it. The WOMAN, *alone, clicks her teeth and mutters. A man walks from the right to the stop, and waits. She looks at him out of the corner of her eye. At length she speaks shyly, hesitantly, with a slight smile.*

Excuse me. Do you know if I can get a bus from here ... to Marble Arch?

Try to answer these questions before reading the commentary that follows:

Does this scene have a shape?

What is the point of the ending?

What effect do the pauses have, especially as they build one on top of the other?

What do you think the reactions of the Small Man are?

What is the Woman in fact doing at the bus stop?

Did you find the sketch funny? Can you say why you did or did not find it funny?

It is difficult to give an example of a short complete play as an illustration, but this sketch is useful in showing how a small incident can provide an entirely satisfactory dramatic situation. The fact that it is practically a monologue makes it all the funnier.

The scene does have a shape. It is, as it were, circular. The ending takes you back to the beginning, and we can imagine the whole scene happening again with another man—unless, of course, his reaction is different from the Small Man's! The fact that the Woman has changed the destination she is pretending to be seeking from Shepherds

Bush to Marble Arch finally clinches in our minds the feel-ing that she isn't really waiting for a bus at all, and that her abuse of the Small Man is due to something rude he has said or his determination to ignore her.

The pauses provide time for laughter, but also lull us into a sense of false security. We think the Woman has finished her abuse and when she suddenly and un-expectedly starts again, time after time, we are surprised and amused. The oftener it happens, the more we are amused, on the same principle as when a man steps on a rake and the handle flies in his face once, we are amused; if it happens twice, it is even funnier; if it happens three times, it is hilarious.

It would probably add to the comic effect if the Small Man ignores the Woman, pretending, as it were, that he is not with her, and she is not speaking to him. Perhaps during the pauses he might cast furtive glances at her or at the others to see if they are listening, only to jerk back into embarrassed rigidity when the Woman starts again.

The Woman is presumably trying to pick the man up. He is not being cooperative, hence the abuse, partly directed at him, but also partly used to cover up her own activity.

Some of the points above suggest why the sketch is funny. Consider the following points: the silence of the Man; the way everyone ignores the Woman; the way the Lady immediately shrieks for a taxi when accosted; the disgruntled abuse of the Woman interspersed with pauses; the build up of these pauses; the change in the Woman's attitude when a new man arrives; the Woman's hesitation before saying '... Marble Arch'; the change from Shepherds Bush to Marble Arch.

If you didn't find the sketch funny, read it again now and see if there is any difference in your appreciation of it.

Write a short play or sketch of about 500 or 600 words on one of the following:

1. A scene between a traffic warden or a policeman and a motorist.
2. A scene between a shopkeeper and a difficult customer.
3. A scene between a housewife and a door-to-door salesman.
4. A play entitled 'The Visitor'.
5. A play entitled 'Trouble in the Family'.
6. A play entitled 'The Waiting Room'.

Check back through your notes on this unit first and make sure you have taken in the points we have made about writing a play. When you have written your play, read it aloud, preferably with your friends taking the parts. Make your own criticisms and improvements.

 # READING AND UNDERSTANDING

Stories

People have always enjoyed reading and listening to stories. There is something about people caught up in events which captures our imaginations. Once caught, we want to know what happens to those people, what happens next. Indeed, here straight away is one of the basic necessities of any story: we must want to know what happens next. If we are not caught, if we don't care what happens to these people, then the story is a failure.

Narrative—telling a story—is obviously an important part of any novel. However, it is impossible to choose a novel—which you may not have read anyway—and to analyse and discuss it in a short space like this. I shall therefore look at a short story (short but complete) and use this as a means by which we can examine the way in which a skilled writer can compel and hold our attention and make us ask, 'What happens next?' and turn the page.

Read this short story by O. Henry.

Witches' Loaves

Miss Martha Meacham kept the little bakery on the corner (the one where you go up three steps, and the bell tinkles when you open the door).

Miss Martha was forty, her bank-book showed a credit of two thousand dollars, and she possessed two false teeth and a sympathetic heart. Many people have married whose chances to do so were much inferior to Miss Martha's.

Two or three times a week a customer came in in whom she began to take an interest. He was a middle-aged man, wearing spectacles and a brown beard trimmed to a careful point.

He spoke English with a strong German accent. His clothes were worn and darned in places, and wrinkled and baggy in others. But he looked neat, and had very good manners.

He always bought two loaves of stale bread. Fresh bread was five cents a loaf. Stale ones were two for five. Never did he call for anything but stale bread.

Once Miss Martha saw a red and brown stain on his fingers. She was sure then that he was an artist and very poor. No doubt he lived in a garret, where he painted pictures and ate stale bread and thought of the good things to eat in Miss Martha's bakery.

Often when Miss Martha sat down to her chops and light rolls and jam and tea she would sigh, and wish that the gentle-mannered artist might share her tasty meal instead of eating his dry crust in that draughty attic.

Miss Martha's heart, as you have been told, was a sympathetic one.

In order to test her theory as to his occupation, she brought from her room one day a painting that she had bought at a sale, and set it against the shelves behind the bread counter.

It was a Venetian scene. A splendid marble palazzio (so it said on the picture) stood in the foreground—or rather forewater. For the rest there were gondolas (with the lady trailing her hand in the water), clouds, sky, and chiaroscuro in plenty. No artist could fail to notice it.

Two days afterward the customer came in.

'Two loafs of stale bread, if you blease.

'You haf here a fine bicture, madame,' he said while she was wrapping up the bread.

'Yes?' says Miss Martha, revelling in her own cunning. 'I do so admire art and' (no, it would not do to say 'artists' thus early) 'and paintings,' she substituted. 'You think it is a good picture?'

'Der balence,' said the customer, 'is not in good drawing. Der bairspective of it is not true. Goot morning, madame.'

He took his bread, bowed, and hurried out.

Yes, he must be an artist. Miss Martha took the picture back to her room.

How gently and kindly his eyes shone behind his spectacles! What a broad brow he had! To be able to judge perspective at a glance—and to live on stale bread! But genius often has to struggle before it is recognized.

What a thing it would be for art and perspective if genius were backed by two thousand dollars in the bank, a bakery, and a sympathetic heart to—But these were daydreams, Miss Martha.

Often now when he came he would chat for a while across the showcase. He seemed to crave Miss Martha's cheerful words.

He kept on buying stale bread. Never a cake, never a pie, never one of her delicious Sally Lunns.

She thought he began to look thinner and discouraged. Her heart ached to add something good to his meagre purchase, but her courage failed at the act. She did not dare affront him. She knew the pride of artists.

Miss Martha took to wearing her blue-dotted silk waist behind the counter. In the back room she cooked a mysterious compound of quince seeds and borax. Ever so many people use it for the complexion.

One day the customer came in as usual, laid his nickel on the showcase, and called for his stale loaves. While Miss Martha was reaching for them there was a great tooting and clanging, and a fire-engine came lumbering past.

The customer hurried to the door to look, as anyone will. Suddenly inspired, Miss Martha seized the opportunity.

On the bottom shelf behind the counter was a pound of fresh butter that the dairyman had left ten minutes before. With a bread-knife Miss Martha made a deep slash in each of the stale loaves, inserted a generous quantity of butter, and pressed the loaves tight again.

When the customer turned once more she was tying the paper around them.

When he had gone, after an unusually pleasant little chat, Miss Martha smiled to herself, but not without a slight fluttering of the heart.

Had she been too bold? Would he take offence? But surely not. There was no language of edibles. Butter was no emblem of unmaidenly forwardness.

For a long time that day her mind dwelt on the subject. She imagined the scene when he would discover her little deception.

He would lay down his brushes and palette. There would stand his easel with the picture he was painting in which the perspective was beyond criticism.

He would prepare for his luncheon of dry bread and water. He would slice into a loaf—ah!

Miss Martha blushed. Would he think of the hand that placed it there as he ate? Would he—

The front door bell jangled viciously. Somebody was coming in, making a great deal of noise.

Miss Martha hurried to the front. Two men were there. One was a young man smoking a pipe—a man she had never seen before. The other was her artist.

His face was very red, his hat was on the back of his head, his hair was wildly rumpled. He clinched his two fists and shook them ferociously at Miss Martha. *At Miss Martha.*

'*Dummkopf!*' he shouted with extreme loudness; and then '*Tausendonfer!*' or something like it, in German.

The young man tried to draw him away.

'I vill not go,' he said angrily, 'else I shall told her.'

He made a bass drum of Miss Martha's counter.

'You haf shpoilt me,' he cried, his blue eyes blazing behind his spectacles. 'I vill tell you. You vas von *meddingsome old cat!*'

Miss Martha leaned weakly against the shelves and laid one hand on her blue-spotted silk waist. The young man took his companion by the collar.

'Come on,' he said, 'you've said enough.' He dragged the angry one out at the door to the side-walk, and then came back.

'Guess you ought to be told, ma'am,' he said, 'what the row is about. That's Blumberger. He's an architectural draughtsman. I work in the same office as him.

'He's been working hard for three months drawing a plan for a new city hall. It was a prize competition. He finished inking the lines yesterday. You know, a draughtsman always makes his drawing in pencil first. When it's done he rubs out the pencil lines with handfuls of stale breadcrumbs. That's better than india-rubber.

'Blumberger's been buying the bread here. Well, to-day—well, you know, ma'am, that butter isn't—well, Blumberger's plan isn't good for anything except to cut up into railroad sandwiches.'

Miss Martha went into the back room. She took off the blue-dotted silk waist and put on the old brown serge she used to wear. Then she poured the quince seed and borax mixture out of the window into the ash can.

Try to answer these questions before reading the commentary that follows.

1. Try to work out the framework of the story, e.g. introduction, setting, establishment of character, encounter, and so on.

2. What kind of impression does the first paragraph establish?

3. What clue is given in the second paragraph as to what the story is going to be about?

4. Do Miss Meacham's deductions about her German customer convince?

5. From whose point of view do we see the events?

6. Does the author make any comments?

7. Where is there a sudden change of mood in the story? What announces it?

8. Does the friend's explanation of the disaster convince?

9. What is the significance of the final paragraph?

10. Is there a change of tone in the final paragraph? Is it effective?

11. What is the effect of the short paragraphs?

The first paragraph establishes a very cosy atmosphere. The shop is quaint, pleasant, old-fashioned. The author makes a personal appeal to the reader by suggesting that it is the type of shop he knows. The second paragraph describes Miss Meacham as getting on a bit, but with money in the bank and a kind heart. The significance is the suggestion in the second paragraph that there is no reason why Miss Meacham shouldn't still marry. The comment appears to be the author's, but it could equally well be Miss Meacham's own thought. The indication here is that the story is going to be about Miss Meacham's dreams of marriage.

Possibly, one could argue that Miss Meacham's deductions about her German customer are reasonable. He was poorly dressed, he only bought stale bread, he had paint marks on his fingers, and he clearly knew something about painting. But are they really? Perhaps he bought the stale bread to feed birds. Miss Meacham only saw the red and brown stain once, and it might not even have been paint. By the time we get to 'No doubt he lived in a garret . . .' Miss Meacham is in the world of fantasy.

The first seven paragraphs are a mixture of factual statements made by the author and suppositions made by Miss Meacham. When the author, in the next paragraph, repeats his comment, 'Miss Martha's heart, as you have been told, was a sympathetic one,' we begin to suspect there is an ironic ring to it, reinforcing our suspicions that Miss Meacham's imagination is carrying her away in her deductions about her customer. When later, the author says, 'But these were day-dreams, Miss Martha,' this is Miss Meacham talking, telling herself not to be so foolish, but it was also the author speaking, the harsh voice of reality which Miss Meacham won't heed. Most of the rest of the story is straight narrative or a description of Miss Meacham's feelings. The final paragraph is objective reporting. Miss Meacham did this, she did that. We have to deduce the significance of what she did for ourselves. She put away her dreams and pretensions and returned to hum-drum reality and the acceptance that she would never get married. The factual reporting of this last paragraph and the lack of a direct comment from the author heightens the pathos. There is no need to comment. The understatement has a much more emotional effect than any moralizing or pointing up of the situation would have.

To return to the body of the story, the dramatic change comes with the paragraph beginning 'The front door bell jangled viciously.' Up to that point, everything had been going smoothly and harmoniously. The jangling door bell is the first false note literally and metaphorically. The change of mood is made audible.

The friend's explanation of what went wrong is perhaps disappointing. It is a bit of a let down that Miss Meacham's misunderstanding depends on a trick of the draughtsman's trade which we may not know about and which we are most unlikely to have guessed. It is ingenious but contrived—but perhaps you disagree!

The effect of the short paragraphs is to lead us on quickly from one to the next. We don't get tired. We move on to the next relevant point easily and can consolidate the essential information as we go along.

To turn now to the framework of the story. O. Henry introduces us quickly into the story. The first paragraph establishes the setting. The second paragraph establishes the character of Miss Meacham and her romantic yearnings. Then the customer is introduced and Miss Meacham's thoughts about him. All of this has been setting up the situation. The first real incident is Miss Meacham's test with the Venetian painting. Then comes her daring kindness with the butter. The jangling bell introduces the unravelling of the misunderstanding. The final paragraph tells us all we need to know about Miss Meacham's reactions and her future. Basically then the plan is as follows:

1. The characters and the situation are set.
2. An action produces
3. a reaction, and
4. the effect on the main character.

There is much more that could be said about the way this short story is written (the way O. Henry calls the character Miss Martha throughout, for instance; the way he uses dialect and German words to create the character of the customer), but I hope enough has been said to show that the story has a very definite shape, that effects are very carefully worked out, and that we are manipulated by the writer into wanting to know what happens next.

O. Henry's words are simple and memorable. He makes his points by straight description or statement, by emotionally leading the reader on and then turning the tables on him, by his use of irony and tone, rather than by his manipulation of words.

READING LIST

Try to read some short stories. Most of them take only fifteen or twenty minutes to read. There are many anthologies, and you may care to dip into one of these until you find an author you enjoy and then search out a volume of stories by that writer to explore more fully. The following writers are particularly skilful in the medium of the short story:

D. H. Lawrence, H. G. Wells, Ernest Hemingway, O. Henry, F. Scott Fitzgerald, Katherine Mansfield, Isaac Babel, Chekhov, Guy de Maupassant, Saki, Somerset Maugham, H. E. Bates, Graham Greene, Dylan Thomas, Ray Bradbury, William Saroyan, Bill Naughton, Frank O'Connor, Liam O'Flaherty, James Joyce, Robert Graves.

VOCABULARY

By now you will have a fair number of words in your notebook—words you have picked out and looked up in your reading as well as words we have chosen in these units. Check them through and make sure you are confident you can understand and use them. Make up more sentences to practise using the words you are slightly doubtful about.

Here is an exercise to check your understanding of some of the words you have studied in this section in previous units. Pick the correct form from the alternatives offered.

1. 'Vulnerable' means susceptible to injury/greedy/easily destroyed/of great worth.
2. He drank a glass of water to assuage/aspire/asperse his thirst.
3. Cliff Richard is a populous/popular star.
4. 'In lieu of' means alongside/in place of/above/after consideration of.
5. After his speech there was a spontaneous/instantaneous burst of applause.
6. The astronaut has to be alert in every facility/faculty.
7. 'Insistent' means continuing obstinately/maintaining emphatically/constant to principles/frequent.
8. I was pleasantly entertained by the traveller's discourse/recourse/concourse.
9. He was suffering from constriction/restriction in his throat.
10. 'Caustic' means callous/expensive/biting/exciting.
11. 'Antagonism' means the study of family relationships/active opposition/suffering pain calmly/the study of insect life.
12. 'Snub' means rebuff/person who looks down on others/catch on a door/neatly-fitting.
13. He made pretentious/preventive/preterite claims for his own worth.
14. The entry of Britain into the European Economic Community was a momentary/momentous occasion.
15. The woodman suffered from the delusion/allusion that he was Napoleon.

LANGUAGE

Punctuation Marks IV

This unit deals with the remaining punctuation marks: the exclamation mark, the question mark, brackets and dashes.

Exclamation Marks

Exclamation marks are used after

1. Words used as exclamations or interjections, e.g.
   Oh!
   Good heavens!
2. Sentences using 'how' or 'what' as exclamations, e.g.
   How senseless you are!
   What a nuisance you are!
3. Sentences expressing strong feeling, e.g.
   I've never been so surprised in all my life!
   Stop thief!

Do not over-use exclamation marks, or they will not be effective. Never use more than one exclamation mark at a time and never use question marks and exclamation marks together as in:

Who do you think you are?!!

Question Marks

The question mark obviously indicates a question, e.g.

Who are you?

Note that both question marks and exclamation marks when used in speech go inside the quotation marks, and if followed by a word of saying, this word of saying has a small letter, e.g.

'What do you want?' she asked.
'How dare you!' she exclaimed.

It is sometimes difficult to decide whether a question mark or an exclamation mark is required. Think carefully which element is the more important in a particular case—the exclamation or the question. Compare:

How could I have known!
How was I to know?

Brackets

Brackets are used to cut off an additional piece of information, an afterthought, an aside, a parenthesis or an extra example from the rest of the sentence. Grammatically the phrase in brackets is an addition to the sentence, and the sentence should still be able to make sense with the phrase in brackets omitted, e.g.

The flowers this year (fuchsias, geraniums and begonias) made a splendid display.

Remember that brackets always come in pairs.

Dashes

Dashes can be used in a similar way to brackets, e.g.

After the performance—the last of the season—the ballerina retired to the country.

When used like this, two dashes, before and after the extra phrase, are needed as with brackets. Where the phrase introduced comes at the end of a sentence, a concluding dash is not needed, e.g.

She gave a magnificent performance—no one could equal her.

Compare this use of the dash with the use of the colon to introduce a summing up of a sentence.
The dash is also used to link a series of disconnected phrases. An example is the speech of Mr Jingle in Unit 6. Here is another:

The autumn trees were a splendid sight—splashes of red—sudden glints of gold and silver—a carpet of russet brown beneath the trunks.

Here is an exercise to test whether you have understood the points made in this section. In the following sentences replace / by the appropriate punctuation mark.

1. The three girls/ Mary/ Elizabeth and Jane/ were all very pretty.

2. 'Who is there/' she called.
3. I want to know why you are here/
4. How dare you interrupt me/
5. It is twelve o'clock/ no one will be up.
6. The screech of brakes/ the judder of lorries/ the shuddering of buses/ these are the noises of traffic that I particularly dislike.
7. 'Help/' she cried.
8. Michael/ aged twelve/ came first in the poetry competition.
9. The police would surround the shop/ a brilliant scheme/
10. When it grew dark/ by 4 o'clock in the winter/ the curtains were drawn for the night.
11. How strange that you should feel like that/
12. How strange did you find him/
13. Read carefully/ failure to do so could lose you marks.
14. That afternoon/ now many summers ago/ will always live in my memory.
15. How can you say such a thing/

(Note that alternative punctuation is possible in some of these examples.)

 # SPELLING

In compound words, a silent final 'e' of the root part of the word is kept when a suffix beginning with a consonant is added; it is dropped when a suffix beginning with a vowel is added (unless the 'e' is preceded by a soft 'c' or 'g'—see 'Spelling' Unit 9), e.g.

care + ful = careful
lone + ly = lonely
safe + ty = safety
like + ness = likeness
move + ment = movement
come + ing = coming
debate + able = debatable
conspire + acy = conspiracy
admire + able = admirable
sense + ible = sensible

Make lists of other words which observe these two rules. Note the following cases where differences occur:
1. Before '-ment' the silent final 'e' of the root is often dropped in the following words: 'abridgment', 'acknowledgment', 'judgment' (in its legal sense). 'Argument' should never be spelt with a silent 'e' in the middle.
2. The silent 'e' is sometimes retained in the following words: 'Hireable', 'likeable', 'rateable', 'saleable', 'sizeable', 'tameable', 'unshakeable'.
3. The silent 'e' is dropped before '-ing' and '-ish' according to the rule except for the following words: 'ageing', 'cueing', 'lungeing', 'routeing' (i.e. 'sending by a route'), 'syringeing', 'singeing', 'swingeing', 'twingeing'. The 'e' is retained in words whose roots end in 'oe', e.g. 'canoeing', 'hoeing', 'shoeing'.
4. The silent 'e' is sometimes retained when adding '-y', e.g. 'bluey', 'cagey', 'clayey', 'gluey'. Most other common words drop the 'e', e.g. 'chancy', 'gamy', 'horsy', 'mousy',

'nervy', 'noisy', 'nosy' (though the form 'nosey' also occurs, especially in the expression 'Nosey Parker').

5. The silent 'e' is retained when adding '-ly' according to the rule, e.g. 'immediately', 'immensely', 'fortunately'. The following are exceptions: 'duly', 'truly', 'wholly'.

6. The words 'acreage' and 'mileage' retain the silent 'e'.

7. The word 'awful' drops the silent 'e', though 'awesome' retains it.

Here is an exercise to check that you have learned this rule. Complete the words in the following sentences:

1. A lighthouse keeper leads a lon— life.
2. No matter how hard you try some animals are quite untam—.
3. He had a car— of passengers.
4. I couldn't follow his argu—.
5. When I received his book, I sent him an acknowledg—.
6. The fireman led the child to saf—.
7. He was praised for his admir— courage.
8. Are you com— to the party?
9. Don't be so nos—!
10. Don't be so nois—!
11. He ended the letter 'Yours tru—'.
12. She waited eagerly for his arriv—.
13. His affair is surrounded by a conspir— of silence.
14. When are you mov— to Barnet?
15. He caught sight of a mov— in the bushes.

 # ASSIGNMENT E

You should spend about an hour and a half on the preparation and writing of Part I and produce at least 500 words. Part II should take about an hour and a quarter.

Part I: Essay

Write a short story mainly in the form of dialogue or a short play on one of the following:

1. The Intruder.
2. Under the Clock.
3. Late Again!
4. The Morning After.
5. Three's a Crowd.
6. The Old Man.
7. Anticipation.

Part II: Comprehension

Read the following short story carefully and then answer the questions below as fully as you can in your own words.

Fur

'You look worried, dear,' said Eleanor.

'I am worried,' admitted Suzanne; 'not worried exactly, but anxious. You see, my birthday happens next week—'

'You lucky person,' interrupted Eleanor; 'my birthday doesn't come till the end of March.'

'Well, old Bertram Kneyght is over in England just now from the Argentine. He's a kind of distant cousin of my mother's and so enormously rich that we've never let the relationship drop out of sight. Even if we don't see him or hear from him for years he is always Cousin Bertram when he does turn up. I can't say he's ever been of much solid use to us, but yesterday the subject of my birthday cropped up, and he asked me to let him know what I wanted for a present.'

'Now, I understand the anxiety,' observed Eleanor.

'As a rule when one is confronted with a problem like that,' said Suzanne, 'all one's ideas vanish; one doesn't seem to have a desire in the world. Now it so happens that I have been very keen on a little Dresden figure that I saw somewhere in Kensington; about thirty-six shillings, quite beyond my means. I was very nearly describing the figure, and giving Bertram the address of the shop. And then it suddenly struck me that thirty-six shillings was such a ridiculously inadequate sum for a man of his immense wealth to spend on a birthday present. He could give thirty-six pounds as easily as you or I could buy a bunch of violets. I don't want to be greedy, of course, but I don't like being wasteful.'

'The question is,' said Eleanor, 'what are his ideas as to present-giving? Some of the wealthiest people have curiously cramped views on this subject. When people grow gradually rich their requirements and standards of living expand in proportion, while their present-giving instincts often remain in the undeveloped condition of their earlier days. Something showy and not-too-expensive in a shop is their only conception of the ideal gift. That is why even quite good shops have their counters and windows crowded with things worth about four shillings that look as if they might be worth seven-and-six, and are priced at ten shillings and labelled "seasonable gifts".'

'I know,' said Suzanne; 'that is why it is so risky to be vague when one is giving indications of one's wants. Now if I say to him: "I am going out to Davos this winter, so anything in the travelling line would be acceptable", he *might* give me a dressing-bag with gold-mounted fittings, but, on the other hand, he might give me Baedeker's *Switzerland*, or *Ski-ing without Tears*, or something of that sort.'

'He would be more likely to say: "She'll be going to lots of dances, a fan will be sure to be useful".'

'Yes, and I've got tons of fans, so you see where the danger and anxiety lies. Now if there is one thing more than another that I really urgently want it is furs. I simply haven't any. I'm told that Davos is full of Russians, and they are sure to wear the most lovely sables and things. To be among people who are smothered in furs when one hasn't any oneself makes one want to break most of the Commandments.'

'If it's furs that you're out for,' said Eleanor, 'you will have to superintend the choice of them in person. You can't be sure that your cousin knows the difference between silver-fox and ordinary squirrel.'

'There are some heavenly silver-fox stoles at Goliath and Mastodon's,' said Suzanne, with a sigh; 'if I could only inveigle Bertram into their building and take him for a stroll through the fur department!'

'He lives somewhere near there, doesn't he?' said

Eleanor. 'Do you know what his habits are? Does he take a walk at any particular time of day?'

'He usually walks down to his club about three o'clock, if it's a fine day. That takes him right past Goliath and Mastodon's.'

'Let us two meet him accidentally at the street corner tomorrow,' said Eleanor; 'we can walk a little way with him, and with luck we ought to be able to side-track him into the shop. You can say you want to get a hair-net or something. When we're safely there I can say: "I wish you'd tell me what you want for your birthday." Then you'll have everything ready to hand—the rich cousin, the fur department, and the topic of birthday presents.'

'It's a great idea,' said Suzanne; 'you really are a brick. Come round tomorrow at twenty to three; don't be late, we must carry out our ambush to the minute.'

At a few minutes to three the next afternoon the fur-trappers walked warily towards the selected corner. In the near distance rose the colossal pile of Messrs Goliath and Mastodon's famed establishment. The afternoon was brilliantly fine, exactly the sort of weather to tempt a gentleman of advancing years into the discreet exercise of a leisurely walk.

'I say, dear, I wish you'd do something for me this evening,' said Eleanor to her companion; 'just drop in after dinner on some pretext or other, and stay on to make a fourth at bridge with Adela and the aunts. Otherwise I shall have to play, and Harry Scarisbrooke is going to come in unexpectedly about nine-fifteen, and I particularly wanted to be free to talk to him while the others are playing.'

'Sorry, my dear, no can do,' said Suzanne; 'ordinary bridge at threepence a hundred, with such dreadfully slow players as your aunts, bores me to tears. I nearly go to sleep over it.'

'But I most particularly want an opportunity to talk with Harry,' urged Eleanor, an angry glint coming into her eyes.

'Sorry, anything to oblige, but not that,' said Suzanne cheerfully; the sacrifices of friendship were beautiful in her eyes as long as she was not asked to make them.

Eleanor said nothing further on the subject, but the corners of her mouth rearranged themselves.

'There's our man!' exclaimed Suzanne suddenly; 'hurry!'

Mr Bertram Kneyght greeted his cousin and her friend with genuine heartiness, and readily accepted their invitation to explore the crowded mart that stood temptingly at their elbow. The plate-glass doors swung open and the trio plunged bravely into the jostling throng of buyers and loiterers.

'Is it always as full as this?' asked Bertram of Eleanor.

'More or less, and autumn sales are on just now,' she replied.

Suzanne, in her anxiety to pilot her cousin to the desired haven of the fur department, was usually a few paces ahead of the others, coming back to them now and then if they lingered for a moment at some attractive counter, with the nervous solicitude of a parent rook encouraging its young ones on their first flying expedition.

74

'It's Suzanne's birthday on Wednesday next,' confided Eleanor to Bertram Kneyght at a moment when Suzanne had left them unusually far behind; 'my birthday comes the day before, so we are both on the look-out for something to give each other.'

'Ah,' said Bertram. 'Now, perhaps you can advise me on that very point. I want to give Suzanne something, and I haven't the least idea what she wants.'

'She's rather a problem,' said Eleanor. 'She seems to have everything one can think of, lucky girl. A fan is always useful; she'll be going to a lot of dances at Davos this winter. Yes, I should think a fan would please her more than anything. After our birthdays are over we inspect each other's muster of presents, and I always feel dreadfully humble. She gets such nice things, and I never have anything worth showing. You see, none of my relations or any of the people who give me presents are at all well off, so I can't expect them to do anything more than just remember the day with some little trifle. Two years ago an uncle on my mother's side of the family, who had come into a small legacy, promised me a silver-fox stole for my birthday. I can't tell you how excited I was about it, and I pictured myself showing it off to all my friends and enemies. Then just at that moment his wife died, and, of course, poor man, he could not be expected to think of birthday presents at such a time. He has lived abroad ever since, and I never got my fur. Do you know, to this day I can scarcely look at a silver-fox pelt in a shop window or round any one's neck without feeling ready to burst into tears. I suppose if I hadn't had the prospect of getting one I shouldn't feel that way. Look, there is the fan counter, on your left; you can easily slip away in the crowd. Get her as nice a one as you can see—she is such a dear, dear girl.'

'Hullo, I thought I had lost you,' said Suzanne, making her way through an obstructive knot of shoppers. 'Where is Bertram?'

'I got separated from him long ago. I thought he was on ahead with you,' said Eleanor. 'We shall never find him in this crush.'

Which turned out to be a true prediction.

'All our trouble and forethought thrown away,' said Suzanne sulkily, when they had pushed their way fruitlessly through half a dozen departments.

'I can't think why you didn't grab him by the arm,' said Eleanor; 'I would have if I'd known him longer, but I'd only just been introduced. It's nearly four now, we'd better have tea.'

Some days later Suzanne rang Eleanor up on the telephone.

'Thank you very much for the photograph frame. It was just what I wanted. Very good of you. I say, do you know what that Kneyght person has given me? Just what you said he would—a wretched fan. What? Oh, yes, quite a good enough fan in its way, but still . . .'

'You must come and see what he's given me,' came in Eleanor's voice over the 'phone.

'You! Why should he give you anything?'

'Your cousin appears to be one of those rare people of wealth who take a pleasure in giving good presents,' came the reply.

'I wondered why he was so anxious to know where

she lived,' snapped Suzanne to herself as she rang off.

A cloud has arisen between the friendships of the two young women; as far as Eleanor is concerned the cloud has a silver-fox lining.

(SAKI, *Fur*)

1. Comment on the following sentences and phrases and the way they are expressed:

'To be among people who are smothered in furs when one hasn't any oneself makes one want to break most of the Commandments.'

'The sacrifices of friendship were beautiful in her eyes as long as she was not asked to make them.'

'With the nervous solicitude of a parent rook encouraging its young ones on their first flying expedition.'

'A cloud had arisen between the friendships of the two young women; as far as Eleanor is concerned the cloud has a silver-fox lining.'

2. Comment on the significance, in terms of the plot, of the following:

'I don't want to be greedy, of course, but I don't like being wasteful.'

'You lucky person,' interrupted Eleanor; 'my birthday doesn't come till the end of March.'

'He would be more likely to say: "She'll be going to lots of dances, a fan will be sure to be useful".'

'But I most particularly want an opportunity to talk with Harry,' urged Eleanor, an angry glint coming into her eyes. Eleanor said nothing further on the subject, but the corners of her mouth rearranged themselves.

UNIT 9

WRITING

Stories

Advice on writing a story.

READING AND UNDERSTANDING

Technical Prose

A look at different types of prose—scientific, specialist, giving information in symbols and in figures as well as in words.

READING LIST

Some recipe books you may enjoy looking at.

VOCABULARY

A study of some of the words in Somerset Maugham's short story *Salvatore*.

LANGUAGE

Prefixes

An account of the usefulness of knowing the meaning of the most common prefixes.

SPELLING

The rule about adding suffixes to words ending in 'soft c' or 'soft g'.

 WRITING

Stories

As suggested in 'Reading and Understanding' Unit 8, the important element in any story that you may be asked to write is to make the reader want to know what happens next. If you don't arouse the interest of the reader, you can't possibly hope to succeed in writing a story. As in other types of writing, the two main features are *what* you say and *how* you say it. But having stated that, it is very difficult to give any definite rules as to how these can be most effectively achieved. Much will depend on your own experience of life and reading, and on your own growing ability to criticize and learn from what you read and to criticize and evaluate what you write. You must learn to alter, adjust, revise, rewrite, reshape, cut and supplement time and time again if your stories are to achieve greater quality and effectiveness. Clearly, in an examination, there is little time for a lengthy process like this, but if you apply

it in your private writing, then there is a chance that some of the analytical and critical skills you learn by going through this process will aid you automatically when you write under examination conditions.

The following notes may help you at least to avoid the obvious pitfalls and to develop some critical attitudes towards what you write.

1. A story need not be full of violent action and dramatic events to be effective. Some students are under the illusion that unless there is a murder or an escape from the police or a tragic accident in their story, then the story is boring and lacks interest. This is not necessarily so. Look again at the stories discussed in Unit 8. What 'happens' in them? In *Witches' Loaves*, a middle-aged woman has her illusions about a romantic attachment shown to be false. In *Fur*, a girl tricks a rich man into buying her a present and gets her own back on a 'friend'. These are hardly epoch-making or violently disturbing events. They are ordinary everyday things that could happen to anyone. There are important events 'off the page' as it were: Miss Meacham's dreams are shattered, but her disappointment is put quietly in its place: the final effect is all the greater for the restraint. Stories can be about ordinary, everyday things that affect and change our lives. If they show insight these ordinary events are transformed through the way you write about them. They don't have to be violent or melodramatic or spectacular or grotesque in themselves. (See the stories by Somerset Maugham and Janet Frame that follow which are about ordinary incidents.)

2. Keep your stories simple. It usually makes more sense to stick to one simple incident rather than to stretch the action of your story over months or years or the whole life history of your main character. If you choose one incident, it is much more likely that you will be able to develop it properly with plenty of atmosphere and detail. If you choose to use a whole series of events, then the 500 or so words will only permit you to skim the surface, and the result will be the outline of a story rather than a convincing study in depth.

3. Your story must have a shape. You must have some idea how your story is going to end before you begin writing. Suppose you are writing a story called 'The Return of the Native', and you intend to show the impact of his home town on someone who hasn't revisited it for twenty years. Before you start writing, you must have clear in your own mind what this impact is, whether the visitor is impressed, nostalgic, depressed, disappointed. You must decide on what episodes you will describe to illustrate this, what people he will meet, and the relative importance of one episode or character to the others. Out of this will come some kind of conclusion—the visitor will decide to return and live there, he will be eager to leave, he will see the missed opportunities of the past.

Getting the relative importance of one episode in your story to another right is extremely important. Often students spend so long on introductory material that the central episode is skimmed over and not given enough detail or emphasis. Before you start writing, you must be able to see the course of the story spread out before you like a map; you must be able to judge that, for instance, the central episode must take up one page of your story and the subsidiary episodes, introductory material and conclusion not more than another page. Cut away any material that is inessential to the framework of your story and clutters it up.

You must also ensure that your story is relevant to the essay title set. It is difficult to set guidelines here. In 'Writing' Unit 3, the point was made that if the title of your essay was 'Flood', you must get to the flood as soon as possible, at least by the beginning of the second paragraph. That is fair enough for descriptive essays, but with stories, it is not possible to be so dogmatic. If the title of your story is 'Night', for instance, most of your story may be about the fears of an old woman as the day grows on to evening, and you may end with the sentence: 'Night had arrived.' Or your story may be called 'Loneliness' in which you describe someone alone in a big city, and the word 'loneliness' may never appear. What you must do is to be constantly aware of the need to be relevant to the title and to check constantly that everything you write is relevant to the title and to the story you are writing. Principally, it means that you must cut out over-lengthy introductions, unnecessary conversations that tell your readers

nothing, long descriptions which take up too much space in the framework of the story, portraits of characters who do not play important roles in the story.

4. Your story must have a point. It must be clear to the reader why you have taken the trouble to write your story. It must have something *to say* to the reader; it must have something that relates to the reader's own life. The way in which a story ends is usually how a point of view emerges. There need not be—indeed, there should not be—a strongly pointed moral. The implications and relevance of your story should be allowed to seep through what you say, to appear between the lines, as it were, rather than be thrust down the reader's throat. But there must be a point. You must have something to say. The reader should be left with some such comment as: 'How true! How strange human nature is! I hadn't thought of people in that light before! How sad! How comic! That's just how I felt!' You must evoke some response in your reader, and the best way of doing this is by making sure that your story has a point. If the reader's reaction after reading your story is 'So what?', then you have failed.

5. The tone of voice. You must decide which tone of voice is best for your story. Are you going to relate the facts objectively? Do you want the reader to sympathize strongly with one of the characters? Do you think a cynical approach would be more appropriate? Do you think a first person narrative would be more effective? Is the first person narrator going to be in fact yourself or are you going to imitate the tone of voice of one of your characters (e.g. a rough hearty truck-driver, a spinsterish lady) in which case the details and the approach will have to be different. It is important for you to decide on questions like these before you start writing so as to ensure that the way you tell the story is consistent. Think back to the stories in 'Reading and Understanding' Unit 8. Compare the tone of *Witches' Loaves* with that of *Fur*. How would you describe the two different approaches?

6. Remember the points made in previous units about characters and descriptions. These referred to essays specifically about a character or requiring a description, but they refer equally to stories which contain elements of both. The characters and settings of your stories must be convincing and the telling descriptive detail or effective use of a phrase can bring them alive for your readers. The only way to convince readers that you know the people you are writing about and have been to the places you describe and have seen these events is by giving concrete detail.

7. Remember too to try to write about what you know. Often students get carried away into writing stories about high society or about exotic places when they have no idea how these people behave or what these places are like. Try to use the material around you in your everyday life as the foundation for your stories. If you look with fresh eyes, it is more likely that this kind of basis will provide something interesting and convincing. Probably most detective novel writers have never met a detective or a murderer, but remember that they are much more experienced writers than you and have been able to do much more research and background reading to verify their facts and to give conviction to their descriptions. If you develop insight into human character and relationships, it may be possible for you to write a story about, say, how a murderer feels and thinks. But writing about things you know nothing of involves risks—you may make blatant mistakes of fact, you may have to be so vague that what you write doesn't carry conviction.

The following story by Somerset Maugham embodies some of the points you have been warned against. Maugham can get away with it (or can he?) because he is an experienced writer, not only in his use of words, but also in life. He also has much more space in which to expand his story than you would have.

Bear in mind the following points as you read:

1. Are the opening and ending effective, or is Maugham really only playing a kind of writer's 'con trick'?

2. Is the pointing of the moral in the last paragraph too blatant?

3. Does the writer try to cover too much ground—practically the whole life history of Salvatore—in too short a space?

4. Is the foreign background convincing? Justify your answer.

Salvatore

I wonder if I can do it.

I knew Salvatore first when he was a boy of fifteen with a pleasant, ugly face, a laughing mouth and carefree eyes. He used to spend the morning lying about the beach with next to nothing on and his brown body was as thin as a rail. He was full of grace. He was in and out of the sea all the time, swimming with the clumsy, effortless stroke common to the fisher boys. Scrambling up the jagged rocks on his hard feet, for except on Sundays he never wore shoes, he would throw himself into the deep water with a cry of delight. His father was a fisherman who owned his own little vineyard and Salvatore acted as nursemaid to his two younger brothers. He shouted to them to come inshore when they ventured out too far and made them dress when it was time to climb the hot, vineclad hill for the frugal midday meal.

But boys in those Southern parts grow apace and in a little while he was madly in love with a pretty girl who lived on the Grande Marina. She had eyes like forest pools and held herself like a daughter of the Caesars. They were affianced, but they could not marry till Salvatore had done his military service, and when he left the island which he had never left in his life before, to become a sailor in the navy of King Victor Emmanuel, he wept like a child. It was hard for one who had never been less free than the birds to be at the beck and call of others; it was harder still to live in a battleship with strangers instead of in a little white cottage among the vines; and when he was ashore, to walk in noisy, friendless cities with streets so crowded that he was frightened to cross them, when he had been used to silent paths and the mountains and the sea. I suppose it had never struck him that Ischia, which he looked at every evening (it was like a fairy island in the sunset) to see what the weather would be like next day, or Vesuvius, pearly in the dawn, had anything to do with him at all; but when he ceased to have them before his eyes he realized in some dim fashion that they were as much part of him as his hands and his feet. He was dreadfully homesick. But it was

hardest of all to be parted from the girl he loved with all his passionate young heart. He wrote to her (in his childlike handwriting) long, ill-spelt letters in which he told her how constantly he thought of her and how much he longed to be back. He was sent here and there, to Spezzia, to Venice, to Bari and finally to China. Here he fell ill of some mysterious ailment that kept him in hospital for months. He bore it with the mute and uncomprehending patience of a dog. When he learnt that it was a form of rheumatism that made him unfit for further service his heart exulted, for he could go home; and he did not bother, in fact he scarcely listened, when the doctors told him that he would never again be quite well. What did he care when he was going back to the little island he loved so well and the girl who was waiting for him?

When he got into the rowing-boat that met the steamer from Naples and was rowed ashore he saw his father and mother standing on the jetty and his two brothers, big boys now, and he waved to them. His eyes searched among the crowd that waited there, for the girl. He could not see her. There was a great deal of kissing when he jumped up the steps and they all, emotional creatures, cried a little as they exchanged their greetings. He asked where the girl was. His mother told him that she did not know; they had not seen her for two or three weeks; so in the evening when the moon was shining over the placid sea and the lights of Naples twinkled in the distance he walked down to the Grande Marina to her house. She was sitting on the doorstep with her mother. He was a little shy as he had not seen her for so long. He asked her if she had not received the letter that he had written to her to say that he was coming home. Yes, they had received a letter, and they had been told by another of the island boys that he was ill. Yes, that was why he was back; was it not a piece of luck? Oh, but they had heard that he would never be quite well again. The doctors talked a lot of nonsense, but he knew very well that now he was home again he would recover. They were silent for a little, and then the mother nudged the girl. She did not try to soften the blow. She told him straight out, with the blunt directness of her race, that she could not marry a man who would never be strong enough to work like a man. They had made up their minds, her mother and father and she, and her father would never give his consent.

When Salvatore went home he found that they all knew. The girl's father had been to tell them what they had decided, but they had lacked the courage to tell him themselves. He wept on his mother's bosom. He was terribly unhappy, but he did not blame the girl. A fisherman's life is hard and it needs strength and endurance. He knew very well that a girl could not afford to marry a man who might not be able to support her. His smile was very sad and his eyes had the look of a dog that has been beaten, but he did not complain, and he never said a hard word of the girl he had loved so well. Then a few months later, when he had settled down to the common round, working in his father's vineyard and fishing, his mother told him that there was a young woman in the village who was willing to marry him. Her name was Assunta.

'She's as ugly as the devil,' he said.

She was older than he, twenty-four or twenty-five, and she had been engaged to a man who, while doing his military service, had been killed in Africa. She had a little money of her own and if Salvatore married her she could buy him a boat of his own and they could take a vine-yard that by a happy chance happened at that moment to be without a tenant. His mother told him that Assunta had seen him at the *fiesta* and had fallen in love with him. Salvatore smiled his sweet smile and said he would think about it. On the following Sunday, dressed in the stiff black clothes in which he looked so much less well than in the ragged shirt and trousers of every day, he went up to High Mass at the parish church and placed himself so that he could have a good look at the young woman. When he came down again he told his mother that he was willing.

Well, they were married and they settled down in a tiny white-washed house in the middle of a handsome vineyard. Salvatore was now a great big husky fellow, tall and broad, but still with that ingenuous smile and those trusting, kindly eyes that he had had as a boy. He had the most beautiful manners I have ever seen in my life. Assunta was a grim-visaged female, with decided features, and she looked old for her years. But she had a good heart and she was no fool. I used to be amused by the little smile of devotion that she gave her husband when he was being masculine and masterful; she never ceased to be touched by his gentle sweetness. But she could not bear the girl who had thrown him over, and notwithstanding Salvatore's smiling expostulations she had nothing but harsh words for her. Presently children were born to them.

It was a hard enough life. All through the fishing season towards evening he set out in his boat with one of his brothers for the fishing grounds. It was a long pull of six or seven miles, and he spent the night catching the profitable cuttlefish. Then there was the long row back again in order to sell the catch in time for it to go on the early boat to Naples. At other times he was working in his vineyard from dawn till the heat drove him to rest and then again, when it was a trifle cooler, till dusk. Often his rheumatism prevented him from doing any-thing at all and then he would lie about the beach, smoking cigarettes, with a pleasant word for everyone notwithstanding the pain that racked his limbs. The foreigners who came down to bathe and saw him there said that these Italian fishermen were lazy devils.

Sometimes he used to bring his children down to give them a bath. They were both boys and at this time the elder was three and the younger less than two. They sprawled about at the water's edge stark naked and Salvatore standing on a rock would dip them in the water. The elder one bore it with stoicism, but the baby screamed lustily. Salvatore had enormous hands, like legs of mutton, coarse and hard from constant toil, but when he bathed his children, holding them so tenderly, drying them with delicate care, upon my word they were like flowers. He would seat the naked baby on the palm of his hand and hold him up, laughing a little at his smallness, and his laugh was like the laughter of an angel. His eyes then were as candid as his child's.

I started by saying that I wondered if I could do it and now I must tell you what it is that I have tried to do. I wanted to see whether I could hold your attention for a few pages while I drew for you the portrait of a man, just an ordinary fisherman who possessed nothing in the world except a quality which is the rarest, the most precious and the loveliest that anyone can have. Heaven only knows why he should so strangely and unexpectedly have possessed it. All I know is that it shone in him with a radiance that, if it had not been so unconscious and so humble, would have been to the common run of men hardly bearable. And in case you have not guessed what the quality was, I will tell you. Goodness, just goodness.

A story that is closer in scope to the kind you may be asked to write in an examination is the following story by Janet Frame.

The Linesman

Three men arrived yesterday with their van and equip-ment to repair the telephone lines leading to the house opposite. Two of the men stayed at work in the house. The third carried his ladder and set it up against the tele-graph pole twenty-five yards from the house. He climbed the ladder and beyond it to the top of the pole where, with his feet resting on the iron rungs which are em-bedded at intervals in the sides of the pole, he began his work, his hands being made free after he had adjusted his safety harness. He was not likely to fall. I did not see him climb the pole. I looked from my window and saw him already working, twisting, arranging wires, screwing, unscrewing, leaning back from the pole, dependent upon his safety belt, trusting in it, seeming in a position of comfort and security.

I stared at him. I was reluctant to leave the window because I was so intent upon watching the linesman at work, and because I wanted to see him descend from the pole when his work was finished.

People in the houses near the telegraph pole had drawn their curtains; they did not wish to be spied upon. He was in an excellent position for spying, with a clear view into the front rooms of half a dozen houses.

The clouds, curds and whey, were churned from south to north across the sky. It was one of the first Sundays of spring. Washing was blowing on the clothes lines in back gardens; youths were lying in attitudes of surrender beneath the dismantled bellies of scooters; women were sweeping the Saturday night refuse from their share of the pavement. Perhaps it was time for me to have some-thing to eat—a cup of coffee, a biscuit, anything to occupy the ever marauding despair.

But still I could not leave my position at the window. I stared at the linesman until I had to screw up my eyes to avoid the bright stabs of spring light. I watched the work, the snipping, twisting, joining, screwing, unscrew-ing of bolts. And all the time I was afraid to leave the window. I kept my eyes fixed upon the linesman slung in his safety harness at the top of the telegraph pole.

You see, I was hoping that he might fall.

Consider the story carefully again from the point of view of the following questions:

1. Does the story have a point? If so, what is it?

2. Is all the detail in the story relevant?

3. Is the ending a surprise, or has the writer prepared the reader? Justify your answer.

Bearing in mind the points raised in this section, write a short story on one of the following titles:

1. Last Chance

2. The Brothers

3. The Lighthouse

4. Escape

5. Getting into Trouble

6. Alone at Last

7. Sunday

8. Tomorrow is Another Day

When you have written your story, read it critically. Reread the points earlier in this unit. Can you see any ways to improve your story? Can you from your experience see any pitfalls to avoid next time? In Assignment F (Unit 10) we will ask you to write a story so don't miss the chance to show yourself your own weaknesses!

 # READING AND UNDERSTANDING
Technical Prose

One of the comprehension passages you may be asked to answer questions on in the examination may be an example of technical prose, using both of these words in a very loose sense. It is technical because it deals with a particular technical subject-matter, which may be scientific, psychological, horticultural or culinary. It is prose because it uses words, though it may also use a great many abbreviations or symbols, as for example, the advertisement of a house for sale, or the instructions of a knitting pattern.

This is one of the types of writing we often meet in our everyday life, and it is useful to be able to get over the feeling of being stumped by unfamiliar vocabulary. It can often be a barrier to taking up a new hobby or following instructions for mending or using an appliance.

One term used for the kind of language found in technical writing is jargon (a term that is also loosely used to describe clumsy, long-winded writing). This refers to the specialized vocabulary often existing in a particular science, art, trade or profession which someone who is associated with this area would be able to understand but which an outsider would have difficulty in following. For example, a musician might talk about counterpoint, harmony, tessitura and bass clef; a gardener might talk about hybrids, cuttings, perennials and herbaceous borders.

Here, immediately, is one of the problems of reading and understanding a piece of technical prose: we may not be acquainted with or be able to understand the vocabulary. Do not worry too much about this as you are unlikely to be asked to answer questions on a passage with so many technical words in it that it is incomprehensible. It means that you have to deduce the meanings of words that you don't know from the passage itself and the general context.

The best way to approach this is to start from the general and work back to the particular. Read the passage through carefully first, not worrying too much about individual words or phrases that you can't understand. A first reading like this should give you a general idea of what the passage is about and what points are being made. You can then go back to areas where you had difficulty, take each in turn, and try to work out the meaning in the light of your understanding of the main ideas contained in the passage.

Read the following scientific passage and see if you can sum up in a sentence the main point being made in each paragraph. There are a lot of scientific terms which you may not know—chlorine, bromine, iodine, halogens, igneous, ionizes, etc.—but the main points should still come through.

What is Fluoride?

Fluorine, together with chlorine, bromine and iodine, is one of the halogens. Being an active element—one of the most active known—it is not found as an element but as a fluoride occurring especially in igneous rock formation as fluorspar, fluorapatite and fluorite, all of which are fluorides of calcium. It also occurs in the endemic regions in soils and rocks, it is present in sea water at a concentration of about one part per million, and it is found in many foods as a trace element.

There is no such thing as chemically pure water in nature. All water contains salts which enter the water as it passes over various rock formations, the relatively insoluble calcium fluoride being one of them. The portion of the salt that dissolves ionizes immediately, fluorine thus appearing in the water as the fluoride ion. It is present in such small quantities that it is measured in parts per million. The whole physiological action depends on this ionization of the fluoride salt, the salt itself ... being of minor importance.

In adjusting the fluoride content of water the relatively insoluble calcium fluoride is not added ... Instead, sodium fluoride is generally used to increase the concentration of fluoride ions. Chemically, the result is the same. No chemist will recognize any difference between fluorides occurring naturally and those added to water.

(from *Symposium on the Role of Fluoride*)

The point the first paragraph is making is that fluoride is a natural substance found in many natural objects.

Paragraph two tells us that all natural water contains 'impurities' of some kind.

Paragraph three suggests that by adding fluoride artificially, we are only doing what Nature does but in a different way.

Read the following recipe by Fanny and Johnnie Craddock:

By switching from beef to veal stock and again using cheese, onions, salt and pepper with the addition of dry white wine, a *bouquet garni* and some oil and butter, you can make a gorgeous French *Soupe à l'Oignon*. Begin by slicing 2 lbs of onions or shallots very thinly indeed. Dissolve a rounded dessertspoonful of butter with 2 tablespoonfuls of oil in a large frying pan. Add the onions.

When this mixture is hot, let it cook very slowly over a low heat until they are soft. Turn them occasionally of course. Then add a heaped tablespoonful of flour and work this well in with the back of a wooden spoon until the mixture becomes pasty. Add a rounded eggspoonful of dry English mustard and 1 gill of wine. Allow this to come to simmering point and then stir to a smooth paste. Add a second gill of water, vegetable water or stock. At this point scrape the whole mixture into a roomy saucepan, put it back over a moderate heat and then thin the mixture down with more of your chosen liquid until it reaches the consistency that you like. Now add another gill and a half, because you are going to simmer it for 35 minutes which will reduce the liquor down to the point where you approved of it. Now taste it and correct the seasoning. If possible, let it get cold and re-heat it the next day. It tastes much better. When it is re-heated, pour it into bowls over little rounds of toasted French bread covered thickly with grated Gruyere cheese.

(from *The Daily Telegraph Cook's Book*)

You may not know some of the technical terms used—stock, dry white wine, bouquet garni, *gill, simmering, seasoning. Nevertheless, it should be possible for you to answer the following questions:*

1. Even though you may not know any French, can you guess what Soupe à l'Oignon *means in English?*

2. Make a list of the ingredients and quantities required.

3. Briefly, outline the process of making this dish step by step.

When it comes to passages using figures, abbreviations and symbols that have to be understood and interpreted, the first thing to do is to make sure that you read all the details very carefully. Only in this way will you be certain that you have understood all the information necessary to answer the questions. It is a matter of taking things easily, carefully and methodically, working through the information and referring from the symbols to where they appear in the context and back again. Where a comparison between two sets of information is involved, take it step by step so that you gradually build up a composite picture.

For practice, look at the two questions that follow and write answers to them in your notebook. They are taken from actual 'O' level examinations.

1. What sort of holiday can you realistically expect from the information provided below? Point out any snags that might occur.

PLAYA DE PALMA
from £29

Weekly departures to Palma

From Gatwick on Saturdays from March 25 to October 21

From Gatwick on Tuesday from April 4 to October 10

From Manchester on Saturdays April 1, 15 and weekly from April 29 to October 14

From Glasgow on Saturdays from May 6 to October 14

Saturday flight depart
    Gatwick 8.45 am   Arrival back 2.10 pm

Tuesday flight depart
    Gatwick 4.40 pm   Arrival back 10.10 pm
Saturday flight depart
    Manchester 10.15 pm Arrival back 6.05 am Sunday
Saturday flight depart
    Glasgow 8.0 am   Arrival back 3.0 pm

Flying time 2 hours from Gatwick, $2\frac{1}{2}$ hours from Manchester, 3 hours from Glasgow

Baggage allowance 33 lbs

Hotel		PARADISO			
Flight from Gatwick	Gatwick		Manchester		Glasgow
Hol No Sat dep	615A 614A	— —	— —		
Hol No Tue dep	621A 620A	— —	— —		
Manchester	— —				
Hol No Sat dep			203A 202A		
Glasgow					
Hol No Sat dep	— —	— —	— —	305A 304A	

	1 wk	2 wks	1 wk	2 wks	1 wk	2 wks
Departure Dates	£	£	£	£	£	£
Mar 25 to Apr 25	35	51	—	56	—	—
Apr 26 to May 23	40	57	45	62	49	65
May 24 to Jun 13	43	62	48	67	52	71
Jun 14 to Jul 11	—	64	—	69	—	73
Jul 12 to Sep 5	—	67	—	72	—	76
Sep 6 to Oct 3	40	57	45	62	49	66
Oct 7	43	60	45	62	49	66
Oct 10	40	—	—	—	—	—
Oct 14	43	60	45	—	49	—
Oct 21	43	—	—	—	—	—

Single room extra	b£1.75	£3.50	b£1.75	£3.50	—	—

Prices from Gatwick are for Tuesday departures. For Saturday departures add £3 except for departures October 7, 14, 21 (from Gatwick) when above prices are for weekend Saturday departures

Supplements code: b = bath

The playground of Majorca—that great sweep of beach that curves eastwards all the way from C'An Pastilla to Arenal. Sunbrellas blossom on the fine white sand, water-skiers glide far out at sea and all the family find plenty to do on this happiest stretch of beach. Cosmopolitan Palma with its cafés, boutiques, discothèques and nightclubs is only minutes away—while in the other direction C'An Pastilla and Arenal vie in the liveliness of their nightlife. If you prefer sophisticated clubs we suggest world-famous Tito's in Palma or perhaps Los Rombos at C'An Pastilla; if you like your music long and loud then try Gaby Rabbit in Palma, or El Granero—but don't say we didn't warn you.

The Paradiso. Opened in 1971 this modern hotel is in a slightly elevated position about 250 metres from the beach at Arenal and enjoys views of the pinewoods and the sea. Sun terraces surround the swimming pool and on the hotel's court you can enjoy a game of tennis. There is dancing in the discothèque and baby-sitting can be arranged. All the well furnished bedrooms have private bathroom and toilet, twin rooms have terraces. There are lifts, and an airy restaurant, beautifully furnished lounge and attractive bar complete the picture.

2. Using the information provided below (which appears in the A.A. Camping and Caravanning Handbook) compare the amenities of the two sites shown, indicating which kind of holidaymaker would be attracted to each.

*▷▷▷**Bude Caravan Park** Maer Lane (Whit–
(Sep 30) ☎2472 ⅓m along Maer Lane, near Crooklets Beach signposted 13 acres (250) grassy, sloping ground, bushes ⌖ lighting of toilets 6 (wc) washrooms (hc) (hc) (⊙) laundry supermarket paraffin Calor gas e Calor gas r bar TV ☎ cold storage ↔ ♂ cinema ⊷ 1 mile 50 50p 50 50p 150 50p 150 vans for hire £6–£20 14 chalets available

*▷▷**Upper Lynstone Farm** (Etr–Sep)
☎2017 ⅓m S of Bude on road to Widemouth Bay signposted 4 acres grassy, sloping ground last arrival 22.30hrs lighting of toilets 4 (wc) (hc) (⊙) ↔ stables ♂ cinema ⊷ 1 mile Tariff not available 12 vans for hire

---

Abbreviations and symbols

ad	charge for adult per night
acres ( )	figure in brackets is total number of touring pitches available
all year	site open all year
am/pm depart	latest departure time
C	century
cdp	chemical closet disposal point
cTV	colour television
car	car charge per night
ch	charge for child per night
E	east
Etr	Easter
Calor gas e	Calor gas bottle exchange
Calor gas r	Calor gas bottle refill
fr	from
(hc)	hot and cold water
ICC	International Camping Carnet accepted
lt	left
ltr	long-term rates
Map	map reference
m	mile
m/c	motor cycle charge per night
N	north
NT(S)	National Trust (for Scotland)
OS ref	Ordnance Survey map reference
rs	restricted service during period stated
rt	right
S	south
☎	public telephone available
☎	site telephone number
TV	black and white television
W	west
wc	water closet
wdn	site patrolled by warden
▷	site with six or more touring caravanning/camping pitches with at least minimum range of facilities
▷▷	more adequate standard and provision of facilities
▷▷▷	greater range of facilities and some services
▷▷▷▷	well-equipped and with good range of services
▷▷▷▷▷	very well-equipped. well laid-out, with full range of services
	towing caravans permitted; maximum number, charge per night
	motor caravans permitted; maximum number and charge per night
	tent campers permitted; maximum number and charge per night
⌖	separate tent enclosure
	bath(s)
(hc)	shower (hot and cold water)
⊙	electric razor points
	shop (on or within 100yds of site)
	swimming pool
	tennis court
	no dogs
	drinking water stand-pipes
	first-aid facilities
*	1973 details
↔	amenities within three miles of site:
⊷	fishing
	boats for hire
♂	golf course

READING LIST

Some people get great pleasure from browsing through cookery books. They find that reading a recipe is almost as good as eating the finished product. If you are interested in food or cooking—and even if you are not—have a look at one or more of the following to see if they whet your appetite.

Fanny and Johnnie Craddock: *Cook's Book*
Robin Howe: *Greek Cooking*
Elizabeth David: *A Book of Mediterranean Food*
Bee Nilson: *The Penguin Cookery Book*
Rosemary Hume and Muriel Downes: *Penguin Cordon Bleu Cookery*
Robert Carrier: *Great Dishes of the World*
Elizabeth David: *French Country Cooking*
Anne Mason: *Cook for Tomorrow*

VOCABULARY

1. Read the short story *Salvatore* again and try to work out the meanings of the following words as used there:

frugal, affianced, uncomprehending, exulted, husky, grim-visaged, masterful, expostulations, stoicism, lustily, candid, unconscious.

2. Look these words up in a dictionary and check with your own definitions.
3. Put each of these words into a sentence of your own. Make a list of any other words used in this unit that you did not fully understand. Look them up in your dictionary and put them in sentences of your own.

LANGUAGE

Prefixes

A prefix is that part of a word placed at the beginning to qualify the meaning of the root part of the word. For instance, in the word 'untrue', the root is 'true' and the prefix which limits or indicates the meaning we are to take from the root is 'un-'. The prefix can therefore be an important element of a word, altering and modifying the meaning of the root, and if we know our prefixes (and roots) this can often help us to deduce the meanings of words which we may not have come across before.

Consider the difference in meaning of 'anti-war', 'prewar', 'post-war', 'pro-war'; 'prelude', 'interlude', 'postlude'; 'include', 'exclude', 'preclude'; 'encamp', 'decamp'; 'regress', 'progress', 'egress'; 'sustain', 'contain', 'obtain', 'retain'; 'exclaim', 'proclaim', 'reclaim', 'declaim'; 'succeed', 'exceed', 'proceed'. Look these words up in a dictionary and study what it says about their derivation, the meaning of the root part of the word and the effect of the prefix on the meaning.

Note that the form of the prefix sometimes changes when joined to a root so as to produce a more pleasant sound, e.g. 'sub-' + 'press' becomes 'suppress'; 'con-' + 'rect' becomes 'correct'. With a little experience, it becomes easy to deduce these changes.

Here are some of the most common prefixes: use your dictionary to find further examples and write them alongside or in your notebook.

1. From Old English
    mis = wrongly, e.g. misinterpret
    out = out, forth, beyond, e.g. outbid
    un = not, e.g. unfortunate
    under = below, incomplete, e.g. underhand
    with = against, e.g. withhold
2. From Greek
    a, ab = without, e.g. amoral
    amphi = on both sides, e.g. amphibious
    anti = against, e.g. antithesis
    arch = chief, e.g. archdeacon
    auto = self, e.g. autobiography
    dia = through, e.g. diameter
    hemi = half, e.g. hemisphere
    hyper = beyond, excessive, e.g. hyper-sensitive
    hypo = under, e.g. hypodermic
    mono = single, e.g. monologue
    pan = all, e.g. panorama
    peri = around, e.g. periscope
    poly = many, e.g. polyglot
    pseudo = false, e.g. pseudonym
    syn = with, e.g. synthesis
    tele = from afar, e.g. television
    tri = three, e.g. triangle
3. From Latin
    a, ab = from, e.g. avert
    ad = to, e.g. admit
    ante = before, e.g. anteroom
    bene = well, e.g. benevolent
    bi, bis = two, e.g. bisect
    circum = around, e.g. circumference
    con = with, e.g. concur
    contra = against, e.g. contradict
    de = down, away from, e.g. descend
    demi = half, e.g. demiparadise
    dis = aside, asunder, e.g. dismiss
        = not, e.g. disuse
    e, ex = out of, e.g. explode
    in = within, e.g. inject

    = not, e.g. indistinct
    inter = between, among, e.g. interfere
    intra, intro = within, e.g. introvert
    male = badly, e.g. malevolent
    mis = badly, e.g. misuse
    multi = many, e.g. multicoloured
    ob = against, e.g. object
    per = through, e.g. pervade
    post = after, e.g. postscript
    pre = before, e.g. predict
    pro = on the side of, e.g. pro-French
    quad = four, e.g. quadrangle
    quasi = as if, e.g. quasi-serious
    re = back, again, e.g. reject
    retro = backwards, e.g. retrograde
    se = apart from, e.g. seclude
    semi = half, e.g. semicircle
    sine = without, e.g. sinecure
    sub = under, e.g. subterranean
    super = above, over, e.g. superabundance
    trans = across, e.g. transfer
    ultra = beyond, e.g. ultraviolet
    vice = instead of, e.g. viceregent

Note: Usually the second part of the word is derived from the same language as the prefix. To understand fully the meaning of each word, look it up in your dictionary, e.g. 'synthesis' is a combination of syn— and thesis, a Greek word meaning 'placing'.

 SPELLING

The letter 'c' is pronounced 'soft' (i.e. the same as 's') before the vowels 'e', 'i' and 'y'. (The French word *ceci* may help you to remember this.) Before other vowels, 'c' is pronounced 'hard' (i.e. the same as 'k'). Compare 'cedar', 'city', 'icy', with 'came', 'comb', 'cute'.

This guide to pronunciation can help when it comes to spelling. When 'c' is pronounced soft but is followed by a suffix beginning with 'a', 'o' or 'u', an 'e' has to be retained or added in order to keep the 'c' soft. Compare 'implacable' and 'irreplaceable'; 'reducing' and 'irreduceable'.

The word 'façade' which is pronounced with a soft 'c' is an exception. The *cedilla* sign under the 'c' shows this. (It is really a French word taken unchanged into English.)

The rule for soft 'g' is less hard and fast. Often 'g' is soft (i.e. pronounced like 'j') before the vowels 'e', 'i' and 'y'. The word 'ginger' should help you to remember. Before the other vowels, 'g' is pronounced hard. Compare 'gesture', 'gipsy', 'cagy' with 'garden', 'go', 'gutter'. There are many exceptions to this including many common words, e.g. 'gaol', 'girl', 'giggle', 'gear'.

However, the tendency is worth remembering because it can sometimes help with spelling. When 'g' is pronounced soft, an 'e' is sometimes required to keep it soft when a suffix beginning with 'a' or 'o' is added. Compare 'courage', 'courageous'; 'exchange', 'exchangeable'; 'manage', 'manageable'.

Here is a chance for you to practise the points made above and to see that you have understood them. Add as many suffixes as you can to the following words and check your spellings in a dictionary.

1. package
2. trace
3. grace
4. finance
5. practice
6. forage
7. range
8. stage
9. place
10. wage

UNIT 10

WRITING
Practical I:
Explanations and Instructions

Advice on and examples of this kind of 'practical writing' assignment.

READING AND UNDERSTANDING
Statistics

Examples to help familiarize yourself with this type of comprehension question.

READING LIST

Some books that take a critical look at the novel, the film and television in preparation for attempting some critical writing in Unit 11.

VOCABULARY

Some words that are often confused for you to check up on.

LANGUAGE
Suffixes

A list of some of the most common suffixes and advice on how they can help you to understand the shades of meanings they give to words.

SPELLING
The Apostrophe

The use of the apostrophe to show that letters have been omitted and to form the possessive case.

ASSIGNMENT F

WRITING

Practical I:
Explanations and Instructions

In earlier units, a distinction was drawn between the two different types of prose you will probably be called upon to write: imaginative and practical. The units so far have dealt with imaginative writing, requiring you to use your own ideas and organize them in a creative way.

Practical writing is more down-to-earth. It requires you to explain a process as simply and clearly as possible; to give directions on how to do something so that a novice can understand and follow; to arrange given facts in a clear, logical and fluent form. Some examples of practical assignments were given in Unit 2. Look at these again and the explanation of what practical writing involves. Here are some further examples of practical writing assignments:

1. Give instructions for boiling an egg.
2. Write a letter to the Box Office Manager of a theatre asking for tickets for a particular performance of a play.
3. Using the following facts, write a report for a local newspaper on a factory fire: the factory made cardboard cartons; employed 50 workers; 30 of these are women; established for 68 years; a small fire occurred 4 years previously; fire started at 3 a.m.; night watchman gave alarm; flames spread very quickly; 10 fire brigades answered call; still smouldering 12 hours later; large section gutted; workers sent home; £50,000 worth of damage done; the owners, Messrs J. H. Graham and Sons, plan to rebuild the factory on a new site; will take 2 years; unemployment meanwhile.
4. Write a report of a speech made by Mr John Taylor to a Ratepayers' Association Meeting, using the following notes: Mr Taylor complained about the poor conditions of the roads; dustbins not emptied regularly; roads not kept clean; many accidents; dangerous crossings; no action taken; letters of complaint not

answered; lack of local amenities; no parking space in shopping areas; inadequate street lighting.

5. State as fully and as clearly as you can the advice you would give to someone going on holiday for two weeks and leaving his house unoccupied.

6. Give advice on looking after a car *or* a dog *or* a garden.

7. Write a short advertisement for a newspaper of something you want to sell. Write a short letter from someone who is interested and wants more details. Write your reply to the letter.

8. Write an explanation of how one of the following works: an electric food-mixer; a vacuum cleaner; an electric shaver.

9. Write a short factual account of the jobs and duties of one of the following: a policeman; an air hostess; a traffic warden.

10. Write an account of Majorca for a holiday brochure, using the following points: largest of the Balearic Islands; off south-east coast of Spain; mild winter climate; plenty of sunshine; 5,000 feet high mountains; terraced vineyards; an abundance of wild flowers; magnificent coastline; sandy beaches and deep-coloured sea; picturesque villages; busy shopping-centres in the cathedral city of Palma; night-clubs, restaurants and bars.

Some of these assignments contain what might be called imaginative elements (for example 5 and 6), but generally, they require you to give a clear statement of facts or instructions so that a reader can understand and follow the process you are describing. Some types of practical writing assignments will be discussed later—Letters in Units 12 and 13; Writing Up Notes in Unit 16. This unit will give advice on the question which requires you to give an explanation or to outline instructions.

Clarity is of the first importance. The main purpose of an exercise of this kind is to see whether you can state facts clearly and logically. The process you are describing must be intelligible to someone who knows very little about the subject. One useful piece of advice is to tabulate the points first so that you have them clear before you write the final account. In this way, you will be able to see whether you have the facts in sequence or not, and whether you have left anything out. In this kind of writing it is also a good idea to use short sentences. There is less danger then that your instructions will become involved and confusing.

The second important point to remember is to be relevant. Give the necessary facts only and keep to the facts. Don't get carried away into flights of fancy which have nothing to do with the basic explanation or instructions. Remember that this is a very down-to-earth kind of exercise where the clear statement and logical arrangement of the facts are what matter, not imaginative touches or original ideas.

The facts must be arranged in a fluent and pleasing way. It is not enough just to give them baldly. You are recommended to use short sentences, but the general effect should not be too blunt or disjointed. The facts must flow easily from one to the next so that the reader is carried smoothly along.

Apart from letters and reports, practical writing assignments of this kind can be divided into three main categories. The first asks you to organize given facts into a specific form; the second asks you to explain a particular process or give a set of instructions on how to operate or do something; the third asks you to give a description of some area of life to see that you can organize all the expected facts. Look again at the ten examples given earlier and say into which of these categories each falls.

Here are three examples of practical writing for you to consider. Ask yourself whether the explanation or instructions given are expressed clearly, logically and fluently in each case, and whether there is any irrelevant material. In your notebook, write a few sentences on each of the passages, commenting along these lines.

1. Q. Write an entry for a guide-book on Potters Bar, using the following information: 14 miles north of London; on Greater London and Hertfordshire borders; surrounded by Green Belt; four-fifths of the borough is open space; industrial development carefully controlled; some sixteenth- and seventeenth-century farmhouses and inns; Great Northern Railway brought about rapid modern development; two modern shopping centres; up-to-date state schools and excellent range of private schools.

A. Potters Bar is situated 14 miles north of London. On the Greater London and Hertfordshire borders, the town is surrounded by the Green Belt. Indeed, four-fifths of the borough is made up of open space. Industrial development in the town is carefully controlled so as to maintain this rural aspect. Some sixteenth- and seventeenth-century farmhouses and inns survive, but the main development of Potters Bar came with the Great Northern Railway. This rapidly created the town we know today. There are two modern shopping centres, and residents have a choice of up-to-date state schools and an excellent range of private schools.

2. Q. Explain how to cook spaghetti.

A. Use a large saucepan two-thirds full of salted water. Bring the water to the boil. Add the spaghetti to the water, using a quarter of a pound or more per person. Bring the water back to the boil and simmer, stirring occasionally. The spaghetti should be simmered from between 12 and 16 minutes depending on taste. If you like it *al dente* (that is, fairly chewy) then cook for 12 minutes. Longer cooking makes the spaghetti softer. Test a piece to see if it is the texture you prefer. When ready, drain the spaghetti carefully and make sure that as much water as possible is removed. Return the spaghetti to the pan (but not over heat), add a generous portion of butter and allow this to melt evenly among the spaghetti. The spaghetti can be served as it is (if enough butter has been used) or with a meat or tomato sauce. Sprinkle parmesan cheese freely over the spaghetti on the plate.

(Note how useful it is in a question like this requiring instructions to use imperatives, that is, orders like 'Do this', 'Do that'.)

3. Q. Without using specific examples, give an account of the main types of programmes found on television.

A. The programmes found on television can be divided into the following categories: news and documentaries; plays, films and dramatized features; entertainment programmes; and programmes designed for special interests.

News bulletins occur at regular intervals throughout the day. Documentaries are programmes that deal with matters of general interest in a factual way. They can range from interviews to filmed reports.

Drama is represented by plays, commercial films from the cinema which have been bought for showing on television, and special series about crime or cowboys or industrial enterprises presented in a fictional setting. Another type of dramatic programme is provided by the adaptation of books as serials.

Entertainment programmes cover such things as variety and song and dance programmes. Many well-known comedians and singers have their own series, either in their own right or as characters in a fictional situation. Quizzes would also come into this category.

The programmes appealing to special interests cover a wide range. The sports enthusiast receives a generous proportion of broadcasting time, and the sports covered range from football to wrestling, from ice-skating to horse-jumping. Programmes are specially provided for children, women viewers, people interested in music and the arts. There are also programmes dealing with religious topics.

(Note that this question requires you to organize your material carefully before giving an answer. It is no good writing about the various programmes as they occur to you. You have to do some thinking first and then arrange your material into some kind of order before you write your answer.)

For practice, look at the ten examples given earlier and see what you can make of one or more of them.

 READING AND UNDERSTANDING

Statistics

We often come across statistics these days on TV or in newspapers. Many people have a mental block about them—can't stand them, mistrust them or can't understand them. It is in fact useful to be able to interpret statistics and the effort involved is actually slight.

The study and comparison of sets of statistics require the same kind of care and attention to detail as was suggested in 'Reading and Understanding' Unit 9. Statistics are sets of figures which in themselves mean very little. It is the comparison of one set with another and your interpretation of the result which gives them meaning.

To take a straightforward example first, look at the following figures which represent the amount of money spent per pupil on class books and school library books in the various London Boroughs:

Q. Which borough spent least per primary pupil and which spent most?

Expenditure on Class Books and School Library Books 1970–1 in England and Wales from *Education Statistics*

London Boroughs	Primary £	Secondary £
Barking	1.12	1.86
Barnet	1.49	2.77
Bexley	0.96	2.17
Brent	1.09	2.62
Bromley	1.37	3.25
Croydon	1.17	3.13
Ealing	1.26	2.73
Enfield	1.34	2.90
Haringey	1.09	2.96
Harrow	1.08	2.77
Havering	1.49	2.00
Hillingdon	1.25	3.45
Hounslow	1.55	2.84
Kingston-upon-Thames	1.48	2.90
Merton	1.45	3.18
Newham	1.24	2.12
Redbridge	1.27	2.52
Richmond-upon-Thames	1.13	2.71
Sutton	1.10	2.68
Waltham Forest	1.53	3.00
Inner London Education Authority	1.53	3.62

A. (It is a simple matter to go down the column representing expenditure in primary schools to find the lowest and the highest figures.) Bexley with £0.96 per pupil spent least; Hounslow with £1.55 spent the most.

Q. Which borough spent least and which most per secondary pupil on books?

A. (The process is the same as above.) Barking with £1.86 spent least; Inner London with £3.62 spent most.

Q. Which borough on average is the most generous, taking into account both primary and secondary schools?

A. (This requires you to add together the primary and secondary sum in each case to find the lowest and the highest. In practice, it is not necessary to add them all up as it soon becomes clear that Barking does not reach a total of £3 which all the others surpass, and boroughs with a secondary spending of £3 + have a clear advantage.) The borough which spends least is Barking with £2.98; Inner London spends most with £5.18.

Q. What would you conclude from a comparison of the figures for primary schools and those for secondary schools?

A. (A quick look down the two sets of figures makes the conclusion obvious.)

More is spent on books per child in secondary schools than in primary schools.

(If you examine the figures more closely, you could say that most of the boroughs spend more than twice as much per head on books for secondary pupils as on books for primary pupils.)

Now for a more complex example, look at the following tables of figures representing various aspects of life in European Community countries (the original Six), other European countries, USA and Japan.

Table 1. Relative income levels $ per year (at current prices)

| | Gross national product per head of population[1] | | Average income per employed person[2] | |
	1958	1970	1958	1970
Belgium	1,154	2,656	1,846	4,198
France	1,196	2,906	1,730	4,264
Germany	1,094	3,028	1,461	4,301
Italy	612	1,710	1,033	3,255
Luxembourg	1,402	(2,929)	2,488[3]	4,286[4]
Netherlands	845	2,398	1,432	4,439
Six	965	2,555	1,455	4,059
UK	1,249	2,175	1,677	3,145
Norway	1,138	2,937	1,873	4,597
Denmark	1,101	3,163	1,757[3]	3,873[4]
Irish Rep.	578	1,321	n.a.	2,324[4]
Ten	1,030	2,476	n.a.	3,364
USA	2,602	4,839	4,703	8,195
Japan	349	1,894	648	2,647

Sources: ECSO [1]At market prices [2]Value of earnings, social-security contributions paid and fringe benefits provided by employers; excludes self-employed and unearned income [3]1960 [4]1969

Table 2. Hours of work (April 1971)

Basic weekly working hours as laid down by law and by collective agreement in major manufacturing sectors, and average hours actually worked

| | Basic working week[1] | | Average hours worked[2] |
	by legislation	by collective agreement	
Belgium	45	42–44	42·2
France	40[3]	40–41$\frac{1}{4}$	44·6
Germany	48	40–41	42·9
Italy	48	40–43	42·2
Luxembourg	44$\frac{1}{2}$	41–44	42·4
Netherlands	48	40–43$\frac{3}{4}$	43·8
UK	—	39$\frac{1}{2}$–40$\frac{1}{2}$	44·9[4]

[1]Adult workers [2]All workers [3]Nominal total only, providing basis for overtime payments [4]October 1970, men over 21 only
Sources: EEC and DE

Try to answer these questions yourself before checking with the suggested answers that follow.

Q. 1. Which country increased its gross national product per head most between 1958 and 1970?

2. Which country has the lowest and which the highest gross national product per head in 1970.

3. Which country increased its average income per employed person most between 1958 and 1970?

4. Which country had the lowest and which the highest income per employed person in 1970?

5. Which country works the shortest and which the longest average hours?

Table 3. Paid holidays
Situation in April 1971 for adult workers in industry

	Legal minimum (working weeks)[1]	Minimum under collective agreements (working weeks)[1,2]	Supplementary holidays (days)[3]	Public holidays (days)
Belgium	3	rare	rare	10
France	4	4	6	8–10
Germany	2$\frac{1}{2}$–3	3–4	6	10–13
Italy	2$\frac{1}{2}$	2$\frac{1}{2}$–3	6	17
Luxembourg	3–4	—	rare	10
Netherlands	3	3–3$\frac{1}{2}$	6	7
UK	—	sometimes 2 generally 3	n.a.	6

[1]Working week may be of 5 or 6 days [2]Varies according to industry
[3]Maximum additional days granted under collective agreements in some industries according to age and length of employment
Sources: EEC and DE

6. What would you say about the amount of holidays given to workers in UK compared with other countries?

7. What do these various tables suggest to you about (a) the way things have developed in UK between 1958 and 1970 as compared with other countries, and (b) the conditions and rewards of working in UK as compared with other countries?

A. 1. Germany increased its gross national product per head most between 1958 and 1970 by nearly trebling it.

2. The Irish Republic with 1,321 had the lowest gross national product per head in 1970; USA with 4,839 had the highest.

3. The Netherlands increased its average income per employed person most between 1958 and 1970.

4. The Irish Republic has the lowest and the USA the highest average income per employed person in 1970.

5. Belgium and Italy with an average of 42·2 work the shortest hours; UK with 44·9 works the longest.

6. Workers in UK get fewer holidays than workers in the other countries specified.

7. (a) The UK has done less well between 1958 and 1970 than other countries. Apart from the USA, it is the only country in the table that has not more than doubled its gross national product per head of the population, and it is well behind a country like Germany which has trebled its gross national product. Only Italy, the Irish Republic and Japan have a lower gross national product than the UK in 1970, whereas in 1958 the UK was third in the table after the USA and Luxembourg. In other words, many countries have overtaken the UK. The same is true of average income. Apart from the USA, the UK is the only country that has not more than doubled its average income per employed person. In 1958, the UK was the seventh in the league for average income; in 1970, it was

89

eleventh in the league, showing a relative decline in its position.

(b) As suggested in 7 (a), the average rewards of an employee in the UK are considerably less than in most of the other countries itemized in the tables. He works longer hours on average than do employees in the Six original countries of the European community, and he has fewer statutory holidays.

Only by keeping alert and working methodically through the tables will you be able to find the information you require for your answers when set a comprehension exercise involving statistics. Make sure you understand what information the question is asking for and search for it in the appropriate table. Reject (after careful consideration) any figures which are not relevant to the question.

 # READING LIST

In the following unit, we shall be looking at ways of writing a critical essay, that is an essay which involves an appreciation and evaluation of a novel, a play, a film or a television programme. As a preparation for this, it would be worth while having a look at one or more of the following books which deal in a fairly approachable way with the criticism of these arts. Look at the contents lists of the books mentioned and choose one which contains something which interests you. You won't, for example, gain much from reading *Ten Novels and Their Authors* if you haven't read any of the novels.

Walter Allen: *The English Novel*
Walter Allen: *Tradition and Dream*
E. M. Forster: *Aspects of the Novel*
H. Coombes: *Literature and Criticism*
W. Somerset Maugham: *Ten Novels and Their Authors*
John Kershaw: *The Present Stage*
John Russell Taylor: *Anger and After*
Bamber Gascoigne: *Twentieth Century Drama*
Penelope Houston: *The Contemporary Cinema*
V. F. Perkins: *Film as Film*
Milton Shulman: *The Least Worst Television in the World*

 # VOCABULARY

There are a large number of words similar in sound or form which are sometimes confused. Here are ten pairs of such words. See if you can distinguish between them:

masterful, masterly
collaborate, corroborate
imperative, imperious
moral, morale
momentarily, momentous
quite, quiet

exhausting, exhaustive
exterior, external
ingenious, ingenuous
inhuman, inhumane

Check the meaning of these words in a dictionary.

Use each of the words in an interesting sentence of your own. Quite often we misunderstand or misuse words because we are confusing them with another similar word. If you catch yourself doing this try to corner both words in your mind, write them both down and learn the differences in meaning straight away. Your vocabulary notes could well have a useful section of pairs of words such as these.

 # LANGUAGE

Suffixes

Suffixes have been mentioned previously when discussing aids to spelling, e.g. whether a silent 'e' is dropped before adding a suffix (in 'Spelling', Unit 8). A suffix is an element placed at the end of a root in order to form a particular part of speech. For example, if the suffix '-able' is added to 'change', the adjective 'changeable' is formed; if '-ize' is added to 'critic', the verb 'criticize' is formed. Consider the effect of adding suffixes to the following words: 'protest', 'nation', 'expect', 'manage', 'employ', 'protect', 'home', 'confess', 'man', 'earth'.

Knowing the meaning and function of suffixes can help you to understand words and how they are used more easily. Here are some of the most common suffixes.

Using your dictionary find more examples and copy them in your notebook.

1. From Old English
   Forming nouns:
   craft = skill, e.g. handicraft
   dom = jurisdiction, condition,
       e.g. kingdom
   er = agent, e.g. employer
   herd = keeper, e.g. shepherd
   hood = state, e.g. boyhood
   ing, ling = diminutive,
       e.g. gosling
   kin = diminutive, e.g. manikin
   man = a person, e.g. swordsman
   monger = dealer, e.g.
       ironmonger
   ness = state, e.g. kindness
   ship = condition, e.g. kinship
   Forming adjectives:
   en = made of, e.g. wooden
   fast = firm, e.g. steadfast
   fold = times, e.g. tenfold
   ful = full of, e.g. beautiful
   ing = present participle ending,
       e.g. wishing
   less = without, e.g. thankless
   like = having the qualities of,
       e.g. manlike

ly = like, e.g. godly
some = causing or characterized
by, e.g. troublesome
Forming verbs:
en = to cause, e.g. stiffen

2. From Greek
Forming nouns:
ad, id, e.g. dryad
ast = agent, e.g. gymnast
ic, e.g. cynic
ism, e.g. communism
ist = agent, e.g. perfectionist
ology = science, e.g. biology
Forming adjectives:
ic, e.g. ironic
astic, e.g. fantastic
Forming verbs:
ise, ize, e.g. criticize
3. From Latin
Forming nouns:
ace, e.g. populace
age, e.g. courage
ance, ence, e.g. occurrence
er, or = agent, e.g. builder
ate = agent, e.g. magistrate
cy, e.g. supremacy
ee, ey = indicating action or
character, e.g. employee,
journey
ess = feminine, e.g. abbess
et, ette = diminutive, e.g.
statuette
ice, ise, e.g. novice
ion = abstract, e.g. opinion
ment, e.g. enjoyment
trix = feminine agent, e.g.
executrix
tude = abstract, e.g. fortitude
Forming adjectives:
able, ible, e.g. changeable
acious, e.g. capacious
al, e.g. vital
ant, ent, e.g. brilliant
ar, e.g. familiar
ary, e.g. contrary
ate, e.g. affectionate
esque = tending to be, e.g.
grotesque
ic = belonging to, e.g. domestic
ior = comparative suffix, e.g.
superior
ique = characteristic of, e.g.
unique
lent, e.g. opulent
ory, e.g. compulsory
Forming verbs:
ate, e.g. agitate
esce, e.g. effervesce
fy = to make, e.g. solidify
ish, e.g. establish

 **SPELLING**

The Apostrophe

The apostrophe is a sign (') used
    1. to show the omission of a letter in a word, and
    2. to show the possessive case.
  1. Examples of the first use are:

    don't (for 'do not')
    it's (for 'it is')
    five o'clock (for 'five of the clock').

Make sure the apostrophe goes in the right place, that is in the space where the missing letter or letters should be. If in doubt, think out what the full version should be.
Make a list of twenty other words that use an apostrophe like this.
Find out the difference in meaning between 'it's' and 'its'; 'let's' and 'lets'; 'won't' and 'wont'. Write sentences containing these words.
  2. The possessive (or genitive) case indicates the possessor or owner of something, e.g.

    the lady's hat (= the hat belonging to the lady)
    the man's suit (= the suit belonging to the man).

The possessive case is formed as follows:
  (a) If the possessor is singular, add 's, e.g. the cloud's shadow, the girl's dress.
(Note that proper names ending in 's' usually just add an apostrophe, e.g. Charles' joke, James' mistake. Other exceptions are 'for goodness' sake', 'for peace' sake'.)
  (b) If the possessor is plural, add an apostrophe only, e.g. the ladies' hats, the boys' school.
(Note that if the plural possessor does not end in 's'—e.g. men, children—the possessive case is formed by adding 's, e.g. the men's department, children's games.)
  An apostrophe is also required in phrases like 'two weeks' holiday', 'five hours' time', 'tomorrow's match', 'out of harm's way'.
  Words like yours, his, her, its (as a personal pronoun), ours, theirs never have an apostrophe.
Learn this section thoroughly
  It is important to try to get this matter of the apostrophe clear as many students spoil otherwise accurate work by failing to use the apostrophe at all or by using it incorrectly. A definite effort to understand its use should help to overcome this deficiency.
In the following sentences, change the words into a possessive phrase using the apostrophe.

1. (The Home of the Old People) is very friendly and well-run.
2. I bought several (toys for children) as Christmas presents.
3. I am going on holiday in (the time of two days).
4. Let's hurry to shelter from (the fury of the wind).
5. (The idea of Thomas) is quite splendid.
6. The council is building a new (lavatory for men) in the town.

7. The native inhabitants make bags out of (the hides of donkeys).
8. I bought (worth of two pounds) of strawberries for making jam.
9. (The leaves of the trees) are changing their colour.
10. (The hooters of the cars) made a dreadful din.

Check your answers carefully against the rules above. If you have several answers wrong spend more time learning the rules.

 # ASSIGNMENT F

You should spend about an hour and a quarter on the preparation and writing of Part I, and your essay should be at least 500 words long. Part II should take about three quarters of an hour and should be about 300 words long. Part III should take about an hour.

Part I: Essay

Write a story on *one* of the following:

1. No Going Back
2. The Retreat
3. Just an Ordinary Man
4. Use the following as the opening sentence for a story: 'The cat from next door had done it again ...'
5. Write a story of which this is the final sentence: 'Now there was no hope left.'
6. Neighbours
7. He Who Laughs Last
8. Meeting at Night

Part II: Practical Writing

Choose *one* of the following:

1. Give clear instructions on how to mend a puncture *or* how to make a cup of tea *or* how to prepare a wall for wall-papering.
2. Write a simple account for a children's magazine giving advice for a beginner on stamp-collecting *or* playing tennis *or* making your own clothes.
3. Write an account for the sleeve of a record of Benjamin Britten's opera *Peter Grimes*, using the following information:
Britten's first major opera—first performed 7 June 1945 at Sadler's Wells Theatre—performed all over the world—based on an episode from George Crabbe's poem 'The Borough'—libretto by Montagu Slater—the central character is a misfit—a fisherman—his apprentice is drowned in strange circumstances—the village is against him—a second apprentice is ill-treated—the village rounds on Grimes—he is helped by the schoolmistress, Ellen Orford—he becomes crazed—is persuaded to drown himself and so escape the hostility of the villagers—the life of the village goes on—a vivid collection of characters—the chorus has an important part—the sea strongly evoked—four sea interludes set the scenes.

Part III: Comprehension

Study the following statistics carefully and answer the questions set below
1. What kinds of crime are most common?
2. At what age are people most likely to commit crimes?
3. Are males or females more likely to commit crimes? Can you give an explanation of this?
4. What would you conclude are the chances of someone proceeded against for a crime being found innocent?
5. What conclusions would you draw from these tables about the crime rate in 1970 as opposed to that of 1951?
6. Comment on the success or otherwise of the police in combating crime as indicated by the following tables.

Table 1. Crime: types of offence: England and Wales

	1951	1961	1966	1967	1968		1969[1]	1970
Indictable offences known to police								
Murder and manslaughter	0·3	0·2	0·3	0·3	0·4	Murder and manslaughter	0·3	0·4
Wounding and assault	6	16	26	28	30	Wounding and assault	36	39
Other offences of violence	0·5	1·1	1·3	1·5	2	Other offences of violence	2	2
Sexual offences	15	20	21	22	23	Sexual offences	24	24
Larceny	355	531	776	784	826	Theft and unauthorized taking	879	915
Breaking and entering	96	165	276	266	287	Burglary and robbery	427	438
Receiving	10	14	22	24	27	Handling stolen goods	32	38
Frauds and false pretences	27	40	51	52	60	Frauds	64	74
Other indictable offences	15	19	27	30	34	Other indictable offences	24	26
Total indictable offences	525	807	1,200	1,207	1,289	Total indictable offences	1,488	1,556
Total per thousand population	*11·9*	*17·5*	*25·0*	*24·9*	*26·5*	*Total per thousand population*	*30·5*	*38·0*
Percentage indictable offences						*Percentage indictable offences*		
cleared up	*47·1*	*44·8*	*40·2*	*41·2*	*41·9*	*cleared up*	*42·1*	*45·0*
Persons proceeded against								
Indictable offences	144	193	250	261	277	Indictable offences	330	350
Non-indictable offences	626	1,014	1,269	1,403	1,388	Non-indictable offences	1,372	1,426
Total	770	1,207	1,519	1,664	1,665	Total	1,702	1,776
Persons found guilty								
Indictable offences:								
Murder or manslaughter	0·1	0·1	0·2	0·2	0·2	Murder or manslaughter	0·2	0·3
Wounding or assault	4	11	15	16	17	Wounding or assault	20	23
Other offences of violence	0·2	1	1	1	1	Other offences of violence	1	1
Sexual offences	5	6	6	6	6	Sexual offences	6	7
Larceny	87	107	136	141	147	Theft or unauthorized taking	168	176
Breaking and entering	22	36	49	48	52	Burglary or robbery	69	70
Receiving	6	9	13	14	16	Handling stolen goods	19	22
Fraud or false pretences	3	5	6	7	9	Frauds	12	12
Other indictable offences	6	7	7	9	9	Other indictable offences	9	11
Total	133	182	233	242	257	Total	304	322
Non-indictable offences:								
Assault	12	12	11	12	12	Assault	12	12
Drunkenness	51	72	67	72	75	Drunkenness	77	79
Motoring offences	291	655	898	1,001	970	Motoring offences	947	970
Malicious damage	9	15	16	16	17	Malicious damage	17	20
Other offences	230	231	237	252	263	Other offences	267	270
Total	593	985	1,229	1,353	1,337	Total	1,320	1,351

Table 2. Indictable offences: age groups of persons found guilty or cautioned

	England and Wales						Per 100,000 population in each sex and age group
	1951	1961	1966	1968	1969 adjusted[1]	1969 actual	1970
Persons found guilty							
Males aged:							
Under 14	1,503	1,425	1,622	1,598	1,522	1,560	1,467
14 and under 17	2,044	2,535	3,199	3,489	3,735	4,252	4,484
17 and under 21	1,164	2,275	2,944	3,496	4,092	4,721	5,102
21 and under 30	938	1,377	1,867	1,990	2,181	2,322	2,420
30 and over	301	300	385	432	480	487	532
All ages	645	818	1,039	1,141	1,248	1,349	1,423
Females aged:							
Under 14	119	142	194	191	187	188	177
14 and under 17	195	310	516	488	501	516	557
17 and under 21	160	265	318	381	456	469	544
21 and under 30	104	152	209	250	296	299	324
30 and over	55	72	93	102	115	115	121
All ages	79	111	150	165	185	187	201
Persons cautioned by the police							
Males aged:							
Under 14	376[4]	560	841	974	1,282	1,302	1,494
14 and under 17	262	410	627	757	1,101	1,188	1,422
17 and under 21	56	133	166	197	227	232	242
21 and under 30	22	37	44	48	25	55	56
30 and over	10	10	14	15		17	18
All ages	68	104	120	139	185	192	221
Females aged:							
Under 14	47[4]	95	187	209	275	276	350
14 and under 17	38	89	198	203	293	296	364
17 and under 21	16	22	26	28	38	39	41
21 and under 30	9	12	16	17	17	19	23
30 and over	5	6	11	15		17	18
All ages	12	21	33	37	47	48	57

Table 3. Indictable offences: age groups and types of offence, 1970

	England and Wales					
	Age groups					
	All ages	Under 14	14 and under 17	17 and under 21	21 and under 30	30 and over
Number found guilty of indictable offences						
All persons	322,898	23,885	50,512	76,926	86,504	85,071
Females	42,681	2,461	5,356	7,284	10,078	17,502
Males	280,217	21,424	45,156	69,642	76,426	67,569
Percentage of males found guilty of						
Murder or manslaughter	0·1	—	—	0·1	0·1	0·2
Wounding or assault	7·6	1·3	5·1	8·5	9·5	8·2
Other offences of violence	0·2	0·1	—	0·2	0·3	0·3
Sexual offences	2·4	0·7	1·6	1·7	2·2	4·2
Burglary or robbery	24·5	44·6	35·8	26·1	21·3	12·6
Theft or unauthorized taking	51·2	45·4	50·0	53·3	49·7	53·0
Handling of stolen goods	7·2	5·8	5·6	5·4	7·8	10·1
Fraud	3·7	0·4	0·7	2·4	5·2	6·6
Other indictable offences	3·1	1·7	1·2	2·3	3·9	4·8
All indictable offences	100·0	100·0	100·0	100·0	100·0	100·0

Note. The 1969 and 1970 figures are not comparable with those for earlier years because the method of classifying offences has been changed. From *Social Trends*, HMSO.

UNIT 11

 WRITING

Critical

Advice on writing an essay requiring an evaluation of a book, a play, a film or a television programme.

 READING AND UNDERSTANDING

Advertisements

Analyses of some examples of the language used in advertisements.

 READING LIST

Some books dealing with advertising.

 VOCABULARY

A look at some words used in the advertisement 'Army Officer'.

 LANGUAGE

Setting Out Letters

Advice on the correct way to set out letters.

 SPELLING

Forming Plurals

The different ways in which the plural of nouns can be formed

---

 WRITING

Critical

One kind of essay assignment is the following: 'Write a critical account of a book you have read or a play, film or television programme you have seen that has impressed you. Say why you found it impressive.'

You may feel critical writing is best left to the experts —the academics, the Sunday newspaper or radio critics. If you start out with that idea you are making your task unnecessarily difficult. Listen to a radio interviewer on a magazine programme talking to a writer or ask yourself the questions the newspaper critic has posed himself about a book. It is easier than you think! Besides, much of the work you have done so far in the 'Reading and Understanding' sections of this course has been critical in a sense. You have looked carefully at a number of stories and extracts; you have examined them for their effectiveness; you have come to some conclusions about them as a result of this examination. This is what the critical process is: close analysis followed by evaluation.

An essay which requires you to take a critical approach will expect you to be able to go through this process.

Of course unless you know a book, film, play or television programme well and can refer to it confidently and constantly, this is the kind of assignment you should avoid. It is no good talking vaguely about the book, etc. You must know it through and through. On the other hand, if you do remember a book, film, play or television programme in detail, then this would be a useful assignment to consider as you will have the necessary facts on which to base your essay. The problem will be how to organize your material and to make sure that you ask the right questions about the work you are studying. The following are points that you should bear in mind and consider, although not all of them will necessarily be relevant to the particular book or film you are writing about.

1. General introduction. Some kind of lead-in to the work is usually helpful. This may tell how you first encountered it. It may describe the general type to which it belongs, e.g. a documentary or a western. It may be an account of the general atmosphere or background against which the work is set.

2. The plot and theme. A brief account of what happens

in the work is useful. This should be not just a retelling of the story but also an indication of the theme. You should consider questions like this: Why did the author write it? What point was he trying to make? What individual point of view comes across? Be careful not to spend too long on relating the plot. One paragraph is quite enough.

3. Characters. Part of your essay could be spent discussing the characters. Are they realistic and convincing? Are they sympathetic or alienating? Are they cynical or sentimental? Are only some characters convincing and the rest shadowy? You might comment particularly on the main character—the one from whose point of view you are meant to see the events of the story—and the relationship of the author to this character. Is the author objective? Does he want you to sympathize with this character? Is he poking fun at him? Is the character a symbol through whom the author can express his own views? If you can quote incidents or phrases from the work to support your opinion, so much the better.

4. Style. Where possible, you should comment on the style of the work, on what gives it its special atmosphere. Is it fast-moving and exciting? Is it contemplative and philosophical? Is it bitter and ironic? What makes it recognizably the work of the person who made it? What makes a Graham Greene novel, a Ken Russell television programme, a John Osborne play or a Hitchcock film immediately recognizable and distinguishable from any other?

5. Audience aimed at and intention behind the work. You may wish to specify the kind of people who would particularly enjoy the work; and this may involve an analysis of why the artist created it. Is it meant simply as entertainment? Is it meant to move or excite? Is it propaganda intended to persuade you towards a particular point of view? There is no good in criticizing a piece of entertainment for not inculcating a moral sense if the latter was no part of the creator's intention. Only when you have worked out why the writer wrote the book can you determine whether it is any good or not, and then you should consider whether it is good of its kind. A serious philosophical novel is quite different from an escapist western, but both can be good of their kind.

6. Personal comment. There is a place in an essay of this kind for your personal opinion. State clearly and honestly how the work affected you. It is possible to enjoy something which you know to be rather mediocre, and it is possible to be left cold by something which is critically held to be of great worth. So long as you justify the opinion you express with well thought out reasons, there is no need to be ashamed of the view you hold. What is not acceptable is dishonest opinions. Gushing comments that Dickens has always been your favourite author or that Shakespeare is a superb dramatist are likely to be unconvincing unless backed up by evidence which clearly comes from your own experience and not from some guide to English Literature.

Here, as an example of the kind of essay you might write, is a critical essay on John Steinbeck's novel *Of Mice and Men*. Even if you haven't read the novel, you should be able to tell whether the essay makes convincing comment or not—it might even encourage you to read it.

Remember that the essay question postulated at the beginning of this section stressed that you should write about a work that *impressed* you, and this is something that must be kept in mind throughout. Similarly, if the question asks you to write about a work that you enjoyed, then the quality of enjoyment you received from the work must be stressed throughout: make sure all your comments are directed towards this.

Of Mice and Men
John Steinbeck's short novel *Of Mice and Men* is a work that impressed me very much when I read it. Its very shortness (it is less than a hundred pages in my edition), the simplicity of its style, and the economy of its story-telling only increase its impressiveness.

The novel concerns the relationship between two men. Lennie is a giant of a man with the mind of a child; George is thin and wiry, shrewd and capable. What holds them together is love—although George would probably never admit this. They try to scrape a living as ranch-hands, forced to move from place to place because Lennie gets them into trouble by causing accidents through not knowing his own strength. It is only George's quick tongue and a hurried departure that keep them out of danger.

The climax of the novel comes when Lennie, who likes feeling silky things, strokes the dress of Curley's wife. She misunderstands his motives, panics and causes Lennie to panic: he breaks her neck. A man-hunt is set up, but George is able to find Lennie first and shoots him—not out of disgust, but out of compassion for his friend who doesn't know what he has done and who would suffer a worse fate at the hands of the enraged ranch-men. It is like killing a pet who is in pain—an incident that occurs earlier in the novel—a blessed release.

What is particularly impressive about the novel is the way the relationship between the two men is built up and the sympathy that is called forth for them. They dream of one day having their own farm where they would be their own bosses and where Lennie would have rabbits that he could stroke and look after to his heart's content. And while they dream, we somehow know that it will never come true. George could have built a life for himself by abandoning Lennie; he could have made something of himself. But his sense of duty and his devotion to Lennie are more important to him than any worldly success. This is not stated in any sentimental way in the novel. Steinbeck allows us to perceive it through the developing relationship between the two men. Lennie is like a child, and George looks after him with something of the devotion of a mother.

Steinbeck has a particular sympathy for the poor and the oppressed. His long novel *The Grapes of Wrath* displays a similar sympathy. George is poor—only a travelling ranch-worker—but he has a dignity too. He is aware of the responsibility of man for man, and the fact that he doesn't boast about it and seems scarcely conscious of it makes him all the more admirable. His final sacrifice—the shooting of Lennie—is the most painful action he has ever had to undertake but also the kindest. It is this awareness of the essential decency and nobility inherent in even the simplest and lowliest of men that makes *Of Mice and Men* an impressive and heart-warming experience.

This is not offered as an ideal essay for you to copy. You may have a number of criticisms to make—read it again and see. It is a competent piece of work which shows a knowledge of the novel, is written in literate English and with a reasonably organized shape, and it keeps in mind most of the time the *impressive* qualities required by the question.

Try your hand at writing an essay on the following subject:

Write an essay about a book, film, play or television programme that you have particularly enjoyed or disliked.

Remember to write down in your notebook your impressions of the books you read and the films you see. These notes could be helpful to you if you decide to write an essay of this type, and you will find that your understanding will gradually deepen. To begin with use the suggestions in this unit as a framework for your notes until you find it easy to go straight to the point.

 READING AND UNDERSTANDING

Advertisements

Advertisements make their appeal in a large number of ways. Some use sex (e.g. the use of a scantily dressed girl who has nothing to do with the product being advertised). Others use fear (e.g. if you don't use X, you won't get a boy-friend); or pseudo-science (all those 'secret' ingredients); or snobbery ('only the best people use ———'); or star personalities (X uses the product, therefore it must be the best); or the desire to conform (*everybody* is using X: if you don't, you must be peculiar); or the desire to be different or exclusive (only people with discernment have discovered ———). And many others. Find advertisements which use the weapons outlined above.

Photographs and art work play a large part in the world of advertising and the appeal of advertisements to the reader. But in these units we are concerned with words, and any comprehension exercise you may have in the examination involving advertisements would concentrate on the words and the kind of manipulation inherent in the use of particular words and their associations. It is important therefore that you should be able to see how the words are being used. It is an exercise in analysis and interpretation as much as examining an extract from a novel or a story and evaluating what the writer's intention is and how he is getting it across. With advertisements, the intention is clear: to sell the product being advertised. What is interesting is to analyse the means used.

On pages 99–104 are some examples for you to study. Before reading the commentaries, try to say what exactly the words are appealing to in you as the reader and consumer, what means are being used (perhaps one of

those suggested above—sex, fear, etc.), and how the words reinforce this appeal.

A. This Girl's In Love With You
B. Spain
C. Slim Kings
D. Cancer Relief
E. Aveleda
F. Premium Bond

A. The words are arranged on the page almost like a poem which creates the right kind of lyrical mood. The advertisement is accompanied by a delicate photograph of a gentle girl's face, but even if you didn't know this, it is clear that sex is being used to sell the airline. We are told twice that the girl is in love with us. The word 'girl' appears four times in the advertisement, and this is no accident. Other aspects of the words besides the arrangement suggest poetry—the repetition, the alliteration (the use of the letter 's' to begin a large number of words), the incantatory effect of the rhythm. All of these build up a lyrical atmosphere of dream fulfilment. But have they really anything to do with flying?

B. The advertisement starts by making a number of claims—'bluer', 'clearer'. Than what? Than where? The wording of the main section of the advertisement seems to be trying to hypnotize you into accepting its claim: 'Think of your holiday ... No doubt you are already dreaming of Spain.' It is putting ideas into your head. The use of imperatives (or are they infinitives?) continues this suggestiveness: 'Toast yourself ... Plunge into the water ... Relax on beaches.' What is the implication behind the statement 'Where only the plane gets more attention than you'?

C. There is clearly a pun on the word 'long'. The suggestion that you should save these cigarettes for special occasions, for the weekend, not every day, implies that there is something special and different about them. But what are 'everyday' cigarettes?

D. This advertisement is appealing—perhaps justifiably?—through fear, our fear of the unknown, our fear of what might happen tomorrow. It is also appealing to our self-interest. If we donate today, we may get more help ourselves tomorrow if we are stricken. The phrasing 'donations from people like you' puts suggestions into our head: it implies that we already donate or intend to donate.

E. This advertisement appeals to our sense of exclusiveness. The product advertised is so good that people want to keep it to themselves, and in any case, those with good taste who have been to Portugal know about it. If you buy this wine, the implication is, you will join that exclusive band of connoisseurs. Notice again the use of imperatives ('Go' ... 'Look' ...) and the poetic touches (the broken sentence structure, the repetitions of 'almost' and 'the way').

F. This advertisement appeals to our greed, to our desire to get something for nothing (or at least a tremendous return on a very modest outlay). Notice the way the money prizes are built up to a climax. The opening headline makes the assumption that your premium bond will come up and you will win a prize. No mention is made of the great odds against this happening.

On pages 106 and 107 is an advertisement which

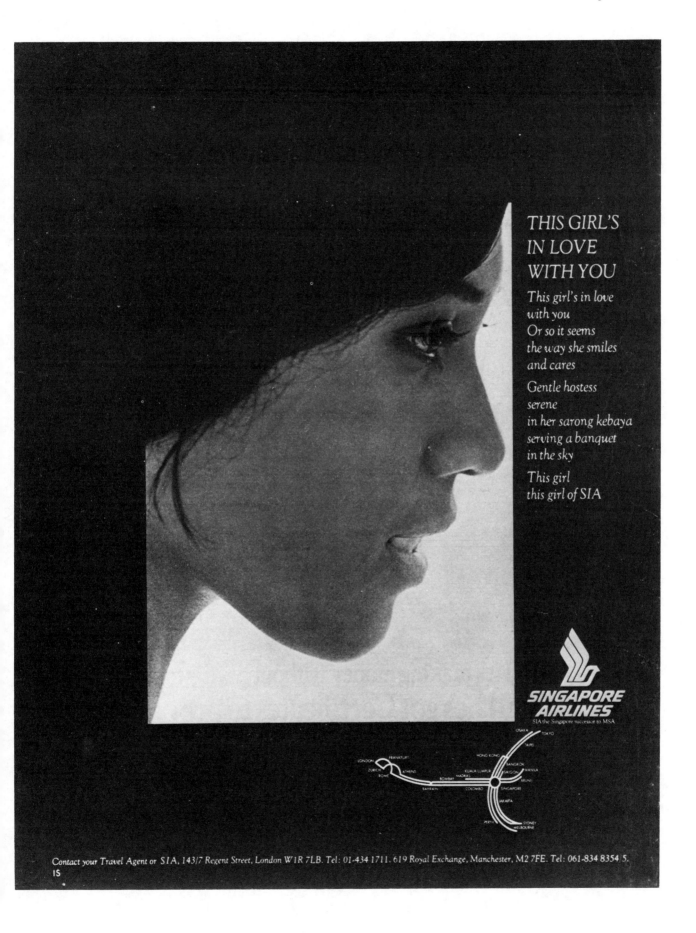

Our sky is bluer.
Our air is cleaner.
And our waters are crystal-clear.

Think of your holiday.

You want to breathe pure air. Toast yourself in the sun. Plunge into the soft, transparent water that makes bathing even more of a pleasure. Relax on beaches of softest sand, washed by crystal waters.

No doubt you are already dreaming of Spain; the land that is so generously endowed with Nature's gifts, and does so much to conserve its inheritance.

Fly to Spain by *Iberia International Airlines of Spain* where only the plane gets more attention than you.

IN SPAIN, EVERY SPANIARD IS A FRIEND.

For further information, contact your Travel Agent, Iberia Airlines or Spanish National Tourist Office, 70 Jermyn Street, London S.W.1.

Today you may be fit as a fiddle

Tomorrow...

Cancer is notoriously unpredictable. Even fit, healthy people are struck down. It affects most of us at some time by attacking a close relation or friend. Maybe you yourself are fated.

Which is why it's vital that more treatment clinics and financial help are made available. NSCR provide both – but only through donations from people like you. So don't hesitate. Send whatever you can afford by cheque or money order to: The National Society for Cancer Relief, Michael Sobell House, 30 Dorset Square, London NW1.

Cancer Relief

Why have the Portuguese kept so quiet about Aveleda?

Go anywhere in Portugal and you'll notice the local populace quietly quaffing away on a light, slightly effervescent, white wine called vinho verde.

By itself. With fish, sea-food, chicken or veal. At parties and celebrations. Almost anytime. Almost anywhere.

Look a little closer and you'll notice the vinho verde they're usually quaffing comes from the famed, old Aveleda estate, near Penafiel, in the Minho province of Northern Portugal.

Well chilled, Aveleda is considered by many to be the most refreshing drink known to man.

You can taste it for yourself. The way the tiny bubbles of the first glass hit your palate and make short work of your thirst.

The way the second icy cold glass starts turning an ordinary meal into an occasion. (And a mundane gathering into a party.)

So why have the Portuguese kept so quiet about Aveleda all these years?

Perhaps it's because there are some things which are too good to share.

Even with your friends.

Aveleda.
The world's finest vinho verde.

What will you do when your Premium Bond comes up?

Isn't there something, secretly, you've always longed to do... if you had the money?

With Premium Savings Bonds there's over £3,500,000 every month to do it with. Shared between at least 90,000 happy winners. It might be £25, or £50, or £100, or £250, or £500, or £1,000, or £5,000, or £25,000. It might even be £50,000.

And the more Premium Bonds you have...the bigger your chance of winning.

Now where else can you win prizes like that...and get your money back?

Over 90,000 prizes won every month.

consists solely of words in its published version. Study it carefully. Consider especially the logic of the statements made, the tone with which the prospective recruit is addressed, and the means used in its appeal. Write an analysis of it.

You might enjoy turning part of your notebook into an advertisement 'scrapbook'. You will only need a couple of newspaper colour supplements or glossy magazines to provide a large store. Write a few notes on each advert on the lines suggested in this unit.

READING LIST

If you want to find out more about advertising, have a look at one of the following books dealing with the subject:

Vance Packard: *The Hidden Persuaders*
John Berger: *Ways of Seeing*
John Pearson and Graham Turner: *The Persuasion Industry*
Denis Thomas: *The Visible Persuaders*
Lionel Birch: *The Advertising We Deserve?*
Ralph Glasser: *The New High Priesthood*
E. S. Turner: *The Shocking History of Advertising*
David Igilvy: *Confessions of an Advertising Man*
Edith Rudinger and Vic Kelly: *Break for Commercials*

VOCABULARY

Read the 'Army Officer' advertisement again and try to work out the meanings of the following words as used there:

idealism, participating, faction, concede, initiative, extrovert, gamut, corporation, spurred, vagrant, misconceptions.

Check the meanings of these words by looking them up in a dictionary.

Use each of these words in an interesting sentence of your own.

Follow the same pattern with any other words in this unit where you were not sure of their meaning.

LANGUAGE

Setting Out Letters

When you write a letter to a friend, it doesn't really matter how you set it out. The relationship between you would be such that each would be able to read between the lines of the other's communication. With business letters, it is rather different. If the transaction is to be carried out efficiently, then you must make sure that you say all you want to say and that you provide all the information the person to whom you are writing requires. For these

reasons, there are certain conventions in the setting out of a business letter that you should conform to. You should give your own address (usually on the top right-hand corner of the page); the address of the person or firm you are writing to (usually below your own address but on the left-hand side of the page); the date (usually directly below your address); an immediate reference in the opening sentence of your letter to previous communications (if any) to enable the addressee to identify your correspondence in files, and to the subject of your letter. It would appear something like this:

> 90, Glebe Avenue,
> Westbury Common,
> London, S.W.15.

Messrs. J. H. Watson and Co.,
55, Dundonald Road,
London, S.12.

> 21st August 1973

Dear Sirs,
    I wish to thank you for your letter of …

Note the punctuation and the capital letter for 'Sirs'. The comma after the street number is optional (indeed there is a tendency now to leave out all punctuation in addresses). The various lines of the address are often indented to the right. For a personal letter—to a relative or friend—you would not put the name and address of the person you are writing to.

The letter may be ended in a number of ways:

1. 'Yours faithfully' or 'Yours truly' if you are writing a business letter to someone you have not written to before or whom you do not know. Usually if you begin 'Dear Sir', you end 'Yours faithfully'.

2. 'Yours sincerely' if you are writing on business to someone you have written to before or whom you know reasonably well in business terms or whom you can address by name. This is the most common form found today.

3. 'Yours' or 'Yours ever' between friends.

4. 'Yours affectionately' between relations.

Note that in endings like these, the first word always has a capital letter and the second never. The phrase usually appears in the middle of the line and is followed by a comma with the writer's name on the next line.

There are, of course, many other informal ways of ending a letter, such as 'Kindest regards', 'With best wishes', 'Love from', depending on the closeness of your relationship with the person you are writing to.

The envelope should be addressed as follows:

> Messrs. J. H. Watson and Co.,
> 55, Dundonald Road,
> London, S.12.

Each line may be indented if so desired and sometimes the punctuation is omitted.

Note that if you use 'Esq.' after a name, you do not use 'Mr.' Thus, either 'Mr. John Williams' or 'John Williams, Esq.'

Write a letter to the Klondyke Travel Bureau asking them to send you their current brochure of holidays in Spain. The address is Klondyke Travel Bureau, 31,

If you're about to decide
career, we hope you've got

You're non violent.

If you're opposed to the use of violence under any circumstances, we respect your idealism. We will leave you in peace, and we genuinely hope the rest of the world will follow our example.

But if there are limits to your non-violence (catching somebody thumping your best friend, for instance) you may be our kind of man.

We are currently participating in the U.N. peace keeping effort in Cyprus. At the moment we're helping to prevent violence between the two factions on the island.

The fact that we haven't yet succeeded in doing this in Northern Ireland is tragic. But even the severest critics of our methods must concede that our purpose is to help restore peace.

In some situations a timely show of force can prevent violence breaking out. Of course, once the action starts it tends to snowball. Particularly if it is paying off. The classic case was Hitler who could have been discouraged relatively easily early on in his violent career by an adequate display of determination backed by force.

Unfortunately there are still people in the world who will use force to gain their ends. While this is so, non-violence is likely to remain an ideal rather than a practical policy.

You think Army life may be monotonous.

An Army Officer enjoys an advantage which does much to ensure him against tedium: he will rarely, if ever be obliged to do the same job in the same place for more than a couple of years.

For example, an Officer in the Infantry could spend two years serving with his battalion in Germany – during which time he could well go to Scandinavia, the Mediterranean area, or Canada on training trips. Maybe even to Singapore on an exercise.

His next job could be behind a desk on a staff assignment. After that, who knows? He might be in action trying to cool a trouble spot. He could find himself flying a helicopter. Or doing a parachute course. The range of possibilities is enormous.

And the Army isn't all Infantry.

The Artillery have some of the most interesting guns and guided missiles in the world, while the Signals have all kinds of fascinating electronic communications equipment.

The Engineers could be tackling anything from throwing a bridge over rapids to laying an air-strip under enemy fire.

The Royal Armoured Corps offers you the chance to command a wide range of technically advanced fighting vehicles, like the 600 h.p. 50 ton Chieftain tank, for example.

Every branch of the Army has its own area of interest and its own pattern of life.

We wouldn't dare to say it's impossible to be bored in the Army. But it's hard to be bored for long.

Army Officers are a lot of stuck-up hearties.

These days we have only fractionally more of them per thousand than does the nation as a whole.

This may surprise you, but we haven't insisted on these characteristics as a condition of entry for some years now.

What we do look for is a combination of energy, initiative and intelligence. We also look for signs that,

against the Army as a better reasons than these.

after training, a chap will be able to get a bunch of knowing professional soldiers permanently on his side.

With the result that most Army Officers are bright, open-minded and slightly extrovert. Much the sort of people you find running things in commerce and industry.

Their accents run the gamut from plum-in-the-mouth to Stow-on-the-Wold. All we ask is that their compatriots can understand them.

But you don't have to take our word for all this. If you're seriously worried about the kind of people you would have to live with in the Army why not meet some of them face to face.

There's no money in it.

If by 'money' you mean a quick million or two don't join the Army. Open a chain of strip clubs or something similar.

But if you'll settle for a good salary and a rewarding way of life, we can offer you both.

Among the rewards mentioned most by Army Officers are things like the variety the life offers; the adventure; the comradeship and the satisfaction that comes from doing a tough, challenging job.

In their less idealistic moments, doubtless they value the holidays that go with the job. Few civilians enjoy 42 days paid holidays a year. Neither do many get the chance to continue full-time education. In the Army you can have both plus the opportunity to travel all over the globe.

And the money itself isn't to be sneezed at. Six months after joining an Officer gets his first pip and a salary of £1,748 p.a.

If he gets to a full General he could end up pulling in £14,000.

It's a hard life – and dangerous, too.

Now this could be a serious worry.

If you're not at all keen on even the slightest whiff of danger or discomfort, head straight for a job in a large secure corporation.

When you're in the Army people throw rocks at you when you're not looking. They try to blow you up. They shoot at you. Not all the time, of course, but you have to face up to the possibility of it happening.

The chances of having to work hours that no union would tolerate and live in conditions that would be spurned by a vagrant are always on the cards.

Then again, as an Officer, you have to get involved in the personal problems of the soldiers under your command. Some of which would test the most patient social worker.

All in all, being an Army Officer is a pretty demanding way of life. It will extend you and challenge you in ways that few civilian occupations will.

If you're going to turn your back on the idea of being an Army Officer we would like to be sure that you're doing it for the right reasons rather than the wrong ones.

We've tried to clear up a few popular misconceptions here. But if you've read this far you may well have questions you would like to put to us.

If so, and you're under 29, write to Major K. S. Robson, Army Officer Entry Dept., A5, Lansdowne House, Berkeley Square, London W1X 6AA, and while you're at it, tell us about your educational qualifications and your interests.

 **Army Officer**

107

Burleigh Drive, London, S.E.23. Check that you have set out the letter correctly.

 SPELLING

Forming Plurals

The plural forms of nouns sometimes cause difficulties in spelling. Most nouns form the plural by adding 's' to the singular, e.g. dog, dogs; girl, girls; book, books.
Note the following cases where difficulties may arise:

1. Nouns ending in -ch, -s, -sh, -ss, -x form the plural by adding -es, e.g. bench, benches; bus, buses; dash, dashes; pass, passes; fox, foxes.

2. Some nouns ending in -f or -fe change this to -ves in the plural. They are: calves, halves, knives, lives, loaves, selves, (yourselves, etc.), sheaves, shelves, thieves, wives, wolves. The plural of hoof can be hoofs or hooves; scarf can be scarfs or scarves; wharf can be wharfs or wharves; staff can be staffs or staves (depending on the sense). All other nouns ending in -f or -fe just add 's', e.g. cliffs, dwarfs, roofs.

3. Nouns ending in -y preceded by a consonant change the 'y' to 'ies' in the plural, e.g. lady, ladies; family, families. Nouns ending in -y preceded by a vowel form the plural by adding 's', e.g. monkey, monkeys; valley, valleys.

4. A number of nouns form the plural by changing the vowel, e.g. foot, feet; goose, geese; louse, lice; man, men; tooth, teeth.

5. Nouns ending in -o preceded by a vowel form the plural by adding 's', e.g. cameos, radios, cuckoos. Nouns ending in -o preceded by a consonant tend to form the plural by adding '-es', e.g. cargoes, echoes, heroes, potatoes, volcanoes. But there are many exceptions, e.g. photos, pianos, solos. The plural of tempo is tempi.

6. Most compound nouns form the plural by changing or adding to the most important word, e.g. brothers-in-law, lookers-on. When 'man' or 'woman' is the first element of the compound, both elements take the plural form, e.g. men-servants, women-writers. Words like 'bucketful' add 's' to the end, e.g. bucketfuls, spoonfuls.

7. Some nouns have the same form in the singular and the plural, e.g. sheep, salmon.

8. Some nouns are almost always used in the plural, e.g. trousers, spectacles.
Note that the apostrophe is never used to form the plural, except in the case of letters as in 'There are two t's in attend'.

In your notebook make a list of plurals that conform to the various types indicated here. Check the words with the dictionary.

UNIT 12

WRITING

Revision

Halfway through the course, we look back and revise some of the points made earlier.

READING AND UNDERSTANDING

Revision

A reminder of some important points about tackling a comprehension exercise, together with some specimen questions and answers.

READING LIST

Some thrillers that you may enjoy reading.

VOCABULARY

A look at some of the words from a passage by J. B. Priestley.

LANGUAGE

Revision

Some questions to test your understanding and memory of previous 'Language' sections.

SPELLING

Foreign Plurals

Some words from other languages that don't follow the rules given in Unit 11.

ASSIGNMENT G

WRITING

Revision

Nearing the half-way stage of this course is a good point to look back at what we have been studying so far and to consolidate the advice and guidance given. We have covered a wide range of the kind of essays you may be asked to write. We have looked at character sketches, descriptive essays, argumentative essays, dialogue, dramatized scenes and stories. For each of these, specific advice has been given on the best methods of approach, but it needs to be stressed that there are a number of general points which apply to any essay you may choose to write regardless of the particular type to which it belongs. These general points have been made previously, notably in Units 1 and 2, but now that you have had actual experience of these various types, it is time to remind ourselves of what these general points are so that they are not forgotten.

1. The beginning. The opening of your essay must arouse interest. It must make the reader want to go on to read what you have to say next. Perhaps too much emphasis was put in the early units on having an opening sentence that surprised or shocked the reader. The first sentence need not in itself be exciting, but there must be something about it which makes the reader want to go on, and certainly by the end of the first paragraph you must make sure that the reader is hooked. For example, sentences like 'It was night' and 'The house was small and compact' are not in themselves very stimulating, but their very abruptness, conciseness and ordinariness could lead a reader on provided that the rest of the paragraph has material in it to engage his attention. So as an alternative to thinking of an exciting opening sentence, you could now think of establishing something in the opening paragraph which would make the reader want to read the rest of your essay.

2. The ending. Remember the kind of effect you want to leave in the reader's mind. Your final paragraph should leave the reader with a sense of fulfilment and satisfaction that what you have attempted in the body of your essay has been rounded off and completed. Your final paragraph should make the point of your essay clear and bang the nail of your argument home. But without repeating anything you have already said, of course. Alternatively, you should leave the reader thinking, either because the ending comes as a surprise or because you have introduced a new angle. Remember that if it is a surprise, it must have been prepared for in the body of your essay and must be seen on reflection to be inevitable; if it is a new idea, it must be relevant to the arguments given previously.

3. Shape. You must have the framework of your essay prepared before you start writing. You must know where you are going, and you must give the reader help (clues and indications) so that he is aware that your essay has a shape and he can see where you are going. Planning an essay before you begin and indicating to your reader the move from one point to another are both essential. If you don't do this, you run the danger of writing an essay that is formless, disjointed and difficult to follow.

4. Point. You must try to make sure that your essay has some point to it, that the subject means something to you and that you have something important to say. The reader at the end of your essay should not be left saying: 'So what? What's the point of this? Why did he bother to write it?' It is up to you to show that you are not just writing because you are required to write.

5. Relevance. Make sure that you understand the subject you choose to write about and make sure that everything you write is relevant to the subject. It is sad to have to give a low mark to a piece of competent writing because it is not relevant. The most common failing has been mentioned earlier where an essay title such as 'Storms' or 'Shipwrecks' either deals with only *one* storm or *one* shipwreck when the title is plural, or where the storms or shipwrecks don't appear until the final paragraph. As you write, keep checking back to the title and make sure that what you are writing is still relevant.

6. Interest. You must maintain the interest of the reader. An essay may be competently written in accurate English, but it can be so flat and boring that it can't possibly get a good mark. There are two elements to maintaining interest: ideas and expression. The things you have to say should be interesting, and you should express them in language that is lively and fresh. Both of these demand thought from the writer.

7. Originality. Try to be different. Don't say the obvious. This again applies to ideas and expression. Possibly the subjects given won't allow for much originality of ideas. For instance, there are only certain standard ideas that could be used in an essay on 'School Uniforms' or 'How to help old people?', but you still have the opportunity of expressing these ideas in a fresh way, and you should as far as possible try to get away from the banal statement of commonplace ideas. Remember that an examiner may have to read a large number of essays on the subject of 'School Uniforms' all saying the same thing, and so when he comes upon one which approaches the subject in an original way his heart will lift with pleasure. Care should be taken, though, not to search after originality for its own sake as there is a danger of facetiousness or silliness taking over. Keep a level head and temper originality with commonsense.

8. Choosing the right subject for you. By now, you have had a fair experience of the different types of essays likely to be asked. You should be developing a sense of which particular genre appeals to you and which you are most successful with. Choosing the right title in the examination is of vital importance. Too often, candidates who fail when they look back on the examination put the blame for their failure on the fact that they chose the wrong essay title. 'I don't know why I wrote about "Gardens",' they say, 'I didn't know anything about it. If only I'd chosen "Pop Heroes".' A calm and careful study of the titles offered, before you make your choice, is time well spent. Choose something you know about and use the awareness of your own abilities which this course should encourage to choose the type of essay you know you are good at. Assignment G at the end of this unit presents a number of titles similar to those you will be given in the examination. Spend time considering each title before choosing the one you think is most suitable for you.

Towards the end of these units, you will be given some actual examination essays to study. In the meantime, here are two examples of good writing which approximate to the kind of essay you should be trying to produce.

First, an extract from J. B. Priestley's English Journey. *This is an example of descriptive writing and might be a response to an essay title like 'The Fair', although it is of course much longer than an essay you might write in exam conditions. Study it carefully and consider its effectiveness as a description before reading the notes that follow.*

The Nottingham Goose Fair

Long before the fair itself came into view you saw its great roof of lighted sky. It had not been allowed to sprawl but was strictly confined to a large rectangular piece of ground—and within this area not an inch of room was wasted—the roundabouts and shows and stalls were laid out in rows and as close together as possible; the lights and the noise buffeted your senses—you seemed to walk into a square of blazing bedlam. Its narrow avenues were so thickly packed with people that you could only shuffle along, pressed close on every side. In this crushing mass of gaping and sweating humanity were little children, some of them hardly more than babies, who had long ago wearied of all these huge glittering toys, who were worn out by the late hour, the lights, the noise, the crowd, and either tottered along like tiny somnambulists or yawned and whimpered over their parents' shoulders. The brazen voices of the showmen, now made more hideous and gargantuan than ever by the amplifiers and loud speakers, battered our hearing, which could not pluck words out of these terrifying noises. The mechanical organs blared in batteries, so closely ranged that the ear could never detect a single tune: all it heard was the endless grinding symphony.

The real patrons of fairs of this kind are youngsters in their 'teens; and there were thousands of them pushing and cat-calling and screaming in the crowd: the boys, their faces grinning and vacant in the whirl of coloured light, sometimes looking like members of some sub-human race surging up from the interior of the earth—the girls, whose thickly powdered faces were little white masks without lines but daubed with red and black, looked like dolls out of some infernal toyshop; and the appearance of them all was fascinating and frightening. And this was Goose Fair, and Merrie England.

I climbed into the tail of a ruby and emerald fish which, after I had paid it threepence, rushed up and down

negro with a mere remnant of a face but with a golden-brown torso that wore the bloom on it of ripe fruit. The men were not boxing, they were simply hitting one another, through round after round, and every now and then the negro, who knew his job as a showman, would stagger about, clutch at the ropes, and even fall, pre-tending a last extremity. At the end of the agreed ten rounds he miraculously revived, looked fierce and made threatening gestures and then the referee, amid an uproar of excited half-wits, announced that they would fight another five rounds later, but in the meantime would come round with the hat. It was not boxing; it was not even genuine fighting—but a nasty and artful

and round and round, and mixed the whole fair into a spangled porridge. At the other end of my car, in the fish's mouth, were half a dozen adolescents, all jammed together, and at every dip the girls screamed and screamed, like slavering maenads. Now and then, high above the topmost cluster of electric lights, outlining the platform from which the diver would plunge into a tank with a surface of blazing petrol, there came a glimpse of a misty moon, mild and remote as the benedic-tion of some antique priest. I went into a boxing show, where, for the benefit of a roaring crowd, a local heavy-weight ('Hit him, Tom,' they cried to him) was battering away at one of the showman's pugs, a thick-set

mixture of slogging and acting, and an insult to any but an audience of bloodthirsty oafs. Having no opportunity of learning the negro's opinion of life, which would have been of more interest than his boxing, I left the show. Close by there were gigantic hoots and screams of laughter coming from a mysterious square building labelled 'Over the Falls'. Never had I heard such brassy bellowings. I paid my threepence, and then found myself in a heaving darkness inside. There were two or three corners to be turned, and at every turn the darkness heaved more violently, and one might have been deep in the hold of a thousand-ton ship in an Atlantic gale. It was then that I realized that the giant laughter, which I could still hear, was not coming from me or from the few others in distress in the dark there, but from a machine. Afterwards I heard several of these machines, hooting and bellowing with satanic mirth. (Probably they are quietly chuckling now, somewhere on the road or at the back of a shed.) When I was finally shot out, on a downward-moving platform, into the gaping crowd, the machine giggled thunderously and then went off into another brazen peal. Even H. G. Wells, in his earlier and wildly imaginative days, never thought of machines that would laugh for us. He can hear them now: not only laughing for us but also, I suspect, laughing at us. I continued my exploration with that laughter still hurting my ears. While circling round in that fish I had caught a glimpse of a show called 'The Ghost Train', which excited my curiosity. When I left the fish, this show had disappeared, but now I suddenly came upon it, with a queue of folk waiting to take their seats in the miniature wooden trains. At last I was given a train, which was immediately pushed through some swing doors and went plunging and bumping into the gloom beyond. It was a perilous journey. Green eyes suddenly glared at me; I rushed to collide with skeletons; hangmen's nooses brushed my forehead in the dark; dreadful screams tore the thick air; the mad little train hurled me straight at an illuminated blank wall that somehow dissolved into dark space again; so that at the end of two or three minutes I felt that I had had a terrific adventure. I should have enjoyed this piece of grim ingenuity much better if while I was waiting I had not seen two tired little children taken into one of these trains by their idiotic parents, who might have guessed that behind those swing doors there was material enough for a hundred nightmares. It is not as if the children were clamouring for these mysteries. The hour had long passed when small children clamoured for anything but home and a bed. It is not always fun being a child in Nottingham during Goose Fair.

(J. B. PRIESTLEY, *English Journey*)

It should be noted, first of all, that this is an extract from a longer work and was not written in isolation, but for the sake of this discussion, we shall regard it as being complete. The sentences and paragraphs are longer than you would be likely to use, and the author has more space at his disposal than you, but there are points that could help you in your own writing.

What is the shape of the essay?

How effective are the opening and the ending?

Comment on Priestley's use of detail and his use of words and ideas that appeal to the senses.

Comment on Priestley's use of the general and the particular.

Does the writer look at the fair with a consistent point of view, and if so, what is this point of view?

The shape of the essay takes you from the general to the particular and then back again to the general. The author shows you the fair from a distance and makes some general comments about its size, the people and its appeal in the first paragraph. In the second paragraph, he experiences particular entertainments and gives examples of the kind of thing to expect at a fair. The essay ends with a general statement. Note how the opening

sentence addresses the reader directly and takes him into the description that follows; how the second paragraph begins with 'I' which is widely used throughout this paragraph to give immediacy—the author himself experiences all of these events; how the final point of the essay is prepared in the first paragraph with the description of the little children 'worn out by the late hour, the lights, the noise, the crowd'. This final point also reinforces the author's general tone throughout the essay which is one of distaste. We generally think of a fair as being a paradise for children, but everything in the essay is directed to showing that the fair is noisy, mindless and hideous. The author's point of view comes through as one of disgust, and the details he chooses and his expression of them leave no doubt of this.

The second example is an editorial from The Guardian. *It starts from a particular incident but goes on to discuss in general terms points which you might make in an essay entitled 'Should we arm the police?' Read it carefully before considering the points raised.*

Arms and the Policeman

Robbing a bank was not a capital offence even before hanging was abolished. Robert Hart therefore paid a higher price than either he or society can have expected for his share in the Kensington bank raid. It was Mr Hart's misfortune that the gang crossed the path of an armed policeman on his way to guard the Jordanian Embassy. In the circumstances the constable had to become involved and an exchange of shots was inevitable. Anything less, and the policeman would have been failing in his duty—regardless of the fact that he was armed originally for a different purpose. He shouted a warning that he was armed before he and his first opponent each fired and fell wounded. To ask that he wait and see whether the gang intended to kill him—letting them fire first, in other words—is tantamount to expecting a voluntary martyrdom by the constable. No one has a right to expect that.

But the incident has predictably polarised opinion. One school of thought holds that the robbers got what they deserved, and that the incident shows that all policemen should be armed. The other, in deploring the killing, also deplores that any constable should be armed (particularly in a busy street). In its extreme form it teeters on the verge of implying that in some way Constable Slimon's action was unfair to armed men who should be able to go about their task without such unexpected and unpleasant shocks.

Often, of course, bank robbers and the like are allowed to go about their work comparatively unmolested. The banks place human life above money. So do we all. Therefore brave resistance by bank clerks or intervention by have-a-go citizens is now discouraged. And if the police are on the scene in time they must grapple with armed men. They are at a disadvantage in weaponry: this does at best inhibit the robber, but at worst it ends with a desperate man killing an unarmed policeman, as did Sewell in Blackpool.

The argument of those who abhor the armed policeman and therefore are shocked by the Kensington incident is greatly coloured by a legitimate fear of a wider

112

use of guns in Britain. In the United States ordinary people often carry weapons for self-defence, so great is the use of guns for attacks in the streets. But we are not as near to the American situation as is sometimes imagined. Our firearms controls, while far from ideal, are in a different world. A majority of our police still do not want to be armed. The number of indiscriminate shootings in the pursuit of criminal gain is not notably greater than before. (There is no appreciable difference, for example, between the number of shots fired at police officers in each of the years 1908–12 and the years 1963–6.)

The arming of police must continue only in special cases. Opposition MPs are already hot on the track of armed guards at embassies, but the case for such precautions is hard to contest for as long as such incidents as that at the Israeli embassy in Bangkok occur. One matter outside any direct public control, but none the less important, will be any change in the attitude of criminals. Will they be more ready to fire at any uniform in future?

Meanwhile they would do well to reflect that they deserve little mercy if they are caught. Domestic violence is still being held in check, in spite of an undermanned police force. The courts can help in this work by treating severely the proven gun-carriers. In general, as we have argued before, prison sentences should be fewer and shorter and more therapeutic. But arms offences must be an exception. This may mean an increase in the central core of long-stay violent prisoners who at large are a menace to society and in prison a problem to their keepers.

(The Guardian)

Does the editorial have a shape? Sum up the theme of each paragraph in a sentence.

Comment on the effectiveness of the use of specific examples.

Sum up the points made for and against arming the police.

Is the argument presented here convincing?

For practice, look at the following list of twenty typical essay titles. Write an opening paragraph for one of them, a closing paragraph for a second, and a paragraph outline for a third.

1. Looking after a Pet.
2. Daybreak.
3. Triumphal Procession.
4. No one should go abroad on holiday until he has explored the pleasures of his own country.
5. 'Light thickens, and the crow
   Makes wing to the rooky wood;
   Good things of day begin to droop and drowse,
   While night's black agents to their preys do rouse.'
6. Write a story that ends with the sentence: 'There was no more to be said.'
7. The Pleasures of Gardening.
8. Beauty Contests.
9. My Ambitions.
10. Friendship: what qualities do you consider are most valuable in a friend?
11. A Rolling Stone Gathers No Moss.

12. A Wood in Winter.
13. The Empty House.
14. Rain.
15. How should we deal with people who commit crimes?
16. Shipwrecked.
17. Champion the claims of the theatre *or* the cinema *or* television as a medium of entertainment and ideas.
18. The Journey.
19. The Wonders of Science.
20. Write an account of cricket *or* fishing *or* golf aimed at convincing someone who knows nothing about it that it is not a waste of time.

READING AND UNDERSTANDING

Revision

It is time we reconsidered our approach to the comprehension exercise. By now, you will have examined and tackled a number of these and should have a much clearer idea of the skills demanded. However, there are some points about the comprehension test which cannot be emphasized or repeated too often.

1. Read the passage carefully several times. Since the passage (and an understanding of the passage) is the whole point of the exercise, you must make sure that you are familiar with it before going on to answer the questions. It is only too easy to skim through a piece of writing and misunderstand it or overlook an important item that provides a clue to the whole meaning or the answer to a particular question. It generally helps to have an understanding of the passage as a whole before you go on to answer questions relating to a particular section of the passage. If the questions are well designed, they should lead you into an understanding of the passage as a whole, and you are therefore helping yourself by getting a full grasp of the piece of writing before you begin answering.

2. Make sure that you understand the question and know what information is being asked for. Look again at the points made in Unit 2 about the different types of questions that may be asked. Again, skimming through the questions can lead you to incorrect conclusions about what is being asked. Make sure you read every word of the question. Stop and ask yourself what the question is getting at. Then seek the information in the passage and check against the question.

3. Answer to the point. Give the information or point of view or explanation asked for, and then stop. Too often, candidates go rambling on and wasting time when they have already answered the question in the opening sentence of their answer.

Study the following passage carefully before trying to answer the questions. It is an extract from Mark Twain's Huckleberry Finn. *Huck has been adopted by a rich widow when his father, who had ill-treated him, arrives unexpectedly. Huck writes in his own Missouri dialect.*

I had shut the door to. Then I turned around, and there he was. I used to be scared of him all the time, he tanned me so much. I reckoned I was scared now, too; but in a minute I see I was mistaken. That is, after the first jolt, as you may say, when my breath sort of hitched—he being so unexpected; but right away after, I see I warn't scared of him worth bothering about.

He was most fifty, and he looked it. His hair was long and tangled and greasy, and hung down, and you could see his eyes shining through like he was behind vines. It was all black, no gray; so was his long, mixed-up whiskers. There warn't no colour in his face, where his face showed; it was white; not like another man's white, but a white to make a body sick, a white to make a body's flesh crawl—a tree-toad white, a fish-belly white. As for his clothes—just rags, that was all. He had one ankle resting on t'other knee; the boot on that foot was busted, and two of his toes stuck through, and he worked them now and then. His hat was laying on the floor; an old black slouch with the top caved in, like a lid.

I stood a-looking at him; he set there a-looking at me, with his chair tilted back a little. I set the candle down. I noticed the window was up; so he had clumb in by the shed. He kept a-looking me all over. By-and-by he says:

'Starchy clothes—very. You think you're a good deal of a big-bug, *don't* you?'

'Maybe I am, maybe I ain't,' I says.

'Don't you give me none o' your lip,' says he. 'You've put on considerable many frills since I been away. I'll take you down a peg before I get done with you. You're educated, too, they say; can read and write. You think you're better'n your father, now, don't you, because he can't? *I'll* take it out of you. Who told you you might meddle with such hifalut'n foolishness, hey?—who told you you could?'

'The widow. She told me.'

'The widow, hey?—and who told the widow she could put in her shovel about a thing that ain't none of her business?'

'Nobody never told her.'

'Well, I'll learn her how to meddle. And looky here—you drop that school, you hear? I'll learn people to bring up a boy to put on airs over his own father and let on to be better'n what *he* is. You lemme catch you fooling around that school again, you hear? Your mother couldn't read, and she couldn't write nuther, before she died. None of the family couldn't, before *they* died. *I* can't; and here you're a-swelling yourself up like this. I ain't the man to stand it—you hear? Say—lemme hear you read.'

I took up a book and begun something about General Washington and the wars. When I'd read about half a minute, he fetched the book a whack with his hand and knocked it across the house. He says:

'It's so. You can do it. I had my doubts when you told me. Now looky here; you stop that putting on frills. I won't have it. I'll lay for you, my smarty; and if I catch you about that school I'll tan you good. First you know you'll get religion, too. I never see such a son.'

He took up a little blue and yaller picture of some cows and a boy, and says:

'What's this?'

'It's something they give me for learning my lessons good.'

He tore it up, and says:

'I'll give you something better—I'll give you a cowhide.'

He set there a-mumbling and a-growling a minute, and then he says:

'*Ain't* you a sweet-scented dandy, though? A bed; and bedclothes; and a look'n-glass; and a piece of carpet on the floor—and your own father got to sleep with the hogs in the tanyard. I never see such a son. I bet I'll take some o' these frills out o' you before I'm done with you.'

(MARK TWAIN, *Huckleberry Finn*)

1. *How had Huck's father ill-treated him in the past?*

2. *Why was Huck afraid at first of his father?*

3. *In your own words, describe the appearance of Huck's father.*

4. *How does Huck feel about the whiteness of his father's face, and how does Mark Twain enable us to understand this?*

5. *What do we learn has happened to Huck since his father last saw him? How does Huck's father think this has changed Huck?*

6. *What reasons does Huck's father give for wanting him still to be illiterate?*

7. *What are his real reasons?*

8. *Give two reasons why Huck's father wants to hear Huck read.*

9. *In what ways are Huck's father's physical reaction to the reading and his tearing up of the picture typical of him?*

10. *Why is Huck's father resentful of Huck's new surroundings?*

11. *Is there any evidence in the passage that Huck is giving himself airs?*

12. *What do you think are the dangers in a situation where a son or daughter receives a better education than his or her parents?*

Now look at the suggested answers below and compare them with your own answers.

1. Huck's father used to beat him.

2. The reason why Huck was afraid of his father at first was because his appearance was so unexpected.

3. Huck's father looked his age which was about fifty. His hair was long, black, greasy and untidy, hanging in front of his face, and he had long unkempt whiskers. His face was pale white. His clothes were ragged and his boots were split.

4. Huck was disgusted by the whiteness of his father's face. Mark Twain tells us that it was enough to make 'a body's flesh crawl'. He also emphasizes Huck's distaste by repeating the word 'white' and by comparing the flesh to unpleasant things like a tree-toad and the belly of a fish.

5. Huck has been looked after decently by the widow and has started his education which he is following successfully. Huck's father thinks this has given him airs and made Huck feel that he is superior to his father.

6. Huck's father gives the fact that none of the family

could read as a good reason for Huck not to learn to read.

7. His real reasons for wanting Huck to remain illiterate are probably fear that he will do better in life than he has and will look down on him, and possibly his jealousy at Huck having opportunities that he never had. He probably also has an irrational hatred of education which he himself has never experienced and which he does not understand.

8. Huck's father wants to hear him read so that he can establish whether the rumours he has heard about Huck being able to read are in fact true. Another possible reason is that Huck's father is secretly proud of his son's accomplishment.

9. Huck's father is clearly a violent man. He used to beat Huck and his remarks to Huck are full of threats of violence. His violent reactions to the reading and the picture are therefore typical of him and suggest that this is the only way he can react to a situation where he is out of his depth.

10. Huck's father resents Huck's comfortable surroundings because he himself has no proper home. He says he has 'to sleep with the hogs in the tanyard'. This may be an exaggeration, but his clothing suggests it is not far from the truth.

11. It depends on what is meant by 'giving himself airs' and from whose point of view you are looking at the situation. Huck answers his father's stare steadily. His reply 'Maybe I am, maybe I ain't' could be interpreted as insolence. But generally, the impression is that Huck is merely standing up for himself, having found that he no longer fears his father, and it is the father's insecurity and jealousy of his son's good fortune that make him accuse Huck of being above himself.

12. In a situation where a son or daughter receives a better education than the parents, there is a danger that a gap will open between them. Their interests and attitudes could change and they could grow apart. The son or daughter could start to look down on the parents because of their ignorance; the parents could feel jealous of the greater opportunity their child has, or they could begin to feel that their child is giving himself airs and getting above himself. These feelings could give rise to conflict.

If you have really understood the implications of comprehension exercises, you ought to be able to do the examiner's job for him. Here is a chance for you to find out if you can. Read the following extract which is another passage from Huckleberry Finn *carefully. Then invent possible questions that might be asked about it and write the answers you would give. Remember such things as the significance of particular phrases as used by the writer, indications of character, the reaction of characters to events or remarks, questions to elucidate understanding of events and reactions.*

But by-and-by, sure enough, I caught a glimpse of fire, away through the trees. I went for it, cautious and slow. By-and-by I was close enough to have a look, and there laid a man on the ground. It most gave me the fan-tods. He had a blanket around his head, and his head was nearly in the fire. I set there behind a clump of bushes, in about six foot of him, and kept my eyes on him steady.

It was getting gray daylight, now. Pretty soon he gapped, and stretched himself, and hove off the blanket, and it was Miss Watson's Jim! I bet I was glad to see him. I says:

'Hello, Jim!' and skipped out.

He bounced up and stared at me wild. Then he drops down on his knees, and puts his hands together and says:

'Doan' hurt me—don't! I hain't ever done no harm to a ghos'. I awluz liked dead people, en done all I could for 'em. You go an git in de river agin, whah you b'longs, en doan' do nuffin to Ole Jim, 'at 'uz awluz yo' fren'.'

Well, I warn't long making him understand I warn't dead. I was ever so glad to see Jim. I warn't lonesome, now. I told him I warn't afraid of *him* telling the people where I was. I talked along, but he only set there and looked at me; never said nothing. Then I says:

'It's good daylight. Le's get breakfast. Make up your camp fire good.'

'What's de use er makin' up de camp fire to cook strawbries en sich truck? But you got a gun, hain't you? Den we kin git sumfn' better den strawbries.'

'Strawberries and such truck,' I says. 'Is that what you live on?'

'I couldn' git nuffin else,' he says.

'Why, how long you been on the island, Jim?'

'I come heah de night arter you's killed.'

'What, all that time?'

'Yes-indeedy.'

'And ain't you had nothing but that kind of rubbage to eat?'

'No, sah—nuffin' else.'

'Well, you must be most starved, ain't you?'

'I reck'n I could eat a hoss. I think I could. How long you ben on de islan'?'

'Since the night I got killed.'

'No! W'y, what has you lived on? But you got a gun? Oh, yes, you got a gun. Dat's good. Now you kill sumfn' en I'll make up de fire.'

So we went over to where the canoe was, and while he built a fire in a grassy open plane amongst the trees, I fetched meal and bacon and coffee, and coffee-pot and frying-pan, and sugar and tin cups, and the nigger was set back considerable, because he reckoned it was all done with witchcraft. I catched a good big cat-fish, too, and Jim cleaned him with his knife, and fried him.

When breakfast was ready, we lolled on the grass and eat it smoking hot; Jim laid it in with all his might, for he was most about starved. Then when we had got pretty well stuffed, we laid off and lazied.

(MARK TWAIN, *Huckleberry Finn*)

 # READING LIST

It has been said a number of times in these units that one of the best ways of improving your understanding of the written word and your ability to write in an interesting way is to read. In addition, reading should be a pleasurable activity. Many people enjoy reading novels which tell an exciting story. Here is a list of some modern novels which are thrillers and recount stories of suspense, crime and espionage. Try one of them. If you enjoy it, try another by the same author. Always try to have a book at hand for when you feel like reading. The books listed here do not have a direct bearing on the topics in the unit but you may find the list useful for reference when looking for a book to read.

Lionel Davidson: *The Night of Wenceslas*
Len Deighton: *Funeral in Berlin*
Graham Greene: *Our Man in Havana*
Patricia Highsmith: *Eleven*
Josephine Tey: *The Franchise Affair*
Raymond Chandler: *The Big Sleep*
Margery Allingham: *The Tiger in the Smoke*
A. Conan Doyle: *The Hound of the Baskervilles*
John le Carré: *The Spy Who Came in from the Cold*
George Simenon: *Maigret's First Case*
Eric Ambler: *The Mask of Dimitrios*

A reminder: you may find it helpful (and enjoyable) to write down in your notebook your comments on the books you read, as suggested in 'Writing' Unit 11.

 # VOCABULARY

Read the passage from J. B. Priestley's *English Journey* again. When examining it, we noticed that it used a large number of ideas that appealed to the senses. Bear this in mind as you try to work out the meanings of the following words as used in the passage:

> sprawl, buffeted, bedlam, gaping, tottered, somnam-bulists, brazen, gargantuan, grinding, cat-calling, infernal, spangled, slavering, maenads, benediction, artful, heaving, bellowing, satanic, clamoured.

Look these words up in a dictionary and check the meanings with your own versions.

Use each of the words in an interesting sentence of your own.

Remember to check up on any other words in this unit that were unfamiliar to you.

 # LANGUAGE
Revision

A lot of ground has been covered in the 'Language' sections so far, and it is important that you should understand the points made there and be able to put them into practice. The 'Language' section in this unit is a revision section intended to give you a chance to check up on the points made about language earlier.

Try to answer the following questions fully and accurately, and then check your answers by referring back to the appropriate section.

1. Why is a piece of writing usually divided into paragraphs?

2. How can we recognize that a new paragraph has begun?

3. What effect can a short paragraph consisting of one sentence have?

4. What is likely to be the effect if you write an essay containing only short and undeveloped paragraphs?

5. What two features should a sentence have if it is to be grammatically accurate?

6. What is required at the beginning of a sentence?

7. What kind of subject-matter could be effectively written about in a series of short sentences?

8. Long sentences would be more appropriate for what kind of writing?

9. What is the difference between single and double quotation marks?

10. What must the first spoken word always have?

11. What always follows a verb of saying which introduces or is in the middle of continuous speech?

12. Does a question mark following a spoken question come inside the quotation marks?

13. What do you do if you have to use quoted words inside speech?

14. Where do we put quotation marks when a speech lasts for more than one paragraph?

15. What is the difference between using a comma and a semicolon to divide two parts of a sentence?

16. When do we use commas and when semicolons to separate the various items of a list?

17. Under what circumstances should the colon be used?

18. When do we use the exclamation mark?

19. What is a phrase in parenthesis?

20. Under what circumstances would it be possible to use either brackets or dashes?

21. What is the effect of the prefixes on the meaning of 'retract' and 'extract'?

22. What is the effect of the prefixes on the meaning of 'transmit' and 'admit'?

23. What is the effect of the various suffixes on the meaning of 'constructive', 'construction', 'constructional', 'constructor'?

24. What is the difference between using 'Yours faithfully' and 'Yours sincerely' at the end of a business letter?

25. Which is correct: 'Dear Sir,' or 'Dear sir,'?

 # SPELLING

Foreign Plurals

The 'Spelling' section in Unit 11 dealt with the usual ways of forming the plural in English. There are, however, quite a number of fairly common words which have come into English from other languages which form their plurals according to the grammatical rules of their original languages. Perhaps the most frequently encountered is the Latin one which requires a singular ending '-is' to become '-es' in the plural, e.g. basis, bases; crisis, crises. Here is a list of the most common foreign plurals formed from Latin and Greek words. Some plurals keep their foreign forms, others are anglicized. You will see they are not consistent so you will need to become familiar with this list. The anglicized forms are marked with an asterisk *.

agendum	agenda
analysis	analyses
antenna	antennae
apparatus	apparatus, apparatuses*
appendix	appendices (medical)
	appendixes* (of a book)
automaton	automata, automatons*
axis	axes
basis	bases
chrysalis	chrysalides, chrysalises*
circus	circuses*
crisis	crises
criterion	criteria
datum	data
dogma	dogmas*
focus	foci, focuses*
formula	formulae, formulas*
fungus	fungi, funguses*
genie	genii (spirits)
genius	geniuses* (people of genius)
gymnasium	gymnasia, gymnasiums*
hippopotamus	hippopotami, hippopotamuses*
hypothesis	hypotheses
ignoramus	ignoramuses*
index	indices (mathematics)
	indexes* (of a book)
larva	larvae
medium	media, mediums*
memorandum	memoranda, memorandums*
millennium	millennia, millenniums*
nebula	nebulae
nucleus	nuclei
oasis	oases
octopus	octopuses,* octopi
phenomenon	phenomena
radius	radii
rhinoceros	rhinoceroses,* rhinocerotes
series	series
species	species
stamen	stamens*
stimulus	stimuli
stratum	strata
synthesis	syntheses
terminus	termini, terminuses*
thesis	theses

Some words from French retain the French form of the plural, e.g.

beau	beaux
bureau	bureaux, bureaus*
madame	mesdames
monsieur	messieurs
plateau	plateaux, plateaus*

From Hebrew come the following plurals:

cherub	cherubim
seraph	seraphim

When in doubt, refer to this list. Add to it any other foreign words you meet in your reading, checking the plurals in the dictionary.

 ASSIGNMENT G

Part I should take about an hour and a quarter and should be at least 500 words long; Part II should take about an hour.

Part I: Essay

These titles give you the chance of writing a description, a character sketch, a story, a dialogue, a piece of criticism, a play, or an argument. Consider them carefully before deciding on the one you will undertake. Try to choose a subject you know something about and a type which you feel you have tackled successfully before:

Write an essay on *one* of the following:
1. Write an account of a book *or* a film *or* a television programme that you have enjoyed and try to analyse what particular features gave you pleasure.
2. Write a story with the title 'On the Run'.
3. Examinations.
4. The Pen is Mightier than the Sword.
5. A True Story.
6. The Salesman.
7. A Room with a View.
8. Is there anything to look forward to when one grows old?

Part II: Comprehension

Read the following passage carefully several times before answering the questions fully in your own words.

The Children at the Wedding
I waited till the procession had gone in, and then I found that the tail of it was composed of Gus, Flora, and Archy, with their nurse. If a bachelor is worth his salt, he will make himself useful. I saw that nurse was in distress and anxious, so I stayed with her.

Archy was really as good as gold till he met with his accident. He walked up the steps with nurse as quiet as possible. But even at first I began to get anxious about Gus and Flora. They were excited. Gus wouldn't walk up the steps; but he put his two heels together, and jumped up them one at a time, and Flora walked backwards, looking at him sarcastically. At the top step but one Gus stumbled; whereupon Flora said, 'Goozlemy, goozlemy, goozlemy.'

And Gus said, 'You wait a minute, my lady, till we get into church,' after which awful speech I felt as if I was smoking in a powder magazine.

I was put into a pew with Gus, and Flora, and Archy. Nurse, in her modesty, went into the pew behind us.

I am sorry to say that these dear children, with whom I had no previous acquaintance, were very naughty. The ceremony began by Archy getting too near the edge of his hassock, falling off, pitching against the pew door, bursting it open, and flying out among the free seats, head foremost. Nurse, a nimble and dexterous woman, dashed out, and caught him up, and actually got him out of the church door before he had time to fetch his breath for a scream. Gus and Flora were left alone with me.

Flora had a great scarlet and gold church service. As soon as she opened it, she disconcerted me by saying aloud, to an imaginary female friend, 'My dear, there is going to be a collection; and I have left my purse on the piano.'

At this time, also, Gus, seeing that the business was well begun, removed to the further end of the pew, sat down on the hassock, and took from his trousers' pocket a large tin trumpet.

I broke out all over in a cold perspiration as I looked at him. He saw my distress, and putting it to his lips, puffed out his cheeks. Flora administered comfort to me. She said, 'You are looking at that foolish boy. Perhaps he won't blow it, after all. At all events, he probably won't blow it till the organ begins; and then it won't matter so much.' ...

I wish those dear children (not meaning them any harm) had been, to put it mildly, at play on the village green, that blessed day.

When I looked at Gus again, he was still on the hassock, threatening propriety with his trumpet. I hoped for the best. Flora had her prayer-book open, and was playing the piano on each side of it, with her fingers. After a time she looked up at me, and said out loud—

'I suppose you have heard that Archy's cat has kittened?'

I said, 'No.'

'Oh, yes, it has,' she said. 'Archy harnessed it to his meal cart, which turns a mill, and plays music when the wheels go round; and it ran downstairs with the cart; and we heard the music playing as it went; and it kittened in the wood-basket immediately afterwards; and Alwright says she don't wonder at it; and no more do I; and the steward's-room boy is going to drown some. But you mustn't tell Archy, because, if you do, he won't say his prayers; and if he don't say his prayers, he will—etc., etc.' Very emphatically, and in a loud tone of voice.

This was very charming. If I could only answer for Gus, and keep Flora busy, it was wildly possible that we might pull through. If I had not been a madman, I should have noticed that Gus had disappeared.

He had. And the pew door had never opened, and I was utterly unconscious. Gus had crawled up, on all fours, under the seat of the pew, until he was opposite the calves of his sister's legs, against which calves, *horresco referens*, he put his trumpet and blew a long shrill blast. Flora behaved very well and courageously. She only gave one long, wild shriek, as from a lunatic in a padded cell at Bedlam, and then, hurling her prayer-book at him, she turned round and tried to kick him in the face.

This was the culminating point of my misfortunes. After this, they behaved better ... Gus only made an impertinent remark about Flora's garters, and Flora only drew a short, but trenchant, historical parallel between Gus and Judas Iscariot.

(HENRY KINGSLEY, *Ravenshoe*)

1. What does the narrator's behaviour in the first paragraph suggest about the kind of person he is?

2. Why was he anxious from the first about Gus and Flora?

3. With what kind of look did Flora regard Gus as he walked up the steps?

4. Comment on the meaning and effectiveness of 'I felt as if I was smoking in a powder magazine'.

5. Why did the nurse sit in the pew behind the narrator and the children?

6. Describe briefly in your own words what happened to Archy in church and how the nurse dealt with the situation.

7. What effect did seeing Gus with the trumpet have on the narrator?

8. Did this worry Gus?

9. Do you think Flora's comment at this point is meant to be reassuring? Give reasons for your answer.

10. What does Flora's story about Archy's cat tell us about Archy?

11. What is the narrator's reaction to this story?

12. Comment on the sentence 'Flora behaved very well and courageously'.

13. What is the effect of the repetition of the word 'only' in the last sentence?

14. What impression do you get from the whole passage of the kind of person Flora is?

15. What elements in the children's characters, the character of the narrator and his reactions to the various catastrophes, and the setting and the occasion contribute to making this piece of writing comic?

UNIT 13

WRITING
Letters I
Business

Having looked at how to set out letters correctly in Unit 11, we now look at the appropriate way of writing business letters.

READING AND UNDERSTANDING
Tone

An examination of the importance of the author's tone in writing and how to distinguish one kind of tone from another.

READING LIST

Some comic books you may enjoy.

VOCABULARY

A look at some of the words in the passage from *Wuthering Heights*.

LANGUAGE
Agreement

Advice on the correct agreement of subjects and verbs.

SPELLING

A spelling rule about when to double consonants.

WRITING

Letters I: Business

It is common to find that the practical writing assignment in the examination requires you to write a business letter. This could be a letter asking for information, replying to an advertisement, applying for a job, ordering tickets or goods, booking a holiday or a hotel room. No great imaginative skill is needed in an assignment like this. What matters is keeping to the point, setting your letter out correctly, and maintaining the necessary formal tone.

1. Keeping to the point. Unless told otherwise, keep to the information you are given in the question. Don't elaborate it and add fanciful details of your own. If you do so, you are only wasting time and effort. This is an exercise in correctness, not of imaginative skill. Conciseness and keeping to the point are what matter.

2. Setting your letter out correctly. The 'Language'

section of Unit 11 indicated how your letter should be set out. A business letter of the kind you are likely to get in the examination would probably be to someone you are not acquainted with and whom you have not contacted before. Therefore, the way you set out your letter should be in the most business-like and formal manner possible. The correctness with which you do this is important.

3. Maintaining the necessary formal tone. Keep things on a business-like, matter-of-fact level. This is not the place for you to become personal and chatty—unless the directions of the question specifically require you to do so. Generally speaking, an assignment like this expects you to remain remote and stick to the facts, leaving out entirely any personal aspects.

The best way to give you advice on tackling this kind of exercise is to present you with some examples to study and learn from. Here are three typical examples.

Q. Write a letter to the Box Office Manager of the Royal Cambridge Theatre booking seats for a performance on a specific date.

119

A.

90, Glebe Avenue,
Westbury Common,
London, SW15 4WT.

The Box Office Manager,
The Royal Cambridge Theatre,
South Street,
London, SW1 5LB.   19th August, 1973

Dear Sir,

I should be grateful if you would send me two tickets for the performance of 'The Seagull' on the evening of Saturday 1st September. I should prefer the stalls, and I enclose a cheque for not more than £4 and a stamped addressed envelope. If no stalls are available for that performance, any other seats would do.

With thanks,
Yours faithfully,
Robert Wilson.

Q. Write a letter asking for more details in reply to an advertisement offering a car for sale.

90, Glebe Avenue,
Westbury Common,
London, SW15 4WT

Box No. 725,
Westbury Echo,
Westbury Parade,
London, SW15 3SL.   19th August, 1973.

Dear Sir,

I was interested in your advertisement in this week's issue of the 'Westbury Echo' offering a Mini Morris for sale. I should be grateful if you would send me further details such as mileage, colour, year of registration, general condition and price asked. I should also be grateful if you would let me know where and when it would be convenient to see and try out the car.

Yours faithfully,
Robert Wilson.

Q. Write a letter to a travel firm asking them to send you their current brochure of holidays, specifying a particular interest.

A.

90, Glebe Avenue,
Westbury Common,
London, SW15 4WT.

Cosmopolitan Travel, Ltd.,
19, Milton Park,
London, W.1.   19th August, 1973

Dear Sirs,

I should be grateful if you would send me a copy of your current holiday brochure. I am particularly interested in holidays in Greece involving car-hire facilities.

Yours faithfully,
Robert Wilson.

Of course, an assignment like this could be elaborated

into a series of letters and replies. Or the letter you are asked to write could be required to go into much more detail. But these three examples show the basic form. It is up to you to study the question carefully to see whether you are required to write more fully and give more detail.

For practice, write a letter to one of the following, setting it out correctly, formally and as fully as you think it requires.

1. G.C.E. Home Study Courses. Helpful 38 page guide. FREE. ABC (Dept. G.T.S. 5), Warmington House, Gravel Road, Salisbury.

2. Come Sailing. Seagull Sailing School, Quay Road, Poole, Hants. Free brochure.

3. Minutes from Monte Carlo. Delightful studio for 2 from £12 to £28 p.w. Box CA 551, The Sunday Times.

4. Any kind of furniture bought for cash. Send details to Daley Bros., 59, Wordsworth Way, Epping.

READING AND UNDERSTANDING

Tone

Tone has been mentioned a number of times already in this course without much explanation of what it means. Some students find it a difficult concept to grasp, but it is so important that it is worth devoting a whole section to it.

When we use the word tone to refer to the way a person talks, it is fairly obvious what is meant. A person can talk in a loud voice or a soft voice; his tone can be intimate or distant; it can be kind or hostile. Even dogs are able to distinguish the difference between one tone and another and respond accordingly.

Clearly, in most cases, the words a person says are related to the tone. If he is friendly, the words will be about friendly matters; if he is being hostile, the words will be wounding and angry. It is possible to deceive a dog by saying angry words in a friendly tone, to say 'You disgusting creature' as though they were loving words, for instance, but this is to employ deception. Generally, kind words demand to be said in a kind way, and angry words in an angry way. It is, in fact, the words themselves which usually determine the tone of voice.

All of these points are relevant when we come to consider the tone of a writer. The words actually being used give us the most obvious indication of the tone of voice a writer is employing. But we must also bear in mind the possibility that the writer is not being straight-forward but has an ulterior purpose behind what appears on the surface: in other words, he may be using deception for a particular purpose, and again it is the words the writer uses that will provide the clues to this.

What kind of thing, then, are we looking for when we consider the tone of voice of a writer? We want to find answers to questions like these: Is he being formal or informal? Is he sympathetic or unsympathetic towards a character he is writing about? Is he being serious or comic? Is he being emotional or restrained? Is he being cynical or sentimental? Is he talking straight or does he have his tongue in his cheek? Is he presenting the facts honestly or is he trying to persuade you to his point of view? All of these are points that we have to know if we are properly to understand what we read, and they are all points where tone is of paramount importance.

What we must do, basically, is to try to capture the tone of voice the author is using by reading the passage in the way we could imagine him reading it. It involves imaginative imitation of the way the author is talking to us, and our success or otherwise depends upon our interpretative skill and the ability of the writer to make his intentions clear. When we read a play, we try to read the speeches of the various characters with the correct dramatic intonation. The same is true of any type of writing: we must try to put ourselves in the place of the author and imagine how he would say it. The words the author uses should provide us with clues as to what his tone is.

Read the following passages carefully. Take each in turn and consider what words you would use to describe the tone of each writer. Then collect the clues from the passage that justify your description.

A. However press on, that's what I always say, which makes any conversation with me so boring. And that's exactly what I did from Athens to Corfu. By a bus as a matter of fact, which starts off at four-thirty in the morning. It was crammed with Corfiotes returning from the capital for the Easter celebrations and it is a journey I can only really recommend to travellers with strong stomachs and even stronger behinds. The route is a fabulous one and crosses several high ranges of mountains. You travel practically the length of Greece and the experience costs around two pounds. (It is just bad luck if you happen to be sitting next to a passenger inclined to bus sickness.) By the end of the journey you feel as if you had shared a deeply emotional and draining experience and know all your fellows intimately. You have joined in the rows about when and where to stop for lunch and partaken of all the sweetmeats and vegetarian delicacies that the Wise Virgins have packed in their dolly-bags, it being fast-time.

Everyone was v. kind to me because (a) I was a foreigner and (b) I looked so frail. By five o'clock in the afternoon we had dropped down into Igoumenitsa, a small seaside town from which there is a fairly frequent ferry-boat service to Corfu. Unfortunately, as the bus came to a grinding halt at the jetty we caught sight of the most recent sailing disappearing round the harbour entrance and no amount of screaming, abuse, or offers of gold would bring her back.

The bus clients, after hasty consultation, decided to take a caïque which was standing by—I imagine for just such an occurrence. Now that I know the idiosyncracies of the Greeks and the adoration of nepotism which runs through the race, I suspect that the bus driver was a cousin of the caïque driver and had timed his arrival to a split second. I didn't give a hoot myself and it was all far more romantic on the small boat. Free coffee (solid grounds as it turned out, only damp ones) was passed through the bridge window. It was indeed an 'aurea taxidi' (beautiful journey) and was accompanied by a great deal of community singing, not 'Roll out the Barrel' type of stuff but sad quiet melodious numeros which went well with the ceiling of stars, which in those parts is so studded that it is sometimes v. difficult to find a bit of black, if you know what I mean.

(PETER BULL, *It Isn't All Greek to Me*)

B. Fourscore and seven years ago our fathers brought forth upon this continent a new nation, conceived in liberty, and dedicated to the proposition that all men are created equal. Now we are engaged in a great Civil War, testing whether that nation, or any nation so conceived and dedicated, can long endure. We are met on a great battlefield of that war.

We have come to dedicate a portion of that field as a final resting place of those who gave their lives that the nation might live. It is altogether fitting that we should do this. But in a larger sense we cannot dedicate, we cannot consecrate, we cannot hallow this ground. The brave men living and dead, who struggled here, have consecrated it far above our power to add or detract. The world will little note, nor long remember what we say here, but it can never forget what they did here. It is for us, the living, rather to be dedicated here to the unfinished work they have thus so far so nobly advanced. It is rather for us to be here dedicated to the great task remaining before us, that from these honoured dead we take increased devotion to that cause for which they gave the last full measure of devotion; that we here highly resolve that the dead shall not have died in vain, that the nation shall, under God, have a new birth of freedom, and that the government of the people, by the people, and for the people, shall not perish from the earth.

(ABRAHAM LINCOLN, *The Gettysburg Address*)

C. This time, I remembered I was lying in the oak closet, and I heard distinctly the gusty wind, and the driving of the snow; I heard, also, the fir-bough repeat its teasing sound, and ascribed it to the right cause: but it annoyed me so much, that I resolved to silence it, if possible; and, I thought, I rose and endeavoured to unhasp the casement. The hook was soldered into the staple: a circumstance observed by me when awake, but forgotten. 'I must stop it, nevertheless!' I muttered, knocking my knuckles against the glass, and stretching an arm out to seize the importunate branch; instead of which, my fingers closed on the fingers of a little ice-cold hand! The intense horror of nightmare came over me: I tried to draw back my arm, but the hand clung to it, and a most melancholy voice sobbed, 'Let me in—let me in!' 'Who are you?' I asked, struggling, meanwhile, to disengage myself. 'Catherine Linton,' it replied shiveringly (why did I think of *Linton*? I had read *Earnshaw* twenty times for Linton). 'I'm come home: I'd lost my way on the moor!' As it spoke, I discerned, obscurely, a child's face looking through the window. Terror made me cruel; and, finding it useless to attempt shaking the creature off, I pulled its wrist on to the broken pane, and rubbed it to and fro till the blood ran down and soaked the bedclothes: still it wailed, 'Let me in!' and maintained its tenacious grip, almost maddening me with fear. 'How can I!' I said at length. 'Let *me* go, if you want me to let you in!' The fingers relaxed, I snatched mine through the hole, hurriedly piled the books in a pyramid against it, and stopped my ears to exclude the lamentable prayer. I seemed to keep them closed above a quarter of an hour; yet, the instant I listened again, there was the doleful cry moaning on! 'Begone!' I shouted, 'I'll never let you in, not if you beg for twenty years!' Thereat began a feeble scratching outside, and the pile of books moved as if thrust forward. I tried to jump up; but could not stir a limb; and so yelled aloud, in a frenzy of fright. To my confusion, I discovered the yell was not ideal: hasty footsteps approached my chamber door; somebody pushed it open, with a vigorous hand, and a light glimmered through the squares at the top of the bed. I sat shuddering yet, and wiping the perspiration from my forehead: the intruder appeared to hesitate, and muttered to himself. At last, he said in a half-whisper, plainly not expecting an answer, 'Is any one there?' I considered it best to confess my presence; for I knew Heathcliff's accents, and feared he might search further, if I kept quiet. With this intention, I turned and opened the panels.

(EMILY BRONTË, *Wuthering Heights*)

A. Words to describe the tone of this passage would be comic, jokey, facetious, colloquial, matey, informal, chatty.

Note the following: the short sentences; the phrases in brackets; the abbreviations; the use of (a) and (b); the use of slang ('dolly-bags', 'I didn't give a hoot', 'type of stuff'); the use of common phrases to fill in the gaps ('that's what I always say', 'if you know what I mean').

B. Words to describe the tone of this passage would be rhetorical, formal, emotional, heightened, grand, dignified.

Note the following: the use of long sentences; the emotional appeal (to 'our fathers', 'liberty', 'a great battlefield', etc.); the rhythmic effect of the prose; the repetition and build up of emotion ('we cannot dedicate, we cannot consecrate, we cannot hallow', and the last sentence); the balancing of one phrase against another ('what we say here ... what they did here', 'of the people, by the people, and for the people').

C. Words to describe the tone of this passage would be urgent, frightened, tense, emotional, passionate.

Note the following: the short phrases; the short snatches of conversation; the exclamations; the exaggeration ('not if you beg for twenty years'); the repetition ('Let me in'); the speed of the events described, happening one after another.

A passage need not consist of only one kind of tone. Lincoln's speech, for instance, builds up to a climax and

is more emotional at the end. In the extract from *Wuthering Heights*, the tone of the phrase in brackets, ('why did I think of *Linton*? I had read *Earnshaw* twenty times for Linton'), could be said to be meditative or puzzled, a moment of repose amid the excited events before the passion starts building up again to greater heights.

 # READING LIST

 # VOCABULARY

Read the extract from *Wuthering Heights* again. This novel was written in the first half of the nineteenth century and some of the words may strike us as pedantic, but note how precisely they describe particular actions and how, in a passage which has a large degree of passion about it, many of the words appeal to the senses. Indeed, this is a general point which you should always bear in mind when looking up a word. You should always consider why an author used a particular word and how it is being used. If a writer is being sentimental, for instance, he will use different kinds of words from the type he would use if he is being cynical. When a piece of writing is written is also relevant here—a nineteenth-century writer is likely to use different words or use words in a different way from a twentieth-century writer. This point becomes even more apparent in the Vocabulary section of the next unit. Give equivalents for the following words as used in the passage:

gusty, teasing, ascribed, importunate, melancholy, disengage, discerned, obscurely, tenacious, lamentable, doleful, frenzy, glimmered.

Look these words up in a dictionary and check with your versions. Use each of these words in an interesting sentence of your own. Check up on any other words used in this unit that you are not sure of.

LANGUAGE

Agreement

One of the grammatical areas of language it is important to know about is agreement. This is concerned with the relationship between a subject and its verb; they should agree, that is, they should both be singular or both be plural. In most cases this is obvious. If we are talking about men working, we realize that the noun 'men' is plural and therefore we use a plural verb—'the men are working', 'the men were working'—automatically. It would be grammatically incorrect to say 'the men is working' or 'the men was working' because in these cases the plural subject ('men') is followed by a singular verb ('is', 'was').

(The subject and verb must also be the same person. 'I', 'me', 'we', 'us' are first person; 'you' is second person; 'he', 'him', 'she', 'her' are third person, and the corresponding forms of the verb must be used, e.g. 'am' for first person; 'are' for second person; 'is' for third person.)

However, there are a number of cases where difficulty can arise.

1. Care has to be taken when using the verb 'to be' to ensure that the verb agrees with the subject. Study the following examples:

There were   fifteen apples in the basket.
plural verb   *plural subject*
The last of the dangers is in sight.
singular subject   *singular verb*
The tin   of beans is   on the shelf.
singular subject   *singular verb*
The troubles of the world are   upon him.
plural subject   *plural verb*

2. When the words 'or', 'either ... or' and 'neither ... nor' join singular nouns or pronouns, a singular verb is needed, and this verb agrees in person with the noun or pronoun nearest to it. Study the following examples:

John or Kate is going to be there.
Neither blue nor green is a suitable colour.
Neither he nor I am likely to be there.
Either he or you are mistaken.
This book or those magazines are enough to take.

3. Care must be taken when a phrase intervenes between a subject and its verb to make sure that the verb agrees with the subject. In cases like this ask yourself what the subject of the verb is and see that both are singular or both are plural. Study the following examples:

Mary with her younger sister is playing in the garden.
The flight of all planes flying to Majorca is delayed.

4. Pronouns such as 'everyone', 'everybody', 'neither', 'either' require a singular verb, e.g.

Everybody was excited by the performance.
Either is an acceptable solution.

5. In sentences containing phrases like 'one of those who', the following verb should be plural agreeing with 'who' and not singular agreeing with 'one', e.g.

He is one of those teachers who delight in taking pains.

6. Collective nouns (the name given to several persons or things of the same kind regarded as one group, e.g. flock, crowd, class, committee) can cause difficulty. Generally speaking, collective nouns are singular and are followed by singular verbs, e.g.

The class was silent.
The flock is grazing on the hillside.

But sometimes a plural verb can be justified if we think of the collective noun as referring to a number of individuals performing different actions, e.g.

The crew were busy at their various tasks.
The government are divided over their policy.

Agreement is necessary not only between subject and verb, but also between the subject and any following pronouns and possessives, e.g.

Each (singular) is entitled to his (singular) opinion.

The same care is needed with collective nouns, e.g.

The pack of wolves descends (singular) on its (singular) prey.
The jury were (plural) undecided on their (plural) verdict.

Note that 'none' can take a singular or a plural verb depending on the sense.

Here is an exercise to test whether you have grasped the points on agreement made in this section. Choose the correct word in these sentences.

1. No one in his/their right mind would agree with you.
2. Neither of the girls was/were ready in time.
3. Neither he nor I am/is/are prepared to give way.
4. The committee is/are undecided on their policy.
5. Beethoven's Choral Symphony is one of those works which inspire/inspires the human spirit.
6. Either he or I go/goes.
7. There was/were plenty of animals to look at.
8. The little boy together with his mother and aunt is/are going on holiday.
9. Mary, as well as her sister, is/are pleased with the present.
10. The management reserve/reserves the right to refuse admission.
11. Everyone did his/their homework.
12. Each must do his/their own work.
13. The town and its surroundings, with its many picturesque sights, is/are worth visiting.
14. The mob is/are pouring angrily through the city.
15. Abortion is one of those subjects that arouse/arouses much controversy.

123

 **SPELLING**

Doubling the Consonant

Here is another spelling rule. It may seem rather difficult at first, but once grasped it can often help you when you are in doubt as to whether or not to double a consonant. The rule is this: When adding -able, -ing (and other suffixes beginning with a vowel) to a word consisting of *one* syllable containing *one* vowel followed by *one* consonant, this consonant is doubled.

The word 'skip' consists of one syllable containing one vowel ('i') followed by one consonant ('p'), therefore this consonant is doubled to form the words 'skippable', 'skipping'. Similarly, 'droppable', 'dropped', 'dropping'; 'trappable', 'trapped', 'trapping'; and all other words of this type.

Words like 'droop' which has two vowels ('oo') do not double the consonant (thus, 'drooped', 'drooping').

Words like 'mind' which has two consonants ('nd') do not double the consonant (thus, 'minded', 'minding').

The rule applies to words of more than one syllable if the stress is on the last syllable consisting of *one* vowel followed by *one* consonant, e.g.

occur becomes occurred, occurring
expel becomes expelled, expelling
compel becomes compelled, compelling.

Words like 'curtail' (the last syllable contains two vowels—'ai') do not double the consonant.

Words like 'remember' (with the stress on the middle syllable) do not double the consonant.

There are a few exceptions:

'Kidnap', 'worship' and 'handicap' double the 'p' ('kidnapped', 'worshipped', 'handicapped') although the stress is not on the final syllable. 'Equip' has the form 'equipped'.

Note that in some words the stress varies from syllable to syllable, and so the doubling of the consonant varies too. Thus:

infer has the forms inferred, inference, inferable
refer has the forms referred, referring, reference, referable, referendum, referential.
prefer has the forms preferred, preference, preferable, preferential.

Note also that words ending in a vowel + a single 'l' double the 'l' before adding the suffix whether the final syllable is stressed or not, e.g. travel, travelling; signal, signalled; quarrel, quarrelling. The only exception is the word 'parallel' which retains a single 'l', e.g. paralleled, parallelogram.

Here is an exercise to test your grasp of this rule. Supply the correct spelling and check your answers with the rules above and in your dictionary.

1. You won't find me (stoop + ing) to such a low level.
2. You have not yet (fulfil + ed) all the requirements.
3. Do you have a (propel + ing) pencil?
4. What an unexpected (occur + ence).
5. Who has the (star + ing) role in the film?
6. What are you (stare + ing) at?
7. Don't shoot the (refer + ee).
8. Stop (hit + ing) that defenceless creature.
9. She wore a closely (fit + ing) dress.
10. Do you think the atom bomb is a (deter + ent)?
11. Can you lend me an ink (blot + er)?
12. The boy (lop + ed) the heads off the flowers.
13. She (step + ed) into a puddle.
14. They (confer + ed) in secret.
15. Are you (plan + ing) a holiday this year?

UNIT 14

WRITING

Letters 11
Personal

Following the advice on business letters in Unit 13, this section deals with how to write a personal letter.

READING AND UNDERSTANDING

Irony

An examination of irony so that you can distinguish this type of tone.

READING LIST

Some satiric novels that use irony.

VOCABULARY

A look at some of the words used in the extract from *Gulliver's Travels*.

LANGUAGE

An examination with examples of various types of writing—the colloquial, journalese, commercialese, purple prose, Johnsonese.

SPELLING

Another spelling rule to help you decide whether there should be a single or a double consonant.

ASSIGNMENT H

WRITING

Letters II: Personal

You could be asked to write a personal letter as a practical or an imaginative writing assignment.

A Practical Writing Assignment: Example

Write a letter in reply to an advertisement offering to exchange holiday houses. Ask for further details of the house offered and give details of your own house and the holiday facilities in your area.

This is a kind of business letter, but it also involves much more personal detail than the examples given in Unit 13. It requires some imaginative skill but basically it is concerned with the arrangement of the details in a logical, fluent and comprehensive manner within the letter. This makes it a practical rather than an imaginative question.

An Imaginative Writing Assignment: Examples

1. Write a letter to a friend giving your impressions of a new town or country you have visited.
2. Imagine you are a soldier at the front line. Write a letter home to your wife or parents.
3. You are working away from your home town. Write a reassuring reply to an anxious letter from one of your relatives, describing how you are getting on.

Essays like these require considerable imaginative skill on your part. The first is really a descriptive essay in letter form; the other two require you to put yourself into the situation of someone else and write sympathetically about that situation: they demand that you impersonate imaginatively that person and understand his thoughts and feelings.

125

Letters like these are organized very much like ordinary imaginative essays with the same kind of care devoted to gathering ideas and arranging them in the most suitable form. Possibly the opening and ending of a letter would have to be more gradual and less dramatic. You would have to lead into the subject of the letter more gradually or more obviously. But you must keep to the subject. In example 1, everything in your letter should be about a new town or country you have visited; 2 should deal completely with your situation and feelings at the front; 3 should describe your new situation reassuringly all the time. This is the respect where a letter like this would differ from a personal letter you might actually write to a friend or relation. A real letter would be much more disjointed and bitty, giving information about things that have happened more or less as they occur to you, not in any specific order and not usually confined to one particular theme. An examination letter where you are required to stick firmly to one subject is therefore in danger of appearing stilted and unnatural. You must be aware of this danger and take steps to overcome it. While keeping firmly to the subject, you must also make it appear natural.

Tone is also important here. You must adopt a tone appropriate to the matter you are writing about and the person you are writing to. If you are asked to write a letter to a wife or husband, or a parent, then the tone should be intimate. If you are asked to write a letter to a friend, then the tone should be reasonably informal and personal. This adoption of the right kind of tone will naturally affect the kind of words you use and the way you write about the subject set.

As suggested earlier, real letters do not follow the requirements of an examination, and it is therefore difficult to give examples of the way a question like this should be answered. However, here are two examples of actual letters which confine themselves to one particular topic in the way that an examination question would require.

The first example is a letter by the eighteenth-century poet William Cowper, giving an eye-witness account of a fox hunt. To our minds, the language may appear rather stilted, but the personal experience and the personal reaction come through vividly. What is Cowper's attitude towards the killing of the fox? Is the ending ironic? (You may be able to answer the second question more easily after studying the 'Reading and Understanding' section.)

To Lady Hesketh

The Lodge, March 3, 1788

One day last week, Mrs Unwin and I, having taken our morning walk and returning homeward through the wilderness, met the Throckmortons. A minute after we had met them, we heard the cry of the hounds at no great distance, and mounting the broad stump of an elm which had been felled, and by the aid of which we were enabled to look over the wall, we saw them. They were all at that time in our orchard: presently we heard a terrier, belonging to Mrs Throckmorton, which you may remember by the name of Fury, yelping with much vehemence, and saw her running through the thickets within a few yards of us at her utmost speed, as if in pursuit of something which we doubted not was the fox. Before we could reach the other end of the wilderness, the hounds entered also; and when we arrived at the gate which opens into the grove, there we found the whole weary cavalcade assembled. The huntsman dismounting, begged leave to follow his hounds on foot, for he was sure, he said, that they had killed him—a conclusion which I suppose he drew from their profound silence. He was accordingly admitted, and with a sagacity that would not have dishonoured the best hound in the world, pursuing precisely the same track which the fox and dogs had taken, though he had never had a glimpse of either after their first entrance through the rails, arrived where he found the slaughtered prey. He soon produced dead reynard, and rejoined us in the grove with all his dogs about him. Having an opportunity to see a ceremony, which I was pretty sure would never fall in my way again, I determined to stay and to notice all that passed with the most minute attention. The huntsman having by the aid of a pitchfork lodged reynard on the arm of an elm, at the height of about nine feet from the ground, there left him for a considerable time. The gentlemen sat on their horses contemplating the fox, for which they had toiled so hard; and the hounds assembled at the foot of the tree, with faces not less expressive of the most rational delight, contemplated the same object. The huntsman remounted, cut off a foot, and threw it to the hounds—one of them swallowed it whole like a bolus. He then once more alighted, and drawing down the fox by the hinder legs, desired the people, who were by this time rather numerous, to open a lane for him to the right and left. He was instantly obeyed, when, throwing the fox to the distance of some yards, and screaming like a fiend, 'tear him to pieces,' at least six times repeatedly, he consigned him over absolutely to the pack, who in a few minutes devoured him completely. Thus, my dear, as Virgil says, what none of the gods could have ventured to promise me, time itself, pursuing its accustomed course, has of its own accord presented me with. I have been in at the death of a fox, and you now know as much of the matter as I, who am as well informed as any sportsman in England.

Yours,
W.C.

The second example is an account by the Earl of Rosebery of his friend Sir Frank Lockwood. From the point of view of the examination letter, note the way the subject is introduced, the way the material is organized, and the natural way the final paragraph leads to an effective conclusion.

To Augustine Birrell

My dear Birrell,

You ask me to write something about Frank Lockwood. It is a labour of love, the more hopeless a task it seems, to convey to those who did not know him what he was to his friends and to society at large. For his position reminds me faintly of that which was occupied by George Selwyn in the last century, who seems to have possessed a fascination, different perhaps in kind, but alike in effect.

What, then, constituted Lockwood's charm? I believe it to be impossible to express this in words, but one may at least touch on one or two obvious points.

In the first place he was a splendid specimen of humanity, and humanity loves to see itself well embodied. His tall, powerful frame, his fine head crowned with picturesque, premature white hair, his handsome, healthy face, with its sunshine of genial, not vapid, good-nature, made him notable everywhere. So powerful was his personality that his entrance into a room seemed to change the whole complexion of the company, and I often fancied that he could dispel a London fog by his presence.

Secondly, his humour, whether in conversation or in caricature, was signal and memorable, for it was as spontaneous and exuberant, though not so brilliant, as Sydney Smith's. Whether any record can give the least idea of it seems to me more than doubtful. Considered apart from the circumstances of the occasion and the personality of the man, his sayings might seem little worthy of publication, and indeed, as I write, I can think of nothing of his that is really worthy of separate record. It would seem as if his reputation for humour will have to rest on his drawings and on the affidavit of his friends.

But there was this about his humour, which is probably unique—it never made him an enemy. He was too much of a man, and too successful a man, not to have had enemies (though I never came across one); but I feel confident that his humour, whether expressed in speech or in drawing, never made him one. Those whom he most loved to rally cherished him all the more. It was, indeed, the peculiarity of his pencil to delineate the humorous aspects of his intimate friends. There was probably an unconscious motive for this—that of these men he was sure they knew him and would not misunderstand him. This was his instinct: they would appreciate his motive; and to make this quite clear he would frequently associate with the sketch his own portrait, the most burlesque of all.

His sketches speak for themselves, as can be seen in the exhibition which was lately held. But even those do not explain themselves as do those of Gillray or Rowlandson or Leech or the Doyles (to cite only dead artists). To understand their charm, one must understand the appositeness, the spontaneousness, the apropos. One must put oneself in the position of a correspondent opening a letter in the welcome handwriting and finding a note summed up with an irresistible sketch; or a lawyer who has had a heavy case enlivened by a succession of droll portraits; or a colleague in the House of Commons who has seen a tedious orator reproduced on a notice paper during a prosaic speech. Frank Lockwood's sketches were the oases of serious life, and it would often need a column of letterpress to explain their full bearing and popularity.

So, too, with his jokes. Written down in black and white they are not like Sheridan's or Canning's, which make the librarian laugh as he takes down the volumes in which they are enshrined. Nor are they like those of Disraeli or Luttrell, elaborate, saturnine, desperately cynical. But then did Disraeli or Luttrell's conversation ever make anyone laugh? Lockwood's well-spring was mirth—his mirth gushed out of him and affected everyone else—it was a general enjoyment, irresistible, contageous, eminently natural. He was of the order of wit who, enjoying his joke himself, conveys at the same time his enjoyment to others. But each was possessed by this exuberant irrepressible drollery. Let me say this last capital word: Lockwood was never coarse.

But, as I said, I can give no specimens. I am writing here alone, far from England, and cannot appeal to his friends for assistance; nor would I if I could, as you want the single impression that he made on one individual. I can only appeal to all who met him as to the impression he made on them as to the quality of his humour, and (to use a dubious expression) as to his magnetism. For one instance I would appeal to those who dined on a certain occasion with Lord Burghclere, if they will ever forget the war of wits between Lockwood and Haldane and yourself. It is pitiful not to be able to quote, for I seem to give away the case, but I cannot; I can only again point to George Selwyn as some parallel to our friend, and remind you that his reputation certainly does not rest on his surviving letters and jokes.

Withal, there is something more to be said of Lockwood which could also be said of Selwyn—he was a good friend. When a man who has shown exceptional qualities of head (especially that of acute and humorous perception) displays also exceptional qualities of heart, he irresistibly attracts his fellow-men. This was the final, subtlest touch of Lockwood's fascination, for it gave the charm to his manners. His manners were the mirror of his soul: the clear pure, sympathetic mirror of a clear, pure, sympathetic soul.

But I am running on—saying nothing but what all who knew him know as well as I do, and what those who did not know him will not appreciate. He is gone, cut off in the flower of a vigorous life, in the springtide of success, in the triumph of popularity. What that means to those who loved him, only those can realize who witnessed the congregation of sorrow that assembled at the little Chelsea church to bid him farewell.

Yours sincerely,
R.

For practice, try one of the following:

1. Write a letter to a friend describing the disruption and excitement of moving to a new home.

2. Write a letter to a friend asking his or her advice on changing your job or leaving home.

3. A friend is moving into the area where you live and has asked whether you would recommend your own or your children's school. Write a letter in reply.

4. A friend is considering taking up the same job you are doing. Write a letter to him describing the advantages and disadvantages of your job.

READING AND UNDERSTANDING

Irony

In Unit 13 the importance of understanding the writer's tone was stressed—whether he is being serious or comic, casual or formal, etc. The most difficult tone to detect is irony, and it is also one of the most important since if you do not realize that a writer is being ironic you may miss the whole point of what he is saying. It is difficult to detect because irony involves the writer in saying something other than what he really means and therefore involves the reader in detective work to find out what the real meaning is.

Irony comes from a Greek word meaning 'dissimulation', that is, pretending to be what you are not. The writer hides his real meaning by saying the opposite of what he means or something different from what he means so that the underlying real meaning will be given more emphasis. For instance, if a child has made a mess of wrapping up a parcel, his father, if he is feeling ungenerous, may say, 'How neat you are with your hands.' This is irony. He says one thing but he means the opposite.

The use of irony involves a shared secret. There is no point in using irony unless it is clear to a reader or a listener that you are being ironic. Someone must be in the secret and know the real meaning. The secret might be shared between a writer and his reader at the expense of a character that is being written about. It is up to the writer to use his skill so that the irony is not too obvious but that it is not so subtle that the fact that it is actually irony is obscure. It is up to the reader to look for the clues the writer provides so that he realizes that irony is being used.

The example above—'How neat you are with your hands'—could be taken at its face value as being a compliment. Only the accompanying situation suggests that the remark is ironic. Similarly, in a piece of writing that is ironic, the general context and hints dropped by the writer will help you to decide whether he is being serious or whether he has his tongue in his cheek.

Read the following passage carefully and consider in what ways the author is being ironic or not.

Obedient to this summons there ranged themselves in front of the schoolmaster's desk, half a dozen scarecrows, out at knees and elbows, one of whom placed a torn and filthy book beneath his learned eye.

'This is the first class in English spelling and philosophy, Nickleby,' said Squeers, beckoning Nicholas to stand beside him. 'We'll get up a Latin one, and hand that over to you. Now, then, where's the first boy?'

THE FIRST CLASS IN ENGLISH SPELLING AND PHILOSOPHY.

128

'Please, sir, he's cleaning the back parlour window,' said the temporary head of the philosophical class.

'So he is, to be sure,' rejoined Squeers. 'We go upon the practical mode of teaching, Nickleby; the regular education system. C-l-e-a-n, clean, verb active, to make bright, to scour. W-i-n, win, d-e-r, der, winder, a casement. When the boy knows this out of book, he goes and does it. It's just the same principle as the use of the globes. Where's the second boy?'

'Please, sir, he's weeding the garden,' replied a small voice.

'To be sure,' said Squeers, by no means disconcerted. 'So he is. B-o-t, bot, t-i-n, tin, bottin, n-e-y, bottiney, noun substantive, a knowledge of plants. When he has learned that bottiney means a knowledge of plants, he goes and knows 'em. That's our system, Nickleby; what do you think of it?'

'It's a very useful one, at any rate,' answered Nicholas.

'I believe you,' rejoined Squeers, not remarking the emphasis of his usher. 'Third boy, what's a horse?'

'A beast, sir,' replied the boy.

'So it is,' said Squeers. 'Ain't it, Nickleby?'

'I believe there is no doubt of that, sir,' answered Nicholas.

'Of course there isn't,' said Squeers. 'A horse is a quadruped, and quadruped's Latin for beast, as everybody that's gone through the grammar, knows, or else where's the use of having grammar at all?'

'Where, indeed!' said Nicholas abstractedly.

'As you're perfect in that,' resumed Squeers, turning to the boy, 'go and look after *my* horse, and rub him down well, or I'll rub you down. The rest of the class go and draw water up, till somebody tells you to leave off, for it's washing-day tomorrow, and they want the coppers filled.'

So saying, he dismissed the first class to their experiments in practical philosophy, and eyed Nicholas with a look, half cunning and half doubtful, as if he were not altogether certain what he might think of him by this time.

'That's the way we do it, Nickleby,' he said, after a pause.

Nicholas shrugged his shoulders in a manner that was scarcely perceptible, and said he saw it was.

(CHARLES DICKENS, *Nicholas Nickleby*)

The basic question is: are we to take the author at his face value or not? What attitude are we to take towards Mr Squeers? Whose side is Nicholas on?

We first begin to doubt whether we are to take Mr Squeers seriously or not when, on learning that the first boy is cleaning the back parlour window, Mr Squeers announces that this is quite in line with his educational principles: he follows the practical mode of teaching. This doubt is immediately reinforced by Mr Squeers' inability to spell 'window'. This pattern is repeated with the spelling of 'botany'. Thus, when we come to Nicholas' comment, 'It's a very useful one, at any rate', we are ready to see the irony in the tone. Squeers takes it as a compliment, ignoring the particular emphasis of the words, whereas the reader has been alerted and is able to share the real meaning with Nicholas at the expense of Squeers. The author's comment that Squeers does not remark 'the emphasis of the usher' makes quite sure that we readers realize there is more to the words than appears on the surface. Squeers thinks that Nicholas is approving, but we know that he is extremely dubious about the benefit of such teaching methods.

The next ironic point comes in Nicholas' comment 'I believe there is no doubt of that, sir', in reply to Squeers' statement that a horse is a beast. The implication is that although it is true that a horse is a beast, there is much else in the preceding that is open to doubt, and this ironic implication is conveyed to the reader. Nicholas' comment 'Where, indeed!' appears to be agreeing with Squeers but is in fact expressive of his whole confusion at and disbelief of Squeers' teaching methods and lack of knowledge.

These clues then indicate that the author and the reader are on the same side as Nicholas watching askance Squeers' inept performance as a teacher. What Squeers says is presented with a straight face, but Nicholas' comments show that we are meant to find it comic and absurd. On the surface, Dickens seems to be presenting Squeers' performance as a perfectly legitimate example of progressive teaching methods, but the words he puts into Squeers' mouth and the way in which Nicholas reacts to the performance show that Dickens is in fact making fun of it. Dickens is using irony.

Here is an extract from Gulliver's Travels. *Read it carefully and consider the following points:*

On the surface, whose view does Swift seem to be wanting us to believe?

In reality, whose side is Swift on?

What clues are there to help us to this conclusion?

To confirm what I have now said, and further, to shew the miserable effects of a confined education, I shall here insert a passage which will hardly obtain belief. In hopes to ingratiate myself farther into his Majesty's favour, I told him of an invention discovered between three and four hundred years ago, to make a certain powder, into a heap of which the smallest spark of fire falling, would kindle the whole in a moment, although it were as big as a mountain, and make it all fly up in the air together, with a noise and agitation greater than thunder. That a proper quantity of this powder rammed into an hollow tube of brass or iron, according to its bigness, would drive a ball of iron or lead with such violence and speed, as nothing was able to sustain its force. That the largest balls, thus discharged, would not only destroy whole ranks of an army at once, but batter the strongest walls to the ground, sink down ships, with a thousand men in each, to the bottom of the sea; and when linked together by a chain, would cut through masts and rigging, divide hundreds of bodies in the middle, and lay all waste before them. That we often put this powder into large hollow balls of iron, and discharge them by an engine into some city we are besieging, which would rip up the pavements, tear the houses to pieces, burst and throw splinters on every side, dashing out the brains of all who came near. That I knew the ingredients very well, which were cheap and common; I understood the manner of compounding them, and could direct his workmen how to make those tubes of a size proportionable to all other things in his Majesty's kingdom, and the largest need not be above an hundred feet long; twenty or thirty of which tubes, charged with the proper quantity of powder and balls, would batter down the walls of the strongest town in his dominions in few hours, or destroy the whole metropolis, if ever it should pretend to dispute his absolute commands. This I humbly offered to his Majesty, as a small tribute of acknowledgment in return for so many marks that I had received of his royal favour and protection.

The king was struck with horror at the description I had given of those terrible engines, and the proposal I had made. He was amazed how so impotent and grovelling an insect as I (these were his expressions) could entertain such inhuman ideas, and in so familiar a manner, as to appear wholly unmoved at all the scenes of blood and desolation which I had painted as the common effects of those destructive machines, whereof, he said, some evil genius, enemy to mankind, must have been the first contriver. As for himself, he protested that, although few things delighted him so much as new discoveries in art or in Nature, yet he would rather lose half his kingdom than be privy to such a secret, which he commended me, as I valued my life, never to mention any more.

A strange effect of narrow principles and short views! that a prince possessed of every quality which procures veneration, love, and esteem; of strong parts, great wisdom, and profound learning, endued with admirable talents for government, and almost adored by his subjects, should, from a nice unnecessary scruple, whereof in Europe we can have no conception, let slip an opportunity put into his hands, that would have made him absolute master of the lives, the liberties, and the fortunes of his people. Neither do I say this with the least intention to detract from the many virtues of that excellent king, whose character, I am sensible, will on this account be very much lessened, in the opinion of an English reader: but I take this defect among them to have arisen from their ignorance, by not having hitherto reduced politics into a science, as the more acute wits of Europe have done.

(JONATHAN SWIFT, *Gulliver's Travels*)

Look again at the extracts from Jane Austen's Emma *in Unit 6. Can you detect irony there?*

 ## READING LIST

Irony is a weapon frequently used in satire which is a means of attacking someone or something in society by making it look ridiculous. Cartoons, for instance, are often satiric in intention. Here are some satiric novels that you may enjoy.

Jonathan Swift: *Gulliver's Travels*
Jane Austen: *Emma*

Samuel Butler: *The Way of All Flesh*
Kingsley Amis: *One Fat Englishman*
Aldous Huxley: *Brave New World*
George Orwell: *Animal Farm*
George Orwell: *Nineteen Eighty-Four*
Evelyn Waugh: *Scoop*
Evelyn Waugh: *The Loved One*
Nathanael West: *The Day of the Locusts*
Joe Heller: *Catch-22*
Michael Frayn: *The Tin Men*
Anthony Burgess: *A Clockwork Orange*

 ## VOCABULARY

Read the passage from *Gulliver's Travels* again. This book first appeared in 1726. The language is precise and the sentences are long, balanced and controlled. The way in which Swift builds up his sentences phrase by phrase, and the effect this has, is an important clue to the meaning he intends the reader to take from the passage. Try to work out the meanings of the following words as used in the extract. At least one of these words has a meaning which is less frequently found today.

ingratiate, agitation, proportionable, dominions, impotent, grovelling, desolation, principles, procures, veneration, endued, nice, scruple, conception.

Look these words up in a dictionary and check with your definitions. Use each of these words in an interesting sentence of your own.

This passage forcefully brings to our attention one of the problems facing us when reading English from previous centuries. Words do develop over time and their meanings and the way they are used can change. The word 'nice', for instance, originally meant 'precise' or 'delicate' or 'scrupulous'. For example, 'There is a nice balance between the two powers' or 'You must not be too nice about the means you use to achieve your ambitions'. This original meaning has now largely fallen into disuse, and a more general meaning such as 'pleasant' has developed. The 'Language' section in Unit 19 will consider some of these changes. Meanwhile, in a piece of older writing do not automatically assume that a word will have its modern meaning. Test this meaning in the context and if it doesn't fit, then use the context to deduce the shade of meaning being used.

Check up on any other words in this Unit that you were not sure about.

 ## LANGUAGE

Types of Writing

It should be apparent by now that writing can be of many different kinds. It can be formal, heightened, poetic, solemn, or it can be casual, chatty, racy, colloquial. It would be useful at this point to get some of the more clearly defined styles of writing more sharply into focus. For instance, the word 'colloquial' has been used a number of times already to describe a tone or approach, but do you understand clearly what the word means?

'Colloquial' describes writing where the language and style are closer to those used in speech than to those used in more formal correct writing. For instance, colloquial writing might use slang (words like 'booze' and 'fed up' that have not been fully accepted into formal English); it might use incorrect grammar; the sentences are likely to be short and may be grammatically incomplete. It is as though the writer is talking to you in a matey (itself a slang word) and informal way. Here is an example:

This pal of mine has a smashing job. He sits in an office all day with his feet up on the desk doing nothing. All day. Every day. How he gets away with it I'll never know. If I was the boss, I'd be down on him like a ton of bricks. But no one seems to pay any attention to him. He gets away with murder. Come the end of the week, there's Harry with a whopping great pay-packet for doing sweet f.a. I don't know. Some people have all the luck.

Read this passage again, picking out the slang expressions and the points where the grammar is doubtful.

Some modern writers use this style of writing (Keith Waterhouse and Alan Sillitoe, for example), and it can be very effective in making a tone realistic and immediate, and in revealing the kind of character who is speaking. But this style of writing would be out of place in a formal essay except in dialogue.

'Journalese' is another kind of writing that has been distinguished by a name. This is the kind of style used by hack journalists, full of stock reactions, hackneyed language and easy sensationalism; the journalist uses the first words that come to hand, those that have always been used, and the effect is stale and pedestrian. Here is an example:

Middleditch, the Giant Killers, have done it again. In the last minute of their game against Cock of the League Arsenal, that god-like centre Morton scored a glorious goal to keep the Amateur team in the F.A. Cup Competition. A draw was a fair result for a match in which Middleditch fought every inch of the way. Arrogant Arsenal will have to look to their laurels at the replay on Wednesday if they are not to bite the dust, and go down before this plucky do-or-die Midlands team. Morton is the man to watch. The hero of the day, he is sure to go out for even bigger and better goals next Wednesday.

Pick out the phrases which are commonplace and hackneyed. Look at the adjectives used and comment on their originality and suitability.

'Commercialese' is the name given to another style that is not recommended. It refers to that kind of language often found in letters dealing with business and commerce. It is stuffy, fulsome and over-formal, using long phrases where short ones would do, and using stilted abbreviations. Here is an example:

Your esteemed and valued order of the 19th inst. is to hand. We beg to thank you for same. Enclosed please find your order packed as per your instructions. We hope that you will favour us with your patronage again in the very near future and assure you at all times of our humble attention.

This kind of approach is less frequent than it was, but it still exists. The main trouble is that it is so verbose. It is possible to say the same thing in half the number of words and still be polite.

Rewrite the letter in half the words and in simple clear English.

Purple passages (or mandarin prose) are at the opposite extreme from 'colloquial' writing. A 'purple passage' is the name given to a piece of writing where the writer has really let himself go and is striving and straining with every trick in his armoury to be poetic, profound, eloquent, sonorous, beautiful. But usually the effect is overdone, the strain is apparent, and the language becomes overblown and exaggerated. Here is the famous description by Walter Pater of Leonardo da Vinci's painting, the Mona Lisa. Note how the writer gets carried away by his subject and how the prose becomes strongly rhythmic, approaching the kind of effect one gets from some poetry.

The presence that thus rose so strangely beside the waters, is expressive of what in the ways of a thousand years men had come to desire. Hers is the head upon which all 'the ends of the world are come', and the eyelids are a little weary. It is a beauty wrought out from within upon the flesh, the deposit, little cell by cell, of strange thoughts and fantastic reveries and exquisite passions. Set it for a moment beside one of those white Greek goddesses or beautiful women of antiquity, and how would they be troubled by this beauty, into which the soul with all its maladies has passed? All the thoughts and experiences of the world have etched and moulded there, in that which they have of power to refine and make expressive the outward form, the animalism of Greece, the lust of Rome, the reverie of the middle age with its spiritual ambition and imaginative loves, the return of the Pagan world, the sins of the Borgias. She is older than the rocks among whom she sits; like the vampire, she has been dead many times, and learned the secrets of the grave; and has been a diver in deep seas, and keeps their fallen day about her; and trafficked for strange webs with Eastern merchants: and, as Leda, was the mother of Helen of Troy, and, as Saint Anne, the mother of Mary; and all this has been to her but as the sound of lyres and flutes, and lives only in the delicacy with which it has moulded the changing lineaments, and tinged the eyelids and the hands. The fancy of a perpetual life, sweeping together ten thousand experiences, is an old one; and modern thought has conceived the idea of humanity as wrought upon by, and summing up in itself, all modes of thought and life. Certainly Lady Lisa might stand as the embodiment of the old fancy, the symbol of the modern idea.

(WALTER PATER, *The Renaissance*)

Johnsonese, also at the other extreme to 'colloquial' writing, is named after the famous eighteenth-century critic, Dr Johnson, whose dictionary was a landmark in language studies. He was a classical scholar and had a fondness for using in his writing a large number of words derived from Latin. Hence Johnsonese is a complex style that contains many Latin words and Latin grammatical constructions and long and balanced sentences. The following extract from Johnson's preface to his dictionary is not too extreme and is easier to understand than some other of his writing where the difficult words and involved constructions bewilder the reader.

When I am animated by this wish, I look with pleasure on my book, however defective, and deliver it to the world with the spirit of a man that has endeavoured well. That it will immediately become popular I have not promised to myself: a few wild blunders, and risible absurdities, from which no work of such multiplicity was ever free, may for a time furnish folly with laughter, and harden ignorance in contempt; but useful diligence will at last prevail, and there never can be wanting some who distinguish desert; who will consider that no dictionary of a living tongue ever can be perfect, since, while it is hastening to publication, some words are budding, and some falling away; that a whole life cannot be spent upon syntax and etymology, and that even a whole life would not be sufficient; that he, whose design includes whatever language can express, must often speak of what he does not understand; that a writer will sometimes be hurried by eagerness to the end, and sometimes faint with weariness under a task, which *Scaliger* compares to the labours of the anvil and the mine; that what is obvious is not always known, and what is known is not always present; that sudden fits of inadvertency will surprise vigilance, slight avocations will seduce attention, and casual eclipses of the mind will darken learning; and that the writer shall often in vain trace his memory at the moment of need, for that which yesterday he knew with intuitive readiness, and which will come uncalled into his thoughts tomorrow.

(SAMUEL JOHNSON, *Preface to the English Dictionary*)

None of these five types of writing is presented to you as a model on how to write. There are dangers inherent in trying to imitate any of them, but you should be acquainted with them. Sometimes, one of the styles may be appropriate (for instance, the colloquial if you want to be racy and realistic; Johnsonese if you want to be serious and learned), but it is probably safer to be able to recognize them in your reading and to avoid them in your own writing.

For practice, to see that you have grasped the main points of each type, write a short passage in the style of each. The best way to do this is to let yourself go and enjoy it!

SPELLING

Here is another spelling rule that may help you in moments of difficulty. As with the rule discussed in Unit 13, it may appear difficult at first, but the examples should help to make it clear. The rule is as follows:

In words of two or more syllables, a vowel pronounced long is followed by a single consonant, and a stressed vowel pronounced short is followed by a double consonant.

(As a help to pronunciation, compare the following:

The 'a' in 'car' is short; the 'a' in 'care' is long.
The 'e' in 'confer' is short; the second 'e' in 'interfere' is long.
The 'i' in 'fir' is short; the 'i' in 'fire' is long.
The 'o' in 'con' is short; the 'o' in 'cone' is long.
The 'u' in 'cur' is short; the 'u' in 'cure' is long.)

Examples of the rule are as follows:

The word 'later' is pronounced with a long 'a', therefore it has a single 't'.	The word 'latter' is pronounced with a short 'a', therefore it has a double 't'.
The word 'fury' is pronounced with a long 'u', therefore it has a single 'r'.	The word 'furry' is pronounced with a short 'u', therefore it has a double consonant.
The word 'pining' is pronounced with a long 'i', therefore it has a single consonant.	The word 'pinning' is pronounced with a short 'i', therefore it has a double consonant.
The word 'holy' is pronounced with a long 'o', therefore it has a single consonant.	The word 'holly' is pronounced with a short 'o', therefore it has a double consonant.

By learning these words and by comparing the pronunciation of doubtful words with these, you can decide whether there should be a single or a double consonant, depending on whether the vowel is long or short.

The only exceptions are the words ending in 'l' mentioned in 'Spelling', Unit 13.

Here is an exercise to test that you have understood this rule. Choose the correct word in the following sentences:

1. The diner/dinner refused to leave the restaurant.
2. The waiter is in the dining/dinning room.
3. The sun was shining/shinning brightly.
4. I wish people would stop staring/starring at me.
5. Vanessa Redgrave is staring/starring in a new film.
6. I was very confused/confussed by all his questions.
7. His head was concused/concussed in the accident.
8. He has been eating and wining/winning all night.
9. He was very wily/willy at getting his own way.
10. When she heard the joke, she let out a silly titer/titter.

ASSIGNMENT H

You should spend about an hour and a quarter on the planning and writing of Part I and about an hour on Part II.

Part I: Essay

Write a composition on *one* of the following:

1. Write a letter to a friend who has shown surprise at and be-littled your interest in football *or* gardening *or* dressmaking *or* car maintenance.
2. Write a letter to a friend whom you want to try to persuade to go on holiday with you and give suggestions as to what kind of holiday it would be.
3. Write a letter to a friend from the place you are staying at on holiday describing your impressions and reactions.
4. You are feeling depressed because of overwork *or* spring-cleaning *or* boredom with the lack of facilities in your area. Write a letter to a friend in which you let off steam.

Part II: Comprehension

Read the following passage carefully several times and answer the questions fully in your own words.

It is a truth universally acknowledged, that a single man in possession of a good fortune must be in want of a wife.

However little known the feelings or views of such a man may be on his first entering a neighbourhood, this truth is so well fixed in the minds of the surrounding families, that he is considered as the rightful property of some one or other of their daughters.

'My dear Mr Bennet,' said his lady to him one day, 'have you heard that Netherfield Park is let at last?'

Mr Bennet replied that he had not.

'But it is,' returned she; 'for Mrs Long has just been here, and she told me all about it.'

Mr Bennet made no answer.

'Do not you want to know who has taken it?' cried his wife impatiently.

'*You* want to tell me, and I have no objection to hearing it.'

This was invitation enough.

'Why, my dear, you must know, Mrs Long says that Netherfield is taken by a young man of large fortune from the north of England; that he came down on Monday in a chaise and four to see the place, and was so much delighted with it, that he agreed with Mr Morris immediately; that he is to take possession before Michaelmas, and some of his servants are to be in the house by the end of next week.'

'What is his name?'

'Bingley.'

'Is he married or single?'

'Oh! single, my dear, to be sure! A single man of large fortune; four or five thousand a year. What a fine thing for our girls!'

'How so? How can it affect them?'

'My dear Mr Bennet,' replied his wife, 'how can you be so tiresome! You must know that I am thinking of his marrying one of them.'

'Is that his design in settling here?'

'Design? Nonsense, how can you talk so! But it is very likely that he *may* fall in love with one of them, and therefore you must visit him as soon as he comes.'

'I see no occasion for that. You and the girls may go, or you may send them by themselves, which perhaps will be still better, for as you are as handsome as any of them, Mr Bingley might like you the best of the party.'

'My dear, you flatter me, I certainly *have* had my share of beauty, but I do not pretend to be anything extraordinary now. When a woman has five grown-up daughters, she ought to give over thinking of her own beauty.'

'In such cases a woman has not often much beauty to think of.'

'But, my dear, you must indeed go and see Mr Bingley when he comes into the neighbourhood.'

'It is more than I engage for, I assure you.'

'But consider your daughters. Only think what an establishment it would be for one of them. Sir William and Lady Lucas are determined to go, merely on that account, for in general, you know, they visit no new-comers. Indeed you must go, for it will be impossible for *us* to visit him if you do not.'

'You are over-scrupulous, surely. I dare say Mr Bingley will be very glad to see you; and I will send a few lines by you to assure him of my hearty consent to his marrying whichever he chooses of the girls; though I must throw in a good word for my little Lizzy.'

'I desire you will do no such thing. Lizzy is not a bit better than the others; and I am sure she is not half so handsome as Jane, nor half so good-humoured as Lydia. But you are always giving *her* the preference.'

'They have none of them much to recommend them,' replied he; 'they are all silly and ignorant, like other girls; but Lizzy has something more of quickness than her sisters.'

'Mr Bennet, how can you abuse your own children in such a way! You take delight in vexing me. You have no compassion of my poor nerves.'

'You mistake me, my dear. I have a high respect for your nerves. They are my old friends. I have heard you mention them with consideration these twenty years at least.'

'Ah! You do not know what I suffer.'

'But I hope you will get over it, and live to see many young men of four thousand a year come into the neighbourhood.'

'It will be no use to us, if twenty such should come, since you will not visit them.'

'Depend upon it, my dear, that when there are twenty, I will visit them all.'

(JANE AUSTEN, *Pride and Prejudice*)

1. Comment on the opening sentence. How appropriate is it to the dialogue that follows? Is there any irony in it?

133

2. What do the statements, 'Mr Bennet replied that he had not' and 'Mr Bennet made no answer' suggest about him and his attitude towards his wife's gossip?

3. What does 'This was invitation enough' imply, and what does it tell us about Mrs Bennet?

4. Why is the fact that Mr Bingley has a fortune 'a fine thing for our girls'?

5. What can you deduce about Mrs Bennet's views on marriage?

6. Pick out and explain four examples of irony in Mr Bennet's comments to his wife.

7. Describe as fully as you can the characters of Mr and Mrs Bennet as revealed by their speech and attitudes.

UNIT 15

 WRITING

Letters III
Opinion

The last section dealing with the writing of letters considers those expressing opinions.

 READING AND UNDERSTANDING

Summary

Although not essential for the examination, this guide on how to summarize should help in the comprehension question.

 READING LIST

Some collections of letters you may find interesting.

 VOCABULARY

A look at some words used in an editorial from *The Listener*.

 LANGUAGE

Jargon and Clichés

An examination of the words and phrases that come into these categories.

 SPELLING

How knowing prefixes and suffixes can help your spelling.

 WRITING

Letters III: Opinion

Having looked at the business letter and personal letters in previous units, we now look at letters expressing opinions in this final section dealing with the writing of letters. Readers' letters make up one of the most popular features in most newspapers and magazines. These letters may be reactions to current events, opinions expressed in articles, or burning local issues. People like to air their views.

An essay in the form of a letter is a likely alternative to a straight argumentative essay. Here are some examples of the way the assignments might be phrased:

1. Write a letter to your local newspaper complaining about the facilities for young people in your area.
2. You have been asked to give your support to a society whose aim is the abolition of blood sports. Write a letter accepting or declining, outlining the reasons for your decision.
3. You are trying to help old people in your area. Write a letter to be distributed in your town giving the reasons why help is needed and explaining how this help can best be given.
4. A recent article in a newspaper advocated the reintroduction of capital punishment. Write a letter to the editor supporting or attacking this view, giving reasons for your opinion.

From these examples it can be seen that letters expressing opinions require the same kind of thought and organization as argumentative essays. Example 1 asks for a consideration of the facilities for young people in your area. You might mention the good points and the bad points, but since it is a letter of complaint, the bad points would have to predominate. You might end with an indication of the main things that have to be done to put things right or a call for action. Example 2 requires arguments for and against blood sports, and you will have to come down finally on one side or the other. In example 3 you would have to consider the difficulties old people face and the ways in which people can help to alleviate these

135

difficulties. Example 4 calls upon you to give arguments for or against capital punishment.

Combined with the ability to organize arguments and facts, however, is the need to write a letter that is natural and convincing. There is a difference between writing an argumentative essay and writing a letter expressing an opinion, and the difference lies in the skill with which you use the letter form to express your arguments freely and naturally. The letter should not appear stilted or artificial with merely a 'Dear Sir' and a 'Yours faithfully' tacked on to an argumentative essay. A letter expressing an opinion generally requires a much more personal and forceful approach than an argumentative essay. You must see it as a kind of dramatic and imaginative exercise where you put yourself in the place of the person writing the letter and express his genuine indignation or annoyance or pleasure, whatever the uppermost emotion may be.

Some general points, some relating to letters, others to presenting arguments, are worth repeating here:

1. Set your letter out correctly. Revise the notes on setting out a letter given in 'Language' Unit 11. Remember to put your own address at the top. If you are writing to a newspaper, you should use the following form:

The Editor,
Berkshire Herald,
County Road,
Maidenhead,
Berkshire.
Dear Sir,
    I was interested in your comment....
Your letter should end 'Yours faithfully,'.

2. As suggested above, your letter should appear natural. One way of doing this is by putting it into a recognizable context. The wording of the question should help you here. If your letter is supposed to be a response to an article or a letter you have received, mention this straight away. Begin something like this:

'I was pleased to see from your editorial last Friday that you are advocating bringing back the birch....' *or* 'Thank you very much for your letter asking me to join your association....'

This kind of approach has the added advantage of getting straight down to the point.

3. Clearly keeping to the point throughout is important. Don't be tempted to add irrelevant material. Stick to the subject raised in the question and omit polite nothings about your correspondent's health or the weather.

4. Make sure the tone of your letter is correct. If it is to a newspaper editor, it should be fairly formal. If it is to a friend, it should be fairly free and personal.

5. The organization of your ideas and arguments is important. Work these out beforehand. Know the points you are going to raise before starting the actual writing of the letter. Make sure that your arguments are in the best order. Bring in as many examples and references as you can to enliven your argument.

6. As always, the ending is important. Don't trail off feebly with something like 'so you can see why I am so annoyed' or 'I therefore support capital punishment'. Make it interesting; make it powerful; make it bite.

Here is an example of a newspaper article written in the form of a letter. Consider the following points as you read it:

1. Is the opening to the point and does it put you clearly in the picture?

2. The tone is conversational and personal. Is this appropriate?

3. Is everything the author writes relevant to the subject?

4. Is the ending effective?

No Old-School Ties
Dear Hazel,

Thank you for your letter inviting me to contribute to the Roedean Development Fund. I must say I am surprised that, in the circumstances, I count as an Old Girl, but your letter certainly brought back memories. I could almost hear the school song in my ears as I read it: a song, you may remember, taken without emendation from Harrow all about the tramp of the 22 men (though I suppose if anyone *had* become the tramp of 22 men, she'd have been expelled).

The Roedean you and I were at was not, of course, typical. Evacuated to the Lake District, we were harangued by the Head from a pulpit in a Methodist chapel, forced by wartime shortages to have icicles *inside* the windows and our eiderdowns *inside* the sheets; and our formative years were spent among the Edwardian splendours of the Keswick Hotel.

A feature of this that I remember was a staircase lampstand in the form of a Negress eight feet high. My father once mortified me by slapping it on its polished flank, saying, 'Distinguished old girl, I suppose.'

The hotel's main advantage from my point of view, however, was a large relief map of the district, which enabled me to plot in some detail the route I would take when, after two years, I finally bicycled away.

The school, to do it credit, was extremely decent about this incident: it required no fees in lieu of notice and even offered to take me back—though this courtesy, as my husband points out, is also extended by H.M. Prisons. And they were a pretty good school from the teaching point of view. The trouble was that it was all at an intellectual level: contact with teachers as human beings was entirely prevented by the knowledge that you would be thought a filthy little sneak if you were seen talking to them.

I admit that a lot of what was wrong was wrong with me; I came from a different school and a different background and had the wrong green uniform of the one, the wrong pink politics of the other. I was so bad at games that they finally gave up trying to teach me; and since in every class there has to be a fat girl who cannot in any circumstances be got over the horse in one heave, the fat girl was, of course, me. And I couldn't take teasing. Looking back on it, I feel better about being teased—it gives one a cosy martyred glow—than about what inevitably followed: I became, as soon as I got half a chance, a bully myself.

At this point, Hazel, you are probably saying that I am wildly overstating it: that even one who, like myself, lost a stone a term from sheer misery must have had

"Well, that's O.K.—now for old 'Stinks'."
(from *Hurrah for St. Trinian's* 1948)

some bright moments. And of course I did. But they shed no light on the surrounding gloom, and it has taken me years to work out why: I think it was the sense of captivity. Never at any point in the 24 hours at boarding school are you free—free of the school, of the other girls' opinions, of the stiff-upper-lip ruling that prevented some girls who were just as unhappy as I was even telling their parents they were miserable. This is the poison gas of boarding schools that Gwen Raverat smells whenever she goes back to one; once smelt, never forgotten.

Still, I realize that not everyone feels like that. The reason you are not, I am afraid, going to get your cheque is not that the toughening process makes the odd girl miserable but that I can't see any point in toughening up girls like this at all. The boys' public schools (not that I hold any special brief for *them*) do make some sort of sociological sense; you take the youths at puberty away from their mothers' softening influence, you give them tough exercises to make them strong warriors and to keep their minds off sex (it says here), you give them a glorious games hierarchy to fight their way up and at the end of it they have been through an initiation. They have no doubt of their identity as British, upper-middle-class, and male. But how can you possibly apply the same tribal techniques to girls, who have the opposite things to learn.

Take, as one classic instance, the boarding school attitude to illness. One house matron is tough: no good going to her because you felt too frightful for cricket practice before breakfast. Another is more sympathetic —and the chances are she is regarded as 'soft.' Yet which are women supposed to be—good at comforting the sick, or good at spotting malingerers, like a sergeant-major?

Well, well, it's all past history now. I am sure that, back in Sussex, it is very different these days; it is years now since I woke from my commonest nightmare of dreaming I was back there. But I must confess it will be all one to me if the jolly old school, far from developing, falls off the Rottingdean cliffs into the sea.

Yours,

Katharine.

(KATHARINE WHITEHORN in *The Observer*)

Here are three examples of actual letters written to newspapers expressing opinion. Consider the points being made in each and how effectively they are made.

A. *Scottish Daily Express*

Other Lives are at Risk

Do climbers (foolhardy ones) ever give a thought to the dangers they cause the people who have to rescue them when they are in trouble through no fault of anyone but themselves?

What good do they get from this stupid pastime? I could think of a dozen ways they could occupy the time they have on their hands. They could volunteer to decorate old people's homes or tidy gardens for hands no longer supple to do these tasks.

Notices should be issued akin to weather reports, and if the rules are broken they should be liable to a fine. After all, if a motorist speeds in a built-up area he is treated as a criminal. I see no difference in these people trying to climb in severe winter weather. They are endangering innocent people's lives when they get into difficulties through their own fault.

B. *The Guardian*

Whose Responsibility?

Sir.—There is a very important fact which seems to escape the two ladies who appeal to the Chancellor to exempt children's clothes from VAT (The Guardian, February 22)—no human being is forced to reproduce, and, as one of those who takes care not to do so, I am tired of hearing from those who don't, about the cost of children's clothes. A quick look around my local shops revealed that were I five years old I could clothe myself for about half what it costs me at 25, which seems quite reasonable.

In addition to this, as a childless person I don't get the benefits of family allowances nor do I use hospital beds just to give birth; indeed, I pay more taxes in order that those with children may pay less.

I deeply regret that April 1 will be the first occasion on which these people will be forced to accept a tiny part of the financial responsibility which should be theirs entirely; and I appeal to the Chancellor to double the VAT on children's clothes in order to recoup some of the tax from which parents have been so unjustly exempt since before the war.

C. *The Observer*

Talking Suburban Posh

SIR, —Your contributor to 'Dissent' (Colour Magazine, 18 February) must surely be writing with her tongue in her cheek, since to protect dialects is to protect the living language at its very roots, as any student of linguistics could tell her.

Variety is the spice of life, yet Diana Cooper would have us reduce language to the colourless uniformity of 'Suburban-Cultural' which, presumably, she would like preserved for posterity. 'Suburban-Snob' perhaps describes more accurately the kind of 'simple English' many Southerners adopt, which capriciously shifts the stress on words and distorts vowels beyond recognition.

If Diana Cooper is anxious to preserve *good* English, as opposed to her 'simple suburban-cultural'—which is often artificial, monotonous and basically insincere (because those who 'talk posh' are, for the most part, more concerned with how they speak than with what they say)—she might campaign rather for *careful* speech. This would mean the elimination of the intrusive 'r'; the avoidance of the solecism 'between you and I,' which more and more 'posh' speakers seem to have adopted in recent years; and the restoration of the short 'o' in words like 'involve,' 'dissolve,' 'revolve,' and 'golf,' which 'Suburban-Culturals' now pronounce with a long 'o,' simply, one suspects, because they equate the use of short vowel sounds with the coarse speech of the less civilised Northerner.

The educated person who speaks correct English is not ashamed of his regional accent, takes pride in his ability to speak and understand his local dialect and is at home in any company. If 'posh talk' becomes obtrusive it has ceased to be 'good' or 'simple' English and, as the writer of the article justly remarks, has become simply another dialect. From what is she dissenting?

For practice, either write a reply to one of these letters or choose one of the examples given at the beginning of the unit.

READING AND UNDERSTANDING

Summary

A summary (or précis as it is sometimes called) is an exercise that requires you to state the main points made in a piece of writing in fewer words than the original passage. It is an exercise that demands the ability to comprehend a passage, to grasp the main things being said, and reproduce these in your own words in a compressed but fluent form. An extract may give the arguments in favour of space exploration in 500 words with examples and references. If you were asked to make a summary of this passage, you would state the arguments in favour of space exploration in about a third of the length, omitting or generalizing the examples and references.

You will not be given a formal summary or précis exercise in the examination, but a summary type question is likely to play an important part in the comprehension exercise in the examination, and some guidance in this area will be valuable. The best way of doing this is to give you a specimen example and then indicate how the answer was achieved.

Read the following passage carefully and then refer back to it as you study the notes on it.

Jargon

'Like respectability in Chicago, Jargon stalks unchecked in our midst'. Nearly fifty years have passed since Sir Arthur Quiller-Couch thundered out these words at Cambridge, when he introduced an attack on jargon into his lectures *On the Art of Writing*. Only a few years earlier H. W. Fowler and his brother had written *The King's English*. These three men were firing the first shots in a campaign still being conducted by distinguished writers and scholars to rid English prose of its burden of clumsy and meaningless phraseology. In a talk that we print today, Alistair Cooke quotes from the United States examples of the writing of jargon, which it would be all too easy to parallel in Britain. Half a century has passed since 'Q' fulminated and since then what have we 'common men' done about jargon? Very little, in spite of the strictures and encouragement of Sir Ernest Gowers, Mr Eric Partridge, Mr Ivor Brown, and others. Ministers of the Crown still 'answer in the negative'. The course at Aintree is still 'of a trying nature'. Men are still 'conveyed to their places of residence in an intoxicated condition'; and when they die the coffins provided are still 'of the usual character'.

It is difficult to know where the remedy lies. This itself is a piece of jargon meaning: what is the cure? To arm schoolmasters and editors with larger and bigger pencils, yes; and to reduce the habit of dictating letters. The number of letters and even articles which are dictated is undoubtedly a cause of jargon that is particular to the modern age. It was noticed by A. P. Rossiter in a talk he broadcast in 1952. He suggested then that the innate self-consciousness of dictation urged a man 'towards a stock impersonal idiom'. Probably the writer was tired, or depressed with routine. 'Tired minds', said Rossiter, 'talk flat whatever is in them'. So everybody should be encouraged to dictate less and write more.

But the greatest danger lies—in Britain as in the United States—in professional jargon. The language of many people today is constantly being shaped by the trade or occupation in which they spend their working lives. W. S. Gilbert was able to make something of this. As an impecunious young barrister he had discovered the legal profession to be one of the favourite nesting places for jargon. He turned the fact to good account in *Trial by Jury*:

'For today in this arena,
Summoned by a stern subpœna,
Edwin, sued by Angelina,
Shortly will appear.'

Nowadays lawyers are probably not the villains they were for darkening their prose with jargon. One has rather to look at the prefaces of most modern textbooks used by chemists or engineers to see how—apart from their necessary use of technical terms—their authors have become a prey to jargon; while the economist and the sociologist are often satirized for using it. Business men with their circumlocutions are serious offenders. But journalists have the least excuse of all. They trade in words in order to entertain and inform the public. Yet in many newspapers and journals (including no doubt our own) can be found such phrases as 'the majority of' when most is meant; and such sentences as 'the possibility of a General Election being held this autumn is not as unlikely as was thought', when the newspaper merely wanted to say that an Election this autumn was now probable.

(*The Listener*)

The first four sentences give a quotation and refer to three critics and two books about the writing of English, but if we are summarizing the main point made in this section we can generalize all of this into the following statement:

1. Fifty years have passed since the first critics spoke out against jargon—a particular type of clumsy and lifeless writing.

The next sentence brings in a modern critic. It can be summarized as:

2. But even today critics complain about its use.

The remainder of the paragraph names critics from the intervening period who have attacked the use of jargon and gives examples of jargon to show that it still exists.

3. In spite of many attacks in the interim, examples of jargon abound today.

The opening sentence of the second paragraph shows us a change in thought. It can be re-expressed as:

4. A solution to the problem is difficult to find.

Some possible ways out are given.

5. School teachers and editors should be more critical.

6. The dictating of letters should be discouraged.

The rest of the paragraph is concerned with attacking the custom of dictating letters and an explanation of why this encourages jargon.

7. The dictating of letters is a modern innovation that encourages the use of jargon.

8. The person dictating feels self-conscious and he uses impersonal hackneyed terms to cover this up.

The opening sentence of the third paragraph again gives the clue to the next point.

9. The main threat comes from 'professional jargon'—the kind of language used in particular jobs.

10. The work people do encourages a particular kind of stereotyped language.

The quotation from *Trial by Jury* is an example of the kind of jargon the writer is referring to, but it does not introduce a new point and can be omitted in a summary.

Possibly the idea behind it and suggested in the first sentence of the last paragraph can be touched on.

11. Once lawyers were among the worst offenders.

The writer then goes on to give examples of modern offenders which are difficult to generalize and which in a summary would probably have to be named.

12. Now the worst offenders are people like chemists, engineers, economists, sociologists and business men with their roundabout way of saying things.

The word 'but' again introduces a new point in the writer's argument.

13. Journalists are also guilty and have least excuse for being so.

The writer then goes on to justify this statement and give examples of journalistic jargon.

14. Their business is concerned with the proper use of words and yet many examples of clumsy circumlocutions occur in newspapers.

The finished summary would read something like this:

Fifty years have passed since the first critics spoke out against jargon—a particular type of clumsy and lifeless writing. But even today critics complain about its use. In spite of the many attacks in the interim, examples of jargon still abound today.

A solution to this problem is difficult to find. School teachers and editors should be more critical, and the dictating of letters should be discouraged. The dictating of letters is a modern innovation that encourages the use of jargon. The person dictating feels self-conscious and tries to cover up this by using impersonal hackneyed phrases.

However, the greatest threat comes from 'professional jargon'—the kind of language used in particular jobs. People are encouraged to use a stereotyped language by the particular work they do.

Once lawyers were among the worst offenders, but now people like chemists, engineers, economists, sociologists and businessmen with their roundabout way of saying things are also guilty. Journalists have the least excuse for using jargon since their work is concerned with the proper use of words, and yet many examples of circumlocutions occur in newspapers.

Through working out this exercise, some general points about making a summary emerge:

1. The best method is to make a list of the main points which can then be combined to form the final summary. Note that some adaptation of the notes has been necessary to make the final summary more fluent and to ensure that it reads better. An example is the use of the word 'however' at the beginning of the third paragraph.

2. Illustrative examples have been omitted. There is no mention of Quiller-Couch, Fowler, Alistair Cooke, etc. No actual examples of jargon are quoted from the original passage. If you have made a general statement, there is no need to give examples. The summary, for instance, states that many examples of clumsy circumlocutions occur in newspapers: there is no need to quote 'the majority of' or 'the possibility of a General Election being held this autumn is not as unlikely as was thought'.

3. Different words have been used as far as possible. Obviously, it is not possible to avoid words like 'chemists', 'engineers', 'economists' and 'sociologists' since these refer to specific professions which it is difficult to describe in any other terms. But you should not follow the phrasing of the original. You should try to translate the ideas into your own language. The point of this is to prove that you have understood the meaning of the passage. It is no good taking out a phrase here and a phrase there and putting them together to provide your summary. In my summary, I have even translated the word 'circumlocutions' as 'roundabout ways of saying things' even though it takes up more words to prove that I know what the word means.

4. The points that require to be mentioned in a summary are not necessarily evenly spaced throughout the original passage. For instance, the first paragraph of the original is the longest, but this is not reflected in the summary. Sometimes a great deal of space is taken up with examples which do not have to be repeated in the summary.

5. It is important to keep your summary clear, simple and natural. The point of a summary exercise is to see whether you have understood the passage and can sift the important from the inessential. To show that you can do this, your final summary should be easily understood by a reader. It should flow naturally as though you are expressing your own ideas and not reproducing in abbreviated form those of someone else.

6. Don't add any ideas of your own. You may know some facts about the subject which the writer does not mention, but don't add these to the summary. The point of a summary exercise is to see whether you understand the passage, not how much you know about the subject of the passage. Your own ideas and feelings are irrelevant.

As an exercise in summarizing here are some more examples of letters expressing opinions. They are concerned with whether young people should be given the vote at 18. Read them carefully and sum up the point of view of each letter in a short sentence. If you like, you can use these ideas to write a paragraph or an essay about the subject.

Give them votes at 18?

1. You asked if people of 18 'understand politics and politicians.' When has that ever been a qualification for voting? Many voters have never heard of half the Government, and at the recent Leyton by-election one man did not vote for Mr Gordon Walker (Labour) 'because of his association with Colin Jordan (National Front)'.

2. A possible answer is that anyone over 18 and under 21 who wants to vote could take an exam in the basic principles of the constitution and in current affairs. Those who pass should be allowed to vote.

3. You ask whether young people want power. I, for one, do. When I see the ghastly mess that Britain is in today, I feel very frustrated at not being able even to vote.

4. Over the last century and a quarter we have seen a righteous widening of the franchise from the privilege of a few to the right of almost every man and woman. Where shall we stop? Let us be sensible and call a halt now. No votes at 18.

5. Lists of electors take months to come into force. General elections are usually held every four or five years. For these reasons the average age at which people cast their first vote in a general election is nearer 24 than 21. Voters at 18 would bring down this average age to about 21.

6. Influence from school could be a danger. Teachers would probably organize discussions on the subject, but is it not possible that they are prejudiced towards a party and might have some sway over their pupils' choice of government? After all, we are human, and it is very difficult to be impartial.

7. It is often overlooked by older people that the youth of today are the product of a better educational system than Britain has ever had before and, consequently, British youth are not only idealistic and concerned about the future of the world, they are also well informed and thinking people and, of course, far less complacent than the average adult.

8. The law as it stands recognizes one essential fact: that the process of growing up is a gradual one. How much more illogical it would be to assume that on the day of, say, my sixteenth birthday I suddenly matured enough to be capable of driving a car, motor cycle or tractor, buying cigarettes and alcohol, getting married and casting my vote, all of which were too great a responsibility the day before.

9. Some would be perfectly eligible for the vote at 18; but they appear to be more than outnumbered by, for example, the thousands of girls suffering from acute Beatlemania, who in their present enraptured state could hardly be considered responsible enough to determine the fate of their country.

10. I would prefer to be free of it all, at least until the age of 21.

11. A vast fund of intelligent ideas is being lost because of the mystique which surrounds the 21st year. An earlier vote would serve to give a very important section of the community a much-needed political vent which would give them an identity and in turn a more responsible and patriotic outlook on life.

12. It was not the exhibitionism of the suffragettes that got votes for women, but their work in the war. In the same way, if the majority of us boys and girls want to vote at 18, we must show more good sense than most older people.

13. Let those who say there will be an irresponsible core of teenagers not forget that there is equally a large core of irresponsibles over 21. These are the 20–30 per cent who did not vote at the last election.

(The Sunday Telegraph)

READING LIST

Still on the subject of letters, it is often interesting to read what great people write in their more intimate and relaxed moments. The letters that an author, for instance, writes to his friends and business associates can give us an insight into the kind of person he is and can make him come alive in a way that is often more immediate than the works for which he is perhaps more famous. Letters (as for example the Paston Letters) can also bring us closer in touch with the intimate details of past centuries and past lives. Try to look at one or more of the following:

The Paston Letters
The Letters of Mozart
The Letters of John Keats
The Letters of Lord Byron
The Letters of Van Gogh
Dearest Child: Letters of Queen Victoria
The Letters of D. H. Lawrence
The Letters of Winston Churchill (in *Winston Churchill*, Randolph Churchill and Martin Gilbert)
The Letters of G. B. Shaw

VOCABULARY

Read again the passage entitled 'Jargon'. It is an editorial from a serious weekly *The Listener* which appeals to an educated audience and is therefore not afraid to use a wide vocabulary. Since it is an editorial, it also tends to speak in a fairly high-flown and dogmatic way, and the vocabulary used reflects this tone. Try to work out the meanings of the following words as used there:

fulminated, strictures, intoxicated, innate, self-consciousness, stock, idiom, impecunious, subpœna, satirized.

Look these words up in a dictionary and check with your versions. Use each of these words in an interesting sentence of your own. Look up any other words in this unit you were not sure about.

LANGUAGE

Jargon and Clichés

The editorial about jargon already used in this unit condemns firmly the use of a particular kind of phraseology. It attacks the use of circumlocutions (longwinded ways of saying something simple) and gives examples of these. It attacks the use of tired stereotyped expressions and the use of technical language. Nothing more need be said on this subject here as it should be clear that these are types of language that you should avoid in your essays.

Clichés are stock phrases, over-used expressions, which people use when they are too lazy to think of a fresh or an original or a personal way of using words. Once the expressions may have been interesting and distinctive, but through over-use they have become stale and automatic. The kind of thing that is meant is the following: 'this day and age', 'the hustle and bustle', 'bag and baggage', 'tooth and nail'. These are stock phrases which have no originality left in them. There are also fashionable phrases which become boring with repetition, for example, 'the generation gap', 'agonizing reappraisal', 'the wind of change'. The automatic choice of an adjective can also produce dull flat writing, things like 'the psychological moment', 'the acid test', 'tumultuous applause'. Many idiomatic and proverbial expressions are now little more than clichés: 'to take the bull by the horns', 'the writing on the wall', 'grist to the mill'. This loose and unthinking use of language, where the first idea is immediately accepted whether it is expressive or meaningful or not, should be avoided in your writing. If something is worth saying, it is worth thinking of a fresh and lively way of saying it.

Newspapers and speeches are fruitful sources of clichés. Be on the look-out for them and make your own collection in your notebook.

In the following sentences, replace the clichés by a more meaningful or precise way of writing, or rephrase the sentences completely.

1. She left no stone unturned in her attempt to gain justice.
2. He is *persona non grata* as far as I am concerned.
3. You'll never get that car to go in a month of Sundays.
4. Heavy showers were the order of the day.
5. Generally speaking, I don't like concerts.
6. His grim determination and private influence enabled him to climb to the top of the ladder.
7. He succeeded in the face of overwhelming odds.
8. What nice weather we are having!
9. His exhortations fell on stony ground.
10. He seized my hand in an iron grip.

SPELLING

The 'Language' sections in Units 9 and 10 dealt with prefixes and suffixes. Revise these sections. Knowing how words are formed and knowing the various prefixes and suffixes can help with spelling. The following rule indicates how:

In cases other than those already mentioned (e.g. the various instances where letters are doubled, where 'e' is dropped before a vowel), when you add a prefix or a suffix, do not drop or add a letter to the root.

For example, 'unnecessary' is made up of the prefix 'un' and the root 'necessary'; therefore the correct spelling is with a double 'n'. 'Disapprove' is made up of the prefix 'dis' and the root 'approve'; therefore there is only one 's'. Here are some further examples:

dis + appear = disappear
dis + satisfy = dissatisfy
lean + ness = leanness
usual + ly = usually
live + ly = lively
ad + dress = address
il + legal = illegal
im + maculate = immaculate
col + lect = collect
cor + respond = correspond
un + noticed = unnoticed

Try to break down a word into its component parts (prefix + root + suffix), and this should help with your spelling. You must, of course, break the word up correctly. For instance, 'inoperable' has one 'n' because it comes from 'in' + 'operable', not 'in' + 'noperable'. Find other examples and make a list of them in your notebook in the form illustrated above.

Here is an exercise to test your understanding of this rule. Choose the correct form in each sentence.

1. That is an illogical/ilogical statement.
2. I have never met such meaness/meanness before.
3. What is the corect/correct answer?
4. That is a fine illustration/ilustration.
5. He is behaving in a very imature/immature way.
6. He is not as inocent/innocent as he looks.
7. I was inoculated/innoculated against smallpox.
8. He spends an inordinate/innordinate amount of his time playing football.
9. She is imensely/immensely rich.
10. I was completely unerved/unnerved by the experience.
11. He suffered from a grave disability/dissability.
12. He was at an unfortunate disadvantage/dissadvantage.
13. She disliked disecting/dissecting animals.
14. He performed a great disservice/diservice by appearing on the scene.
15. I was surprised by her thiness/thinness.

Note. Make sure you check your answers in a dictionary.

UNIT 16

WRITING
Practical II
Writing Up Notes

Advice on how to turn notes into continuous prose.

READING AND UNDERSTANDING
Imagery

An examination of how imagery works and how to analyse its effectiveness.

READING LIST

Some novels dealing with love and human relationships.

VOCABULARY
Revision

LANGUAGE
Figures of Speech

An explanation of the main figures of speech involved in imagery—simile, metaphor and personification.

SPELLING

Revision.

ASSIGNMENT I

WRITING

Practical II: Writing Up Notes

In the 'Reading and Understanding' section of the previous unit, we had a look at how to make a summary. One of the questions you may be asked in the examination as an assignment in practical writing is to make a report using certain facts given to you. This is, in effect, the converse of making a summary. You are given certain details in abbreviated form, and you are required to combine them fluently, to put flesh on them as it were. Here are some examples of the kind of assignment I mean:

1. Write an account in continuous prose of the life and work of the writer Graham Greene using the following notes: b. Berkhamsted 1904; educ. Berkhamsted Sch. and Baliol, Oxf.; m. Vivien Dayrell Brourig;

s. 1; d. 1. Author; Foreign Office 1941–44; Special Duties in West Africa 1942–43; Sub-Ed. *Times* 1926–30; Lit. Ed. *Spectator* 1940–41; Novels include *The Man Within, Stamboul Train, A Gun for Hire, Brighton Rock, The Power and the Glory* (Hawthornden Prize 1940), *Our Man in Havana, Travels with My Aunt.* Travel books include *The Lawless Roads, Journey without Maps.*

2. Re-write the following notes on the flower phlox as a piece of continuous prose: richly flowering perennial—many colours from white through every shade of pink to red and purple—form clumps of firm stalks—thrives best in deep, loose, well-drained soil—needs watering during dry periods—sunny position best—used in borders—easily propagated by dividing the clumps.

3. Write an account of the city of Athens using the following notes: capital of Greece—on ill-watered Attic plain—4 miles from its harbour Piraeus—modern Athens dates from 1833 when it became the capital of independent Greece—grew from village of 5,000 people to a city of 561,250 in 1951—now one connurbation with

143

Piraeus, total pop. 1,368,142—a business centre—manufacturing town with factories to the S and SW—textiles, light engineering, printing, clothing—best roads in Greece radiate from the city—3 airports—Piraeus has sea links with all major Greek ports.

4. Write an account of the Philippines using these notes: Official name: Republica de Filipinas; area—300,000 sq. kil.; pop. 27,087,685 (census of 15 Feb. 1960) consisting of 26,867,999 Filipino citizens and 219,686 aliens (181,626 citizens of China); ethnic composition: mainly Malay; many languages: 44·37% were able to speak Tagalog; 39·46% could speak English; religions: 92·9% Christian (83·75% Roman Catholic) and 4·9% Islam; capital: Quezon City (pop. 397,990); conquered by Spain 1565; ceded to USA 1889; independent republic 1946.

5. Write an account of volcanoes for a children's encyclopedia using the following notes: an opening in the earth's crust through which heated matter is brought to the surface—tends to be conical in shape—originally used to describe Etna and some of the Lipari Islands—name comes from Vulcan, the god of fire in Roman mythology—most v. give off smoke or vapour—in eruption shoot up lava—can cover the countryside around with dust, ashes or cinders—can flow at a rate of 40 m. an hour—some v. are extinct—others remain dormant for many years before erupting—basic cause is the internal heat of the earth—pressure forces the lava out—between 300 and 400 active in the world—range from Japan to Equador—famous European v. at Etna, Vesuvius, Stromboli and Santorin.

6. Write a letter to parents inviting them to a school fête using the following details:
Takes place on 15th June—opened by Richard Walker, the famous TV interviewer—at 2.30 p.m.—on school field—entertainment—Donkey Derby—Aunt Sally—raffles—refreshments—jumble stalls—books—flowers and plants—cakes—in aid of the swimming pool fund—programmes 3p.—lucky programme prize.

7. Write a report of the speech made by an opponent of comprehensive education at a public meeting using the following details:
Destroys good schools—grammar school pupils need special teaching—comprehensive schools encourage bad discipline—lower standards—prevent pupils who want to learn from working—force grammar school pupils to mix with children from all types of backgrounds—bad influence—restrict choice of subjects—exam results are poorer—fewer go to university—take away parental choice.

Here is a possible answer to No. 7.

At a public meeting about comprehensive education, Mr Johnson complained bitterly that the introduction of comprehensive schools would destroy the good schools that already exist. He said that grammar school children needed a special kind of teaching and they would not get this in the comprehensive school. He claimed that comprehensive schools encouraged bad discipline and lowered standards; pupils who wanted to work were prevented from doing so in the comprehensive schools because grammar school children were forced to mix

with children from all kinds of backgrounds and this was a bad influence on them. There were fewer subjects in the comprehensive school for children to choose from and the exam results were poor. This was shown by the fact that fewer pupils from comprehensive schools than from grammar schools went to university. Above all, the abolition of grammar schools and the introduction of comprehensive schools took away the element of parental choice.

This example shows that putting the notes into an acceptable form is fairly straightforward. You should make sure that you use complete sentences. Add details or join one idea to another where this seems appropriate or logical (e.g. a connection is made in the example above between children being prevented from learning and their having to mix with children from different backgrounds, an idea that is not necessarily present in the notes; the last point is made the most important by introducing it with 'Above all', which is again an element not fully implied by the notes). Remember to angle your report in the direction suggested by the question. The example above is a report of a public speech by an opponent of comprehensive education, and this is kept in mind by using phrases like 'he complained bitterly', 'he said that', 'he claimed'. Assignment 6 would have to be in the form of a letter with a clear view of the audience aimed at (parents) and the purpose of the letter (to encourage parents to come). Assignment 5 would have to present the facts in a form suitable for a children's encyclopedia.

As when making a summary, you should not add facts or information of your own which are not in the notes or implied by them unless you are specifically asked to. The point of this kind of exercise is to see whether you can express notes in acceptable continuous prose. By all means dress the notes up in a suitable manner, but don't add irrelevant or additional material.

For practice, tackle one of the examples given at the beginning of the section.

READING AND UNDERSTANDING

Imagery

Study the following carefully. Each contains an example of imagery. Can you deduce from them what imagery is?

1. The Thunder Lizard raised itself. Its armoured flesh glittered like a thousand green coins. (Ray Bradbury, *A Sound of Thunder*)

2. Why should I let the toad *work*
   Squat on my life? (Philip Larkin, *Toads*)

3. October's lemon-coloured sun,
   Quietly as shadows, softly as a cat,
   Walks across the fields and paths ... (Gillian Stoneham, *The Tramp*)

4. The rather dense light fell in two places on the overfoldings of her hair till it glistened heavy and bright, like a dense golden plumage folded up. (D. H. Lawrence, *Daughters of the Vicar*)

5. Since every family has its black sheep, it almost

follows that every man must have a sooty uncle. (D. H. Lawrence, *Rex*)

6. This was a lashing, pitiless rain that stung the windows of the coach. (Daphne du Maurier, *Frenchman's Creek*)

7. The emphasis was helped by the speaker's square wall of a forehead, which had his eyebrows for its base, while his eyes found commodious cellarage in two dark caves, overshadowed by the wall. (Charles Dickens, *Hard Times*)

8. As far as the eye can see, scarlet men are marching. The hillside is in bloom with them. (Leon Garfield, *The Drummer Boy*)

9. A hot burning stinging tingling blow like the loud crack of a broken stick made his trembling hand crumple together like a leaf in the fire: and at the sound and pain scalding tears were driven into his eyes. (James Joyce, *A Portrait of the Artist as a Young Man*)

10. The young moon recurved, and shining low in the west, was like a slender shaving thrown up from a bar of gold. (Joseph Conrad, *Lord Jim*)

11. Life's but a walking shadow, a poor player
    That struts and frets his hour upon the stage,
    And then is heard no more.

    (Shakespeare, *Macbeth*)

12. A deafening din of machinery halted young Harry Ackers on the threshold of the weaving shed. It hit him the moment he pushed open the old thick door. (Bill Naughton, *Weaver's Knot*)

13. That kitchen, worn by our boots and lives, was scruffy, warm and low, whose fuss of furniture seemed never the same but was shuffled around each day. (Laurie Lee, *Cider with Rosie*)

14. But there he was always, a steaming hulk of an uncle, his braces straining like hausers, and breathing like a brass band; or guzzling and blustery in the kitchen over his gutsy supper, too big for everything except the great black boats of his boots. (Dylan Thomas, *A Story*)

15. The sea is a hungry dog,
    Giant and grey. (James Reeves, *The Sea*)

To state it simply, imagery is the use of comparisons or associations to connect one object or idea with another so that the first object or idea can be more effectively understood and imagined. It is a fanciful and non-literal way of describing things so that they become more vivid to the reader. For instance, in example 12, it states that the din of machinery *hit* Harry Ackers when he opened the door. The din did not literally hit him; noise does not have any physical force. But by implying that the noise hit him, the writer is able to create more vividly the powerful effect of the noise. The writer is saying that the noise was so loud that it was as though Harry had been struck by a physical force. Had the writer merely stated the literal fact, namely that Harry *heard* the din the moment he opened the door, the effect would not be so strong. By using the image of the din hitting Harry, the din is made almost alive as though it has a power of its own with the ability to do physical harm to the hearer. The use of the word 'hit' also makes the meaning more precise. If 'he heard' were used, we would not know whether the noise was welcome or distasteful, pleasant or unpleasant. 'Hit', with its suggestion of violence, gives us a clearer impression of the character's

attitude towards the noise. In addition, the image 'hit' conveys the idea that the noise is hostile and destructive. It suggests a hostility between the noise and the character.

It should be clear from this example why writers use imagery. A good image or comparison can give us more information about what is being described and can set it more precisely in our minds; it can create a much more vivid impression; it can set up reverberations and associations which enrich the experience.

Not all images are effective, of course. Sometimes writers use hackneyed images which are so stale that they add nothing to the effectiveness of the writing. Examples of these can be found in the 'Language' sections of Units 14 and 15.

In the comprehension test in the examination, you will probably be asked to explain an image or to explain the effectiveness of an image or metaphorical expression. When you are asked to explain an image, what you must do is to make clear the idea the writer has in mind, the comparison he is drawing, the extra information or richness which the image gives which a literal statement would not. When you are asked to explain the effectiveness of the image, you must decide whether the comparisons made or the associations implied are appropriate to the situation, and whether what is gained by using an image and not a literal statement is helpful in making the situation more vivid. You must also justify the conclusions you reach.

Look again at example 8. The author uses the image of the hillside being in bloom with scarlet men (soldiers in eighteenth-century uniform). What does he mean by this image? He is comparing the soldiers to flowers, firstly because of the colour of their uniforms (the scarlet is like poppies) and secondly because of the way they are scattered over the hillside. There is also the idea of density: there are so many soldiers it is as though the hillside were covered with them just as flowers might sprout up and cover the ground. Is it an effective image? The visual effect works: the scarlet of the soldiers' uniforms is associated with flowers, and this association helps us to see the colour more precisely; the comparison with flowers massing on a hillside also helps us to picture the formation of the soldiers more clearly. But there is one element that at first sight may seem incongruous. Soldiers are instruments of destruction: flowers are symbols of beauty and growth. We could stop here and say that the image is inappropriate. But can we explore it more deeply? Flowers have a short life, beautiful in their prime but soon to wither and die. Isn't it possible to say the same about soldiers—splendid in their youthful vitality but soon to be cut down and die? The implications of the image can then be seen to go deep. There is a poignant ironic contrast between the beauty of the soldiers and the flowers and the fate that is in store for them. The image carries out the requirements of a good image: it gives us information about the situation so that we can see it more precisely; it makes us see this situation in a much more vivid way; it sets up reverberations which enable us to understand the situation more deeply.

If you were asked to explain the effectiveness of this image in the comprehension test, your answer should be something like this:

The writer is drawing a comparison between the scarlet men and flowers spread over a hillside. By comparing them with flowers we are able to visualize the colour of the men's uniforms and the way they are set out on the hillside more precisely. The writer may also be implying that just as flowers are beautiful in their prime but soon die, so the soldiers splendid in their finery are soon to be cut down. This gives a sense of doom and a poignant irony to the image.

Now look at the other examples of imagery at the beginning of this section and explain their effectiveness.

READING LIST

Here are some novels mainly about love and human relationships that you may enjoy.

Lynne Reid Banks: *The L-Shaped Room*
Stan Barstow: *A Kind of Loving*
Colette: *Chéri*
Margaret Drabble: *The Millstone*
Daphne du Maurier: *My Cousin Rachel*
Paul Gallico: *The Snow Goose*
Graham Greene: *The End of the Affair*
F. Scott Fitzgerald: *Tender is the Night*
Ernest Hemingway: *A Farewell to Arms*
Penelope Mortimer: *The Pumpkin Eater*
Iris Murdoch: *The Sandcastle*
David Storey: *This Sporting Life*
Evelyn Waugh: *Brideshead Revisited*

VOCABULARY

Revision

Here is a chance for you to check how effectively you have studied the 'Vocabulary' sections between Units 9 and 15. Choose the correct word or phrase in the following sentences.

1. The Christmas cake was rich with currants, raisins and candid/candied peel.
2. After the accident he was subconscious/unconscious for several hours.
3. He was so strong and masterful/masterly that he swept her off her feet.
4. That is an ingenious/ingenuous idea for an exciting new advertising campaign.
5. An introvert/extrovert is a person with a lively outgoing nature.
6. It is a complete fiction/faction to say that I have been misleading you.
7. The player had to concede/accede that his opponent had the victory.
8. The painting showed that the student had considerable artful/artistic ability.

9. The recently discovered manuscript has been ascribed/proscribed to a long-forgotten poet.
10. The boy's important/importunate demands soon grew tiresome.
11. I feel that I can rely on your innate/inert good nature to do what is right.
12. Impecunious means having no money/sinful/unstable/untrustworthy.
13. Fulminate means to meditate/to thunder forth/to eat too much/to chew the cud.
14. Ingratiate means to bring to the attention/to be overwhelmed by/to lie down in front of/to bring oneself into favour with.
15. Tenacious means holding fast/high-spirited/pertaining to a tenant/noisy.

Make sure you check your answers by looking the words up in a dictionary or in your notebook.

LANGUAGE

Figures of Speech I

This is the general name given to those tricks of the trade in the use of words which can help to give vividness and emphasis to writing or speech. They are the rhetorical and technical devices writers use. A large number of these have been defined and it is not necessary to know them all. Some have been described already (irony in Unit 14; circumlocution in Unit 15). The most important of the remainder are allegory, alliteration, antithesis, hyperbole, metaphor, onomatopoeia, paradox, personification, rhetorical question and simile, and they will be dealt with in this unit and the next.

In the 'Reading and Understanding' section of this unit, we discussed imagery. Most imagery involves the use of metaphor, personification or simile, and it is vital that you should be able to understand and differentiate between these if you are to appreciate fully how imagery works.

1. A simile is a comparison in which one thing is said to be like another in one or more aspects. A similarity is drawn between one object and another so as to make the first object clearer and more vivid. For example,

Her hair was like gold.

This is a simile in which hair is being compared with gold. The aspects they have in common are the colour and the shining effect.

The snowflakes were as light as feathers.

This is a simile in which snowflakes and feathers are being compared. The aspect they have in common is the lightness and the lack of weight. (Another aspect referred to may be the way they move through the air, how they float softly.) A simile can usually be recognized by the word 'like' or 'as . . . as'.

2. A metaphor is a compressed simile. Instead of saying one thing is like another, we say one thing *is* another, although we know that literally this is not so. For example,

The boy is an ass.

This obviously is not meant to be taken literally. A comparison is being drawn between the boy and an ass who share some such quality as stupidity. In a metaphor the aspect the two objects have in common is left to the reader's imagination or ingenuity. This means that a metaphor can be more vague than a simile, but it can also be more powerful because a whole range of qualities in common may be implied. Here are some more examples:

Her presence at the party lit up the whole room for him.

This is a metaphor in which the presence of the woman has as great an effect for the man as a light in a dark room.

The surface of the lake mirrored the trees by its edge.

This is a metaphor in which the surface of the lake is said to be a mirror which in literal fact it is not. What is meant is that the surface of the lake is like a mirror in that it reflects the trees at the edge of the water. The silvery surface of the water may also give the appearance of a mirror.

3. Personification is a kind of metaphor in which an inanimate object or a non-human animal is said to have the qualities or emotions of a human being. The *person* part of the word personification should help you to remember this. For example,

The birds were chattering in the trees.

Birds don't literally chatter. Human beings do. This is an example of personification whereby the birds are said to be chattering as though they were human beings.

Disease held the city at ransom.

Disease cannot literally do this. Here disease is treated as though it were a human being with the power to threaten a city.

Here are some further examples of similes, metaphors and personification. Identify each and explain its effectiveness.

1. The shop is opening another branch in a neighbouring town.
2. The pupils came thundering down the corridor like a herd of elephants.
3. The wind in the trees crooned softly.
4. The wind played upon the surface of the lake.
5. The car was knifed in two in the smash.
6. Time hung heavy on his hands.
7. The tramp looked like a bundle of old rags.
8. The reverberations of his discovery spread throughout the world.
9. The water was so clear it was like glass.
10. Brick by brick he rebuilt his shattered life.
11. The news of his dismissal came with the suddenness of a flash of lightning.
12. The sun smiled gently on the summer scene.
13. 'Break his heart!' Miss Havisham cried.
14. The old man's hand was like a gnarled withered root.
15. Anger soared like a flame through his body.

You ought also to try to use images in your own writing. Write a sentence containing an image about each of the following:

1. The Sun
2. A fire
3. Water
4. Sand
5. A tree
6. A smile
7. An athlete
8. Television
9. Knitting
10. A book

 SPELLING

Revision

The following exercise is to check that you have learned and understood the spelling rules outlined in Units 9 to 15. Choose the correct form in each sentence.

1. The weather is very changeable/changable today.
2. There is no point in arguing with him: he is implacable/implaceable.
3. That is the best boys' school/boy's school in the district.
4. Children's clothes/childrens' clothes are becoming even more expensive.
5. The donkies/donkeys stood patiently on the sand.
6. The buses/busses were all crowded.
7. The pack of wolfs/wolves skulked around the cabin.
8. We passed only three oasises/oases in our whole journey.
9. All my friends seem to be geniuses/genii, and I am the only one with no brains.
10. The revolution was niped/nipped in the bud.
11. The sprinter was pipped/piped at the post by the Australian.
12. He said that he would see me later/latter.
13. The decorator made a good job of tiling/tilling the bathroom.
14. Charles II is usually regarded as being rather disolute/dissolute.
15. He did not leave a forwarding adress/address.

Make sure that you check your answers in a dictionary or in the previous 'Spelling' sections. You do not want to be left remembering the wrong spelling.

 ASSIGNMENT I

Part I should take about an hour and a quarter for preparation and writing, and your finished essay should be at least 500 words long. Part II should take about an hour.

Part I: Essay

Write a composition on *one* of the following:
1. Write a letter to a friend who has been on strike, condemning his action or giving him your support. Justify the views you express.

2. A friend of yours has just sold his television set. Write him a letter saying why you think this is a sensible or a short-sighted action.

3. In a letter try to convince a friend that your enjoyment of pop music *or* classical music is justified.

4. Write a letter to your local newspaper giving your views on public transport *or* traffic problems in your town *or* the proposed building of a high office block in the town centre *or* the proposed demolition of a building of historic interest *or* the closure of the town's last cinema.

Part II: Summary

Read the following passage carefully. Make a summary of the main points in about 200 words. (The passage contains 523 words.)

Wild Over the West

Nowadays one has to be pretty politic over what one says about 'Westerns', although they have been going for a long time. In a talk which we publish on another page on 'The Western Gunfighter' Colin Richards states that the first 'Western' film was made in 1903. The days of the silent movies in the 'twenties were a wonderful era of cowboy films—William S. Hart, Tom Mix, and Douglas Fairbanks Senior were among the 'stars' of those distant days and nobody thought then that they were morally debasing. Their adventures were particularly suitable to the dumb actors and the tinkling pianos which accompanied them. When the 'Westerns', after suffering a temporary setback, received a new lease of life, first in 'talking pictures' and then upon the television screens, it was discovered that the heroes riding their horses into the purple sunsets or toting their guns in the saloon bars still necessarily had to remain fairly silent. A talkative cowboy somehow appeared to be a contradiction in terms. And as G. K. Chesterton once remarked, a strong, silent man is usually silent because he has nothing to say.

Many efforts have been made to 'debunk' the cowboy or the gunfighter, but yet he retains his eternal appeal to those of us whose lives are glued to typewriters and who rarely become dangerous except when driving motor-cars. It is of course saddening to be informed that 'the average cowboy was no gunman' and that he carried a pistol to protect himself from snakes. Or, again, that the 'badman' seldom drank and rarely smoked and made a practice of killing his victims by shooting them in the back. But that is how things are: the romantic lover later divorces his wife, the professional funny man is a bore at the dinner table, the angelic philosopher loses his temper along with his collar stud. It is a chastening thought that there is scarcely one of the Great Victorians who basked in evangelical moralities who has not now been exposed as living a private life filled with perversions or secret self-indulgences. As one grows older, one discovers that the world lives upside down; but when we were young we liked it to be simple and even thought that it was so.

And so it can be argued that even the modern 'Westerns', generally more sophisticated than those of forty years ago, are not always as black as they are painted. Maybe they are 'cathartic'; in any case, as the recent committee writing on 'Children and Television Programmes' pointed out: 'Criticism' that 'has been levelled most commonly against the Western . . . might equally be raised against the filmed series based on the activities of present-day police squads', etc. Mr Tom Driberg observes in *The New Statesman* that Dickens could be horrific, while 'Bronco' is often kind to Indians. The children today, poor mites, have been born into a world of nuclear war-heads, and even the most conscientious parent finds it difficult to prevent them from ransacking the bookshops for war stories. Compared with an age in which the inhabited globe may be blown to pieces by pressing a button, the Western frontier attracts us as a haven of civilized security.

(The Listener)

UNIT 17

WRITING

Using Imagery

Advice on using imagery to make your own writing more lively and interesting.

READING AND UNDERSTANDING

Poetry

How to tackle reading a poem and a look at some of the problems that might arise if you are given a poem to study in a comprehension exercise.

READING LIST

Some modern poets and anthologies you may enjoy.

VOCABULARY

Some words that are often confused.

LANGUAGE

Figures of Speech II

An explanation with examples of allegory, alliteration, antithesis, hyperbole, onomatopoeia, paradox, rhetorical question.

SPELLING

-able, -ible

Lists of words ending in these suffixes for you to learn.

WRITING

Using Imagery

The 'Reading and Understanding' section of Unit 16 explained how and why writers use imagery. Clearly, in your own writing, imagery can help to enliven what you say and make it more interesting and effective. As suggested in the previous unit, imagery can give more precise information; it can make a much more powerful visual effect; it can provide a richness and suggestiveness which a plain literal statement does not.

Imagery in Descriptive Writing

One would expect imagery to be most effective in descriptive writing where it is important to create an atmosphere or to enable the reader to visualize the scene through the words being used, and this is partly true. Descriptive writing demands a sensitive use of words, an

appeal to the senses of the reader, and the evocation of the right kind of atmosphere. In all of these, imagery can help. For instance, compare the following pairs of sentences:

1. (a) It was autumn and the hillside was aflame with bracken.
   (b) It was autumn and the hillside was covered with reddy-brown bracken.
2. (a) The old man's face was dry and wrinkled like a withered apple.
   (b) The old man's face was dry and wrinkled.
3. (a) The sun suddenly burst from behind a cloud.
   (b) The sun suddenly appeared from behind a cloud.
4. (a) Her laughter tinkled like ice in a glass.
   (b) Her laughter was high-pitched and staccato.
5. (a) The waiting passengers stormed the train.
   (b) The waiting passengers pushed and shoved their way on to the train.

The first sentence in each pair uses an image; the second is a plain literal statement. In the first pair, the use of the image of the reddy-brown bracken being like flame sweeping across the hillside is much more vivid than the plain statement. The literal statement gives you only the colour of the bracken; the image gives you the colour and a sense of movement and energy as well. As an idea 'aflame' is much more vital than 'reddy-brown'.

Look at the other pairs of sentences and say in what ways the first is more interesting and more informative than the second. Try to write down your ideas as we have above—don't just let it pass as a vague idea in your mind.

Imagery in Argumentative and Factual Writing

Imagery can also be used effectively in argumentative essays or in essays which involve the use of facts. Consider the following pairs of sentences:

1. (a) There are more stars in the universe than there are grains of sand on all the seashores of the world.
   (b) It is impossible to count the number of stars in the universe.
2. (a) If all the people in China were laid end to end, they would stretch right round the equator.
   (b) The population of China is very great.
3. (a) The motor car is throttling the life blood of our cities.
   (b) The motor car is blocking up the roads of our cities.
4. (a) To try to prevent the building of the new airport is to be like King Canute trying to stem the inevitable advance of the sea.
   (b) To try to prevent the building of the new airport is foolhardy and impossible.
5. (a) You have no more idea of what happens in a comprehensive school than a monkey has of an opera house.
   (b) You have no idea of what happens in a comprehensive school.

Again, the first sentence in each pair uses an image or an analogue (a kind of comparison) to make its points; the second is a plain literal statement. In the first example, for instance, instead of just saying the number of stars in the universe is vast or innumerable, the image gives us an idea of *how* vast the number is by comparing the number to that of the grains of sand on the seashores. The immensity is presented to us in visual terms and in terms that we can all understand. We can imagine how vast the number of grains of sand must be, and we can transfer this awareness to the number of stars which is a much more difficult and abstract idea to grasp. The use of an image makes the concept much easier to comprehend.

Look at the other examples above and comment on whether the first sentence in each pair is more effective than the second. If so, how?

Stories can also be made more alive and dramatic by the use of imagery. Consider the following sentences:

1. (a) The sight rooted him to the spot.
   (b) The sight made him stop moving.
2. (a) He suddenly felt the icy grasp of fear at his heart.
   (b) He suddenly felt very afraid.
3. (a) His emotions were a tangled web.
   (b) His emotions were very confused.
4. (a) He plunged into the midst of the argument.
   (b) He joined the argument.
5. (a) The news burst like a thunderclap on his consciousness.
   (b) He suddenly became aware of the news.

The first sentence in each pair uses an image to establish the dramatic effect more forcefully. In the first example, for instance, the use of the image 'rooted' brings in the idea of solidity and fixedness that we associate with a tree firmly rooted in the ground. This conveys more strikingly the effect of the sight upon him; it made him as immovable as a tree; he became inanimate and fixed. This produces a much more effective picture in the reader's mind than the literal statement 'made him stop moving'.

Comment as before on the effectiveness of the other images above.

Hazards in Using Images

It should be clear from these examples that imagery can make your writing more exciting and vivid. But there are dangers which should be avoided.

1. Make sure that your images are fresh and interesting. Often there is a danger that we reach for the nearest comparison and use it because we are familiar with it. Stale imagery of this kind should be avoided. The kind of thing I mean is: 'he was as cool as a cucumber'; 'his face was as red as a beetroot'; 'his muscles were like steel'. Images such as these don't really enhance the situation: they are merely expressions of a lazy mind.

Perhaps some of the examples given above come into this category. Look at them again and decide.

2. Don't overdo imagery. If every sentence contains an image, the effect can be over-rich and over-fanciful. Ration yourself to using images when they are needed, when their use can have a definite visual or illustrative effect. Writing that is peppered with comparisons can appear mannered, artificial and falsely poetic.

Look again at the extract by Walter Pater in Unit 14. Pick out the images in the passage.

3. Be careful not to mix your imagery. Sometimes, one starts describing something in terms of one image and then develops it in terms of another image. If this second image is inappropriate to the first, the effect can be incongruous, e.g.

We must put our shoulders to the wheel and leave no stone unturned.

There are two ideas here which don't really match. If we have our shoulders to the wheel, how can we leave no stone unturned? The technical name for this kind of illogicality is mixed metaphors. Incongruities of this kind should be avoided.

Love poetry often contains exaggerated comparisons praising the loved one. To round off this section we give you to read for enjoyment one of Shakespeare's sonnets, in which he manages to praise his love by making fun of the overloaded compliments and stale images used by other poets.

My mistress' eyes are nothing like the sun;
Coral is far more red than her lips' red:
If snow be white, why then her breasts are dun;
If hairs be wires, black wires grow on her head.
I have seen roses damask'd, red and white,
But no such roses see I in her cheeks;
And in some perfumes is there more delight
Than in the breath that from my mistress reeks.
I love to hear her speak, yet well I know
That music hath a far more pleasing sound:
I grant I never saw a goddess go,—
My mistress, when she walks, treads on the ground:
    And yet, by heavens, I think my love as rare
    As any she belied with false compare.

READING AND UNDERSTANDING

Poetry

We are now going to look at the special problems in reading and understanding that poetry may set. It is quite possible that one of the passages you will be given for comprehension in the examination will be a poem. People sometimes have fixed preconceptions about and an antipathy towards poetry. They regard it as 'effeminate' or 'arty' or 'difficult'. These comments may be true of some poems, but they are not true of poetry as a whole. Sometimes, poems require a greater effort on the part of the reader but equally they can give the reader a satisfaction commensurate with this effort. The more you put into reading a poem, the more you are likely to get out of it.

It is difficult to generalize about poetry, but the basic difference between prose and poetry is the latter's economy. A novel may contain 80,000 words, a short story 5,000: the writers of these have room to expand and fill in detail. The poet is usually working on a much smaller scale: he is trying to catch a moment or create an effect or pass on a thought, and he may use only 200 words in doing so. It follows then that if he is to make an impression on the reader at all, these words must be chosen with great care so that they have the maximum impact. A writer of a novel or a short story can afford to be expansive, he can afford to some extent to waste words or write about irrelevancies: a poet can't.

The pattern imposed on a poem by its verse-form also acts as a discipline on the poet. A novelist or a short story writer doesn't necessarily have to worry too much about the rhythm of his words or the lengths of his paragraphs: a poet has to concern himself much more with how the words fit into a particular pattern and the need for the words to carry on a particular rhythm.

It follows then that the words in poetry are likely to be more packed with meaning than in prose. The poet has to take into consideration the sound of the words he uses, their rhythm, the associations they call forth in the reader's mind, much more than a prose writer, because the poet has to make a much more powerful effect in a smaller space. For the same reasons, imagery, allusions, double meanings, symbolic references are much more important to the poet than to the prose writer. Because of this need for concentration and depth of meaning, a poem may well require closer study and examination on the part of the reader than prose if he is to appreciate fully what a poem is saying and the skill with which it is being said.

In looking at poetry, it is useful to understand the points about imagery made in this and the previous unit and the comments on figures of speech made there and in the 'Language' section that follows. But the kind of appreciation expected at this stage does not require you to know whether a poem is a sonnet or an epic in order to be able to understand what it is saying and how effective it is.

When reading a poem, the first thing you should try to do is to get the general drift of the meaning or a grasp of the kind of mood the poet is creating. At first, this may seem rather vague, but further readings should strengthen your first impressions. Gradually, ideas will fall into place, and points that had seemed obscure will become clear. The relevance of particular words or images will show themselves. The technical skill of the poet in manipulating rhythm and structure and language will become more apparent. A reader can usually get something from a first reading of a poem, and it is on this general understanding that a deeper grasp of the subtlety and skill of the poem is built.

Read this poem carefully several times before reading the commentary on it that follows:

Dulce et Decorum Est

Bent double, like old beggars under sacks,
Knock-kneed, coughing like hags, we cursed through sludge,
Till on the haunting flares we turned our backs
And towards our distant rest began to trudge.
Men marched asleep. Many lost their boots
But limped on, blood-shod. All went lame; all blind;
Drunk with fatigue; deaf even to the hoots
Of tired, outstripped Five-Nines that dropped behind.

Gas! GAS; Quick, boys!—An ecstasy of fumbling,
Fitting the clumsy helmets just in time;
But someone still was yelling out and stumbling
And flound'ring like a man in fire or lime . . .
Dim, through the misty panes and thick green light,
As under a green sea, I saw him drowning.

In all my dreams, before my helpless sight,
He plunges at me, guttering, choking, drowning.

If in some smothering dreams you too could pace
Behind the wagon that we flung him in,
And watch the white eyes writhing in his face,
His hanging face, like a devil's sick of sin;
If you could hear, at every jolt, the blood
Come gargling from the froth-corrupted lungs,
Obscene as cancer, bitter as the cud
Of vile, incurable sores on innocent tongues—
My friend, you would not tell with such high zest
The old lie: Dulce et decorum est
Pro patria mori.

(WILFRED OWEN)

Before you read the commentary make sure you have gathered some idea of what the poem is about. If you don't know, can you guess what the Latin words mean? (They are translated in the commentary below.)

In general terms, Wilfred Owen's poem is describing a specific example of the horror and squalor of war. While trudging back from the front line, there is a gas attack. One soldier is too late in putting on his mask and is gassed. The poet will never forget his suffering, and it makes him realize how hollow is the old idea that it is brave and fitting to die for your native land. So it is important that the poet makes the suffering and squalor as strong as possible so that we accept his view that dying for your country is not something glorious and noble. Let us look at the poem in more detail to see how he achieves this.

The first two lines establish the indignity of the soldiers struggling back to their position. They are 'bent double'; they are 'like old beggars', not young but moving like old men destitute of everything; 'knock-kneed' and 'coughing' stress how out of sorts they are; 'like hags' compares them to old women deprived of all humanity. The use of the verb 'cursed' to describe their movement suggests how difficult it is, how physically enfeebled they are that only by cursing can they make their way through the mud. The simple statement 'Men marched asleep' emphasizes their exhaustion. The bluntness of the expression 'blood-shod' brings home to us the hardship the soldiers are suffering. 'Lame', 'blind', 'drunk', 'deaf' show how the senses of the soldiers are stopped up: they are so exhausted they can no longer feel. Even the noise of the bombs that drop behind them cannot penetrate their numbed minds.

Having established the tiredness of the men in the first verse, the second verse shocks the reader—and the soldiers— with actual words spoken: 'Gas! GAS! Quick, boys!' Suddenly there is violent movement described as 'an ecstasy of fumbling' in contrast to the heavy weary movement of the first verse. The word 'ecstasy' usually describes supremely happy feeling. Here the excitement associated with the word is applied to something that can affect life or death. 'Fumbling' and 'clumsy' emphasize the difficulty the exhausted soldiers have in getting their masks on. Then comes the description of the soldier who couldn't fit his mask in time—'Like a man in fire or lime'—Owen uses this comparison to get over the effect: the gas is made into something concrete ('fire or lime') that we can visualize eating the man up. Then comes the image of the man drowning—appropriate because the man is gasping for air as though drowning and because he is being viewed through the green cellophane-like window of the gas mask the poet is wearing which makes the whole world look as though it is under water.

With the next short verse, the poet comes up to the present, stating how his dreams ever since have been haunted by this figure. The use of the word 'plunges' by its violent action, suggesting the man almost attacking the poet in his effort to get help, is in the present tense as though the action is still taking place, being repeated and repeated in dreams. It also reinforces the idea of drowning with its suggestion of plunging through water. 'Guttering' and 'choking' by their very sound—harsh, hard, unpleasant—bring to mind the fate the man has suffered.

The final verse brings the reader in and places before him the situation Owen had to face. The gassed soldier is thrown on a wagon. His eyes 'writhe' in agony; his blood comes 'gargling' from his lungs. Both of these words suggest violent effort and pain. The associations of the comparisons 'like a devil's sick of sin', 'froth-corrupted', 'obscene as cancer', 'bitter as the cud/Of vile, incurable sores on innocent tongues'—all emphasize the horror of the occasion.

And so Owen reaches his conclusion. If you had experienced something like this, you would realize that the old saying 'Dulce et decorum est pro patria mori' (It is sweet and fitting to die for your native land) is a lie. The very restraint of the language after the grim description of the gassing itself emphasizes how bitter the tone is, and how resentful Owen is that people should still believe in such a sentiment.

There are many other points about the poem which could be discussed, but this should give you some idea of the richness of ideas and associations which the words suggest. The concentration of the poem itself is shown by the fact that it has taken me three or four times as many words to describe the poem and its effect as are actually in the poem. And I have still not fully discussed the implications of the poem.

Here are the kinds of questions you might be asked on a poem like this. See if you can answer them convincingly. Some—but not all—of the information will be found in the commentary above.

1. Why does Owen say the soldiers are 'like old beggars'?
2. Why does he compare the soldiers with 'hags'?
3. What is implied by saying 'Men marched asleep'?
4. Explain what the poet means by 'blood-shod'.
5. What does the poet mean by 'drunk with fatigue'?
6. What change in the action is brought about by the words 'Gas! GAS! Quick, boys!'?
7. Comment on the poet's use of the word 'ecstasy'.
8. Explain why the soldier was 'flound'ring like a man in fire or lime'.
9. Why does the poet see him 'as under a green sea'?
10. Comment on the appropriateness or otherwise of the sound of the words 'guttering' and 'choking' when applied to the meaning and situation here.
11. Why does the poet regard the idea that it is noble to die for your country as 'the old lie'?

Many people regard the close study like this of a poem as a kind of sacrilege. They think that you should be able to understand a poem straight away and that taking it to pieces like this destroys it. On the contrary, I feel that you can't really get to know and appreciate a poem unless you have some insight into how the poet works and what he is trying to achieve. There is no harm in taking a poem to pieces so long as you put it together again and re-read the poem with a deeper understanding and appreciation.

Before moving on to the next section read the poem again straight through and preferably aloud. You will probably agree that its effect has been strengthened by the effort we have put into understanding it.

READING LIST

Poetry

Students unused to reading poetry will probably find modern poems more readily accessible, but even in this area the choice is so great that it is difficult to make recommendations. It is often a matter of personal taste. Try one of these, and if you are put off, try another.

Brian Patten: *Notes to the Hurrying Man*
Vernon Scannell: *Walking Wounded*
Roger McGough: *After the Merrymaking*
John Betjeman: *Collected Poems*
Carl Sandburg: *Collected Poems*
E. E. Cummings: *Selected Poems*
Philip Larkin: *Whitsun Weddings*
Ted Hughes: *The Hawk in the Rain*
R. S. Thomas: *The Bread of Truth*
Wilfred Owen: *Collected Poems*
Stevie Smith: *Not Waving but Drowning*
D. H. Lawrence: *Selected Poems*

Perhaps an easier way to find out poets with whom you may have a sympathy is to look through an anthology and then follow up the poets you like. Some anthologies, mainly of modern poems, are:

Voices, ed. Geoffrey Summerfield
Themes: Conflict; Imagination; Men and Beasts; Generations; Town and Country; Men at Work, ed. Rhodri Jones
The New Poetry, ed. A. Alvarez
The Mersey Sound (Penguin)
The Beat Poets (Penguin)
Children of Albion, ed. Michael Horovitz

 VOCABULARY

Here are some words which are often confused. Try to distinguish between them.

muscle, mussel
imaginary, imaginative
libel, slander
psychiatrist, psychologist
vacation, vocation
veracious, voracious
accessary, accessory
alternate, alternative
amoral, immoral
draft, draught

Check the meaning of these words in a dictionary.
Use each of them in an interesting sentence of your own.
Check up on any other words used in this unit that you were not sure about.

LANGUAGE

Figures of Speech II

In Unit 16, we looked at the figures of speech mainly concerned with imagery—simile, metaphor, personification. In this unit, we shall look at the remaining figures of speech that it is useful to know.

1. Allegory. This is the name given to a story that works on two levels at the same time. On the surface, the story may be about a series of adventures, but underneath, the characters and events described stand for or symbolize other things. For instance, Bunyan's *The Pilgrim's Progress* is an allegory. On the surface, it is about the adventures that happen to the hero Christian, but Christian is also symbolic of the Christian soul on its journey towards salvation, and all the other characters (e.g. Giant Despair, Hopeful) have a religious significance.

2. Alliteration. This is the device whereby the same letter or sound is repeated to produce a particular effect, e.g.

He clasps the crag with crooked hands.

In this description of an eagle, the use and repetition of the hard 'c' sounds can be said to represent the hardness of the eagle and of the crag he clings to. Alliteration can create an appropriate sound or emphasize important words.

3. Antithesis. This is the balancing of one word or one phrase against another usually suggesting an idea opposite in meaning, e.g.

Better to reign in Hell, than serve in Heav'n.
To lose one parent, Mr Worthing, may be regarded as a misfortune: to lose both looks like carelessness.

4. Hyperbole. The use of exaggeration for the sake of emphasis, e.g.

I feel a million times better.
I wouldn't give it you for all the tea in China.

5. Onomatopoeia. The device whereby a particular word is used because the sound of the word echoes the sense, e.g.

The pile of plates crashed to the ground.

The word 'crashed' suggests by its sound something of the kind of action that happened to the plates.

The moan of doves in immemorial elms
And murmuring of innumerable bees.

This is a more subtle example. Here the repetition of 'm's and 'l's echoes the drowsy peaceful scene.

6. Paradox. A statement that on the surface seems to be absurd or self-contradictory but which on closer study is seen to have something wise to say, e.g.

If a thing is worth doing, it's worth doing badly.
The child is father to the man.

7. Rhetorical question. This is a question which is asked for effect only, not because an answer is wanted.

153

Indeed, the answer is usually obvious and is implied in the question. The device is often used in public speaking as an emotional appeal to rouse an audience, e.g.

Are we to lie down beneath this vile attack?
Will no one help to root out this scourge from our midst?

The following sentences contain examples of the figures of speech explained above. Identify them.

1. To sin is mortal; to forgive, Divine.
2. The crack of the whip urged the horse on.
3. The long day wanes; the slow moon climbs.
4. Who could fail to be moved by such a touching appeal?
5. The boy stood on the burning deck.
6. The fair breeze blew, the white foam flew,
   The furrow followed free.
7. A terrible beauty is born.
8. Had I a thousand sons I should sacrifice them all for my country.
9. Are we downhearted?
10. The bare black cliff clang'd round him.
11. It was a bitter sweet experience.
12. The man who does not know fear cannot claim to be truly brave.
13. Spare the rod and spoil the child.
14. The heavy door closed with a clang.
15. Set a thief to catch a thief.

 # SPELLING

The suffixes '-able' and '-ible' are often confused. There is no rule to help decide which is the correct form. It is simply a case of learning which words end in '-able' and which in '-ible'. Here are some of the most common examples:

acceptable	accessible
admirable	admissible
charitable	audible
conceivable	collapsible
considerable	contemptible
excusable	credible
hospitable	divisible
immovable	edible
inconsolable	eligible
indescribable	fallible
indistinguishable	feasible
inescapable	flexible
inevitable	gullible
inextinguishable	intelligible
inflammable	invincible
invaluable	irrepressible
irritable	irresistible
passable	legible
practicable	negligible
regrettable	ostensible
reliable	perceptible
variable	permissible
	responsible
	sensible
	susceptible

Note that verbs ending in silent 'e' drop the 'e' except after soft 'c' and soft 'g' where the 'e' must be kept to indicate the soft pronunciation, e.g. changeable, noticeable. See 'Spelling', Unit 9.

In the following sentences, complete the words by adding '-able' or '-ible'.

1. His statement is not compat— with the facts.
2. The performance left an indel—impression in my memory.
3. Is this solution reduc—?
4. The sands of the sea are immeasur—.
5. His hatred was implac—.
6. His playing was impecc—.
7. The atmosphere was so tense that it was almost tang—.
8. The fortress was impreg—.
9. There was a scarcely percept— draught.
10. The story was so strange that it was hardly cred—.

Check the spelling of these words in a dictionary.

154

UNIT 18

WRITING

Poetry

After analysing a poem in the previous unit, we look at the use of poetic extracts as stimuli to encourage your own writing.

READING AND UNDERSTANDING

Personal

An examination of how we can learn about the writer of autobiographical prose from what and how he writes.

READING LIST

Some autobiographies you may enjoy.

VOCABULARY

Some words often confused for you to study.

LANGUAGE

Slang

An explanation of the term 'slang' and advice on its use—or non-use.

SPELLING

'-ise', '-ize'

An indication of how to distinguish between these two suffixes.

ASSIGNMENT J

WRITING

Poetry

In the 'Reading and Understanding' section in the previous unit, we studied a poem and saw how much more concentrated and intense the language of a poem is compared with that of prose. You will not be asked to write a poem in the examination (nor would I advise you to try), but a piece of poetry may be suggested as the starting point for an essay. The reason for this is clear from the nature of poetry itself: the language *is* concentrated and intense; it can evoke an atmosphere or call forth an idea; it can suggest things to the mind which a straightforward prose statement cannot.

Read the following brief snatches of poetry and see what response each makes in your mind, what ideas are evoked.

1. Not a leaf, not a bird—
   A world cast in frost.
2. The very air is veined with darkness, hearken!
   The brown owl wakens in the woods now.
3. A lonely cab-horse steams and stamps.
   And then the lighting of the lamps.
4. Night's candles are burnt out, and jocund day
   Stands tiptoe on the misty mountain tops.
5. It seemed that out of battle I escaped
   Down some profound dull tunnel, long since scooped.
6. It was a high day, a crisp day,
   The clearest kind of Autumn day
   With brisk intoxicating air, a
   Little wind that frisked ...
7. I see him old, trapped in a burly house
   Cold in the angry spitting of the rain
   Come down these sixty years.

155

8. Two vast and trunkless legs of stone
   Stand in the desert. Near them on the sand,
   Half sunk, a shatter'd visage lies.
9. These are the sprigs; flash boys, uncaught,
   Treading the reedy springboard of green days.
10. Today I think
    Only with scents.
11. From hidden sources
    A mustering of blind volcanic forces
    Takes her and shakes her till she sobs and gapes.
12. The leafy boughs on high
    Hissed in the sun;
    The dark air carried my cry
    Faintingly on.
13. The noise of silence, and the noise of blindness
    Do frighten me!
    They hold me stark and rigid as a tree!
14. An evil creature in the twilight looping,
    Flapped blindly in his face. Beating it off,
    He screeched in terror, and straightway something
        clambered
    Heavily from an oak ...
15. And then I pressed the shell
    Close to my ear,
    And listened well.
16. Out of the wood of thoughts that grows by night
    To be cut down by the sharp axe of light—
    Out of the night, two cocks together crow.

(The sources of these extracts are given at the end of this section, but don't look them up yet. They have been deliberately separated from the extracts themselves so that you will not be influenced in your impressions by the titles.)

When faced with an assignment like this, the first thing to do is to try to understand the piece of poetry as fully as you can. Since it is usually an extract taken out of context, this is not necessarily easy, but you should try. (Whether your interpretation gives a convincing view of the whole poem does not matter as we are only concerned with the extract given.) Explore the imagery if there is any; savour the words and the implications and the meanings which may lie beneath the surface. Work out, if you can, what the subject-matter appears to be—a description of night? a soldier in battle? an old man?

Having got some idea of what the extract is about consider what type of essay you could write using this piece of verse as a stimulus or as a starting off point. Remember the various categories open to you—character-sketch, description, story, argument. Could you write a story with this as a beginning? Could you use this as a character in a story? Could you write a description using this as one of the details? Could you write an account of a character with this as your starting off point? You must explore the possibilities before deciding on your actual method of approach.

The main problem with an assignment of this kind is the question of relevance. Usually, you will be asked to write anything that the scrap of poetry suggests to you. On the face of it, this leaves the field wide open: you could write about anything and claim that it was suggested by the poem. But since you will not be at the

examiner's elbow to argue your case, it is wiser to make sure that there is something in your story or description that shows a quite definite connection with the poem that inspired it. The poem may only be a starting point, or it may suggest a mood that you develop in your essay, or it may only provide a detail that you make use of; but the source of your inspiration must be patently clear in your piece of writing. That is why it is important that you understand the poetry given as fully as possible. A quick look at the verse may suggest an idea for you to write about which has no bearing on the original verse, and therefore any chance of your showing the relevance of your writing to the source of inspiration is impossible.

As an example of the process you should go through, look at the piece of verse given in 1. First, we must explore the verse. It appears to be a description of a frosty day. The world is cast—moulded, fixed fast as a piece of metal that is cast is moulded or set into a pattern—in the shape of frost. Frost has taken over and transformed the whole world. Frost has fixed the world fast in its icy grasp. There is 'not a leaf' because it is winter; there is 'not a bird' because they have all migrated or are sheltering from the cold. The absence of leaf and bird adds to the desolation of the atmosphere.

Next we must see what ideas for development the extract suggests, what types of essay it lends itself to. The most obvious one is a descriptive essay dealing with frost, showing how the coming of frost affects plant and bird and transforms the appearance of the world. Or you could use the idea of the frost as the setting for a story: the opening paragraph creates a desolate wintry scene in which something happens—perhaps an animal is trapped or a journey is made difficult or, using a contrast, skating is possible on a lake and there is an accident.

Finally, having chosen how to deal with the idea and having chosen an appropriate form, you must check that your essay remains relevant to the initial inspiration. A descriptive essay dealing with frost, its appearance and effect is likely to remain safely on the right lines. If you tell a story, however, you should try to make sure that the events of the story itself are affected by frost—an opening description of a frosty scene is probably not enough. If you then go on to tell a story about a boy maltreating his cat, this is not really relevant to the poem. If you show that the boy maltreats his cat through boredom because the frost prevents him from playing outside, then this is relevant.

Examine the other extracts from poems given at the beginning of this unit and explore them in the same way as outlined above. Write the essay that comes to mind for one of them.

(The sources of the extracts are as follows:

1. The Horses: Ted Hughes
2. Wales: R. S. Thomas
3. Prelude: T. S. Eliot
4. Romeo and Juliet: William Shakespeare
5. Strange Meeting: Wilfred Owen
6. The Soul Longs to Return Whence it Came: Richard Eberhardt
7. A Pauper: George Barker
8. Ozymandias: P. B. Shelley

READING AND UNDERSTANDING

Personal

Clearly, every writer reveals something of himself when he writes. His subject-matter may be related to events in his life or his background; his characters may be based on people he knows; the tone in which he writes, and the style of his work, may tell us about the kind of person he is. One would expect, therefore, that a writer would reveal himself most fully when he is writing directly about himself and his own life, and it is worthwhile looking at some autobiographical extracts to see how far this is true, and how a reader can build up a more complete picture of the writer from this kind of writing. (See the extracts from *Below Stairs* by Margaret Powell and *A Cackhanded War* by Edward Blishen in Unit 4 for other examples.)

Read the following extract carefully, bearing in mind these two questions: A. What do we learn about the writer from the attitudes indicated towards what she is describing? B. What do we learn about her from the style she uses? The extract is the opening of Billy Holliday's life story as told in Lady Sings the Blues *(written in conjunction with William Dufty).*

A Couple of Kids

Mom and Pop were just a couple of kids when they got married. He was eighteen, she was sixteen, and I was three.

Mom was working as a maid with a white family. When they found out she was going to have a baby they just threw her out. Pop's family just about had a fit, too, when they heard about it. They were real society folks and they never heard of things like that going on in their part of East Baltimore.

But both kids were poor. And when you're poor, you grow up fast.

It's a wonder my mother didn't end up in the workhouse and me as a foundling. But Sadie Fagan loved me from the time I was just a swift kick in the ribs while she scrubbed floors. She went to the hospital and made a deal with the head woman there. She told them she'd scrub floors and wait on the other bitches laying up there to have their kids so she could pay her way and mine. And she did. Mom was thirteen that Wednesday, April 7, 1915, in Baltimore when I was born.

By the time she worked her way out of hock in the hospital and took me home to her folks, I was so big and smart I could sit up in a carriage. Pop was doing

what all the boys did then—peddling papers, running errands, going to school. One day he came along by my carriage, picked me up, and started playing with me. His mother saw him and came hollering. She dragged at him and said, 'Clarence, stop playing with that baby. Everybody is going to think it's yours.'

'But, Mother, it *is* mine,' he'd tell her. When he talked back to his mother like this she would really have a fit. He was still only fifteen and in short pants. He wanted to be a musician and used to take lessons on the trumpet. It was almost three years before he got long pants for the wedding.

After they were married awhile we moved into a little old house on Durham Street in Baltimore. Mom had worked as a maid up North in New York and Philly. She'd seen all the rich people with their gas and electric lights and she decided she had to have them too. So she saved her wages for the day. And when we moved in we were the first family in the neighbourhood to have gas and electricity.

It made the neighbours mad, Mom putting in the gas. They said putting pipes in the ground would bring the rats out. It was true. Baltimore is famous for rats.

Pop always wanted to blow the trumpet but he never got the chance. Before he got one to blow, the Army grabbed him and shipped him overseas. It was just his luck to be one of the ones to get it from poison gas over there. It ruined his lungs. I suppose if he'd played piano he'd probably have got shot in the hand.

(BILLY HOLLIDAY and WILLIAM DUFTY,
Lady Sings the Blues)

Here are some more specific questions to help you answer the two basic questions:

A. 1. How are we intended to react to the opening paragraph?
   2. What can we tell about Billy's attitude towards the white family by the way she describes their reactions to her mother—'they just threw her out'?
   3. What can we tell about Billy's philosophy of life by her view 'When you're poor, you grow up fast'?
   4. Does the sentence 'And she did,' indicate anything of Billy's attitude towards her mother?
   5. Is the exchange between Clarence and his mother meant to be serious or comic? How does Billy regard these events?
   6. Can we tell how Billy felt about being the first family in the neighbourhood to have gas and electricity?
   7. Comment on the way the existence of rats in Baltimore is described.
   8. What can you tell about Billy's attitude to life by her comment 'I suppose if he'd played piano he'd probably have got shot in the hand?'

B. 1. Pick out examples of slang words used. What effect does this use have? What does it suggest about Billy?
   2. A number of sentences begin with 'And ...' What effect is intended?
   3. Sum up the tone of the extract.

Now read the following commentary:

A. From this extract, we get the impression that Billy Holliday knows what life is about. She has had to face the realities and has suffered. Yet she is able to look at life with a kind of wry amusement: it may have been tough, but she has survived so far and she can laugh about it.

The opening paragraph may be intended to be comic, but it is more likely that the intention is to shock. Immediately, Billy Holliday establishes that she lived in a world where illegitimate children occurred, and she has no intention of hiding the fact. Our attention is captured by the unexpectedness of the facts and by the honesty with which they are stated.

'They just threw her out' indicates surprise and indignation that the white family could behave in such a way—it is the use of the word 'just' that shows this.

Billy's statement 'When you're poor, you grow up fast' suggests that she is speaking from personal experience. Life is hard, and if you want to survive, you have to learn fast how to adapt yourself to these conditions.

'And she did' gives the statement emphasis. Billy's mother did exactly what she said she would do, and her determination and success are indicated by the sentence. It also suggests an element of admiration on Billy's part for her mother.

The exchange between Clarence and his mother is set up as a comic dialogue. The reader already knows that the baby is his, so we are amused by his mother's warning as it comes too late. Clarence's emphasis of the fact that the baby *is* his completes the comic situation. He is admitting with seeming eagerness to something he ought to be concealing. With affectionate amusement Billy is recreating the events which she could not have remembered.

There is an element of pride about being the first family in the neighbourhood to have gas and electricity. The way in which the incident is described, the build up of sentences, and the effect on the neighbours (it made them mad) with its suggestion of amused malice confirm this.

The existence of rats is understated. Billy says Baltimore was famous for rats, but she doesn't go into great unpleasant details about them. She leaves it at that and allows the reader's imagination to put two and two together.

Billy's comment about her father 'I suppose if he'd played piano he'd probably have got shot in the hand' shows her fatalistic and pessimistic attitude towards life. Misfortune is bound to happen and it's bound to happen in the most awkward and inconvenient way.

So a picture of Billy emerges that shows her tough, pessimistic though not down-trodden, looking with affection and amusement at her parents and the struggles they had. She is aware that life is difficult, that in the end she will probably be defeated, but she is not going to let that get her down.

B. Examples of slang used are 'a couple of kids', 'a swift kick in the ribs', 'out of hock', and many more. The effect of the use of slang is to put us immediately in touch with Billy: it is as though she is speaking directly to us. This kind of approach suggests that Billy is down to earth, she doesn't put on airs, she's not going to pretend to be someone special; she's just going to talk to us the way she'd talk to anyone, the way she's always talked.

The sentences beginning 'And ...' give emphasis to the various statements. Again, the speaking voice is captured. This, together with an emphatic expression on the face, is how a point would be given greater force in speech.

The use of slang establishes the general tone. It is racy, intimate, personal. The writer is speaking directly to the reader about herself. The short sentences and paragraphs also support this.

This brief examination of the style tells us something about the kind of person Billy Holliday was: she was eager to communicate, she wanted to speak face to face to people, she was down to earth and had no pretensions.

I have said before that what a writer tells us and how he tells it can reveal a great deal about the writer. This is most true of autobiography, but it requires close study and analysis on the part of the reader to see that this is so. You must be constantly open to receive the merest hint or clue that will indicate the truth or reality behind the words.

Here is another autobiographical extract. Read it carefully bearing in mind these two basic questions: A. What do we learn about the writer from the facts he describes? B. What do we learn about the kind of person he is from the style he uses?

1, Ashwell Terrace

The house in which we lived in Caerleon was No. 1, Ashwell Terrace, one of a row of cottages that have since been condemned. My father took it because it was cheap—and because he was married, young, and a carpenter only just starting in business as a cabinet-maker. I remember that when I played on the bit of pavement outside I could look right through the cottage as though it was a telescope, through the front door seeing the back garden so close I was afraid of being stung by bees. The reason was that the cottage was only one room wide—there was one room downstairs for cooking, eating, and living in, and one room upstairs for all of us to sleep in.

There was no gas in the house: cooking was done on an open fire or in an oven at its side heated by hot embers, the embers being scraped with a steel rake from the fire to a space under the oven. For lighting we had an oil lamp which stood in the middle of a beautiful pear-wood table made by my father. That oil lamp was a beauty, too: made simply to be practical it was as graceful in profile as a piece of Samian ware. Its brass curved sides were as full of little squares and circles of reflected daylight as a polished bed-knob, and through its globe of translucent porcelain you could see shadowy images of the furniture on the other side of the room. It was my father's job to light the lamp in the evening. To me this was a ritual and a spectacle that invested him with priestly power and glory. He held a match to the wick and the wild wick snatched the flame from his hand and threw it up in the air and bounced it on the floor and hurled it up to the ceiling and flung it from wall to wall: it was a rough and playful exhibition of the eternal conflict between the forces of light and darkness. Majestically my father turned the lamp's brass wheel

and the romping flame was hauled instantly back into the lamp like a tiger into its cage: the ceremony, short, brilliant, and daunting, was over. Now a cone of sunshine radiance hung placidly from the lamp to the floor, and until it was time for me to be put to bed I scrambled about in a bell-tent made of light.

In the daytime I played in the back garden, where my father grew leaves. There were millions, billions, trillions of them. Leaves were my ceilings, walls, partitions: they pressed me down and shut me in, and when I resisted they tugged at my hair, slapped my face, pushed themselves up the legs of my short trousers, sealed my nostrils, gagged my mouth, tolled at my ears, jazzed before my eyes; and sometimes my forehead smarted and ached from the brutal rebuff of wood as a branch denied my thrusting head. All the same, I liked the leaves, and spent hours in the thousands of acres where they grew, breathing foreign green air and getting tipsy on sappy, fruity smells.

After these exotic holidays in the leaves I made my way back to everyday life by staggering across our living-room to the street. It wasn't a street really—it was more of a lane. In it there was our row of cottages, whitewashed and blue-roofed, the white walls stained, broken and mildewed, but seen by me now through a haze of years that gives them a dairy sweetness; and alongside them were the few flagstones of pavement, then a dirt roadway, then a hedge with a wicket gate, and then beyond the hedge, as far as I could see, nothing—though a grown-up could have looked over the hedge and viewed fields and beyond them Tyn Barlym mountain hunched low to let the clouds pass over.

(CLIFFORD DYMENT, *The Railway Game*)

These questions may help you to reach a more definite conclusion:

A. 1. What does Clifford tell us about the size and quality of the house?
   2. What does he tell us about the objects in the house? What does this suggest?
   3. What action invests his father with a special quality? What does this tell us about Clifford's attitude towards his father?
   4. What indications are there that Clifford appreciates beauty and is imaginative?

B. 1. What does the writer's use of comparisons suggest? —e.g. 'as though it was a telescope', 'like a tiger into its cage', 'a bell-tent made of light'.
   2. Comment on the style of the paragraph beginning 'In the daytime ...'
   3. Comment on the contrast between 'these exotic holidays' and 'everyday life'.
   4. What indications are there that the writer is a poet?

 # READING LIST

Some autobiographies have been recommended incidentally earlier in this course, but here is a more complete list. Other people's lives can be very interesting, and they can often throw light on our own lives. They can provide an insight into experience and the pleasure of recognition as we realize that other people have passed through the same situations and emotions as ourselves. Try to read one of the following:

Billy Holliday and William Dufty: *Lady Sings the Blues*
Clifford Dyment: *The Railway Game*
Dannie Abse: *Ash on a Young Man's Sleeve*
Maurice O'Sullivan: *Twenty Years A-Growing*
Laurie Lee: *Cider with Rosie*
Margaret Powell: *Below Stairs*
Maxim Gorki: *My Childhood*
Richard Church: *Over the Bridge*
James Kirkup: *The Only Child*
Arthur Barton: *Two Lamps in Our Street*
Edward Blishen: *A Cackhanded War*
Robert Graves: *Goodbye to All That*
Frank Norman: *The Lives of Frank Norman*
V. S. Pritchett: *A Cab at the Door*
Denton Welch: *A Voice Through a Cloud*
W. H. Davies: *The Autobiography of a Super Tramp*
Caitlin Thomas: *Left Over Life to Live*

 # VOCABULARY

Here are some more words that are sometimes confused. Try to distinguish between them.

agnostic, atheist
antiquated, antique
informant, informer
inedible, uneatable
hoard, horde
historic, historical
human, humane
ostensible, ostentatious
re-enforce, reinforce
serge, surge

Check the meaning of these words by looking them up in a dictionary.

Use each of them in an interesting sentence of your own.

Check up on any other words used in this unit you were not sure about.

 # LANGUAGE

Slang

The word 'slang' has already been used a number of times in this course, and so it would be a good idea to have a clearer impression of what it means. It is sometimes difficult to distinguish between slang and colloquialism which was discussed in the 'Language' section of Unit 14. Both are forms of language which are rather inelegant and should normally be avoided in good writing except for dialogue or for naturalistic effect. Slang is even less refined than colloquial language; it is the use of a new or unusual name for an object invented by one group

160

of people and taken up by others, so as to appear fashionable or clever whereas colloquialism is the name given to an expression that may be accepted in speech but which one would not use in formal written Standard English. One can imagine a kind of sliding scale or table in which Standard English is in the first division, colloquialism in the second, and slang very definitely in the third. Some examples should make this clear.

Standard English	*Colloquialisms*	*Slang*
man	chap	bloke
fight	scrap	bundle
friend	pal	mate
mad	off his head	off his nut

Other examples of current slang are 'fed-up', 'browned off', 'booze', 'mug' (=face), 'mit' (=hand), 'bird' (=girl), 'shambles' (= chaos).
Slang can often become dated or hackneyed (e.g. 'smashing' or 'super'=very good; 'shower'=useless collection).

Some writers try to make slang 'respectable' by putting it into quotation marks, e.g.

When I lived in Spain, I studied the 'lingo'.

This isn't really acceptable, and it is safer to avoid slang altogether unless you are using it to provide a certain local colour because, although there is no denying that slang can sometimes help to make writing lively, examiners do not always look upon it with favour. (To see how effectively slang can be used to capture a particular tone of voice and personality read again the extract from *Lady Sings the Blues*. This could easily be defended as good writing of its kind, but you are not encouraged to copy it.)

It can be an amusing and interesting pastime to collect examples of slang. Write down as many instances as you can in your notebook and add to your list whenever you come across other examples.

Find Standard English and/or colloquial equivalents for the examples given above and for the following:

1. Leave him alone—he's only a kid.
2. They went out on a binge.
3. Why don't you use your loaf?
4. You must be thick if you can't work out the answer.
5. He makes a muck-up of every job he's given.
6. A pint of wallop, please.
7. My poor old plates of meat are giving me hell.
8. Why don't you shove off?
9. I was sorry to hear that he had kicked the bucket.
10. That's a nice bit of stuff.

 # SPELLING

'-ise', '-ize'

There is sometimes confusion about when a word ends in '-ise' or '-ize'. The form '-ise' is permissible in most cases. The form '-ize' tends to have the meaning 'to alter something in a particular way', e.g. 'naturalize' = 'to make something natural' (usually to a particular country).

Where this meaning is not present in the word, it is safe to use '-ise'. Examples where '-ize' is used are:

anglicize, authorize, bowdlerize, capsize, civilize, emphasize, fertilize, generalize, harmonize, humanize, minimize, naturalize, organize, prize, realize, recognize, seize, sympathize, visualize.

The following words *must* be spelled with '-ise':

advertise, advise, apprise, chastise, circumcise, demise, despise, devise, disguise, enterprise, excise, exercise, franchise, improvise, incise, prise, promise, revise, supervise, surmise, surprise, televise.

The ending '-ise' and '-ize' are pronounced the same, namely as though with 'z' except for 'promise' where it is pronounced as 's'. Check up on the meanings of the words given above, particularly the difference in meaning between 'prize' and 'prise', 'advise' and 'advice', 'devise' and 'device'.

Here is an exercise to test whether you have understood these notes. In some instances either '-ise' or '-ize' may be possible. Check your answers with the dictionary. Add the correct ending in each case.

1. If we are to improve, we must maxim— our efforts.
2. If we are to make a success of the project, we must capital— our resources.
3. You are emphasi—ing the wrong word.
4. How dare you critic— my behaviour.
5. Do you real— how rude you are being?
6. Please categor— these specimens.
7. Please exerc— some restraint.
8. The holy man was canon—d a hundred years later.
9. It's essential that you cauter— the wound.
10. At the party, please try to social— as much as possible.

 # ASSIGNMENT J

Part I should take about an hour and a quarter for preparation and writing, and your finished essay should be at least 500 words long. Part II should take about an hour.

Part I: Essay

Write an essay suggested by *one* of the following:

1. Late August, given heavy rain and sun
   For a full week, the blackberries would ripen.
2. For a touch of her fingers
   In a darkened room ...
3. They looked long at the moon and called it
   A silver button, a copper coin, a bronze wafer.
4. When the waltz throbbed out on the long promenade
   O his eyes and his smile they went straight to my heart.
5. They keep me sober,
   The old ladies
   Stiff in their beds,
   Mostly with pale eyes
   Wintering me.

Part II: Comprehension

Read the following poem carefully and then answer the questions set on it.

My Last Duchess

That's my last Duchess painted on the wall,
Looking as if she were alive. I call
That piece a wonder, now: Fra Pandolf's hands
Worked busily a day, and there she stands.
Will't please you sit and look at her? I said
'Fra Pandolf' by design, for never read
Strangers like you that pictured countenance,
The depth and passion of its earnest glance,
But to myself they turned (since none puts by
The curtain I have drawn for you, but I)
And seemed as they would ask me, if they durst,
How such a glance came there; so, not the first
Are you to turn and ask thus. Sir, 'twas not
Her husband's presence only, called that spot
Of joy into the Duchess' cheek: perhaps
Fra Pandolf chanced to say 'Her mantle laps
Over my lady's wrist too much,' or 'Paint
Must never hope to reproduce the faint
Half-flush that dies along her throat': such stuff
Was courtesy, she thought, and cause enough
For calling up that spot of joy. She had
A heart, how shall I say?—too soon made glad,
Too easily impressed; she liked whate'er
She looked on, and her looks went everywhere.
Sir, 'twas all one! My favour at her breast,
The dropping of the daylight in the West,
The bough of cherries some officious fool
Broke in the orchard for her, the white mule
She rode with round the terrace—all and each
Would draw from her alike the approving speech,
Or blush, at least. She thanked men,—good!—but thanked
Somehow—I know not how—as if she ranked
My gift of a nine-hundred-years-old name
With anybody's gift. Who'd stoop to blame
This sort of trifling? Even had you skill
In speech—(which I have not)—to make your will
Quite clear to such an one, and say, 'Just this
Or that in you disgusts me; here you miss,
Or there exceed the mark'—and if she let
Herself be lessoned so, nor plainly set
Her wits to yours, forsooth, and made excuse,
—E'en then would be some stooping; and I choose
Never to stoop. Oh sir, she smiled, no doubt,
Whene'er I passed her; but who passed without
Much the same smile? This grew; I gave commands;
Then all smiles stopped together. There she stands
As if alive. Will't please you rise? We'll meet
The company below, then. I repeat;
The Count your master's known munificence
Is ample warrant that no just pretence
Of mine for dowry will be disallowed;
Though his fair daughter's self, as I avowed
At starting, is my object. Nay, we'll go
Together down, sir. Notice Neptune, though,

Taming a sea-horse, thought a rarity,
Which Claus of Innsbruck cast in bronze for me!

(ROBERT BROWNING)

1. Who is speaking in the poem?
2. What is he doing?
3. Who is allowed to look at the portrait?
4. Describe the expression on the face of the portrait.
5. How does the speaker explain away the expression?
6. What is the speaker's main criticism of the character of the sitter for the portrait?
7. Why did the speaker refrain from reprimanding her?
8. What do you understand by 'I gave orders'?
9. Who is the speaker speaking to?
10. What is being planned?
11. Why does the speaker say 'Notice Neptune, though,/ Taming a seahorse, thought a rarity'?
12. What impression do you get of the speaker's character?
13. What impression do you get of the character of the Duchess?

UNIT 19

WRITING

Personal

A further look at autobiographical writing, this time from the point of view of writing it and how much livelier writing can be when you write from your own experience.

READING AND UNDERSTANDING

Style

A gathering together of the various points about style already touched on, and how to set about analysing the style of a prose passage.

READING LIST

Some war books that you may find interesting.

VOCABULARY

Some more words that could be confused.

LANGUAGE

Degeneration of Words

A look at how some words have lost their original power through misuse or overuse.

SPELLING

A section on careless spelling mistakes.

WRITING

Personal

Compton Mackenzie, giving advice to budding authors about their first novel, said, 'Write about something you know.' This advice was also given to you in the early units of this course when you set about choosing a subject for an essay. The full implications of this piece of advice have not been fully explored till now. Why should you write about something you know? Clearly because you will be acquainted with some facts, details, ideas about the subject that will be useful when you write about it. But even more important, if you are writing from personal experience, then your writing is likely to be more original, more interesting and more lively than if you are inventing it all.

We looked at some personal writing—autobiographical writing—in the 'Reading and Understanding' section of the previous unit. The extracts given there showed the authors remembering their parents and their childhood.

Read them again, and consider how much the amuse-ment, affection and admiration Billy Holliday shows for her parents comes from the fact that she is writing about people she knows, and how much the vividness of the portrait of 1, Ashwell Terrace comes from the fact that Clifford Dyment is describing a place that he knows and remembers personally.

People's lives, backgrounds and attitudes may have many similarities, but no two are likely to be identical. Therefore, if you write out of your own experience, you will be writing about what will be in many ways a unique experience and you will view it from a unique stand-point. This kind of originality of view can give writing about personal matters a freshness which it might not otherwise have.

Some students may think that their personal experience in childhood or within the family is too ordinary or trivial to be of interest to anyone else. In this they would be mistaken. Nothing is more fascinating than other people, and if you present your experience clearly and honestly then the fact that you are writing about yourself and remembering things that happened to you in a way that they didn't happen to other people will in itself make your writing interesting.

Other students may feel a reserve about writing about

163

their personal experience. After all, an examination is an impersonal affair, and lessons are conducted with people whom you don't know all that well, and you may regard it as a breach of privacy to be expected to pour out your personal feelings and describe things that happened to you. And this is a perfectly justifiable reaction. That is why, although some of the titles suggested for essays previously have dealt with personal themes, the idea of personal writing has not been raised till now and there has been no compulsion about writing personally. But it is unlikely that you will be asked to reveal intimate secrets or write about painful or unpleasant experiences. Most assignments about personal matters will be of the 'ordinary and trivial' nature mentioned in the previous paragraph. If you feel that you can tackle assignments like this, do so because they are likely to embody genuine feeling and fresh details that will be interesting. If you feel shy about this kind of writing, look for another title that you can feel easy about tackling.

As an example of how fresh and lively personal writing can be, read the following extract from *Twenty Years A-Growing*. The subject is 'Hallowe'en' which you may think is hackneyed and difficult to make interesting. I think Maurice O'Sullivan makes his description lively because he portrays in a straightforward way the events of a Hallowe'en from his Irish childhood. The short sentences, the Irish rhythms and names, the high spirits of the events, all contribute to the effectiveness of the description, but above all the exuberance and clarity come from the fact that the writer is remembering the way that he himself spent Hallowe'en.

Hallowe'en

When the long cold nights came the boys and girls spent them in our house. How happy we were waiting for Hallowe'en, and playing the old Gaelic games—the Ring, the Blind Man, Knucklestones, Trom-Trom, and Hide-and-Seek; a fine red fire sending warmth into every corner, bright silver sand from the White Strand on the floor glittering in the lamplight, two boys and two girls going partners at a game of knucklestones in one corner of the house, four more in another corner.

It was Hallowe'en, and most of the boys were in Dingle. We were expecting a great night of it, when they would come home with the apples, oranges, and sweets. Maura and Eileen had the hearth swept and scrubbed, a glowing fire was burning, the lamp alight, and we waiting.

'Aren't they a long time coming?' said Eileen, with a glance at the fire and then at the door.

'They won't be long now,' said Maura, and soon we heard the chatter and laughter approaching.

The door opened and the clamour and clatter poured into the house. You would think they had been in prison for many a long day and had only just been let out.

The games began. A cord was tied to the rafters and a big red apple tied to the cord. One goes down to the door and takes a running leap up towards the apple. He misses it. Then another. The third succeeds in getting a bite. So they go on till the apples are all eaten. Then another game begins. There is a big bowl of water at the fireside and they are roasting beans. Every boy and girl who are great with each other get two beans, a little one

for the woman and a big one for the man. They put the two beans in the fire. As soon as they are roasted they draw out the beans and throw them into the bowl of water. If they sink it is a sign that those two have great love for each other, and I tell you they are the two who would sleep happily that night.

Tomas Owen Vaun and I were amongst them, but we were too small to try for the apples. But when one of the boys would get one in the leap, he would give it to us, that way we had our bellies full all night long.

When the apples and sweets and everything else were eaten, Padrig Peg stood up: 'I am going to make a short speech,' he said, 'and I hope all will agree with what I have to say.'

Everyone claps hands.

'Now,' said he, 'this is Hallowe'en, and it is not known who will be living when it comes again, so I am going to propose another plan to make a night till morning of it. We will all go in twos and threes with lanterns through the island hunting thrushes, and when we have made our round let everyone come back here. See you have a good fire down for us, Maura, and there is no fear but we'll have a roast for the night.'

'Very good,' said one. 'A great thought,' said another. Everyone agreed.

They began to look for bottles to knock the bottom out of them, for there is no lantern so handy as such a bottle with a candle stuck into the neck. Everyone was ready to go, all except Maura and Maura O'Shea, who were to stay in the house baking bread and cakes.

(MAURICE O'SULLIVAN, *Twenty Years A-Growing*)

Here is another example, an account of an eleven-year-old boy's visit to the synagogue. The description is more impressionistic and includes the boy's thoughts as well as an account of the events, but again it is the personal quality—the fact that the author is remembering his own experience and can see it clearly in his mind's eye—that makes it vivid and interesting.

When breakfast was over, I had to go to the synagogue, rain or shine, for it was Saturday morning. I used to sit next to Bernard and Simon. We would wear our skull caps and whisper to each other beneath the chant of the Hebrew prayer. A man with a spade-shaped beard would stutter and mutter at us now and then and again. 'Shush, shush,' his eyes said. Such and these times, we would stare at the prayer book and giggle. It seemed natural that the prayer book wasn't in English, but written and told in some strange language one read from right to left, some mystical language one couldn't understand. Obviously, one couldn't speak to God in everyday English. We stood up when the congregation stood up and sat down when they sat down. The men were segregated from the women lest they should be deviated from their spiritual commerce with God. The women prayed upstairs nearer to heaven; the men downstairs nearer to hell. The sermon would begin and I would stare at the red globe that burned the never-failing oil. The Rev. Aaronowich, a man with an enormous face, gave the sermon. Usually his tone was melancholy. Every New Year, Rosh Hashana, he would begin his speech, raising his hands, eyes round, mournfully direct, 'Another year has passed . . . another nail . . . in the coffin.' The congregation knew this preface to his sermon by heart. They could have joined in, if they so wished, in some sorrowful chant; instead (except for the elders who nodded their heads slowly as if watching vertical tennis) each would nudge and pinch his neighbour.

However, this Saturday morning in 1934, the Rev. Aaronowich was almost gay. I stopped staring at the red globe and ignored the scrubbings and scratchings of Simon and Bernard. He spoke in English, with a Russian and Welsh accent, throwing in a bit of Yiddish when his vocabulary failed him. I think I could understand what he was saying. I believe he proclaimed that it was an honour to be alive, good to breathe fresh air, miraculous to be able to see the blue sky and the green grass; that health was our most important benediction and that one should never say 'no' to the earth. (Also, that the congregation should as Jews avoid ostentatiousness.) Never to despair, for when one felt dirty inside, or soiled, or dissatisfied, one only had to gaze at the grandeur of the windswept skies or at the pure wonder of landscapes—one only had to remember the beauty of human relationships, the gentleness and humour of the family, the awe and tenderness when a young man looks upon his betrothed—all things of the earth, of the whole of Life, its comedy, its tragedy, its lovely endeavour and its profound consummation—and I understood this for only that morning my brother Leo had read me from a little blue book words that sounded like 'Glory be to God for dappled things'—though, then, I didn't know what 'dappled' meant. And the Rev. Aaronowich spoke such beautiful things in such a broken accent that his voice became sweet and sonorous and his huge mask-like face rich, ruffled, handsome.

Afterwards, there was nothing to do but to stare at the red globe again, as the congregation offered thanks to God. In that red globe the oil of Jewish history burned, steadily, devotedly. Or was it blood? Blood of the ghettoes of Eastern Europe. My brother Wilfred said a world flickered in that globe: the red wounds of Abel, the ginger hair on the backs of the hands of Esau, the crimson threaded coat of Joseph, the scarlet strings of David's harp, the blood-stained sword of Judas Maccabeus—David, Samson, Solomon, Job, Karl Marx, Sigmund Freud, my brother said lived in that globe. Gosh.

The service seemed interminable, the swaying men, the blue and white *tallisim* around their shoulders, the little black *yamakels*, the musty smelling prayer books, the wailing cry of the Rev. Aaronowich, the fusty smell of sabbaths centuries old. Thousands of years of faith leaned with the men as they leaned—these exiled Jews whose roots were in the dangerous ghetto and in dismayed beauty. Their naked faces showed history plainly, it mixed in their faces like ancient paint to make a curious synthesis of over-refinement and paradoxical coarseness. One received a hint, even as they prayed, a hint of that unbearable core of sensual suffering. As they murmured their long incantations, I saw in their large dark eyes that infinite, that mute animal sadness, as in the liquid eyes of fugitives everywhere. I was eleven years old then: I could not have named all this but I knew it . . . I knew it all.

(DANNIE ABSE, *Ash on a Young Man's Sleeve*)

For practice, write an essay on one of the following subjects. They are all intended to be examples of personal writing, but if you do not feel able to write personally, treat the title as the subject for a story. Of course, your personal writing doesn't have to be totally true to your experience and accurate: it could be based on personal experience with extra details and ideas supplied by your imagination.

1. My First Day at School
2. Christmas Day
3. Sunday Morning
4. My First Date
5. In Hospital
6. My Parents

READING AND UNDERSTANDING

Style

A number of points about the criticism and appreciation of style have been made in these units, and it is now time to gather these together so that we have a clearer idea of the kind of things we are looking for when we study the style of a piece of writing. You are unlikely to have a question in the examination asking you to comment on the style of a whole passage, but as indicated in Unit 2, there will almost certainly be questions about specific stylistic points. There are three main areas that need to be examined.

1. Sentence structure (and punctuation). Look at the passage and work out whether the sentences tend to be long, or short, or a mixture of both, or long followed by a short one. This should not be difficult to determine. Next you must decide what effect the sentence structure has and whether this effect is appropriate to the subject-matter. If the sentences are long, does this give a heavy ponderous effect? Is the subject serious? Do the two relate? If the sentences are short, does this give a fast intense atmosphere to the writing? Is the piece of writing about a fast-moving action? Do the two correspond? Are the sentences made up of a number of phrases neatly balanced (antithesis)? Is the writing a detailed argument? Are the sentence structure and the subject compatible?

Questions about punctuation relate more to individual points than to a consideration of the style of a whole passage, but you must be able to explain why a colon, for example, has been used at a particular point, or a semicolon, or quotation marks, and say why it is appropriate—or inappropriate.

2. Language and imagery. You must be able to look at a passage and generalize about the type of language used. Does the writer use a lot of colloquialisms? Is the language learned and formal? Are there lots of images and comparisons? Next you must relate this to the subject-matter and say whether it is suitable or not, whether the use of colloquial language, for instance, is appropriate to what is being written about and helps to make the subject-matter more effective. An account of a fish and chip shop in learned language, for instance, would be rather strange unless there were some satiric intent. Another point to consider is the kind of words used. Does the writer use expressive verbs suggesting movement? Does he use words because their sound is appropriate (onomatopoeia)? Does he use a large number of adjectives?

3. Tone. This has been dealt with fully in previous units (13 and 14) but a brief summary here may be useful. You must be able to decide whether an author is being serious or comic, personal or impersonal, sympathetic or hostile, ironic or persuasive. Next you must determine whether this is an appropriate tone for what he is writing about. If, for instance, an account of the funeral of the writer's father strikes you as comic, you must decide whether this is intentional or unintentional. If it is unintentionally comic, then it is a bad piece of writing. If it is intentionally comic, you must then go on to consider whether this is appropriate. It is not the kind of treatment one would expect, so what lies behind this kind of treatment of this solemn subject-matter? Is he being satiric? Is he being comic to hide his real feelings? Is he being comic because he has no feelings for his father? Only when you have found the answers to questions like these can you decide whether the tone is appropriate or not and how effective it is. This requires careful thought and consideration.

Here is a short passage for you to study. The writer is in hospital. Examine the style according to the three headings given above before reading the commentary that follows.

Someone had put a dahlia in a pencil-thin vase on the table in the middle of the room, and as I saw the sun glint on its tongue petals, flashing them into scarlet spears, and on its smaller spoon petals, making them brim over with molten sealing-wax, I was filled with an extraordinary upsurge of delight, a fierce renewal of pleasure. For a moment my whole body was concentrated on the flower; its perfection and pungent colour, and the wonder of its paper-smooth flesh—the face it had on it, somehow all innocence and guile together. I was in the state to make it human: that vibrating scarlet ball set me thinking of everything beautiful away from the ward.

It was autumn now, with the plane leaves falling in the square. I thought of the iron railings, just waiting for the orange winter rust; and I longed to get away.

If I could be lying in a field of spongy grass, close to the fiery wood where the light under the leaves was yellow, like lamplight! If I could hear the cold grass-snake slithering close to me, polishing a tunnel through the razor grasses. If I could see again the grim hut in a field near my grandfather's, where a wild beast man lived with his goat, his beehive and the skeleton of a child's perambulator. He swore at passers-by and made horrible faces, showing his jagged fangs.

If I could go to the bottom of Spring Hill and drink water so bitingly clear that it had almost the 'black'

look of old glass, I would cup my hands, or sink my face in, wetting my forelock.

I thought of all these things. And then they came to get me up and into a wheel-chair, with a red blanket over my knees.

(DENTON WELCH, *A Voice Through a Cloud*)

1. **The opening sentence is long.** It builds phrase on phrase, and reflects the emotion of the writer, his joy in exploring the beauty of the flower. Later, there are a series of sentences beginning 'If I could . . .' These also build up a strong emotional response. The writer's longing to be among nature and to revisit beloved places is emphasized by this repeated pattern of sentences. The two sentences of the last paragraph show the writer being brought back to the reality of his situation. They are short statements of fact.

2. **The passage is strongly metaphorical.** The dahlia in the first paragraph has 'tongue petals', 'scarlet spears', 'spoon petals'; its petals 'brim over with molten sealing-wax'. The writer wants us to see the flower with the same intensity and delight that he experiences, and so he uses these vivid images so that we are able to imagine the flower with a new perception. Later, when describing the life he would like to be living—'lying in a field of spongy grass', hearing the grass-snake 'polishing a tunnel through razor grasses', drinking water 'so bitingly clear that it had almost the "black" look of old glass'—the writer again wants us to experience these things and know what they mean to him. His images appeal to the senses and help us to visualize and understand his deep longing. The imagery helps to make the experiences more immediate.

Notice too how the writer affixes an adjective to nearly every noun—'pencil-thin vase', 'tongue petals', 'scarlet spears', 'spoon petals', 'molten sealing-wax', 'extraordinary upsurge', 'fierce renewal', 'whole body', 'pungent colour', 'paper-smooth flesh'. Everything has to be qualified so that the reader can see and experience what the author is describing. (This habit could also be seen as a fault in the style as it sets up a pattern which could become repetitive and monotonous.)

3. **The passage is not categorized by one particular tone,** other than that associated with someone meditating on the present and the past. Some of it is concerned with factual reporting; other parts with personal reactions and emotions. It is a mixture of objective writing and emotional response. The writer sees everything from his own point of view so the passage is intensely personal. Perhaps the most distinctive example of tone is contained in the sentences beginning 'If I could . . .' which reveal the writer's sensuous longing for the pleasures of nature. Nostalgia is an important element of the tone here.

In the same way, analyse the following passages:

1. And we pumped. And there was no break in the weather. The sea was white like a sheet of foam, like a cauldron of boiling milk; there was not a break in the clouds, no—not the size of a man's hand—no, not for so much as ten seconds. There was for us no sky, there were for us no stars, no sun, no universe—nothing but angry clouds and an infuriated sea. We pumped watch and watch, for dear life; and it seemed to last for months,

for years, for all eternity, as though we had been dead and gone to a hell for sailors. We forgot the day of the week, the name of the month, what year it was, and whether we had ever been ashore. The sails blew away, she lay broadside on under a weather-cloth, the ocean poured over her, and we did not care. We turned those handles, and had the eyes of idiots. As soon as we had crawled on deck I used to take a round turn with a rope about the men, the pumps, and the mainmast, and we turned, we turned incessantly, with the water to our waists, to our necks, over our heads. It was all one. We had forgotten how it felt to be dry.

And there was somewhere in me the thought: By Jove! this is a deuce of an adventure—something you read about; and it is my first voyage as second mate—and I am only twenty—and here I am lasting it out as well as any of these men, and keeping my chaps up to the mark. I was pleased. I would not have given up the experience for worlds. I had moments of exultation. Whenever the old dismantled craft pitched heavily with her counter high in the air, she seemed to me to throw up, like an appeal, like a defiance, like a cry to the clouds without mercy, the words written on her stern: '*Judea*, London. Do or Die'.

O youth! The strength of it, the faith of it, the imagination of it! To me she was not an old rattle-trap carting about the world a lot of coal for a freight—to me she was the endeavour, the test, the trial of life. I think of her with pleasure, with affection, with regret—as you would think of some one dead you have loved. I shall never forget her . . .

(JOSEPH CONRAD, *Youth*)

2. I trotted on along the edge of the field bordered by the sunken lane, smelling green grass and honeysuckle, and I felt as though I came from a long line of whippets trained to run on two legs, only I couldn't see a toy rabbit in front and there wasn't a collier's cosh behind to make me keep up the pace. I passed the Gunthorpe runner whose shimmy was already black with sweat and I could just see the corner of the fenced-up copse in front where the only man I had to pass to win the race was going all out to gain the half-way mark. Then he turned into a tongue of trees and bushes where I couldn't see him anymore, and I couldn't see anybody, and I knew what the loneliness of the long distance runner running across country felt like, realizing that as far as I was concerned this feeling was the only honesty and realness there was in the world and I knowing it would be no different ever, no matter what I felt at odd times, and no matter what anybody else tried to tell me. The runner behind me must have been a long way off because it was so quiet, and there was even less noise and movement than there had been at five o'clock of a frosty winter morning. It was hard to understand, and all I knew was that you had to run, run, run, without knowing why you were running, but on you went through fields you didn't understand and into woods that made you afraid, over hills without knowing you'd been up and down, and shooting across streams that would have cut the heart out of you had you fallen into them. And the winning post was no end to it, even though crowds might be

cheering you in, because on you had to go before you got your breath back, and the only time you stopped really was when you tripped over a tree trunk and broke your neck and fell into a disused well and stayed dead in the darkness for ever. So I thought: they aren't going to get me on this racing lark, this running and trying to win, this jogtrotting for a bit of blue ribbon, because it's not the way to go on at all, though they swear blind that it is. You should think about nobody and go your own way, not on a course marked out for you by holding mugs of water and bottles of iodine in case you fall and cut yourself so that they can pick you up—even if you want to stay where you are—and get you moving again.

(ALAN SILLITOE, *The Loneliness of the Long Distance Runner*)

3. The virtue of Marcus Aurelius Antoninus was of a severer and more laborious kind. It was the well-earned harvest of many a learned conference, and many a midnight lucubration. At the age of twelve years he embraced the rigid system of the Stoics which taught him to submit his body to his mind, his passion to his reason; to consider virtue as the only good, vice as the only evil, all things external as things indifferent. His *Meditations*, composed in the tumult of a camp, are still extant: and he even condescended to give lessons of philosophy, in a more public manner than was perhaps consistent with the modesty of a sage or the dignity of an emperor. But his life was the noblest commentary on the precepts of Zeno. He was severe to himself, indulgent to the imperfections of others, just and beneficent to all mankind. He regretted that Avidius Cassius, who excited a rebellion in Syria, had disappointed him, by a voluntary death, of the pleasure of converting an enemy into a friend; and he justified the sincerity of that sentiment by moderating the zeal of the senate against the adherents of the traitor. War he detested, as the disgrace and calamity of human nature, but when the necessity of a just defence called upon him to take up arms, he readily exposed his person to eight winter campaigns on the frozen banks of the Danube, the severity of which was at last fatal to the weakness of his constitution. His memory was revered by a grateful posterity, and above a century after his death, many persons preserved the image of Marcus Antoninus among those of their household gods.

(EDWARD GIBBON, *The Decline and Fall of the Roman Empire*)

READING LIST

Many people enjoy reading war books. Often, these books are shallow, gloating over the atrocities and violence, or glamorizing the exciting adventure and gallant bravery. Here are some books that try to go more deeply below the surface of war and show the reality behind it.

Joe Heller: *Catch-22*
Ernest Hemingway: *A Farewell to Arms*
Stephen Crane: *The Red Badge of Courage*
H. E. Bates: *Fair Stood the Wind for France*

Norman Mailer: *The Naked and the Dead*
The Diary of Anne Frank
E. E. Cummings: *The Enormous Room*
Robert Graves: *Goodbye to All That*
C. S. Forester: *The Ship*
Evelyn Waugh: *Men at Arms*
Anthony Powell: *The Valley of Bones*
Siegfried Sassoon: *Memoirs of an Infantry Officer*
Ford Madox Ford: *Some Do Not*

 VOCABULARY

Try to distinguish between the following words which are sometimes confused.

dingy, dinghy
flaunt, flout
imperative, imperious
imply, infer
gorilla, guerrilla
nationalize, naturalize
negligent, negligible
observance, observation
temporal, temporary
classic, classical

Check the meaning of these words by looking them up in a dictionary.

Use each of them in an interesting sentence of your own.

Check up on any other words you have met in this unit that you were not sure about.

 LANGUAGE

Degeneration of Words

Some words began with precise and powerful meanings, but through over-use or carelessness in their use, the meanings have become weakened. The word 'epic', for instance, originally referred to a narrative poem celebrating the deeds of a hero. *The Iliad* and *The Odyssey* of Homer are epics: they deal with the mythical and larger than life exploits of heroes and gods. But nowadays, the word is used loosely to describe something on a large scale, e.g.

After an epic struggle for control of the ball, Wilson
    scored the winning goal.
Adelaide Grande is the star of the latest epic from
    Olympic Studios.

These examples show the word 'epic' being used in a common but debased way. Neither Wilson nor Adelaide Grande can really be compared with the god-like heroes of Greek poetry. By using the word in this way, it has degenerated and lost much of its power. It has become little more than a cliché. As with clichés, this kind of loose use of language is the sign of a lazy imprecise mind and should be avoided. Look out for examples of language used in this way in the popular newspapers, particularly in headlines.

168

Here are some further examples of words which have been degraded by over-use or imprecise use. Find out what the words originally meant.

Appalling, awful, colossal, dreadful, fabulous, fantastic, frightful, ghastly, great, horrible, mammoth, nice, sensational, terrible, tragedy, tremendous.

Use each in a sentence in its original sense.

 SPELLING

The most frequent spelling mistakes are the results of carelessness, haste or lack of thought. A student might write 'That is the house were I was born. There where five of us.' If it is pointed out to him that there is something wrong with the spelling in these sentences, he can nearly always find the mistakes ('were' should be 'where' and 'where' should be 'were'). It is easy to see how the mistakes occurred in the haste of writing; the words are pronounced practically the same, and the writer was thinking too fast to bother about the correct forms. Here are some more common errors of this type. Check that you can distinguish between the words.

allowed, aloud	peal, peel
ascent, assent	pedal, peddle
advice, advise	peer, pier
bare, bear	plain, plane
bean, been	practice, practise
boar, bore	pray, prey
brake, break	prise, prize
buy, by	quiet, quite
coarse, cause	rain, reign, rein
council, counsel	review, revue
chord, cord	right, write
creak, creek	ring, wring
flair, flare	sail, sale
gamble, gambol	sea, see
gorilla, guerrilla	seam, seem
groan, grown	sear, seer
hail, hale	soar, sore
hair, hare	some, sum
heal, heel	sort, sought
hear, here	stair, stare
hew, hue	stear, steer
hoard, horde	stile, style
leak, leek	storey, story
mail, male	tea, tee
manner, manor	team, teem
meat, meet	their, there, they're
miner, minor	threw, through
moan, mown	troop, troupe
muscle, mussel	vain, vane, vein
naval, navel	waist, waste
of, off	wait, weight
pail, pale	waive, wave
pain, pane	weak, week
pair, pare, pear	weather, whether
pale, pall	were, where
passed, past	yoke, yolk.
peace, piece	

UNIT 20

PRE-EXAMINATION RECAPITULATION

Essays

A summary of advice on how to set about an essay in the examination, together with some examples of examination essays for you to study and evaluate.

SPELLING

A list of words commonly mis-spelled for you to check up on and learn.

ASSIGNMENT K

An actual examination paper of the type you are likely to be set for you to attempt.

PRE-EXAMINATION RECAPITULATION

Essays

The time has come for us to gather together the various points about the imaginative essay you will be required to write in the examination. Much advice has been given about the general approach to the essay and about specific types of essays in previous units. It is up to you to revise these carefully now. The notes that follow give only the briefest indication of the points you need to remember if you are to do yourself justice.

It is worth reminding you that you will probably have to show yourself capable of coping effectively with two types of writing: the imaginative and the practical. The first requires you to make up or invent a story or a description or to reproduce in an interesting way an account of some aspect of your life or to organize your views about some controversial topic. The second requires you to present facts (sometimes supplied to you) in a clear and fluent way. Most of the advice that follows refers to both types of writing.

1. Where there is a choice (and there usually is a choice) **choose your subject carefully.** If it is an imaginative essay, make sure you choose a title you know something about, one you can develop in an interesting and original way because you have plenty of ideas and material at your disposal.

2. Study your chosen subject carefully and investigate the various possible ways it can be developed. If it is an imaginative subject, would it be better as a story, as a description, as an argument?

3. Plan and organize your material carefully. Have in mind some overall shape for your writing. Know before you start writing how you are going to begin, how you

are going to develop your material, how you are going to end.

4. Spend time working out an effective opening and ending. Ask yourself what is the best way to begin and end. Consider a number of alternatives. Decide on what seems to you the best. Ask yourself whether your opening would encourage a reader to go on, and whether your ending leaves him satisfied or stimulated.

5. Make sure that what you write is relevant to the subject. This means that you must be certain in the first place that you have understood the implications of the title. Then you must keep asking yourself whether what you write is still relevant and whether you are sticking to the point.

6. Keep an eye on the quality of your writing. Are you using stereotyped hackneyed phrases or is your writing fresh and alive? Have you managed to use interesting comparisons and examples? Does your essay give the impression that you yourself are involved in it and have something urgent to say? Are you relating the words you use and the kind of sentences you write to the subject-matter of the essay? What kind of response are you trying to arouse in your reader and do the words and sentences you use help to produce this response?

7. Keep an eye on the technical quality of your writing. Is your spelling accurate? If you can't remember how to spell a particular word, is there another word that you can spell which would do just as well, or can you turn the phrase round another way? Are you punctuating your sentences correctly? Are you putting in all the full stops in the right places? Are you paragraphing effectively so that each paragraph is complete in itself and yet leads on fluently to the next?

If you are to do all of this successfully, you need to develop strong powers of self-criticism, and hopefully this is what this course has been guiding you towards. By studying the writing of others, and by learning what works and what does not, what is effective and what is flabby, you should be able to look objectively at what you yourself write. You ought to be able to judge when you are writing well and when you are being ineffective, when you have expressed your arguments clearly and when they are woolly and vague, when you have gone deeply into a subject and when you have floated superficially on the surface.

Some Sample Essays

Now we are going to look at some actual essays written by students under examination conditions. The kind of questions and comments made on these are the kind of questions and comments you should ask about your own essay when you write one for practice and when you write one in the examination.

The subject for the first two essays we are going to look at was as follows: 'This is an age of popular idols, especially in sport and entertainment. Do you think that these "idols" deserve the hero-worship, publicity and money they receive?'

This is clearly an argumentative type of essay. The obvious way to organize the material for such an essay would be to consider why these idols deserve hero-worship, publicity and money on one side, and why they do not on the other. Under the first heading, we might consider things like the pleasure they give to people, the possible shortness of their popularity, the arduousness of the life; under the second heading would come points like this: they present a false set of values; they don't perform an essential service; in some cases they don't even possess any discernible talent. As a general introduction, one might make a comparison between the rewards of pop singers and those of nurses, for example. One point to note about the title is that it raises three areas for discussion: hero-worship, publicity and money. Each of these needs to be fully discussed if the essay is to be regarded as being on the subject.

Here is an examination essay written on this title. Read it carefully and consider it under the following headings suggested earlier:

1. Does it develop the subject effectively?
2. Is the material planned and organized?
3. Are the opening and ending effective?
4. Is all the material relevant?
5. Is the writing effective? Is it fresh, interesting and lively?
6. Is the writing technically accurate as regards spelling, punctuation, expression and paragraphing?

The essay is reproduced as written and an asterisk appears in the margin opposite every line in which there is a technical mistake. Correct these.

    I think that sportsmen and pop singers get far too
* much money for their work and this is the cause for
    some of them behaving badly. Pop singers do get
** through alot of work; writing and composing the
    music, going to recording studios nearly every day of
the week, thinking up new records that will please their fans and the public. I think this is no excuse, though, for behaving the way some of them do.
* Smoking pot, violence, orgies; all these accusations, some of them true, have been levelled at pop singers at one time or another.
**   Those who are guiltly of these things, should not be paid and, as smoking pot and the other accusations are all criminal offences, should be put into prison. Of course there are many pop stars who do
** not endulge in this sort of behavior and work only for the satisfaction of their fans and the public. I think the price of concerts should stay as they are now and should not go any higher.
    It is the same with sportsmen. They train very
* hard for their one particular sport and it is expected from them to give a good show of skill to the public.
** In some sports eg football the prices of transfers and
* the amount the players recieve has gone way out of proportion. The majority of the players all have a certain amount of skill but it must be a disgrace for their fans when some of them are arrogant and play dirty on the pitch. Also I think that if any sort of sportsman swears while he is playing his sport he cannot be called a real sportsman. When these things happen I think he is letting his fans down and does not deserve his pay or the publicity he gets. The majority of sportsmen, though, play their sport fairly and train and work only for the joy of perhaps breaking a record and the satisfaction of their fans. In some sports if players swear or make rude signs they are fined a certain amount of money. These penalties are good and make players think twice before they
* commit an unjust offence but I think that after a while, if the penalties do not seem to work, they should be threatened with a long ban or completely banned from the game. The pop singers and sports-
* men must also be more quieter in their private lives. They are always in the public eye and they must not carry on the way some of them do.
*   If these 'idols' do something well they are
* applauded and complemented for it. They expect this sort of treatment as they are stars.
**   Therefore if they do something bad I think they must expect to be punished and not argue or be temperamental when that time comes. They must
* remember that they have and image to keep and to protect. If they carry on the way some of them do,
* this image will be shattered and they must expect this to happen if they behave badly.

Answering the questions above should have led you to some conclusions about the quality of the essay. Do you think it deserves a pass mark in the examination?

Here are my comments. The opening sentence is ineffective. It is too long for a start and doesn't arouse interest. Having stated his opinion at the very beginning, there is little encouragement to read further. It would have been more interesting if the essay had been an exploration with the writer reaching a conclusion at the end, not at the beginning.

Look at the sentences in the opening paragraph. Do

they have any continuity? They can be summarized as follows: 1. Pop-heroes are paid too much and some of them behave badly. 2. They have to work hard. 3. This is no excuse for their behaviour. 4. They have been accused of bad behaviour. There is not really any logical connection between these statements. Even if there were, I doubt whether it is really an effective introduction to the subject. This same lack of logic can be found in other paragraphs. For instance, what does the last sentence of the second paragraph have to do with the point being made in that paragraph?

Paragraph 3 begins with a statement that tries to link the argument with the preceding thought, but it is so vaguely expressed that the connection is not really clear. 'It is the same with sportsmen,' says the writer. What does 'it' refer to?

And so the essay goes rambling on. The final sentence is a repetitive statement of the obvious: what it says is 'If they behave badly, their image will be shattered, and they must expect their image to be shattered if they behave badly.' Hardly a very profound thought on which to close.

The main trouble is that the writer has not understood the point behind the question. He makes the statement that if pop-heroes misbehave they should be punished, whereas the question is asking whether pop-heroes (whether they misbehave or not) deserve more money (and hero-worship and publicity, which the writer largely ignores) than nurses, for instance. There is very little understanding of this in the essay.

The actual writing of the essay is flat and pedestrian. The sentences tend to be too long. Points are not made effectively. There are no illuminating or vitally expressed examples. Technically, too, the essay has its weaknesses. The punctuation is sometimes odd and the paragraphing is inadequate. There is some awkward phrasing and the expression 'I think' occurs far too often. I would consider this essay to be well below the standard required for a pass.

Here is another example on the same subject. Consider it from the same point of view as the previous essay, answering the same questions before you read on.

It seems to me that although it would at first appear that the 'popular idols' of today are grossly overpaid
* and overrated in every way, it is only fair to think a little more deeply into the work they do.

Footballers, for example, some people seem to feel, are paid incredibly high sums considering the work they do. However, what these people don't
* seem to realise, is that the way a player plays in a match is just the end-product of much hard work and methodical training. Not that it is really the actual work that the players do for their clubs which makes me feel they ought to be paid better. The stresses and strains of playing perhaps as many as sixty or seventy games a season, all of which are vitally important, must surely justify the high wages some players earn. I also feel that it is necessary to
* point out that there are really only a 'handful' of footballers in Britain (when compared with the total number of players) who earn, say, £200 a week and can be classed as idols. Therefore it seems to me

that if a player becomes an 'idol', he is really at the
* peak of his proffesion, and deserves all the money he can get. I feel that it should also be pointed out that the small number of footballers who get to the top are there, usually, for as little as about ten years,
* and thus must 'make hay while the sun shines, and that footballers are very prone to injuries which can ruin their careers.

* In the field of sport, footballers in this country at any rate, are the sportsmen who are usually thought of as being highly-paid. Other highly-paid sportsmen include some jockeys, racing drivers and boxers, but only the really best of these can earn the vast sums of those at the top. It therefore seems to me that they are entitled to every penny they can get.

In the world of entertainment, there are also very highly paid idols. Perhaps some of the highest paid are film stars and pop stars. However, as with foot-ballers, the number of idols earning vast amounts
* for doing 'next to nothing' as some people would put it, is very, very small. For every pop star or film
* star etc. there must be hundreds of people in show-
* buisiness who struggle to earn a living. It can there-
* fore be seen that those people 'at the top' make up a very small percentage of the actual number of
* people in show-buisiness, and for that reason I feel
* that the people who are 'worshipped' up and down the country deserve all the money they earn, as they are the best of their kind.

* It should also be noted, I feel, that top buisiness men are also capable of earning vast sums of money, and yet they have done no more than the 'popular
* idols' of today—got to the top of their proffesion.
* As few people seem to dispute that top-buisiness men
* should earn a lot, I feel it is only fair that 'top-
* people' in show-buisiness and sport should also be allowed to earn large amounts of money. I also
* feel that whereas if a person in ordinary 'big-buisiness' is liable to have quite a long stay at the top, with little danger of him becoming redundant, the idols of entertainment have far greater risks to run. An injury to a footballer, for example, can ruin his whole career,
* and therefore his whole life, a pop-star is liable to be,
* at one time or another faced with the prospect of
* drug-addiction, and the risks to a racing driver are only too obvious. Another reason why I feel that all 'popular idols' deserve all the money they can earn is that they provide an essential service to our community today. Without the stars of entertainment and sport the lives of many people would become very drab indeed. Therefore, even for the simple
* reason that the 'idols' provide an 'essential' ingredient
* in the part of so many peoples' lives, I believe that however much money they earn, they deserve every penny of it.

This essay is at least on the subject and shows an understanding of the implications behind the title. The writer gives examples and puts up a persuasive case. The opening is too obvious, the ending rather repetitive, and the writing itself is not particularly interesting. But there are ideas here, and they are presented lucidly.

171

Unfortunately, the writer deals only with 'money' and doesn't explore fully enough the implications of 'hero-worship' and 'publicity'. He also has some difficulty with hyphens, quotation marks and the spelling of some words. The fact that he has not dealt properly with every aspect of the question would certainly lead to a loss of marks. But for these omissions, the essay would probably have gained a pass mark.

Another examination title was 'An Outing by Motor-coach'. This could be treated as a story, a description, or an example of personal writing. *Bearing in mind particularly the points already suggested, read the following essay written under examination conditions in response to this title.*

* I was touring in the North of Spain, it was a cheap
**** holiaday,. But I didnt want to go on a typical Bus-
** man's holiaday. So I moved around the country.
* I stayed at small hotels and usaully moved on the next day. I visited places of interest to me, not having to please a whole family. Some of the places I found were really beautiful, and it gave me a thrill and sensation to imagine that I was the first person to explore this part of land.
One day out of the 14 days was cloudy and
** miserable. So on this day I thought I take an outing on a coach. The coach was going into a town called
* Monserrat, what I wanted to see were the mountains around there. They surrounded the town, and were an impressive sight. The journey took about one and a half hours, and the time went very quickly looking at scenery.
The coach arrived at the top of the road on Mt Monserrat. The driver said we could get out and look around, and then go back and have lunch down
* in the town. There was a magnificaent view from
* the top, I could have gazed around all day.
* The driver called us back and we started the steep journey downhill to the town. I was sitting at the front of the coach near the driver. It all happened
** very suddenly and I didnt have time to think. The
* driver slumped forward on to the wheel seemingly
* unconcious. We were hurtling down the mountain side at about 40 m.p.h. I pushed the driver away
* and took control of the bus. Then it dawned on me, I had never driven before in my life. 30 people were
* on the coach and I was holding all our lives. When I
** located the brake, it was useless, it wasn't work-
* ing. My mind was in a turmoil. I steered frantically, every corner seemed to be a lifetime long. The coach
* gained acceleration and I could do nothing but steer. I heard screams from the back, but ignored
* them. I could see the village if I could only make
* it to there?
* As we neared the village I saw a car coming up,
** I hooted loudly and it just pulled aside, the driver
* looked amazed at our high speed coach. Before we
* got to the town the speed was slowing down.
* When I woke up 2 days later I found out that we
* had crashed into a haystack and all the passengers were alive. I had a broken arm which had got stuck
*** in the wheel. After I was relesed I was quite a hero,

with the townspeople. They set up celebrations and a party for me.
** In a way I did have a Busman's Holiaday.

The first point about this essay that strikes a critical reader is the weak sentence structure. The writer doesn't know how to use full stops. (Read the essay again and make sure that you know where there should be full stops.) The spelling also gives some cause for alarm.

Then there is the story itself. The writer spends a lot of time on unnecessary preliminaries before getting to the subject of the story—*the outing.* The description of the mountains surrounding Monserrat is very vague. The writer tells us that it was 'an impressive sight' and he 'could have gazed around all day', but he doesn't really give the reader any idea what it was like; there is no attempt at descriptive detail. The runaway bus is described with some excitement, but the details are not very convincing, and we can't really believe in it. It shows the danger of writing about something you have not experienced. An incident like this would be difficult for a professional writer to bring off successfully, and it is therefore rather foolhardy of this writer to attempt it. He is writing about something he has never experienced, and it shows. The ending is an attempt to round the story off neatly. It has been prepared for in the opening, but it nevertheless strikes me as rather contrived and unconvincing—an artificial way of giving the story a specious unity. It isn't really clever or original enough—nor does the writer seem to know what the expression 'a busman's holiday' means. With these deficiencies, the essay would have been unlikely to get a pass mark in the examination.

Here are two more essays on the subject 'An Outing by Motor-coach'. One of them is sentimental, unnatural, unconvincing and stilted; the other is lively and convincing with inventive and believable detail. One of them is just silly; the other is a pleasure to read. One would fail the examination abysmally; the other would pass splendidly. It should not be too difficult to tell which is which. *Study each carefully, correct any technical mistakes and consider each critically under the various headings that have already been suggested.*

Mr Wells, a well-known figure in the history of the
* old peoples' home, did not glance up from his desk in answer to a gentle knock on the door, but he made sure that he had signed and blotted the letter he was
** writing, before he raised his grey eyebrows and peer
* out of his horn-rimmed spectacles did he answer, 'Come!' The heavy doorknob turned slowly round, and the oak door was pushed slightly open. A young, cheerful face of a man swung round the door, and said smiling, 'Sir, may I see you for a moment,
* please.' This request was granted positively, and an athletic figure of a male stepped into the grey room.
'Yes, what is it you want?'
The young man, who in fact was a helper at the
* old-people's home began to inquire about an idea
* that he had struck upon. As it was the summertime now, the thought of an outing for the people in the home by a motorised vehicle seemed a pleasant idea. If the thought could be accepted, the young man

would arrange the majority of the things to be done.

'Please sir, they would enjoy it immensely—seeing as now they are fairly tired with their routine life.'

'Yes, you can do it,—but what is wrong with the running of the place, you know that when I was an assistant here, I used to ...'

The young man, who was called Jim, didn't bother to hear the rest of the statement and was too happy to hear the words of acknowledgement that he could go with the old-people. He thanked the man and left his office down a long corridor to the main building where he informed the majority of the old persons of the surprise he had previously promised them. He set to work.

Jim began the arrangements. He first phoned a reliable motor-vehicle hire service.

'Hello, is that the "Golden-Horse car-hire" firm. Good. Could I order a motor-coach for about thirty-five persons. with a good ventilation system, for the 2nd August. Thank-you.'

Jim organised the luncheon-hall at their destination. By popular vote, the result was Sunspot-On-Sea, a scenic seaside town on the south-coast.

After a great-deal of excitement the day came. Thirty-five old-age pensioners were helped into the motor-coach which had arrived at ten o'clock.

The most prominent characters on the trip were; Mr Jake Thrinsop, a great old man. In the home he had quite an influence on the other people. His gaeity and incredible wit, which very often burst through his clump of grey-white beard and moustache, was a joy to the others. Major John Riverdale D.S.O., R.A.C.M.M.B.E. was known as 'the old master.' His piercing voice still has the 'full of enjoyment' tone of life that he owned fifty years back. Miss T. Brown was the dearest of all ladies. Confined to a wheel-chair after only thirty years of her life, she had made up for it with her marvellous humour. Her lovable eyes still blue could hold a 'devil' paralysed. Her strong point is her melodious voice which delighted the old-people whenever she burst into song.

Along the route, on the way to the resort, a great deal of singing and talking was done. The old-people's faces had begun to gleam once again.

The coach arrived at 1 o'clock, and Jim hadn't realised the time flash away three hours, as he really was enjoying himself.

At Sunspot, they all spent a long, enjoyable day, on the yellow, warm sands and paddling in the deep-blue, sun-reflecting water. The old boys went along the west Pier and had a great time.

It soon had to end. In the early-evening, they once again boarded the coach, with serene, happy faces. They felt youthful at heart again, though perhaps not physically.

Arriving late back at the home, they were greeted by the smiling face of the Governor, happy to see their joyful faces. Jim stepped last off the coach, thanking the driver.

It was a day *very* well spent.

The one day in the year when I get up early is for our work's outing. Opening my eyes to a faint, early morning light which I see only on one morning in every three hundred and sixty five, I managed to fall out of bed, and miraculously arrived at the factory gates on time, at our last outing. It was seven in the morning and those of us who had actually managed to wake up, stood screwing our eyes and rubbing them, for we had only just managed to awaken. As usual, nearly half of us weren't there and so a long half hour was spent waiting for the remnants to stumble up to where they should have been thirty minutes ago, but it was usually these latecomers, who, having been sworn at and given long glares, had remembered to bring the survival kits of Watney's 'Red Barrel' and one or two very thick bags for the weaker travellers amongst us.

Eventually, our self-appointed works-outing leader nudged the driver and told him we were ready, as though the two had been life-long friends. I had settled down near the back of the coach where all the fun would be, but sat, or rather 'dug in' to the seat next to me I had to have 'Porker' who bulged in all directions, in clothes bursting at the seams and trousers only being held on by a pair of braces, straining like hausers, which stretched round to define the roundness of his stomach. He had started sweating already and beneath his shirt droplets of sweat were running down causing dark lines to run down the white. The stench was overpowering.

This was to be my outing for the day, as only the smell of beer could overthrow the pungent smell of Porky's B.O. What's more, when everyone else was trying to sing, it was Porky's idea to drown everyone else out with his own versions, which were much more earthy, but which didn't quite have the subtlety of the usual songs. I tried to join in, in an effort to drown out Porker, but it was practically useless, as I watched the bellow of his stomach breath out yet another sordid chorus and vibrate the windows with each off-key note.

From what I can remember, we were supposed to be going to Southend that year. However, one pub looks much the same as another to me, and all the others, so I couldn't say with confidence exactly where we ended up. I remember the beer on the coach ran out somewhere near Chingford, and we made the driver stop and fill up; but after that, the coach began to fill with smoke, much to the dismay of the driver, but it was only a cheap brand of cigars which had been handed around, and the mist made looking out of the window extremely difficult, along with the condensation, not that there were many of us who were bothering.

Contrary to what you may think, I do not like beer, and stick with cider, which puts me under suspicion from the 'manly' point of view, according to the looks I get when I call for a half of Bulmer's. However, it has taken eight works-outings to get me used to the smell of beer, so I doubt if it will be before another eight until I start drinking it.

Dirty jokes, besides dirty songs, are the favourite pastimes for us when wives and girlfriends are not present. From the way some of them tell these long, complicated stories you'd have thought they stayed up for half the night learning them. However, all * jokes I'm glad to say, keep to a very good standard of * filth, as noone dares tell a bad joke, which would probably earn him a wall of blank faces and then a lot of nasty rumours about his sexual habits.

Surprisingly few stops were made for nature as I think we are conditioned to holding in drink for long periods of time by now, and the rhythm of the coach only brought one casualty, who regurgitated out of the window, which unfortunately left a mark on the outside which was only partly covered by the condensation.

By nightfall another works-outing had come to a close, with very little to say for itself. I was tired out, but somehow felt it was all worth it, for at least it kept me in the good books of the others for the next rivet-punching year, until tomorrow, when it all begins again ...

 # SPELLING

In most of the 'Spelling' sections in previous units, we have looked at rules which can help us when we are in doubt about the spelling of a word. But the intricacies and idiosyncrasies of the English language are so great that rules do not take us very far. For most words, we have to sit down and memorize the correct form. Therefore, the remaining 'Spelling' sections in this course will consist of lists of words which are commonly mis-spelled. It is up to you to learn them (and of course check up on the meanings if you are not sure of them).

abridgment
abysmal (but 'abyss)
accelerate
accidentally
accommodate
acknowledgment (or acknowledgement)
acquaintance
acquire
acquit
adjacent
advantageous
aisle (=passage in church)
alley (=lane)

allowed (=permitted)
aloud (=not in a whisper)
altar (=part of a church)
alter (=change)
amiable
angel (=heavenly spirit)
angle (=geometric figure)
appalling
ascent (=upward movement)
assent (=agree to)
assassin
awkward
bachelor
bailiff
behaviour
benefit
bicycle
cannibal
capital (= main town)
caricature
catarrh
caterpillar
cellar
cemetery
centenary
clamour
commemorate
committee
conscience
definite
democracy
develop
development
different
disappear
discreet
disease
dissatisfy
eerie
embarrass
endeavour
exaggerate
exceed
except
excite
exercise
exhilarating
extravagant
extreme

ASSIGNMENT K

This assignment is based on the type of examination you may be sitting. Treat it as a trial examination. Time yourself carefully so that you complete the examination within the time limit.

ENGLISH LANGUAGE—Paper 1

One and three-quarter hours allowed

You are advised to spend **one hour** *on Section A (30%), and* **45 minutes** *on Section B (20%).*
Write on **one** *of the subjects in Section A and attempt* **one** *of the tasks in Section B.*

Section A

Write on *one* of the following subjects. You should write between 400 and 600 words. Credit will be given for relevant and well-ordered ideas, use of appropriate language, careful spelling and punctuation.

1. The Visit
You may like to write about a building, a factory, a town or a country you have visited. Or you may like to write about an occasion when someone visited you or when you paid a visit to friends or relations.

2. Taking Part
Describe an occasion when you took part in some communal or social activity. It could be a school play or a jumble sale or a sponsored walk or any other appropriate activity.

3. The Stranger

4. My Education
Looking back on your experience of school, write about how you think you have benefited and how you think things could have been improved.

5. 'Adults just don't understand young people. They insist on applying their standards to us, and these are mostly out of date. Surely we have a right to shape our own lives.' (A teenager's view.)
'Young people need guidance. We owe it to them to give them all the benefit of our experience, whether in success or failure.' (An adult's view.)
Discuss these two viewpoints.

6. A Close Shave

7. The Crowd
Describe a scene where the crowd plays an important part.

8. 'I can't stand people who are always showing off.'
Write about the qualities in people that you approve of and disapprove of.

Section B

Read the following article carefully and then do *one* of the tasks set after the passage.

Lost and Found
The Salvation Army's Missing Persons Bureau is described as the largest and most successful inquiry agency in the world. Glenn Gale pursues his own inquiries into their good work.

After spending nearly two years on a fruitless search for her brother, with whom she had lost contact in 1950, Glasgow housewife Meg Blair sought the help of the nearest Salvation Army centre.

A week later her questionnaire reached Col. Bramwell Pratt, head of the Salvation Army's Missing Persons Bureau*. Details were a bit sketchy, but Col. Pratt noticed that the last correspondence from the brother was postmarked Brighton. He turned to the Brighton phone book, and *voila!* Within 10 minutes the brother had been tracked down.

Some inquiries take a little longer—one took Col. Pratt seven years to unravel. Three months is average.

The Bureau was formed by William Booth in 1885 as Mrs Booth's Inquiry Agency, and operates from a drab Victorian pile within earshot of Petticoat Lane. Last year it handled 5562 inquiries, with a 72 per cent success rate. 'We have no magic formula,' insists Col. Pratt. 'We grind away applying a great deal of common sense, some psychology, anticipation of the missing person's intentions, and immense patience in following up every clue.' As well as his staff of 24, the Colonel can call upon the aid of 24,745 'agents' in 83 countries.

The tremendous demands made on the Bureau mean its inquiries must be restricted, on the whole, to missing relatives. Only in exceptional circumstances are inquiries undertaken for friends.

Sometimes investigations turn up relatives the inquirer didn't even know existed. An Australian nurse was anxious to trace her foster brother here. When found, he didn't want to know. But Col. Pratt discovered she had 10 brothers and sisters—eight still living—and she flew to England for a grand reunion.

All inquirers are invited to pay a registration fee of £3; otherwise, the service is free. It does sometimes reap rich rewards, though. A Lincolnshire businessman who had been reunited with his sister, left the Salvation Army £1 million in his will.

The Bureau has a reputation for integrity in respecting all confidences. No address is divulged without consent, but it will act as an intermediary by forwarding letters. No inquiry is pursued if it is felt it might cause pain or embarrassment, or if the motive is suspect. 'Our sole object is reconciliation. If we feel our inquiries will not achieve that purpose, we will not pursue them.'

Last year they succeeded in reuniting two sisters who hadn't seen each other for 79 years. One for the *Guinness Book of Records*?

* *The Salvation Army Missing Persons Bureau can be contacted at 110 Middlesex Street, London E1 7HZ.*

(RADIO TIMES)

Write *one* of the following.

1. As part of your school's community service scheme, you regularly visit an old person. You learn that he or she has lost contact with a brother or sister, wants to get in touch again, but is uncertain how to go about it.

Write down in play form a conversation in which you attempt to persuade him or her to consult the Salvation Army's Missing Persons Bureau. Credit will be given for well-developed persuasive arguments that use evidence in the article above. You should write approximately 200–250 words. Do not try to write a story; just put the name of the speaker in the margin, and then the words spoken.

OR

2. The committee of your youth club decides it would be a good idea to publicise the work of the Salvation Army Missing Persons Bureau among old people in your area. You are given the job of drawing up a leaflet which will be distributed among them. Write the leaflet, basing it on the information given in the article above. Use approximately 200–250 words.

ENGLISH LANGUAGE—PAPER 2

One and three-quarter hours allowed

*You are advised to spend **45 minutes** on Section A (15%),
and **45 minutes** on Section B (15%).*
*Answer **all** questions in Section A and **one** question in
Section B.*

Read the following poem and then answer the questions that
follow.

Sledging

Blotches of people in crimson or lilac or tan
Inhabit the intricate slope, not so massive as trees,
Nor so gracious, nor obstinate; children are gliding
    between,
5 Through a forest of trousers and blurring colours and
    knees
('That child'll kill someone!')—one of them parts from
    his sledge,
Which darts among people who giggle or scatter or
10 dodge.

In lemon and indigo sweaters that burn on the snow
They greet and collide with each other, they guffaw
    and shout,
Isn't it lovely? or icy? or years since we met!
15 Through the speckles of chatter, the flurry, the limbs
    in his way
My son goes careering, unable to stop or to steer.
Somehow each time the rooted spectators step clear.

Each swerve that he takes tears a muscle inside me;
20   each time
He lets go he goes tumbling down a slope in my head,
Knocking over the colourful thoughts, and paying no
    heed.
(This time nobody dodges): the white
25 Hill of my hopes is all littered with bodies, and still
He goes falling and bruising my flesh, till he falls out
    of sight.

                   (LAURENCE LERNER)

Section A

Answer *all* the following questions.

(a) Why does the poet say there are '*blotches* of people' (line 1)? (2)

(b) The poet compares the people to trees (line 2)—'not so massive, Nor so gracious, nor obstinate'. Explain what he means by each of these. (3)

(c) Pick out two words later in the poem which continue this comparison with trees. (2)

(d) In your own words, express clearly what is being described by
      'that burn on the snow' (line 7) (2)
and   'the speckles of chatter' (line 10). (2)

(e) In your own words, describe what is going on in the poet's mind in the last verse. (6)

(f) The poet uses scraps of conversation in the poem. Pick them out and say what effect they have on the description of the scene. (4)

(g) Does the poem gain by being written in the present tense (as if it is happening now)? Refer to the poem in your answer. (4)

(h) The poet uses many words which describe movement or activity. Why do you think this is? (2)
Pick out three such words and explain precisely the movement or activity described by each. (3)

(Total 30 marks)

Section B

Choose *one* of the following.

Credit will be given for your ability to describe scenes, people, thoughts and feelings, and for your choice of words. You should write between 200 and 250 words.

1. Imagine you are 'the son' in the poem. Write a letter to a friend describing your day sledging.

OR

2. Put yourself in the place of the poet in this poem. Write down the conversation he has with his wife when he returns home and describes what happened and his fears. (In writing your playscript, just put the speaker's name in the left-hand margin, and then the words spoken.)

(30 marks)

Note: Remember that you will also be expected to undertake an oral test and to provide course work in your examination. See Appendixes II and III.
Check the examination requirements of the examining board for which you are sitting.

UNIT 21

 WRITING
Pictures

This is another possible starting-point for essays, and this section indicates the procedure to go through when tackling an assignment of this kind.

 READING AND UNDERSTANDING
Comic

Some suggestions about the kind of thing which produces comic effects in writing.

 READING LIST

A reference to the comic books suggested in Unit 12.

 VOCABULARY

More commonly confused words for you to distinguish between.

 LANGUAGE
Ambiguity

An exploration with examples of how writing can be confused and misunderstood through the careless use of words, through lax punctuation, etc.

 SPELLING

A continuation of the spelling list.

 WRITING

Pictures

One form of stimulus you may be given in the examination has been left till now. You may be presented with a picture and asked to write an essay suggested by it. The approach is similar to that outlined when discussing the use of a poetic image to spark off an idea and an essay. (Look again at 'Writing', Unit 18.)

The picture you will be given is likely to be a dramatic one suggesting a relationship between the people in the photograph or depicting an event or a place. What you must do is to study the picture carefully and see whether the people in it or the place shown gives you an idea for a story or a description. Ask yourself questions about the picture. Who are these people? What are they saying to each other? Are they related? Where are they? What are they doing? Are they friends or enemies? What has just happened? What is going to happen next? In this way, you can explore the situation of the people in the picture and can consider the various possibilities for development that the picture calls forth.

As with the use of the poetic image as a stimulus to writing, there is no right answer about what you write in response to a picture. It is an open-ended response. The picture may in fact show a crowd at a strike meeting, but if there are no clues in the picture to particularize it in this way, it would be perfectly legitimate to see it as a picture of a crowd in some quite different situation. Some people find visual stimulus more evocative than simply a title or a verbal suggestion, and that is why a picture is sometimes used as one of the topics for writing. Care must be taken, though, to make sure that what you write is relevant to the picture and can be seen to be relevant. The response is open-ended, and a situation can be interpreted and developed in a large number of ways, but the interpretations must be convincing and clearly connected with the original situation. For instance, you may be given a picture of two girl football fans, beribboned and ecstatic because their team has scored a goal. This might suggest to you the idea of writing about a football match or about the enthusiasm of football supporters. If you merely describe a football match or describe two *boy* fans going to the match, then this would not really be on the point. You would have to use the two girls as your viewpoint as the picture is about them rather than about football.

179

The process of using a photograph as stimulus is therefore as follows:

1. Study the picture carefully and explore all its implications.
2. Decide how you are going to treat it—a story, a character-sketch, a description.
3. Check before you start writing that your approach is relevant to the picture and can be seen to be a genuine response to the picture. Refer back frequently as you write to the picture to make sure that what you are writing is still relevant.

As an example, look at the picture on page 180. The picture shows a large number of people. There is no clue as to where it might be. The central feature of the picture is the woman's face and the expression on it. But what exactly are her feelings? The expression can be interpreted in a number of ways. Is it anger? Astonishment? Fear? Her mouth is open and her eyes are wide. Has she been caught in the middle of animated conversation? The man in the background seems to be half-smiling, and this may provide a clue, but he is not looking at the woman or in the same direction as the woman. Who is the woman talking to or looking at? There are a large number of hands in the photograph. They form a kind of pattern. What are they doing? Are people shaking hands? Are they greeting each other? And now we see that someone—the person the woman is looking at or talking to?—is grasping her by the wrist. The hand is large and looks like a man's hand. Who is this person? Why is he grasping the woman's wrist? Where are they? What is happening?

These are the kind of questions that run through your mind as you explore the picture, and these are the kind of questions you must ask in order to fill in the background before you can begin to see how you are going to treat the picture.

You could disregard the importance of the woman and treat the picture as a general description with the woman as just one of the figures in the crowd, though doing something appropriate to her expression and the man's hand on her wrist. It could be a crowd of people waiting at the airport for the arrival of friends from abroad, perhaps refugees seeking asylum—there is a slightly foreign look about some of the faces. It could be a crowd on a quayside saying goodbye. It could be a crowd in a city street or at a railway station or at some sporting event.

On the other hand, you could treat the picture as a story with the woman as the central character. She has gone to the airport in the hope that her husband has managed to get a place on the last plane out of their native-country which has been taken over. In the crowd, he doesn't seem to be there. She is just giving up in despair when a hand grasps her wrist. She looks round in astonishment and disbelief: he is there.

Or the scene could be set in a crowded department store. There is a sale on, and people are frantically searching for bargains. The woman sees a scarf she wants. She slips it under her coat when she thinks no one is looking. Suddenly a hand grips her wrist, and she looks terrified at an attendant: she has been caught.

These outlines give some idea of the way a picture can be developed. There are a great number of ways of looking at a picture. Some facts are fixed and have to be complied with, but after that, you are free to interpret the picture in any way you like. Do seriously consider tackling the picture assignment in the examination, if there is one, as it can often help by providing a start, by stimulating ideas, and by providing details.

For practice, consider carefully the possibilities of the pictures on the pages that follow. Take each in turn. Explore it and outline the ways it could be developed. Write an essay suggested by one of them.

READING AND UNDERSTANDING
Comic

What makes people laugh? It is very difficult to define and analyse what makes a piece of writing comic. Yet being able to pick out the comic elements in a passage and say why they are comic is an important aspect of analysing the style of a piece of writing that is intended to be funny. Here are some points that can lie behind humour.

1. Misfortune. As people, we are often rather callous and find the misfortunes that happen to other people comic. I don't think we would laugh if someone's wife died or if his house were burned down, but if someone falls in a pond and gets wet through, or if he stands on a rake and the handle hits him on the nose, we may burst out laughing. It is strange that when misfortunes like this happen to people, we find it funny. This is the secret perhaps of the popularity of practical jokes—the popularity of them to other people, that is, except the victims. If the person is by nature a bit pompous or conceited or vain or self-satisfied, then the practical joke or the misfortune that makes him look a fool and brings him down more to our level is all the more pleasing.

2. The unexpected. When we expect one thing to happen and in fact something else occurs, this can have a comic effect. For instance, someone may be expecting a birthday present. A parcel arrives. He unwraps it and finds a box inside. He opens it and takes out another box, and so on, until in the centre he finds a marble wrapped in tissue paper. Or a young man thinks he has made a big hit with a girl at a dance. He thinks she likes him and is going to take her home. He imagines the marvellous time they are going to have. And then she walks off with his best friend. The unexpected is similar in mood to the misfortune. Baldly stated here, these examples could seem rather sad: the comedy would depend as much on the telling as on the actual situation. Again, there is an element of deflation: the self-satisfied person expecting success is suddenly dealt out failure.

3. The incongruous. When someone behaves in a way that is inappropriate to the situation or the surroundings, this can be comic. An example would be where someone unused to polite company has to attend an important dinner party. Because he does the wrong things and doesn't know how to behave in these circumstances, we find it funny. Have a look at the passage given in Assignment G which is an example of this. The children don't

know how to behave properly in church at a wedding and their riotous behaviour is so unsuitable to the formal dignity of the occasion that it is comic.

4. The eccentric. 'There's nowt so queer as folk' goes the Yorkshire proverb, and the strangeness and peculiarity of people can be comic. There is the character in the play by N. F. Simpson who buys a do-it-yourself kit of the Old Bailey and builds it in his living room. Or another character who collects speak-your-weight weighing machines and is teaching them to sing the Hallelujah Chorus. Eccentricity on this scale can't help but be comic.

5. Sick humour. The element of cruelty is at its strongest in what is known as 'sick' or 'black' comedy. This is the name given to a kind of ghoulish humour that makes comedy out of a situation which is really rather serious or even tragic. The description of cigarettes as 'cancer sticks' can be called sick humour. Another example is the joke in which the little boy asks his mother why he always walks in a circle. 'Shut up,' his mother replies, 'or I'll nail your other foot to the floor.' The element of incongruity is very strong here too: we treat distressing situations in a flippant and irreverent manner.

6. The verbal. The preceding notes refer to situations or characters that are comic, but just as vital in producing a comic effect are the words a writer uses and the way

he uses them. There are a number of ways in which a writer can do this.

(i) The most obvious is probably the pun which is a play on words where two possible meanings of a word are referred to, one of them the expected meaning, the other an absurd or comic meaning in the context. For example,

> Ben Battle was a soldier bold,
> And used to war's alarms:
> But a cannon-ball took off his legs,
> So he laid down his arms!

In this example, it is the words themselves, or the vision called up by the words, that is comic.

(ii) Another way in which words can indicate comedy is by the care and neatness with which they are balanced against each other—in other words by using antithesis. For example, here are some epigrams by Oscar Wilde:

> A man cannot be too careful in the choice of his enemies.
> The only way to get rid of temptation is to yield to it.
> It is better to be beautiful than to be good. But . . . it is better to be good than to be ugly.

(These examples also illustrate how the unexpected can be comic: Wilde says the opposite of what we expect.)

184

(iii) Another way in which words can create a comic effect is by their outrageousness—in a comparison, for example:

> The angry councillor looked like a bloated bluebottle. His shiny red cheeks were puffed up like a balloon about to burst. I wanted to stick a pin in him and watch him shrivel into a scrappy end of rubber.

(iv) Understatement is another use of words that can underline that a piece of writing is meant to be comic. For instance, a character may have had a whole series of disasters: he woke up late, went to work without any breakfast, missed his train, posted letters in the wrong envelopes, spilled ink over his boss's new suit, ruined a contract by treating an important client like an office boy, etc. And the account could end with the comment: 'It had been a trying day.'

(v) But the most important way in which words can create a comic effect is through the tone used. Irony has already been mentioned, and its use is often comic: the writer is laughing at his characters—at their vanity, their pretensions, their snobbery—and he wants us to laugh at them with him. It is largely through examining the tone that we can determine whether a piece of writing is meant to be comic or not. We must ask questions like these: Is the author being serious? Is he being mock-serious, keeping a straight face while in fact laughing? Do his comparisons and the details of his descriptions make the characters look silly? Are the characters' reactions and the things they say sensible or absurd? Are we meant to laugh at the way the characters behave? How is the writer using words? Is there a contrast between the seriousness of the characters and the absurdity of the situation? Do the words heighten this contrast?

These are only a few indications of the kind of thing that may suggest that a piece of writing is meant to be comic. There are probably many others, but these will provide you with a start. Remember though the warning made earlier about the fact that different people have different senses of humour and what is funny to one person may not be funny to another.

Read the following extract from Three Men in a Boat *and say how you know it is meant to be funny and how the writer gets his comic effects.*

The Maze

Harris asked me if I'd ever been in the maze at Hampton Court. He said he went in once to show somebody else the way. He had studied it up in a map, and it was so simple that it seemed foolish—hardly worth the two-pence charged for admission. Harris said he thought that map must have been got up as a practical joke, because it wasn't a bit like the real thing, and only misleading. It was a country cousin that Harris took in. He said:

'We'll just go in here, so that you can say you've been, but it's very simple. It's absurd to call it a maze. You keep on taking the first turning to the right. We'll just walk round for ten minutes, and then go and get some lunch.'

They met some people soon after they had got inside, who said they had been there for three-quarters of an hour, and had had enough of it. Harris told them they could follow him if they liked; he was just going in, and then should turn round and come out again. They said it was very kind of him, and fell behind, and followed.

They picked up various other people who wanted to get it over, as they went along, until they had absorbed all the persons in the maze. People who had given up all hopes of ever getting either in or out, or of ever seeing their home and friends again, plucked up courage, at the sight of Harris and his party, and joined the procession, blessing him. Harris said he should judge there must have been twenty people following him, in all; and one woman with a baby, who had been there all the morning, insisted on taking his arm, for fear of losing him.

Harris kept on turning to the right, but it seemed a long way, and his cousin said he supposed it was a very big maze.

'Oh, one of the largest in Europe,' said Harris.

'Yes, it must be,' replied the cousin, 'because we've walked a good two miles already.'

Harris began to think it rather strange himself, but he held on until, at last, they passed the half of a penny bun on the ground that Harris's cousin swore he had noticed there seven minutes ago. Harris said: 'Oh, impossible!' but the woman with the baby said, 'Not at all,' as she herself had taken it from the child, and thrown it down there, just before she met Harris. She also added that she wished she never had met Harris, and expressed an opinion that he was an imposter. That made Harris mad, and he produced his map, and explained his theory.

'The map may be all right enough,' said one of the party, 'if you know whereabouts in it we are now.'

Harris didn't know, and suggested that the best thing to do would be to go back to the entrance, and begin again. For the beginning again part of it there was not much enthusiasm; but with regard to the advisability of going back to the entrance there was complete unanimity, and so they turned, and trailed after Harris again, in the opposite direction. About ten minutes more passed, and then they found themselves in the centre.

Harris thought at first of pretending that that was what he had been aiming at; but the crowd looked dangerous, and he decided to treat it as an accident.

Anyhow, they had got something to start from then. They did know where they were, and the map was once more consulted, and the thing seemed simpler than ever, and off they started for the third time.

And three minutes later they were back in the centre again.

After that they simply couldn't get anywhere else. Whatever way they turned brought them back to the middle. It became so regular at length, that some of the people stopped there, and waited for the others to take a walk round, and come back to them. Harris drew out his map again, after a while, but the sight of it only infuriated the mob, and they told him to go and curl his hair with it. Harris said that he couldn't help feeling that, to a certain extent, he had become unpopular.

They all got crazy at last, and sang out for the keeper, and the man came and climbed up the ladder outside, and shouted out directions to them. But all their heads were, by this time, in such a confused whirl that they were incapable of grasping anything, and so the man told them to stop where they were, and he would come to them. They huddled together, and waited; and he climbed down, and came in.

He was a young keeper, as luck would have it, and new to the business; and when he got in, he couldn't get to them, and then *he* got lost. They caught sight of him, every now and then, rushing about the other side of the hedge, and he would see them, and rush to get to them, and they would wait there for about five minutes, and then he would reappear again in exactly the same spot, and ask them where they had been.

They had to wait until one of the old keepers came back from his dinner before they got out.

Harris said he thought it was a very fine maze, so far as he was a judge; and we agreed that we would try to get George to go into it, on our way back.

(JEROME K. JEROME, *Three Men in a Boat*)

READING LIST

Look again at the list of comic books and novels suggested in the Reading List for Unit 12. Have you read any of them? If not, try now to get one of the books from your library.

VOCABULARY

Here are some more words which are often confused. Try to distinguish between them.

adapt, adept
advice, advise
affect, effect
wreath, wreathe
weather, whether
intelligent, intellectual
judicial, judicious
laudable, laudatory
marital, martial
incredible, incredulous

Check the meaning of these words by looking them up in a dictionary.

Use each of these words in an interesting sentence of your own.

Check up on any other words in this unit where you were not sure of the meaning.

LANGUAGE

Ambiguity

The whole point of writing is to be able to communicate your meaning to your reader. If you use words awkwardly so that the meaning is confused, then you have failed. A statement is ambiguous when it is possible to take two meanings out of it, and there is no way of telling, except by using your commonsense and the context, which is the meaning the writer intended. You must make sure that ambiguity does not obscure the meaning of your writing. Here are some common cases where careless writing can lead to ambiguity.

1. Take care to place a qualifying clause after the word it describes, e.g.

There is a lovely house in the town where I live.
(Does 'where I live' refer to 'house' or 'town'?)

2. Be careful of using 'because' after a negative, e.g.

He was not popular because he was good at his lessons.

(Does this mean 'The reason he was not popular was because he was good at his lessons' or 'He was popular but not because he was good at his lessons but because of some other reason'?)

3. Sometimes the omission of a hyphen can lead to ambiguity, e.g.

My father is a hard working man.

(Does this mean 'My father is an unfeeling working man' or should it be 'hard-working', that is, 'conscientious'?)

4. Be careful to make participial phrases refer to the right word, e.g.

Walking down the road, the church came into view.

(What was walking down the road? The church?)

5. Be careful where you place the word 'only' in a sentence. Make sure it refers to the right word, e.g.

Only gym shoes are to be worn.

(What? Nothing else?)

6. Make sure that when you use personal pronouns it is clear to whom they refer, e.g.

Mary asked her sister if she could hear her new record.
(Whom do 'she' and 'her' refer to?)

7. Care needs to be taken with punctuation. You should remember in particular to put quotation marks round titles, e.g.

Adam Bede is next on my list.

(Presumably the novel 'Adam Bede' is referred to, but as written above it could be the name of a person.)

8. Words can sometimes mean two things, perhaps one a literal and another a metaphorical interpretation. Make sure that what you write isn't open to this confusion, e.g.

The man looked round the bend.

(Did he literally look round the corner of something, or is the slang expression meaning 'mad' referred to?)

There are other instances, but these should be enough to indicate the kind of dangers to be on the look-out for. If you think about what you write and study it carefully afterwards to make sure that it makes sense, then you should be able to prevent yourself from writing anything that is ambiguous.

186

Rewrite the examples given above so as to remove the possibility of misunderstanding.

Here are some more examples for you to examine:

(a) *State why each is ambiguous.*

(b) *Write an unambiguous version.*

1. Fresh fruit only supplied.
2. I am making a study of old peoples' living conditions.
3. Looking towards the left is Chipping Barnet Parish Church.
4. There is an apple tree in the garden which needs much attention.
5. The chemist exploded when the experiment went wrong.
6. There are now only forty odd inhabitants on the island.
7. When I was young my mother told me stories like Ali Baba.
8. He was not successful because he treated people well.
9. Jane asked her where she had left her purse.
10. The mayor's enthusiasm for fireworks set the whole town on fire.

 # SPELLING

The list of words whose spelling you must learn is continued here.

favour
favourite
feasible
February
fervour
fictitious
flavour

foreign
forfeit
gawky
glamour
glamorous
government
grammar
grievous
handkerchief
harass
hindrance
humour
hypocrisy
hypocrite
idiosyncrasy
independence
independent
inflammable
innocent
intelligent
intrigue
intriguing
irrelevant
jewellery
judgement (though 'judgment' is found in legal contexts)
khaki
laboratory
leisure
lieutenant
lightning
likable (though 'likeable' is also common)
listener
livelihood
loneliness

UNIT 22

 WRITING
Miscellaneous

A mixed bag of suggestions for different approaches to the essay: science fiction, comedy, an interview, philosophical, stream of consciousness.

 READING AND UNDERSTANDING
Variety of Prose

A look at prose written at different times during the last 400 years and the effect the time of writing has on the style.

 READING LIST

Some science fiction novels and stories you may enjoy.

 VOCABULARY

Some more words that are commonly confused for you to distinguish between.

 LANGUAGE
Revision

Questions to test your understanding of the points made in Units 13–21.

 SPELLING

A continuation of the spelling list.

 WRITING

Miscellaneous

Previous 'Writing' sections in this course have indicated various ways of treating the imaginative essay assignment. The title may suggest a description, a character sketch, an argument, a story, a dramatic scene. In this miscellaneous section dealing with writing, I want to indicate briefly five further possible approaches which may not have occurred to you, and which may spark off an idea in your mind when faced with a series of titles, none of which at first glance inspires you. Some dangers to be avoided are also indicated.

1. Science Fiction. Some students enjoy reading science fiction very much and feel at home in this fictional world. If you are one of these, think about writing a science fiction story. Often a very ordinary title such as 'The New Arrival' or 'Lost' if given a science fiction slant can suggest an exciting and original approach. Some students have the knack of inventing new worlds and

filling them with convincing and ingenious details. They find it easier to describe a completely imaginary world than to use words to depict the real world. See if you can manage this.

The danger to avoid is making your science fiction so fantastic that the reader can't accept it. Avoid, if possible, bug-eyed monsters and weird Martians. Keep your story simple and on an even keel rather than make it fanciful and too much out of this world. A few convincing details in a realistic setting are much more effective than extravagant fantasy.

2. Comedy. Comic writing was discussed in 'Reading and Understanding' Unit 21. Some people have a natural gift for telling humorous stories. When it comes to writing them, it is more difficult. Your touch has to be light and confident. If you think you can manage it, you might try your hand at it. The dangers inherent in this type of writing are heavy-handedness on one hand, and facetiousness on the other. As already suggested, not everyone has the same sense of humour, and to write a comic story successfully is not something to be undertaken lightly. If the comedy is too obvious, the story can fall flat or become leaden; if it is too far-fetched, it can seem just plain silly and childish. You must guard against both extremes.

3. An Interview. Interviews with people, famous or unknown, are popular in newspapers, on radio and on television. If an essay title suggests a character sketch, you might consider writing this in the form of an interview. You would include some description to set the scene and depict the character, the questions you ask and the answers the interviewee gives. In this way, you would be able to use a lot of the words of the person himself to describe his character—telling his life-story or expressing his opinion. Care must be taken to ensure that the whole is presented naturally, the character growing out of the setting, and the character's remarks growing out of the questions. To start like this—'I went up to this tramp in the park and asked him, "Where were you born?" He replied ...'—is much too abrupt. Try to make it more subtle. Try to read some of the interviews that frequently appear in *The Guardian* or those depicting nineteenth century down-and-outs in *Mayhew's Characters*.

4. Philosophical. Between the wars something called 'belles lettres' were very popular. These were essays about nothing really, exercises in writing interestingly about any subject that comes to mind. Writers like Robert Lynd, E. V. Lucas and G. K. Chesterton used to spin out words on such subjects as 'Walking' or 'Dreams' or 'The English Countryside', showing off their wit or their learning or their urbanity in the process. Something of the same kind can be seen today in the weekly columns of newspaper writers ranging from Jean Rook to Keith Waterhouse and Katharine Whitehorn, though today they tend to be much more down-to-earth.

It is possible that a title such as those suggested above will be set in the examination, and you may care to consider taking this fanciful philosophical approach, using the subject as a peg on which to hang interesting and personal ideas. The difficulty with this type of approach is that to carry it off successfully you need to be able to write sophisticatedly and to have interesting and original ideas. You need to be able to scatter references and quotations liberally through your essay. You need to be able to bring in scientific or artistic points and show off your knowledge. And above all, you need to maintain a thread of relevance, no matter how far-ranging your thoughts may be. All of this suggests that this kind of discursive approach should only be undertaken by someone who is confident that he has a sufficient width of interest and command of a witty style to carry it off. It may be wiser to set your sights lower and aim at something more prosaic and mundane—an account of a walking holiday or a firmly organized essay on how dreams affect different people—but something which can be achieved with competence.

5. Stream of Consciousness. Simply stated, this is the name given to the kind of writing where a character's thoughts are allowed to pour out on the page without any apparent sequence or order. It is the kind of style used by Virginia Woolf and James Joyce among others. Of course, the thoughts are not haphazard, but carefully controlled to give a picture of the character and the way he reacts to events.

A title might suggest this kind of approach to you in an essay. A character is thinking aloud. He is unhappy, say, and he allows his mind to go back over the events that led up to his present state of unhappiness, and the whole story is told as it passes through his mind. This kind of 'interior monologue' can often be very effective, and it has the advantage of imposing a shape on your essay. You begin with the state of the character at the moment; you go back over past events; you return to the present and the dominant state with which you began.

The stream of consciousness method can also be used successfully to describe a mood. The Title may be 'Loneliness', and you may feel that the best way of dealing with this would be to imagine that you are a character who feels lonely—an old woman perhaps, or someone working away from home in a big city—and allowing that character to pour out his thoughts and feelings.

Approaching Essays

When you are presented with essay titles in the examination, don't just stare at them blankly. Try out the ideas suggested here. See what kind of approach you can adopt —whether a title would be better treated this way or that, whether this approach or that would provide for richer or more interesting development. Always important, of course, are your powers of self-criticism. You must know what you are capable of doing and what you can do best. There is no point in trying a philosophical approach if you know that you are not very successful at this rather vague abstract style. There is no point in trying to write a comic essay if you know that your previous attempts have been feeble and flat. The old adage 'Know thyself' is nowhere more relevant than in your own awareness of your own strengths and weaknesses as a writer.

It is also worth mentioning here that you should not try to attempt a new approach in the examination itself. Always choose an approach you have previously practised and found you can manage successfully. To attempt something new without prior evidence that you can do it is to court disaster.

For practice, write essay plans for some of the following and write one or more essays.

1. Science Fiction
(a) The Last Inhabitant
(b) The Day it Rained Forever
(c) 2050 AD
2. Comedy
(a) The Day I Put My Foot In It
(b) He Who Laughs Last
(c) Caught in his own Trap
3. An Interview
(a) The Tramp
(b) My Hero
(c) The Sea Captain
4. Philosophical
(a) Gardening
(b) Past Ages
(c) Cities
5. Stream of Consciousness
(a) Alone
(b) Too Late Now
(c) Those Were The Days

READING AND UNDERSTANDING

Variety of Prose

Much has been made of the way in which writing varies according to the tone of voice used or the intention behind the writing. Writers employ different styles—formal or colloquial, solemn or ironic—depending on the purpose they have in writing or the particular subject-matter. But writing also varies according to the time it was written. Eighteenth-century prose is very different from contemporary prose: we are in some ways different people, we use words in different ways and we have different lifestyles. To take a very simple example, with television as a rival medium of entertainment and with other pressures on our time, few of us could think of sitting down to read a 600 or 800 page novel. Yet a novel of this dimension (perhaps in instalments or in three volumes) was the popular medium of the middle of the nineteenth century: the prose in which it was written was correspondingly leisurely and discursive. Nowadays, we are lucky if a novel is 200 pages long, and the language is correspondingly more immediate and personal.

In the examination, the passages you will be asked to study are likely to be modern, or at least twentieth-century. It is, however, worth looking at some examples of prose from the past so that we can recognize that the style of a piece of writing is to some extent influenced by the time in which it was written. These are not presented as models of how to write but as indications of how people wrote in the past.

Read the following passages carefully and then study the notes on them.

1.   *Of Studies*

Read not to contradict and confute, nor to believe and take for granted, but to weigh and consider. Some Books are to be tasted, others to be swallowed, and some few to be chewed and digested; That is, some Books are to be read only in parts; others to be read but not curiously, and some few to be read wholly, and with diligence and attention. Some Books also may be read by deputy, and extracts made of them by others; but that would be only in the less important arguments and the meaner sort of Books; else distilled books are like common distilled waters, flashy things. Reading maketh a full man; Conference a ready man; and Writing an exact man; and therefore, if a man write little he had need have a great memory; if he confer little he had need have a present wit; and if he read little he had need have much cunning, to seem to know that he doth not. Histories make men wise; Poets, witty; the Mathematicks, subtile; Natural Philosophy, deep; Moral, grave; Logik and Rhetorick, able to contend; *Abeunt studia in mores.*

(FRANCIS BACON, *Essays*; 1561–1626)

2.   *The Footprint*

It happened one day, about noon, going towards my boat, I was exceedingly surprised with the print of a man's naked foot on the shore, which was very plain to be seen in the sand. I stood like one thunder-struck, or as if I had seen an apparition. I listened, I looked around me, I could hear nothing, nor see anything. I went up to a rising ground, to look farther. I went up the shore, and down the shore, but it was all one; I could see no other impression but that one. I went to it again to see if there were any more, and to observe if it might not be my fancy; but there was no room for that, for there was exactly the very print of a foot—toes, heel, and every part of a foot. How it came thither I knew not, nor could in the least imagine. But after innumerable fluttering thoughts, like a man perfectly confused and out of myself, I came home to my fortification, not feeling, as we say, the ground I went on, but terrified to the last degree, looking behind me at every two or three steps, mistaking every bush and tree, and fancying every stump at a distance to be a man; nor is it possible to describe how many various shapes affrighted imagination represented things to me in, how many wild ideas were found every moment in my fancy, and what strange, unaccountable whimsies came into my thoughts by the way.

When I came to my castle, for so I think I called it ever after this, I fled into it like one pursued. Whether I went over by the ladder, as first contrived, or went in at the hole in the rock, which I called a door, I cannot remember; no, nor could I remember the next morning, for never frighted hare fled to cover, or fox to earth, with more terror of mind than I to this retreat.

(DANIEL DEFOE, *Robinson Crusoe*; 1661–1731)

3. The extract from *Gulliver's Travels*; by Jonathan Swift (1667–1745) Unit 14, page 129.

4. The extract from *Preface to his Dictionary*; by Samuel Johnson (1709–1784) Unit 14, page 132.

5. The extract from *Pride and Prejudice*; by Jane Austen (1775–1817) Unit 14, page 133.

6.   *On Going a Journey*

One of the pleasantest things in the world is going a journey; but I like to go by myself. I can enjoy company in a room; but out of doors, nature is company enough for me. I am then never less alone than when alone.

The fields his study, nature was his book.

I cannot see the wit of walking and talking at the same time. When I am in the country I wish to vegetate like the country. I am not for criticizing hedge-rows and black cattle. I go out of town in order to forget the town and all that is in it. There are those who for this purpose go to watering-places, and carry the metropolis with them. I like more elbow-room and fewer encumbrances. I like solitude, when I give myself up to it, for the sake of solitude; nor do I ask for

a friend in my retreat,
Whom I may whisper solitude is sweet.

The soul of a journey is liberty, perfect liberty, to think, feel, do, just as one pleases. We go a journey chiefly to be free of all impediments, and of all inconveniences; to leave ourselves behind, much more to get rid of others. It is because I want a little breathing-space to muse on indifferent matters, where Contemplation

> May plume her feathers and let grow her wings,
> That in the various bustle of resort
> Were all too ruffled, and sometimes impair'd,

that I absent myself from the town for a while, without feeling at a loss the moment I am left by myself. Instead of a friend in a postchaise or in a Tilbury, to exchange good things with, and vary the same stale topics over again, for once let me have a truce with impertinence. Give me the clear blue sky over my head, and the green turf beneath my feet, a winding road before me, and a three hours' march to dinner—and then to thinking! It is hard if I cannot start some game on those lone heaths. I laugh, I run, I leap, I sing for joy. From the point of yonder rolling cloud I plunge into my past being, and revel there, as the sun-burnt Indian plunges headlong into the wave that wafts him to his native shore. Then long-forgotten things, like 'sunken wrack and sunless treasuries', burst upon my eager sight, and I begin to feel, think, and be myself again. Instead of an awkward silence, broken by attempts at wit or dull common-places, mine is that undisturbed silence of the heart which alone is perfect eloquence. No one likes puns, alliterations, antitheses, argument, and analysis better than I do; but I sometimes had rather be without them. 'Leave, oh, leave me to my repose!' I have just now other business in hand, which would seem idle to you, but is with me 'very stuff o' the conscience'. Is not this wild rose sweet without a comment? Does not this daisy leap to my heart set in its coat of emerald?

(WILLIAM HAZLITT, *Table-Talk*; 1778–1830)

7. The extract from *Wuthering Heights* by Emily Brontë (1818–1848) Unit 13, page 121.

8. The extract from *Nicholas Nickleby* by Charles Dickens (1812–1870) Unit 14, page 128.

9. *Clara Middleton*

She had the mouth that smiles in repose. The lips met full in the centre of the bow and thinned along to a lifting dimple; the eyelids also lifted slightly at the outer corners and seemed, like the lip into the limpid cheek, quickening up the temples, as with a run of light, or the ascension indicated off a shoot of colour. Her features were playfellows of one another, none of them pretending to rigid correctness, nor the nose of the ordinary dignity of governess among merry girls, despite which the nose was of a fair design, not acutely interrogative or inviting to gambols. Aspens imaged in water, waiting for the breeze, would offer a susceptible lover some suggestion of her face; a pure smooth-white face, tenderly flushed in the cheeks, where the gentle dints were faintly intermelting even during quietness. Her eyes were brown, set well between mild lids, often shadowed, not unwakeful. Her hair of lighter brown, swelling above her temples on the sweep of the knot, imposed the triangle of the fabulous wild woodland visage from brow to mouth and chin, evidently in agreement with her

taste; and the triangle suited her; but her face was not significant of a tameless wildness or of weakness; her equable mouth threw its long curve to guard the small round chin from that effect; her eyes wavered only in humour, they were steady when thoughtfulness was awakened; and at such seasons the build of her winter-beechwood hair lost the touch of nymph-like and whimsical, and strangely, by mere outline, added to her appearance of studious concentration. Observe the hawk on stretched wings over the prey he spies, for an idea of this change in the look of a young lady whom Vernon Whitford could liken to the Mountain Echo, and Mrs. Mountstuart Jenkinson pronounced to be a 'dainty rogue in porcelain'.

(GEORGE MEREDITH, *The Egoist*; 1828–1909)

10. The extract from *The Loneliness of the Long Distance Runner* by Alan Sillitoe (b. 1928) Unit 19, page 167.

11. They stayed in the bedroom for half an hour or so, talking, looking at the things, talking; and Clara remembered thinking at the time that it was just such a honey-suckle-filtered, sunny conversational afternoon that would in years to come, whatever those years might bring, cause her the most sad and exquisite nostalgia. She was sad in advance, and yet at the same time all the happier, doubly happy, for knowing that she recognized her happiness, that it was not slipping by her unheeded, for knowing that she was creating for herself a past. She found Clelia's company extraordinarily entertaining, and bracing herself only in so far as she liked to be braced; she could not follow a word, for instance, of the art references in her conversation, but Clelia managed somehow to combine a great air of erudition and abstruseness with a marked facility for making explanations, so that ignorance was no bar to amusement. She was puzzled only by the unmistakable largesse of the confidence proffered to her, because try as she might, she could not persuade herself that Clelia could talk like this, so wittily and intimately and inquiringly, to everyone; she could not believe that she could talk like this to many. And she even dropped from time to time the odd and flattering hint about the unique nature of her interest. So that Clara, although she found it hard to believe that she herself was thus chosen, had no alternative to believing it. And once she had admitted that it might be possible, she could see that all the evidence pointed clearly in that one direction; so she thought that she might take it on trust. For, after all, it was not humility that restrained her from believing herself to be the equal even of Clelia Denham; it was simply a deference to the law of probability. And the law of probability seemed, for once, to have slipped up, and to have permitted her a striking piece of good luck.

(MARGARET DRABBLE, b. 1939, *Jerusalem The Golden*)

Many other passages could have been chosen. Look back at the extracts used to illustrate this course and see if you can tell approximately when they were written.

1. Note the logical presentation of the argument in

short phrases, one carefully weighed against another. The passage is full of antithesis. The sharpness of the brain behind the words is apparent. The writer is intent on presenting his ideas clearly and in convincing the reader that his ideas make sound sense. He is a moralist concerned with persuading the reader. Note also the impersonal tone of the writing.

2. Note the simplicity of the language. Each thought and action is described clearly. There is too a logical development from one fact to the next. Although simple, every eventuality is covered so that a complete picture of Crusoe's feelings is built up. The writer is concerned with making sure that the reader can visualize exactly what is taking place and what thoughts and fears go through Crusoe's mind.

3. Note still the logical development and presentation of ideas. The line of the argument is clearly defined, step by step, with phrase qualifying phrase. But this time, the author is working on two levels at the same time. He seems to be presenting Gulliver as a simple honest fellow-countryman whom we should believe and respect, while at the same time he shows him up to be a callous insensitive human being. Swift is using irony. There is a growing sophistication.

4. Note the increased complexity of the language and the sentence structure. The ideas are presented logically and clearly but the language is so learned and difficult that it sometimes endangers understanding.

5. This passage again employs irony, but it is of a lighter more subtle kind than that used by Swift. Note the ease with which the irony is used and the ease with which information is given in a conversation which is realistic and natural. Jane Austen catches the tone of a typical middle class conversation of her time which still convinces today.

6. The writing here is more personal, more fanciful and more emotional. Hazlitt gets carried away by his own enthusiasm. His comparisons are exotic, and he becomes passionate. There is much less discipline to the ideas than is shown in previous extracts. (This could be taken as an example of the philosophical type of essay mentioned in 'Writing'.)

7. Emotion is also the key-note of this extract. Although the sentences are long, they are broken up into short breathless phrases mirroring the agitated emotions of the narrator.

8. Dickens' irony is much more flamboyant and exaggerated than that of Jane Austen. He is more colourful, larger than life. He is also writing comedy, but where Jane Austen's comedy is gentle and subtle, Dickens's is loud and closer to farce.

9. This is a minute description of a character, but somehow it is too minute. It is in danger of becoming precious and artificial. The comparison at the end sums up this artificial literary quality. While effective and making its point, it is really too extreme and far-fetched.

10. The language is much more down-to-earth and colloquial. It is the way people might speak today. The sentences are long, but not because they are carefully built up of logical phrase upon phrase, but because they convey the thoughts pouring out of someone's mind. The language is simple and everyday.

192

11. Comment on the style of this passage.

Looking at the extracts again and considering the notes, outline the main changes that emerge as having occurred to English prose during the last 400 years.

 READING LIST

Science Fiction

Some people who don't usually enjoy reading novels find that they become devotees of science fiction. If you have never read any, try one or more of the following:

H. G. Wells: *The War of the Worlds*
Olaf Stapledon: *The Last and First Man*
James Blish: *A Case of Conscience*
Isaac Asimov: *Foundation*
C. S. Lewis: *Out of the Silent Planet*
Fred Hoyle: *The Black Cloud*
John Wyndham: *The Chrysalids*
John Christopher: *The Death of Grass*
Ray Bradbury: *The Day It Rained Forever*
Ray Bradbury: *Fahrenheit 451*
J. G. Ballard: *The Drought*
Philip K. Dick: *Time Out of Joint*

 VOCABULARY

Here are some words commonly confused. See if you can distinguish between them.

    act, bill
    allusion, illusion
    amend, emend
    amoral, immoral
    antiquated, antique
    appreciable, appreciative
    astrology, astronomy
    authoritarian, authoritative
    avenge, revenge
    barbaric, barbarous

Check the meaning of these words in a dictionary.

Use each of these words in an interesting sentence of your own.

Check up on any other words in this Unit you were not sure of. Look especially carefully at the extracts in the Reading and Understanding section, watching out for words which are little used today or have changed their meaning in modern English.

 LANGUAGE

Revision

Here is a chance for you to check that you have understood and remembered the points made in the 'Language' sections since Unit 13. Answer the following questions.

1. What do you understand by agreement?
2. What problems over agreement arise with collective nouns?
3. Is the agreement in this sentence correct?—Everyone was in their places.
4. Is the agreement in this sentence correct?—He is one of those people who finds fault with everything.
5. What do you understand by colloquial language?
6. Give three examples of colloquial language.
7. What do you understand by commercialese?
8. Write a sentence that could be described as commercialese.
9. Explain what Johnsonese is.
10. What is a cliché?
11. Give three examples of clichés.
12. What is jargon?
13. Give three examples of jargon from a particular profession.
14. What are figures of speech?
15. What is a simile?
16. Give three examples of similes.
17. What is a metaphor?
18. Use the word 'root' as a metaphor.
19. Give three examples of metaphors.
20. What is personification?
21. Give three examples of personification.
22. Explain with examples what antithesis is.
23. Explain with examples what onomatopoeia is.
24. Explain with examples what alliteration is.
25. Give three examples of slang and explain what it is.
26. Explain what you understand by the degeneration of words, and give three examples of words that have degenerated in meaning.
27. Explain the ambiguity in the following sentence— Two year old houses are hard to come by.
28. Explain with examples why you have to be careful where you place the word 'only'.
29. Explain how it is that the word 'because' coming after a negative statement can cause ambiguity.
30. Give three examples of sentences that contain ambiguities.

Check your answers by finding the information in the relevant 'Language' sections from Units 13–21.

 SPELLING

The list of words often mis-spelled is continued here. Learn these words.

manoeuvre
mantelpiece
mattress
medicine
Mediterranean
miniature
minute
mischievous
necessary
neighbour
obscene
occurrence
outrageous
pastime
Piccadilly
pigeon
piteous
Portuguese
possess
possession
precede
proceed
pretension
privilege
professor
pursue
quarrel
queue
rarefy
recommend
relevant
resistance
restaurant
rhyme
rhythm
rigour
rigorous

UNIT 23

 PRE-EXAMINATION
RECAPITULATION

Comprehension

A summary of the advice on tackling a comprehension exercise, together with some specimen answers which indicate the right and the wrong way to set about it.

 SPELLING

The completion of the list of commonly misspelled words for you to learn.

 ASSIGNMENT L

An actual examination paper for you to attempt to help you time your answers so that you do not waste time or find you have not finished the paper.

 PRE-EXAMINATION
RECAPITULATION

Comprehension

Now for a final revision of the comprehension question. There is not really much new to say about it as all the points have been stated and stressed already. The important thing is to keep alert so that you are open to all the implications of the passage and the questions and don't miss important facts that could alter the whole complexion of the passage. Here again are the basic points you must remember when tackling a comprehension exercise.

1. Read the passage carefully several times. Don't be content with merely skimming through the passage. This is not enough if you are to understand it sufficiently to answer questions on it. Passages for comprehension are not chosen idly. Passages are chosen that will test your powers of understanding and interpretation. They require thought and study if they are to be properly understood. Time spent on studying the passage and the questions before you start writing is time well spent.

2. Read the questions carefully. Make sure you understand what is being asked. Often students lose marks because they answer what they think from a quick glance is being asked, not what is in fact being asked. Your answer must give the information the question demands, and if you don't examine the question carefully, you won't be able to do this. If necessary, play about with the wording of the question and rephrase it in your own words. Ask yourself what kind of information each ques-

tion requires. The earlier units of this course suggested the different types of question that might be asked. Revise these notes and use the ideas there when it comes to the examination.

3. Finally, write the answers. Here there are two points to remember. The first is that the information you give in your answers must be relevant to the question. The second is to know when to stop. There is no need to go rambling on. This only wastes time. If you have given the required information, stop. When you have written your answer, always go back to the question and check that you have in fact answered the question being asked. This final act of revision is very important.

Now we shall look at a comprehension passage set in a GCSE type examination and compare some of the answers given by candidates. *Read the following passage carefully. Then read the questions and consider the answers you would give. Write your answers before looking at the notes that follow. You should take about one hour over this exercise.*

My life was fulfilled on my fourth birthday. By which I mean everything that has happened since has been an anticlimax and has failed to match the joy and satisfaction I experienced on that day. My mother had taken me for a holiday to Bishop's Hull, a small village outside Taunton. A farm-labourer, who lived in an adjoining cottage and who had lost an arm in the war, offered to take me fishing. I had been fishing before, but only for sharks from the upturned kitchen-table. I had never held a real rod or had my hook dangling in genuine water. Now the prospect alone of this expedition made me so excited that I ran a temperature and did not sleep at all the night before. I even forgot the grey hunter which I had discovered stabled in a pub opposite. The

194

15 shutter of my mind must have been full open that day, for every detail of the river still remains in sharp focus. My cousin and I followed the man along the river-bank. It was my first river: then he stopped at a deep pool by a weir: it was my first pool; deep, bottomless. Branches
20 of ash reached out so that half was in the shade; the sunlight shone on the other half, and the whole was so still that flies could walk upon the invisible skin of the water.

I watched the fisherman take from his pocket a small
25 tobacco-tin full of worms. Then breathlessly I saw him hold his rod against his body with his iron arm and watched him dexterously fix a worm on the hook with the other. Then he cast his line, and for the next half-hour I sat too excited to speak, my eyes riveted on the
30 scarlet float almost unmoving on the still water. But we caught nothing.

That evening I could not even eat my supper, I was too possessed. My mind was completely filled with the images of fish swimming beneath the water. I felt resent-
35 ment against them for avoiding being caught. I lay in bed imagining I was a fish to find out how long it would be before hunger made me take the temptation of the hook.

That problem was promptly resolved the next morn-
40 ing by my mother who took me into Taunton to buy me a fishing line and one or two other pieces of necessary equipment. As soon as she got off the bus, I raced her towards the pool, found a worm and cast the float on to the water. Then I closed my eyes and prayed 'Dear God,
45 please make the trout hungry. Dear God, please make them like worms, not any worms, but my worm which I've put on that hook, for Thine is the Kingdom for ever and ever, Amen.'

I have never prayed so fervently or succinctly. It was
50 not a particularly odd prayer. As a child I always imagined God as a grocer, order-book and pencil in hand, giving me the courtesy due to a customer. I sat willing the fish towards the worm. My whole soul was screwed up into my eyes riveted on the float. I kept this
55 up for half an hour or so, till my mother asked me to go and pick her some cowslips from the meadow behind her. Grudgingly I complied, running back with the flowers.

'Why don't you see now if you've caught a fish,' my
60 mother suggested casually; 'it seems to me your float's quite low in the water.'

'Yes, it is,' I cried, hauling in, nearly falling into the water.

I can state, but I cannot express, the pleasure I felt as
65 a great fish broke the water.

'You've never seen a trout as big as that, have you?' I asked my mother confidently.

'Never,' she said truthfully.

'I shall eat it for supper,' I said, 'and perhaps I'll give
70 you a bit for buying me the line. But tomorrow you can have all the fish. There's bound to be another tomorrow.'

That evening I broke my fast and ate the whole of the fish. There was another fish on my hook the next day. And for every day that week. I never suspected that
75 there was any coincidence in the fact that the fishes took my bait only while I was off picking flowers.

No doubt my mother's subterfuge was justifiable. I never suspected it and was seventeen before she punctured my boast about the trout I used to catch, by telling me they were herrings. But it was too late then. Conse- 80 quently I have gone through life always sublimely confident that wherever I flung my hook an obliging fish would swallow it. And the incident has had other psychic repercussions.

(RONALD DUNCAN, *All Men are Islands*)

(a) How old was the author when he first fished with a real rod in genuine water?

(b) Suggest a word or phrase to describe the only fishing he had done before that time.

(c) The farm-labourer who taught him to fish is depicted as having *an iron arm* (line 26).

　(i) What do you understand by *an iron arm*?
　(ii) How did the farm-labourer come to have one?

(d) In lines 64–65 the author says 'I can state, but I cannot express, the pleasure I felt as a great fish broke the water.' What does he mean by *I can state, but I cannot express*.

(e) Give briefly and clearly the meaning of the italicized words:

　(i) everything that has happened since has been *an anticlimax* (line 3);
　(ii) and watched him *dexterously* fix a worm on the hook (line 27);
　(iii) I was *too possessed* (line 33);
　(iv) so fervently or *succinctly* (line 49);
　(v) Grudgingly I *complied* (line 57).

(f) In a sentence or two for each, describe the small boy's feelings towards

　(i) the trout he was trying to catch;
　(ii) his mother;
　(iii) God.

(g) *No doubt my mother's subterfuge was justifiable* (line 77).

Write a paragraph to make clear what the subterfuge was, why the boy's mother would see it as justifiable, and what effect the author feels it has had upon him.

(a) This question asks you to find a particular fact in the passage. It is a simple question to begin with so that you can feel confident to proceed to the other questions. Here are three answers that were given. Which do you think is the best answer?

1. The author was four years old when he first fished with a real rod in genuine water.

2. The author first fished with a real rod in genuine water on the day after his fourth birthday when his mother bought him a rod.

3. It was on his fourth birthday that he first fished. (Answer 1 is too vague. The author was four years old for 365 days. Answer 3 is incorrect. The author himself did not fish on his fourth birthday but on the day after his fourth birthday. Answer 2 gives the precise information required.)

(b) This question asks you to sum up an aspect of the passage in a word or a phrase. Consider these answers.

1. Imaginary fishing.

2. He had 'pretended' to fish before he really went fishing.

3. A word to sum up the kind of fishing the author had done before would be 'make-believe'.

(Answer 1 is correct but it is not expressed as a complete sentence. Answer 2 also gives the correct implication but it is awkwardly phrased and the information given is not directed towards answering the question in the clear and direct manner that it is stated in answer 3.)

(c) (i) This question asks for an explanation of a term used in the passage.

1. By this I understand that he had an imitation arm.

2. By 'an iron arm', I understand that the farm-labourer had a false arm made of metal.

(Answer 1 is not precise enough. Who is the 'he' referred to in the answer? I think too that the term 'iron' requires some explanation. Answer 2 is a more precise answer. Would it be too much to expect in the answer some suggestion that the word 'iron' may be used in a metaphorical sense as well as a literal sense? That as well as indicating an artificial arm, it also indicates that the arm is very strong, as strong as iron?)

(c) (ii) This question asks you to find a particular fact from the passage.

1. The farm-labourer lost his arm during the war.

2. During the war the farm-labourer had lost his arm. It was replaced by the hospital for this iron arm.

3. The farm-labourer came to have an iron arm because he had lost his real arm in the war.

(Faced with an answer like answer 1 I would be inclined to say, 'So what?' The candidate has the right information, but he hasn't directed it properly to answering the question. Answer 2 has some odd phrasing, and the candidate introduces '*the* hospital' which is not in the passage. Answer 3 gives the answer clearly and directly.)

(d) This question asks you to read between the lines and interpret what the author means by using these words. It asks what the implications are.

1. What the author implies by this phrase is that he cannot simulate the feeling inside him as he caught his first fish. Stating his pleasure is just an abrupt phrase saying that he had great pleasure in seeing the fish as he reeled it in. Expressing his feelings would actually require an analysis of his feelings as he caught the fish.

2. The phrase 'I can state, but I cannot express' means that although he could write down the event that happened, he could not express the joy that he felt in words. It was purely an inner experience.

3. When the author says, 'I can state but not express,' he means that the joy of that moment was so great that it would be impossible to put this feeling into words. He can only tell us as a fact that it was great, but he cannot find words strong enough to describe it.

(Answer 1 is long-winded and inarticulate. It is really impossible to say whether the candidate understands the question and has answered it or not. Answer 2 is halfway there; the only trouble is that it uses the word 'express' without explaining what it means. Answer 3 goes to the heart of the matter.)

(e) This question asks you to explain what the author means when he uses a particular word or phrase. First,

you have to explain what the word means and then you have to explain its significance in the context.

(i) 1. The word 'anticlimax' means that his life after that day has never lived up to the joy and satisfaction that the author experienced on that day.

2. Anticlimax is a disappointing end to something that had a good start.

3. 'An anticlimax' is something which does not match up to previous experience or expectation. In the passage, the author implies that every experience after his experience of fishing was a disappointment and a let-down.

(Answer 1 explains the word in the context, but it doesn't really say what 'an anticlimax' is. Answer 2 explains roughly what an anticlimax is, but it doesn't explain the significance of the word in its context. Only answer 3 does both.)

(ii) 1. In the passage given, the word 'dexterously' gives the meaning of carefully and in fact implies that there is an art of fixing a worm on a fishing-hook. The fisherman fastened the worm in a way that he thought would best attract the fish.

2. I think this means he carefully and with the utmost concentration placed the worm on the hook.

3. 'Dexterously' means with great skill in the use of the hands. In the context, it means that he fixed the worm on the hook with great neatness and expertise, making no mistakes about it.

(Answer 1 is long-winded and gives extraneous information. 'Dexterously' does not mean the same as 'carefully': it is not precise enough. Therefore answer 1 and answer 2 are in this respect inaccurate. Answer 3 gives the full information required.)

(iii) 1. 'Too possessed' means when you are wholly involved in something.

2. He was too possessed or thinking too much about fishing. All his thought, nothing else could enter his mind.

3. 'Too possessed' means 'caught up with or involved in to an excessive extent'. Here it means that the boy was so full of the idea of fishing that he had lost his appetite.

(Answer 1 is incomplete. It doesn't explain the word in its context. Answer 2 is an inadequate explanation. It repeats the words the candidate is supposed to interpret and gives an alternative version—'thinking too much about'—which while adequate does not explain the phrase in its context. Answer 3 is a complete answer.)

(iv) 1. 'Succinctly' is on and on, over and over again.

2. The word 'succinctly' means 'enthusiastically'.

3. 'Succinctly' means briefly and to the point. In the context, it means that the author wasted no unnecessary words in his prayer but said exactly what he wanted in the fewest words required.

(Answers 1 and 2 are incorrect. The word has not been understood. Answer 3 gives the complete answer.)

(v) 1. He did what his mother asked him. Grudgingly I gave in to what my mother asked of me.

2. This means that he agreed but very unwillingly.

3. 'Complied' means 'acted in accordance with someone's wishes'. The boy agreed to gather some flowers for his mother.

(Answer 1 is confused. It goes into the first person which is unsuitable for an answer. It doesn't explain the word in its context. Answer 2 gives the word a connotation ('unwillingly') which is not necessarily in the context. Answer 3 gives a full answer.)

(f) These questions require you to read between the lines, to deduce feelings and attitudes from actions and comments.

(i) 1. The boy looked towards the trout as a reward for his work. When he catches the fish he feels he has been rewarded and can then stop fishing for the day.

2. He thought that the trout should take the bait because he had prayed for it to do so. He also regards the trout's job is to be caught by fishermen.

3. The boy's attitude towards the trout is a self-centred one. He thinks the trout's only purpose in being there is to be caught by him, and he tries by prayer and will-power to lure the trout on to his hook.
(Answer 1 seems rather vague and fanciful. It doesn't really get to the heart of the matter. The boy's prayer to God and the sentence 'I sat willing the fish towards the worm' are the material from which the answer is to be drawn. Answer 2 is better but not sufficiently related to the boy himself. Answer 3 keeps very much to the point and refers to the clues in the text.)

(ii) 1. The small boy's feelings towards his mother were such that he always had to show her what he was doing or had done, as he 'raced her towards the pool' and then needed her comment on the size of the fish. Thus he must have admired her, looked up to her and valued her judgment, as well as being obedient in picking the flowers.

2. He was grateful to his mother for buying the rod but also hated her for sending him to pick flowers when he could be fishing.

3. To some extent the boy tends to treat his mother rather casually and take her for granted. She is somebody to show off to (when he boastfully shows her the fish). But he also has some consideration for her as he picks some flowers for her when he would far rather have continued with his fishing, and is prepared to give his mother a bit (but only a bit) of the fish he has caught.
(There are three elements which need mentioning in this answer: the fact that the boy obeyed his mother and picked some flowers when he would have preferred to go on fishing; his pride in showing the fish he has caught to his mother; and his grudging offer of a bit of the fish to his mother as a reward for buying the rod. Answer 1 is rambling and poorly expressed. The ideas are not convincing or logically expressed. Answer 2 is much too strongly expressed (the boy didn't 'hate' his mother) and omits too many other important points. Answer 3 makes a convincing deduction from the facts.)

(iii) 1. He thought that God was a grocery man with an order book and pencil ready to note down anything he wanted and get it for him.

2. As he said himself, he believed in God as anything, anyone who could help him.

3. He regarded God as a convenience, someone who should serve him and not someone that he should serve, and so he thinks of him as a shopkeeper who should always keep him (the customer) happy by doing what he wants.
(The relevant information for this answer is the prayer and the image of God as a grocer. Answer 1 keeps too closely to the words of the original and has not been

properly translated into the candidate's own words. Answer 2 is confused and doesn't really make sense. Answer 3 gets to the heart of the question. Perhaps the points that the boy always expected to get his own way and the boy's complete faith that God would supply it could have been emphasized more.)

(g) This question demands reading between the lines and searching out facts. The first part is factual: what was the subterfuge. The other two parts are interpretative.

1. 'No doubt my mother's subterfuge was justifiable.' The subterfuge in this case was the telling of the mother to the boy about the actual truth about the trout. She related to him how the fish were herrings and not trout. The boy's mother felt that the truth was needed, as he was 17, and that his life in fishing should not have been such a reality to him. The effect it had on him was one of great psychological strain. His views on fishing were now completely altered, and he suffered severe nervous strains due to it.

2. His mother's subterfuge was the way by which she continually tricked him into believing that he had caught a fish. His mother might see it as justifiable because it would help him to believe in God, encourage him to take up fishing as a hobby and keep him away from the kitchen where he probably made himself a nuisance. The author feels that these early experiences have always affected him by making him think that all he had to do was to set a simple trap and anything he intended to catch would fall for it. He also feels that the experiences had psychological repercussions.

3. The boy's mother's subterfuge was to put a herring on the fishing line when her son was picking flowers for her. She saw this as perfectly justifiable because she knew that her son would be disappointed if he did not catch a fish, and she wished to spare him this disappointment. The author considers that these events caused him always to expect to be lucky and always to get what he wanted in ventures throughout his life as well as causing other differences in his attitude towards life.
(Answer 1 does not understand the meaning of the word 'subterfuge'. Nor does it see that the phrase 'wherever I flung my hook an obliging fish would swallow it' is meant to be taken metaphorically and not literally. Answer 2 understands and explains the word 'subterfuge', but it goes into irrelevant and invented detail (the boy 'probably made himself a nuisance in the kitchen'). In the explanation of the final image, the idea of 'trap' is not really appropriate. Answer 3 is clear and to the point.)

Now look again at your own answers and see where you went wrong.

 SPELLING

Here is the continuation of the list of words you ought to know how to spell. Learn them.

safety	seizure
satellite	separate
scandal	sergeant
seize	sheriff

siege

silhouette

skilful

slander

solemn

splendour

sprightly

squalor

squawk

stomach

stubborn

stubbornness

succeed

success

surprise

tendency

terrible

tragedy

treachery

twelfth

tyranny

vapour

veterinary

vigorous

vigour

visitor

weird

wilful

withhold

woollen

yacht

yield

ASSIGNMENT L

This assignment is based on the type of examination you may be sitting. Treat it as a trial examination. Time yourself carefully so that you complete the examination within the time limit.

ENGLISH LANGUAGE—Paper 1

Two and a quarter hours allowed

Answer **all** *questions.*
Each **section** *carries a total of 50 marks.*
The marks at the side of the page will give you a guide to the amount of material required in your answers.

Section A

Read the short story below carefully and then answer the questions that follow.

Sixpence

Children are unaccountable little creatures. Why should a small boy like Dicky, good as gold as a rule, sensitive, affectionate, obedient, and marvellously sensible for his age, have moods when, without the
5 slightest warning, he suddenly went 'mad dog', as his sisters called it, and there was no doing anything with him?

'Dicky, come here! Come here, sir, at once! Do you hear your mother calling you? Dicky!'
10 But Dicky wouldn't come. Oh, he heard right enough. A clear, ringing little laugh was his only reply. And away he flew; hiding, running through the uncut hay on the lawn, dashing past the woodshed, making a rush for the kitchen garden, and there dodging, peer-
15 ing at his mother from behind the mossy apple trunks, and leaping up and down like a wild Indian.

It had begun at tea-time. While Dicky's mother and Mrs Spears, who was spending the afternoon with her,

were quietly sitting over their sewing in the drawing-room, this, according to the servant girl, was what had 20 happened at the children's tea. They were eating their first bread and butter as nicely and quietly as you please, and the servant girl had just poured out the milk and water, when Dicky had suddenly seized the bread plate, put it upside down on his head, and 2 clutched the bread knife.

'Look at me!' he shouted.

His startled sisters looked, and before the servant girl could get there, the bread plate wobbled, slid, flew to the floor, and broke into shivers. At this awful point 3 the little girls lifted up their voices and shrieked their loudest.

'Mother, come and look what he's done!'

'Dicky's broke a great big plate!'

'Come and stop him, mother!' 3

You can imagine how mother came flying. But she was too late. Dicky had leapt out of his chair, run through the french windows on to the veranda, and, well—there she stood—popping her thimble on and off, helpless. What could she do? She couldn't chase 4 after the child. She couldn't stalk Dicky among the apples and damsons. That would be too undignified. It was more than annoying, it was exasperating. Especially as Mrs Spears, Mrs Spears of all people, whose two boys were so exemplary, was waiting for her in 4 the drawing-room.

'Very well, Dicky,' she cried, 'I shall have to think of some way of punishing you.'

'I don't care,' sounded the high little voice, and again there came that ringing laugh. The child was 5 quite beside himself . . .

'Oh, Mrs Spears, I don't know how to apologise for leaving you by yourself like this.'

'It's quite all right, Mrs Bendall,' said Mrs Spears, in her soft, sugary voice, and raising her eyebrows in 55 the way she had. She seemed to smile to herself as she stroked the gathers. 'These little things will happen from time to time. I only hope it was nothing serious.'

'It was Dicky,' said Mrs Bendall, looking rather helplessly for her only fine needle. And she explained 6 the whole affair to Mrs Spears. 'And the worst of it is, I don't know how to cure him. Nothing when he's in that mood seems to have the slightest effect on him.'

Mrs Spears opened her pale eyes. 'Not even a whipping?' said she. 6

But Mrs Bendall, threading her needle, pursed up her lips. 'We never have whipped the children,' she said. 'The girls never seem to have needed it. And Dicky is such a baby, and the only boy. Somehow . . .' 7

'It's such a mistake,' sighed Mrs Spears, 'to be weak with children when they are little. It's such a sad mistake, and one so easy to make. It's so unfair to the child. That is what one has to remember. Now Dicky's little escapade this afternoon seemed to me as though 75 he'd done it on purpose. It was the child's way of showing you that he needed a whipping.'

'Do you really think so?' Mrs Bendall was a weak little thing, and this impressed her very much.

198

'I do; I feel sure of it. And a sharp reminder now and then,' cried Mrs Spears in quite a professional manner, 'administered by the father, will save you so much trouble in the future. Believe me, my dear.' She put her dry, cold hand over Mrs Bendall's.

'I shall speak to Edward the moment he comes in,' said Dicky's mother firmly.

The children had gone to bed before the garden gate banged, and Dicky's father staggered up the steep concrete steps carrying his bicycle. It had been a bad day at the office. He was hot, dusty, tired out.

But by this time Mrs Bendall had become quite excited over the new plan, and she opened the door to him herself.

'Oh, Edward, I'm so thankful you have come home,' she cried.

'Why, what's happened?' Edward lowered the bicycle and took off his hat. A red angry pucker showed where the brim had pressed. 'What's up?'

'Come—come into the drawing-room,' said Mrs Bendall, speaking very fast. 'I simply can't tell you how naughty Dicky has been. You have no idea—you can't have at the office all day—how a child of that age can behave. He's been simply dreadful. I have no control over him—none. I've tried everything, Edward, but it's all no use. The only thing to do,' she finished breathlessly, 'is to whip him—is for you to whip him, Edward.'

In the corner of the drawing-room there was a what-not, and on the top shelf stood a brown china bear with a painted tongue. It seemed in the shadow to be grinning at Dicky's father, to be saying, 'Hooray, this is what you've come home to!'

'But why on earth should I start whipping him?' said Edward, staring at the bear. 'We've never done it before.'

'Because,' said his wife, 'don't you see, it's the only thing to do. I can't control the child ...' Her words flew from her lip's. They beat round him, beat round his tired head. 'We can't possibly afford a nurse. The servant girl has more than enough to do. And his naughtiness is beyond words. You don't understand, Edward; you can't, you're at the office all day.'

The bear poked out his tongue. The scolding voice went on. Edward sank into a chair.

'What am I to beat him with?' he said weakly.

'Your slipper, of course,' said his wife. And she knelt down to untie his dusty shoes.

'Oh, Edward,' she wailed, 'you've still got your cycling clips on in the drawing-room. No, really—'

'Here, that's enough.' Edward nearly pushed her away. 'Give me that slipper.' He went up the stairs. He felt like a man in a dark net. And now he wanted to beat Dicky. Yes, damn it, he wanted to beat something. My God, what a life! The dust was still in his hot eyes, his arms felt heavy.

He pushed open the door of Dicky's slip of a room. Dicky was standing in the middle of the floor in his night-shirt. At the sight of him Edward's heart gave a warm throb of rage.

'Well, Dicky, you know what I've come for,' said Edward.

Dicky made no reply.

'I've come to give you a whipping.'

No answer.

'Lift up your night-shirt.'

At that Dicky looked up. He flushed a deep pink. 'Must I?' he whispered.

'Come on, now. Be quick about it,' said Edward, and, grasping the slipper, he gave Dicky three hard slaps.

'There, that'll teach you to behave properly to your mother.'

Dicky stood there, hanging his head.

'Look sharp and get into bed,' said his father.

Still he did not move. But a shaking voice said, 'I've not done my teeth yet, Daddy.'

'Eh, what's that?'

Dicky looked up. His lips were quivering, but his eyes were dry. He hadn't made a sound or shed a tear. Only he swallowed and said huskily, 'I haven't done my teeth, Daddy.'

But at the sight of that little face Edward turned, and, not knowing what he was doing, he bolted from the room, down the stairs, and out into the garden. Good God! What had he done? He strode along and hid in the shadow of the pear tree by the hedge. Whipped Dicky—whipped his little man with a slipper—and what the devil for? He didn't even know. Suddenly he barged into his room—and there was the little chap in his night-shirt. Dicky's father groaned and held on to the hedge. And he didn't cry. Never a tear. If only he'd cried or got angry. But that 'Daddy'! And again he heard the quivering whisper. Forgiving like that without a word. But he'd never forgive himself—never. Coward! Fool! Brute! And suddenly he remembered the time when Dicky had fallen off his knee and sprained his wrist while they were playing together. He hadn't cried then, either. And that was the little hero he had just whipped.

Something's got to be done about this, thought Edward. He strode back to the house, up the stairs, into Dicky's room. The little boy was lying in bed. In the half-light his dark head, with the square fringe, showed plain against the pale pillow. He was lying quite still, and even now he wasn't crying. Edward shut the door and leaned against it. What he wanted to do was to kneel down by Dicky's bed and cry himself and beg to be forgiven. But, of course, one can't do that sort of thing. He felt awkward, and his heart was wrung.

'Not asleep yet, Dicky?' he said lightly.

'No, Daddy.'

Edward came over and sat on his boy's bed, and Dicky looked at him through his long lashes.

'Nothing the matter, little chap, is there?' said Edward, half whispering.

'No-o, Daddy,' came from Dicky.

Edward put out his hand, and carefully he took Dicky's hot little paw.

'You—you mustn't think any more of what happened just now, little man,' he said huskily, 'See? That's all over now. That's forgotten. That's never going to happen again. See?'

'Yes, Daddy.'

'So the thing to do now is to buck up, little chap,'
205 said Edward, 'and to smile.' And he tried himself an
extraordinary trembling apology for a smile. 'To forget all about it—to—eh? Little man ... Old boy ...'
Dicky lay as before. This was terrible. Dicky's father
sprang up and went over to the window. It was nearly
210 dark in the garden. The servant girl had run out, and
she was snatching, twitching some white clothes off the
bushes and piling them over her arm. But in the
boundless sky the evening star shone, and a big gum
tree, black against the pale glow, moved its long leaves
215 softly. All this he saw, while he felt in his trouser
pocket for his money. Bringing it out, he chose a new
sixpence and went back to Dicky,
'Here you are, little chap. Buy yourself something,'
said Edward softly, laying the sixpence on Dicky's pil-
220 low.
But could even that—could even a whole sixpence—
blot out what had been?

(KATHERINE MANSFIELD)

A1. From lines 1 to 45 explain how Dicky has mis-
behaved. (3)
A2. Describe how his sisters react. (3)
A3. 'It was more than annoying, it was exasperating,'
thinks his mother (line 43). Explain what this
means about her feelings. (2)
A4. Why doesn't Mrs Bendall follow Dicky into the
garden? (3)
A5. Describe Mrs Spears' attitude towards whipping
and explain her justification for her views (lines
71 to 86). (6)
A6. Describe Mrs Bendall's tactics in getting her husband to beat Dicky (lines 99 to 129). Is she being
entirely honest in what she says? (6)
A7. 'He felt like a man in a dark net' (line 132).
Explain how he felt and why. (3)
A8. Explain what makes Mr Bendall feel so upset
after beating his son (lines 162 to 179). (4)
A9. Taking into consideration the attitudes and re-
sponses of Mrs Spears, Mrs Bendall and Mr Bendall to the beating and the way the author describes them, what attitude do you think the
author wants to encourage in the reader by writing this story? (6)
A10. What evidence is there in this story to suggest
that the events described do not take place in the
present day? (4)
A11. Imagine Mr Bendall at work next morning talking to a friend. Write at least half a page on what
he said about what he did to his son and how he
felt. (10)

Section B

Item A is a newspaper article about school uniform.
Items B, C and D are letters from readers responding
to the article. You are advised to read through all the
material before starting the questions.

Item A

*Why the arguments for uniform are wearing rather
thin*

The issues in the present furore over education have been
aired in public before and rightly so. Another which should
have a good airing is school uniform. Now, while the educational melting pot is on the boil, it is time to question the
existence of this perennial thorn in the flesh. It is an outdated
imposition embroiling parents, teachers and pupils.

Who really wants school uniform? The parents? Certainly
not the pupils. As a housemistress and teacher of many years,
I say we should abolish school uniform, and most of my
colleagues agree.

What are the arguments in favour? One is that it prevents
class distinction in the classroom. Another is that it makes
sure even the poorest child has clothes suitably warm for
winter. Both arguments no longer apply since most families
buy the items of uniform from the cheaper large department
stores or by mail order.

It is argued that uniform provides the children with a sense
of pride in belonging to their school. Also that it helps teachers to recognise their own pupils easily on school outings,
especially at multi-school gatherings such as Wembley
matches and London book exhibitions for schools. When I
have been supervising such outings, most schools seem to
wear navy blue and white, the only small distinguishing feature being the blazer pocket badge—not quickly visible in a
crowd.

Most pupils would like to wear their 'own clothes'—as
they call non-uniform garments. If they are asked to think of
any possible advantages of having school uniform the only
answer they produce is that it saves their own clothes for
evenings and weekends. A valid point.

Sometimes pupils have been allowed a special non-uniform
day at the end of term—which incidentally makes nonsense
of having the rule in the first place. At such times it struck
me how pleasant it was to see cheerful colour in the classroom. How much easier it was to recognise your children as
individuals.

Nobody dressed outrageously and far from the tatty look
that many pupils achieve in their hated uniforms, they actually took a pride in their appearance. There was no
apparent increase in class distinction. Most of their clothes
were from the same department stores.

I once heard it argued that it's better to keep school uniform so that the children can rebel over that rather than over
more important things. I suggest that it is a godsend to

trouble-makers who want to create mischief and provoke friction between pupils and those teachers who diligently try to uphold the school rules.

It is much more important to provide an atmosphere in which young people can work and discuss and be themselves, within a sound discipline framework, based on sensible principles of mutual courtesy and good behaviour rather than on what a person is wearing.

So who really wants school uniform. Do you?

(HILARY BROCKLEHURST, *the Guardian*)

Item B

Adopting a uniform approach

UNLIKE Hilary Brocklehurst (Education Guardian, August 6), I welcome the fact that my daughter's comprehensive school insists—with considerable success—on the wearing of uniform.

For me it is a symbol that the pupils identify with the values of the school, as opposed to those of the peer group, whose competitive power is in so many respects so arbitrary, so strong, and so often anti-educational.
John Honey,
5 Woods Close,
Oadby,
Leicester.

Item C

MY SONS, aged 5 and 11, have just endured a year with a dictatorial, newly-appointed headmaster for whom adherence to school uniform was the paramount concern. Unfortunately, the cajoling and bullying to conform was not simply directed towards parents, the children themselves were subjected to comment and questioning although few people would expect children of primary school age to select and purchase their own clothing. I found fear of being thought incorrectly dressed caused stress in my younger child and was most divisive at a time when one was anxious to establish a good home/school relationship.

Fortunately both my children are moving to new schools this autumn, my elder son entering a comprehensive where children are expected to dress 'in a reasonable way.' Reasonableness must be one of the most vital lessons to be learned. My younger son is transferring to a first school where the realistic and sensible headmistress says: 'Uniform is not compulsory but we suggest grey trousers, etc. . . . Simple, easy-to-change clothes make school life happier.' My son will be happier, freed from a concern which should never have blighted his adjustment to school.

I, too, shall be happier—no more early morning panics when THE school jumper has failed to dry; no more arguments over short trousers as required by headmaster versus long trousers as required by English climate. School life will be happier without a specific uniform, and homelife will as well.
Pamela Hodgkins (Mrs),
Warwick.

Item D

The grey brigade

I FIND the arguments for and against school uniform interesting (Education Guardian, August 6 and 13) because as a parent I have tried through letters in my local newspaper and school magazine (with another like-minded parent) to get our local comprehensive to abandon school uniform. We found that the same old arguments were presented to us and we failed to persuade the majority of parents
(a) that school uniform is *not* a leveller. Both of us came from hard up, working class homes. We experienced the humility of wearing secondhand, worn out or too small uniforms when the better off children had new ones regularly replaced. Children know who lives in a big posh house and who lives on a council estate and what their fathers do for a living, if anything. School uniform levels no one. Our class system has seen to that;
(b) that school uniform is *not* cheaper. Read the Child Poverty Action Group's pamphlet 'Uniform Blues.' It contains many letters from distressed parents who cannot afford school uniform and have been refused a local authority grant;
(c) school uniform does *not* necessarily engender pride in a school. My children have attended primary schools in the Midlands where uniform was not worn. Both schools were happy and well disciplined and pride came naturally from the way the schools were run—not from forcing children to look alike.

For the odd individual determined on non-cooperation school uniform will make no difference. Social workers who have persuaded habitual truants to return to school can see all their work undone by a head teacher sending that child home again because he has not worn a tie. Although it is the head teacher who sends the child home it is the parents who can be prosecuted for non-attendance. The principle behind the 1944 Education Act was that school education should be free and available to all children but the law is that parent are only entitled to free education if they first buy extra clothing!

European schools manage very well without uniforms and vandalism is not as rife there as it is here and it is widely acknowledged that they generally have a higher standard of education. Every year French children from our twin town in Normandy attend our comprehensive in their colourful clothes. Our French girl commented that the English children look as if they are going to a funeral in their drab grey. Needless to say, these children do not behave like barbarians—nor do the English children when they to go to school in France without school uniforms.

I would like to free the teaching profession from the time-wasting dialogue needed to enforce this out-dated tradition so that they can get on with the job of educating my children to the best of their ability, and within the funds allowed (and I wish they could have more Sir Keith!). I will give them every support in their

201

efforts but I object to teachers, head teachers and local authority education committees telling me how to spend my money on clothes I do not wish to buy and my children do not wish to wear.

Pat Mathewson.
Bridport, Dorset.

B1. In the first paragraph of Item A, the writer calls school uniform 'an outdated imposition embroiling parents, teachers and pupils.' Explain three criticisms stated or implied by these words. (3)

B2. From Item A, state five of the arguments in favour of school uniform which the writer refers to. (5)

B3. What is the attitude of pupils towards school uniform according to the writer of Item A? (3)

B4. Why does the writer of Item A end with the question, 'Do you?'? (2)

B5. In your own words, explain why the writer of Item B approves of school uniform. (4)

B6. In your own words, explain why the writer of Item C welcomes the move of her children to new schools. (4)

B7. From paragraph 1 of Item D, it would appear that which group of people approves of school uniform? (2)

B8. In your own words state what are, in the view of the writer of Item D, 'the same old arguments'. (3)

B9. Why does the writer of Item D compare British and European schools? (3)

B10. From the material as a whole, pick out two arguments which the writer supports by giving evidence, and two arguments which are expressions of opinion without supporting evidence. (4)

B11. Write a letter suitable for a local newspaper or your school magazine giving your reasons for supporting *or* attacking school uniform. (15)

ENGLISH LANGUAGE—Paper 2

Two and a quarter hours allowed

Answer all **three** *questions.*
You are advised to spend some time planning your answer in each case.

1. Write about *one* of the following topics. You are advised to spend about an hour on this question. (50 marks)
The quality of your writing is more important than its length, but as a general guide, your work should cover 2 or 3 sides of the pages of your answer book.

(a) A good day's work.
Describe an occasion when you were involved in an activity that required effort but left you with a sense of satisfaction—papering a room, digging a garden, collecting for some good cause, for example.

(b) My earliest memories.

(c) Spring, Summer, Autumn, Winter.
Which season do you prefer and why?

(d) Lost!

(e) The View.
Imagine you have climbed to the top of a hill or a cliff. Describe the journey and the view you have at the end of it.

(f) Write about the qualities you think are needed to be a good parent.

2. Write on *one* of the following topics. Read the question carefully before beginning to plan your answer.

(30 marks)

(a) Write your views on advertising and advertisements, referring, if you wish, to the following extracts from 'The British Code of Advertising Practice':
—All advertising should be legal, clean, honest and truthful.
—Advertisements should not contain any description which is misleading about the product advertised.
—Medical advertisements should not contain copy which is exaggerated, e.g. the use of the words 'magic', 'miraculous'.

(b) Write about what you think are the main problems facing someone who is unemployed.

(c) If you were involved in the planning of a new town, write about the leisure facilities you think ought to be provided for young people in the area.

(d) 'You can't tell the boys from the girls. They all look scruffy.' 'There's no quality in the clothes. They won't last.' 'Ridiculous! Why don't they wear something sensible?' Write your views on the clothes young people wear today, commenting, if you wish, on the above criticisms.

(e) Assume that the following letter appeared in a newspaper. Write your own letter to the Editor on the subject of blood sports. It is up to you whether you agree or disagree with S. Johnson's views, but you should make some reference to the letter.

(You do not need to supply addresses in your letter, and you should note that the printed letter below is *not* intended as a guide to the length of your own letter.)

Sir,

I am heartily sick of people who attack so-called 'blood sports'. I have a deep and genuine love of the countryside and everything in it. I also shoot and fish. No doubt the opponents of blood sports would find this an incredible contradiction. I do not.

Thousands of people, rich and poor, shoot and fish in this country, and I believe that most of them share similar opinions. I certainly feel no shame in expressing mine.

I detest cruelty of any kind. But I do not approve of hypocrisy either. There are millions of people in our civilized country who eat meat. My meat comes from the butcher's shop and from the animals I kill and prepare myself.

I derive great pleasure from my ability to use a gun and cast a fly line. The majesty of unspoilt countryside heightens that pleasure.

I wonder how many opponents of 'blood sports' are vegetarians. They seem to regard only wild creatures as having a right to live, but what about cows, pigs, lambs and domestic fowl?

People who claim that these animals are killed 'humanely' should visit a slaughterhouse. The sight of what goes on would come as a real shock.

Contrary to what people might think, I am a conservationist. Anyone who hunts wild animals must be. If the countryside were to die, so would shooting.

I do not kill for the sake of it, and I do not kill creatures which I cannot use as food. I feel I can justify my attitude just as much as someone who has bacon for breakfast or turkey for Christmas dinner. The only difference is that I am being honest about it all.

Your faithfully,
S. Johnson

3. Answer *one* of the following questions. (20 marks)

EITHER

(a) Your school provides a brochure for new pupils, giving them information about the school and its activities. Included is information about clubs and societies. Write a description of *one* of these clubs or societies, providing relevant information for someone who may be thinking of joining.

OR

(b) Using the information below, write an article giving general advice on the kinds of building society accounts available, the kind of investor each is intended to appeal to, and any advantages and disadvantages in each that you think investors ought to bear in mind before choosing.

INTEREST RATES

		Net Rate %	Gross Equivalent Rate* %
Five Star Account Instant access to your funds —no loss of interest. Just £500 gets you in and as your balance increases, so does your interest rate.	£500 up to £1,999	8.75 PA	12.50
New	£2,000 up to £4,999	9.00 PA	12.86
	£5,000 up to £9,999	9.25 PA	13.21
	£10,000 plus	9.50 PA	13.57
Higher Interest Account Only £500 to get in, with monthly income. Withdrawals subject to 90 days' notice or 90 days' interest charge.		9.50	13.57
Cheque-Save Only £100 to get in. Maximum investment £90,000. (Single or joint account.)	Up to £2,499	5.50	7.86
	£2,500 up to £9,999	8.81	12.59
	£10,000 up to £24,999	9.05	12.93
	£25,000 plus	9.50	13.57
Build-Up Share For regular savings. From £1 to £200 per month.		8.00 PA	11.43
Share Account No charges—and a minimum investment of £1.		7.00	10.00

*Gross Equivalent Interest is paid net of tax at the basic rate. To achieve the same net return on your investment from taxable interest you would need to receive a rate at least equal to the gross figure quoted.

Your total investment in all Abbey National Accounts must not exceed £250,000 (£500,000 for Joint Accounts).

Note: Remember that you will also be expected to undertake an oral test and to provide course work in your examination. See Appendixes II and III.

Check the examination requirements of the examining board for which you are sitting.

UNIT 24

ADVICE ON TAKING THE EXAMINATION

General Comments

1. The purpose of this course has been to make you familiar with the kind of assignments you will be asked to perform in the examination, to give you practice in trying your hand at these assignments, and to enable you to find out something about your own abilities—your weaknesses and your strengths. Out of this should come confidence and self-criticism. You should feel confident that you know the kind of question that is going to be asked, and you should be aware of the kind of thing you do best and the particular areas where you have to proceed with additional care. You are now ready to approach the examination with confidence, even with pleasure. Here is a chance for you to show how much you know, how skilful you are at writing and understanding, how much you enjoy writing and getting to the heart of an author's meaning. If you can convey this element of enjoyment to the examiner, you are halfway there. Remember that an examiner has to wade through paper after paper of dreary pedestrian mediocre standard. If you can show by your essay and your answers that you actually enjoy writing and reading the comprehension passage, the examiner will be highly gratified and in the mood to reward you accordingly.

2. The appearance of your examination answers is

important. Handwriting has not been mentioned in this course, but clearly if your writing is difficult to read, your work begins with a distinct handicap as far as the examiner is concerned. If he has to spend time and effort trying to decipher what you say, he is unlikely to look upon your answers with much favour. He may not deliberately deduct marks but, being only human, he may allow the difficulty of deciphering your answers to influence his attitude. Some examination papers in English Language actually state that marks will be deducted for bad handwriting.

The lay-out of your answers is also important. Make sure that the question you are answering is clearly indicated by number or letter alongside your answer. It may seem pedantic to suggest ruling a line after each answer—and it certainly is not essential to do so—but it can make your examination paper look neater and it can make things clearer to the examiner. Make sure that if there are any instructions on the writing paper you are given for the examination—for example, write only on one side, or do not write in the margins—that you obey these instructions.

3. Another factor on which the neatness of your examination paper depends is what you do when you make a mistake or do work in rough. If you wish to change a word, draw a single line through it and put the new word above. Do not try to obliterate the first word by blocking it out completely in ink. This only creates an untidy impression. If you have done some rough work, for instance notes and an outline for an essay, or notes

204

for a summary type question in the comprehension exercise, rule it off and draw a single oblique line through this section. You may also prefer to do this rough work in pencil. If you cancel rough work clearly in this way, the examiner will ignore it, and he will in any case be too busy reading the relevant parts of your answers to bother with it. But you must see that rough work is clearly and neatly cancelled, otherwise it could lead to confusion and lost marks. Alternatively, of course, you may be able to use rough paper which will not be handed in with your examination paper.

4. Make sure you read the questions carefully and know what is being asked. This point has been stressed a number of times already, but there is an aspect of it that has not been commented on before that needs to be remembered. Sometimes a question contains two parts: you must make sure you answer both parts fully. An essay title, for example, may run as follows: 'Describe a scene you remember well, and say why you remember it.' If you spend most of your essay describing a scene and then tack on a final few lines saying why you remember it, you are not answering the question properly. Both sections may not require equal treatment, but both require *full* discussion. In the comprehension exercise, there may be two parts to a question under one numerical heading, e.g.

5. How is Mrs Bull dressed? In what ways is this typical of her?

You must not neglect to answer the second part of the question by an oversight.

5. You must allow yourself time to revise your work. Only in this way can you be sure that you have in fact written what you intended to write. It is all too easy to think that you have answered the question when a closer examination shows that you haven't answered it at all. The second element of revision is to check that your writing is accurate and makes sense, that words are correctly spelled, that sentences are correctly constructed, and that words requiring capital letters have them.

6. Time is an important element in any examination. Look carefully at the question paper to see how long you are allowed (these times can vary from paper to paper and from examining board to examining board). Divide the time available between preparation, writing and revision. For instance, you may be allowed an hour to write an essay. You might use 10 or 15 minutes in preparation (making notes, organizing your material, writing an outline); 40 minutes for the actual writing of your essay; 5 or 10 minutes for revision and alterations. It is unlikely that you will have time to write a complete rough draft of your essay, therefore the time at the beginning for preparation is important. The same applies to the comprehension exercise: allow yourself about a quarter of the time—perhaps even more—for reading the passage several times, reading and grasping the meaning of the questions, and finding the material for the answers. Then write the answers, allowing yourself 5 or 10 minutes at the end to check that your answers cover all the points asked for in the questions and that they make sense. You should make out for yourself a timetable along these lines in the examination and try to keep to it. Otherwise, there

will be a danger that you will spend too much time on one aspect of the paper and find that you are only halfway through another when the time limit is up.

Another aid to timing is the mark allocation. Not all examining boards give the marks for each question, but if the paper you are sitting does this, take advantage of it. For instance, in the comprehension question if one question is allocated 3 marks and another 15, it is clear that you should spend longer on the second question and that your answer should be much longer and more detailed.

7. While we are all capable of making spelling mistakes when we don't have a dictionary to refer to, there is one kind of inaccuracy which is unforgivable in an examination, and that is the mis-spelling of words that occur in the question paper. This refers particularly to proper names used in the text, but also to ordinary words which you may have to use in your answers. Keep an eye on the question paper and make sure that if a particular word occurs there that you spell it correctly when you use it in your answer.

8. When preparing for the examination, it is a mistake to leave everything to the last minute, till the last two or three days before the examination. There are many sections in this course that could usefully be revised; there are your notebooks to go through to check up on words and ideas that might be valuable; there is your written work to re-read so that you know your weak points and the things to be on the look-out for. But to cram all this into the period before the examination is a mistake. You need to work out a timetable for your revision, beginning perhaps a fortnight before the examination, so that you have time to go through this material and consolidate it well before the deadline. Probably the best way to spend the evening before the examination itself is to read something interesting and of quality so that you are relaxed and yet have the image of good writing before you. This is why a Reading List has been included in this final unit.

 THE ESSAY

In addition to the general remarks above and the specific points about writing an essay made in previous units, which you ought to revise, it is worth making three final points about the essay.

1. Writing an essay that means something and is worth reading requires effort and concentration. It is no good going at it half-heartedly and letting ideas and words slip out in a slovenly way. An intense effort is required. You must concentrate hard on the writing so that everything else is excluded for the 40 minutes or so of your actual writing. After all, it is an act of creation, and the effort should take something out of you. At the end, you should feel as though you have given something of yourself, you should have used up considerable emotional and intellectual energy in your writing, and you should have a feeling of satisfaction at having accomplished something worth accomplishing. Unless you can achieve this kind of intensity, your writing is likely to be superficial and uninvolved.

2. In writing an essay, a conflict sometimes arises between content and accuracy of expression. Which is

more important: what you say or the grammatical correctness with which you say it? My advice is to concentrate on the first and let the second to some extent take care of itself. If you have fresh, interesting and original ideas, if what you say catches the imagination of the reader, then occasional faults in spelling and expression can be forgiven. There is nothing more depressing than a piece of writing that is correctly spelled and correctly expressed which is boring, superficial and saying absolutely nothing. Don't allow doubts about the spelling of a particular word to interfere with your writing. Get the ideas down while they are fresh and vigorous, and then you can use your revision time to check on things like spelling, sentence structure and grammar. It is more important, in the first instance, to be interesting than accurate.

3. Avoid extremes in writing your essay. I am thinking in particular of those students who think that a story must be full of melodrama and contrived coincidences if it is to be effective. A story does not have to be full of wild and violent events in order to be exciting. Keep it simple; keep it true to life and realistic. What gives a story authenticity is detail. Give as much convincing detail as you can to create the impression that you know what you are writing about.

COMPREHENSION

The main points about tackling a comprehension exercise have been made in previous units. Revise them. Suffice it here to restate the difference between the two types of passages you are likely to be asked questions on. One passage will be factual; the important thing is to get clear in your mind the information or arguments given. The other passage will be imaginative; you must be able to read between the lines and interpret the author's tone and the relationship between the characters and events. Bear this distinction in mind when you read the passages set for comprehension and study the questions.

READING LIST

It was suggested earlier that it is a good idea to include some reading as part of your revision for the examination, perhaps even devoting the last evening of your revision to this. You may care to look at some of the previous reading lists and choose a work by an author that you have enjoyed. Or you may care to read some more short stories by one of the authors named in the Reading List in Unit 8. Whatever you read, however, it is important that it should be of a reasonable literary standard and that you should read it with pleasure and as a relaxation, not as an examination chore. As an alternative, here is a list

of novels that could be described as modern classics. They represent the best that has been written in this century. The idea is not that you should read these with any idea of trying to copy the ideas or style in the examination, but that you should get an impression of the richness, concentration and verbal skill that good writing requires and provides.

Arnold Bennett: *Anna of the Five Towns*
Albert Camus: *The Plague*
Joyce Cary: *The Horse's Mouth*
William Faulkner: *Intruder in the Dust*
F. Scott Fitzgerald: *The Great Gatsby*
E. M. Forster: *Howards End*
Graham Greene: *The Heart of the Matter*
Ernest Hemingway: *The Old Man and the Sea*
Aldous Huxley: *Brave New World*
Christopher Isherwood: *Mr Norris Changes Trains*
Henry James: *The Turn of the Screw*
Henry James: *Washington Square*
James Joyce: *Dubliners*
James Joyce: *A Portrait of the Artist as a Young Man*
Franz Kafka: *The Trial*
D. H. Lawrence: *Sons and Lovers*
George Orwell: *Animal Farm*
George Orwell: *1984*
Alan Paton: *Cry, The Beloved Country*
J. D. Salinger: *The Catcher in the Rye*
Evelyn Waugh: *Decline and Fall*
Evelyn Waugh: *Brideshead Revisited*
Angus Wilson: *Hemlock and After*
Virginia Woolf: *The Years*

LAST WORD

There is an element of luck in all examinations—how you feel on the particular day, whether you have slept well, whether the paper asks the right questions for you, whether you have revised the right things. This element of luck is even more strongly present in the English Language examination where subjectivity plays such a large part—there may not be an essay title that appeals to you, the comprehension passages may be about areas of experience that you are ignorant of.

One of the purposes of this course has been to try to eliminate the element of luck—or at least reduce it to a minimum—by preparing you through experiencing the various aspects of the examination and giving you confidence that you can tackle any kind of question that may occur. However, it would be foolish to claim that luck plays no part still, and churlish of me not to wish you luck in the examination. I wish you every success.

Appendix I

THE MULTIPLE-CHOICE COMPREHENSION TEST

1. What is it?

The multiple-choice comprehension or objective test as it is sometimes called is becoming a common feature of examinations, not only in science subjects and economics, but in English as well. Basically, questions are asked to which four or five alternative answers are given. What the candidate has to do is to select one of the answers, the one that seems to him to be correct or most likely.

There are a number of reasons why tests of this kind are being introduced. If only one answer is correct, then it eliminates any possibility of bias on the part of the examiner. A test like this is easier to mark since the answer sheets can be fed into a computer. It is also felt that a much more precise examination of the candidate's knowledge of the subject is possible by using this method.

This may be true of what can be termed factual subjects such as physics and even economics where there are usually correct answers to particular questions. But when it comes to a subject like English, and particularly English literature, things are less straightforward. Normally the objective test in English takes the form of questions with alternative answers to be selected based on a piece of writing. As has been suggested a number of times in *A New English Course*, part of the richness of the English language depends on the fact that words convey several different nuances. The question of interpretation comes into it, and there may well be more than one 'correct' answer. You may even feel that none of the given answers fits the particular shade of meaning which you get from the passage.

For example, read the following poem, *To Daffodils* by Robert Herrick:

> Fair daffodils, we weep to see
> You haste away so soon:
> As yet the early-rising sun
> Has not attain'd his noon.
>
> Stay, stay,
> Until the hasting day
> Has run
> But to the evensong;
> And, having pray'd together, we
> Will go with you along.
>
> We have short time to stay, as you,
> We have as short a spring;
> As quick a growth to meet decay,
> As you, or any thing.
> We die,
> As your hours do, and dry
> Away,

> Like to the summer's rain;
> Or as the pearls of morning's dew
> Ne'er to be found again.

One of the questions on this poem might be as follows:

The poet is sad to see the daffodils 'haste away so soon' because
  A it is too early in the day for them to fade
  B he likes flowers and doesn't enjoy seeing them die
  C he feels they have such a short life
  D the flowers are so beautiful.

All of these answers could be 'correct'. A is what the poet literally says. B is implicit in the whole poem. C is also convincing because he wants the flowers to go on living longer. D is perhaps less plausible, although he does call the daffodils 'fair' and weeps for them. The deeper and more satisfying answer is not given as a possibility, namely that the poet is sad to see the daffodils 'haste away so soon' because their transience reminds him that man's life is also very short.

Of course, I haven't been playing fair, and I have deliberately chosen an example which presents problems of interpretation. Normally questions would be more carefully balanced so that one of the statements is more likely than the others.

For instance, supposing the question had been as follows:

The poet is sad to see the daffodils 'haste away so soon' because
  A he is particularly fond of yellow flowers
  B he wanted to pick the flowers that afternoon
  C he feels they have such a short life
  D he wanted to decorate the church with them for
     evensong.

Given this choice, it is obvious that C is the correct answer. The deeper implications of the answer that was preferred above could be explored in later questions.

The first example, nevertheless, does highlight the kind of danger inherent in this type of test when it is applied to creative writing. It also shows the kind of care and attention the candidate must employ when approaching it. It is not our brief here to question the validity of the multiple-choice comprehension as a genuine test of the candidate's understanding and appreciation of English literature: if this kind of exercise is set by the examining board that the candidate is sitting for, then he must be prepared and know how to tackle it.

2. Specimen Multiple-Choice Comprehension

Read the following passage carefully and then study the questions below:

This is the history of Silas Marner, until the fifteenth year after he came to Raveloe. The livelong day he sat in his loom, his ear filled with its monotony, his eyes bent close down on the slow growth of sameness in the brownish
5 web, his muscles moving with such even repetition that their pause seemed almost as much a constraint as the holding of his breath. But at night came his revelry: at night he closed his shutters, and made fast his doors, and drew forth his gold. Long ago the heap of coins had
10 become too large for the iron pot to hold them, and he had made for them two thick leather bags, which wasted no room in their resting-place, but lent themselves flexibly to every corner. How the guineas shone as they came pouring out of the dark leather mouths! The silver
15 bore no large proportion in amount to the gold, because the long pieces of linen which formed his chief work were always partly paid for in gold, and out of the silver he supplied his own bodily wants, choosing always the shillings and sixpences to spend in this way. He loved the
20 guineas best, but he would not change the silver—the crowns and halfcrowns that were his own earnings, begotten by his labour; he loved them all. He spread them out in heaps and bathed his hands in them; then he counted them and set them in regular piles, and felt
25 their rounded outline between his thumb and fingers, and thought fondly of the guineas that were only half earned by the work in his loom, as if they had been unborn children—thought of the guineas that were coming slowly through the coming years, through all his life,
30 which spread far away before him, the end quite hidden by countless days of weaving. No wonder his thoughts were still with his loom and his money when he made his journeys through the fields and lanes to fetch and carry home his work, so that his steps never wandered
35 to the hedge-banks and the lane-side in search of the once familiar herbs: these too belonged to the past, from which his life had shrunk away, like a rivulet that has sunk far down from the grassy fringe of its old breadth into a little shivering thread, that cut a groove for itself
40 in the barren sand.

(GEORGE ELIOT, *Silas Marner*)

1. When the author says Silas Marner sat in his loom 'the livelong day' (1. 2), she means
    A he worked the whole length of the day
    B he worked only when he was feeling lively and enthusiastic
    C he worked this way to make his livelihood
    D he worked only when the day was pleasant.
2. The author describes the noise of the loom as
    A very loud and deafening
    B unvaried and repetitive
    C pleasant
    D reverberant.

3. *All* of the following are brought out in the second sentence *except*
    A the regularity with which Silas Marner did his work
    B the concentration with which Silas Marner did his work
    C the repetitiveness of the work Silas Marner did
    D the enjoyment with which Silas Marner did his work.
4. The word 'revelry' (1. 7) usually means
    A accounting
    B locking up
    C evening activity
    D merry-making.
5. 'Lent themselves flexibly to every corner' (1. 12) means
    A filled the whole space available
    B was available to be borrowed by anyone
    C burst out of the bags and scattered over the floor
    D were hidden in different corners of the room.
6. One of these statements describes Silas Marner's feelings:
    A he preferred the gold to the silver
    B he preferred the silver to the gold
    C he liked both equally
    D he preferred the gold but he also loved his silver.
7. When the author says Silas thought about the as yet half-earned guineas 'as if they had been unborn children' (1. 27), she means
    A he thought of them with the same love as other people might have for their children
    B he thought how much they would buy for his children
    C he was saving up so that he could marry and have children
    D he knew he would never have any children.
8. When the author compares Silas Marner's way of life to a rivulet (1. 37), she means
    A it is lively like a fast-moving stream
    B Silas no longer lived beside a river
    C it has grown narrow and confined like a once-broad river that is silted up with sand
    D it had become narrow and confined because he could no longer collect herbs.
9. *All* the following are metaphors *except*
    A mouths (1. 14)
    B bathed (1. 23)
    C rivulet (1. 37)
    D thread (1. 39)
10. From the passage as a whole we gather that Silas Marner was
    A someone who lived only for his work
    B someone who lived only for his money
    C someone who liked helping people
    D someone who lived only from one day to the next.

Here now are some suggested answers showing the thought and argument that goes into reaching a satisfactory decision.

1. Arriving at an answer to this question depends to some extent on knowing what 'livelong' means. However, going through the various alternatives can reduce the

number of possibilities. B is obviously not the answer since there is no suggestion in the passage that Silas Marner was lively and enthusiastic. D can also be eliminated since there is no mention of working on some days and not on others. It must therefore be either A or C. It might be felt that C with its use of the word 'livelihood' is a likely contender, but it is hardly the kind of phrase to use to describe the word 'day'. It must therefore be A. This is reinforced by the fact that a contrast is being made between 'day' at the beginning of the second sentence and 'night' at the beginning of the third. 'The whole length of the day' therefore makes good sense.

2. First, find the relevant words in the passage from which the answer must come. These are 'he sat in his loom, his ear filled with its monotony'. There is no suggestion in these words that the noise was A loud, C pleasant or D reverberant—though one or more of these might have been present. The descriptive word given is 'monotonous' which means B unvaried and repetitive.

3. Study the second sentence. Regularity, concentration and repetitiveness are all suggested, especially by the use of the image that were he to stop his work it would be as though his breathing had stopped. There is no hint that Silas Marner enjoyed his work. Therefore D is the answer.

4. Like question 1 the answer to this depends to some extent on having come across the word before. If you don't know the word 'revelry', perhaps you know the word 'to revel' or 'revels'. If 'revelry' means 'accounting' or 'locking up', why go on to mention both these things separately in the rest of the sentence? Wouldn't it be too obvious to say 'But at night came his evening activity'? That leaves only 'merry-making', and the use of the word can then be seen as an ironic comment on the kind of relaxation Silas Marner indulged in after the monotony of the day's work.

5. Almost one can decide that A is correct without testing the other alternatives. B is not applicable since the passage shows that Silas is unlikely to lend money to anyone. The corners referred to are the corners of the leather bags, not the room.

6. The salient words here are 'He loved the guineas best, but he would not change the silver . . . he loved them all'. The statement that fits these words is D.

7. Any statement that suggests that Silas was thinking about children is immediately out, so that eliminates B, C and D. There is no suggestion in the passage that he has or wants children. What the passage says is that the guineas were *like* children to him. A is therefore the closest in meaning.

8. A is unacceptable since there is no indication that Silas Marner is lively—rather the reverse. B is also out because there is no hint as to where Silas Marner used to live. The words say that Silas's life is 'like a rivulet' in some way, and C seems to explain this similarity. D can be rejected because there is no indication that Silas Marner wanted to collect herbs.

9. C is the answer here as 'like a rivulet' is a simile. The others are metaphors.

10. A is not correct, because Silas also lived to gloat over his money. There is no evidence for C. D is not convincing because the weaver did have a purpose in life,

namely to accumulate money. B is correct—working was a means to this end.

It should be clear from this that the thought processes that have to be gone through in order to reach a correct deduction are quite considerable. It is not just a case of picking the first solution that seems to make some kind of sense. You must go through all the possibilities, considering, judging and eliminating until there is only one that fits into the logic of the question and the information you have gathered from the passage.

3. Advice on How to Proceed

1. Read the passage carefully several times. As with any comprehension exercise it is not enough to skim through the passage quickly once and then assume that you will be able to answer the questions. Read the passage at least twice. Then read the questions and see where the information for the answers is to be found in the passage. Then read the passage again before you actually start to answer the questions.

2. Test the validity of each of the alternatives in turn. Isolate each of them in your mind and refer to the appropriate section of the passage before accepting or rejecting. Even when you are certain that the first solution given is the correct one, go on to check the others just to make sure.

3. Remember that it is the *most likely* solution that you are looking for, or the one that contains the *most truth*. There may be elements in each of the statements which could justifiably be considered correct, but it is the one that is 'most correct' (if that makes sense) that you are looking for.

4. If you don't know the answer and can't work it out, have a guess. The mathematical chances of your guessing correctly are rather slim, but you never know—you might be lucky! In any case, it's better than leaving a blank.

5. Most of the points made about comprehension exercises in *A New English Course* apply also to objective tests of this kind. Revise the appropriate sections in *A New English Course*: an approach to comprehension, pp. 9–11; revision, pp. 113–14; comprehension, pp. 196–9.

4. Assignment

Here is a multiple-choice comprehension of the type that you may be asked to undertake in your examination. Read the passage carefully and select the letter A, B, C or D in each of the questions that follow. You should take about one hour over this exercise.

Mr Bounderby was a rich man; banker, merchant, manufacturer, and what not. A big, loud man, with a stare, and a metallic laugh. A man made out of a coarse material, which seemed to have been stretched to make so much of him. A man with a great puffed head and 5 forehead, swelled veins in his temples, and such a

strained skin to his face that it seemed to hold his eyes open and lift his eyebrows up. A man with a pervading appearance on him of being inflated like a balloon, and
10 ready to start. A man who could never sufficiently vaunt himself a self-made man. A man who was always proclaiming, through that brassy speaking-trumpet of a voice of his, his old ignorance and his old poverty. A man who was the bully of humility.

15 A year or two younger than his eminently practical friend, Mr Bounderby looked older; his seven or eight and forty might have had the seven or eight added to it again, without surprising anybody. He had not much hair. One might have fancied he had talked it off; and
20 that what was left, all standing up in disorder, was in that condition from being constantly blown about by his windy boastfulness.

In the formal drawing-room of Stone Lodge, standing on the hearth-rug, warming himself before the fire, Mr
25 Bounderby delivered some observations to Mrs Gradgrind on the circumstances of its being his birthday. He stood before the fire, partly because it was a cool spring day, though the sun shone; partly because the shade of Stone Lodge was always haunted by the ghost of damp
30 mortar; partly because he thus took up a commanding position, from which to subdue Mrs Gradgrind.

'I hadn't a shoe to my foot. As to a stocking, I didn't know such a thing by name. I passed the day in a ditch, and the night in a pig-sty. That's the way I spent my
35 tenth birthday. Not that a ditch was new to me, for I was born in a ditch.'

Mrs Gradgrind, a little, thin, white, pink-eyed bundle of shawls, of surpassing feebleness, mental and bodily— who was always taking physic without any effect, and
40 who, whenever she showed a symptom of coming to life, was invariable stunned by some weighty piece of fact tumbling on her—Mrs Gradgrind hoped it was a dry ditch.

'No! As wet as a sop. A foot of water in it,' said Mr
45 Bounderby.

'Enough to give a baby cold,' Mrs Gradgrind considered.

'Cold? I was born with inflammation of the lungs, and of everything else, I believe, that was capable of in-
50 flammation,' returned Mr Bounderby. 'For years, ma'am, I was one of the most miserable little wretches ever seen. I was so sickly, that I was always moaning and groaning. I was so ragged and dirty, that you wouldn't have touched me with a pair of tongs.'

55 Mrs Gradgrind faintly looked at the tongs, as the most appropriate thing her imbecility could think of doing.

'How I fought through it, I don't know,' said Bounderby. 'I was determined, I suppose. I have been a deter-
60 mined character in later life, and I suppose I was then. Here I am, Mrs Gradgrind, anyhow, and nobody to thank for my being here but myself.'

Mrs Gradgrind meekly and weakly hoped that his mother—
65 'My mother? Bolted, ma'am!' said Bounderby.

Mrs Gradgrind, stunned as usual, collapsed and gave it up.

(CHARLES DICKENS, *Hard Times*)

210

1. Mr Bounderby's laugh was
   A hard and brassy
   B thin and high-pitched
   C loud and hollow
   D simpering and tremulous
2. When the passage says Mr Bounderby was 'made out of a coarse material, which seemed to have been stretched' (1. 3), it means
   A he had a rough skin
   B he had crude manners
   C he looked as though he could hardly hold in his fatness
   D his clothes were made of low-quality cloth.
3. *All* the following words are used to describe Mr Bounderby's physical grossness *except*
   A puffed (1. 5)
   B swelled (1. 6)
   C strained (1. 7)
   D pervading 1. 8).
4. Mr Bounderby 'could never sufficiently vaunt himself' (1. 10) means
   A he was always lying about being …
   B he could never have enough of boasting about being …
   C he never had enough of thinking about being …
   D he was always talking about being …
5. A 'self-made man' (1. 11) is
   A one who has made a success of his life through his own efforts
   B one who has made a lot of money
   C one who is very ambitious
   D one who is always thinking about himself.
6. When the writer says that Mr Bounderby was 'the bully of humility' (1. 14), he means the character was
   A humble and modest
   B always fighting and bullying other people
   C a defender of ambitious achievements
   D proud and boastful.
7. *All* the following words are used as metaphors *except*
   A metallic (1. 3)
   B a coarse material (1. 3)
   C a balloon (1. 9)
   D speaking-trumpet (1. 12).
8. Which *one* of the following qualities does Mr Bounderby *not* possess, judging from the first paragraph?
   A boastfulness
   B consideration for others
   C pomposity
   D conceit
9. When the passage says Mr Bounderby's friend was 'eminently practical' (1. 15), it means
   A he had a sound commonsense and got things done
   B he was good at making things
   C he was a man of distinction as a craftsman
   D he had a very thriving practice.
10. The writer imagines that Mr Bounderby is practically bald because
    A he is getting old
    B he talked so much that he was suffering from a disease
    C his loud boastfulness has blown his hair off
    D he doesn't wear a hat and the winds have blown his hair off.

11. While 'warming himself at the fire' (1. 24), Mr. Bounderby was

   A presenting Mrs Gradgrind with a birthday card

   B expressing his views on his birthday

   C wishing it were his birthday

   D looking about the room on his birthday.

12. Stone Lodge was

   A dank

   B warm

   C haunted

   D shady.

13. Mr Bounderby 'stood before the fire' (1. 27) for *all* the following reasons *except*

   A he wanted to be in a position of dominance

   B he was cold

   C he knew what the house was usually like

   D he was afraid of ghosts.

14. When the writer says Mr Bounderby wanted to 'subdue' (1. 31) Mrs Gradgrind, he means the character wanted to

   A flatter her

   B please her

   C intimidate her

   D impress her.

15. As a child, Mr Bounderby was

   A without any clothes

   B without a home to live in

   C fond of playing in ditches

   D employed looking after pigs.

16. One of these phrases describes Mrs Gradgrind:

   A fluffy and feminine

   B small and attractive

   C weak in mind and body

   D pink of complexion.

17. The word 'physic' (1. 39) means

   A advice

   B offence

   C exercise

   D medicine.

18. One of the following words is connected by context with the word 'physic' (1. 39)

   A stunned (1. 41)

   B weighty (1. 41)

   C symptom (1. 40)

   D fact (1. 41)

19. When the writer says Mrs Gradgrind 'was invariably stunned by some weighty piece of fact tumbling on her' (1. 41), he means

   A she was always having accidents

   B she could not face reality

   C she was in a state of concussion

   D she was constantly having things thrown at her.

20. When Mrs Gradgrind 'hoped it was a dry ditch' (1. 42), she was

   A trying to show concern for Mr Bounderby's past suffering

   B interested in finding out what the conditions were really like

   C being sarcastic at Mr Bounderby's expense

   D showing how bored she was with hearing Mr Bounderby's story.

21. 'As wet as a sop' (1. 44) is

   A a simile

   B a metaphor

   C a statement of fact

   D a non sequitur.

22. Mrs Gradgrind's reaction 'Enough to give a baby cold' (1. 46) is

   A too strong

   B too weak

   C too sympathetic

   D too cynical.

23. Mr Bounderby's statement 'I was born with inflammation of the lungs' (1. 48) is

   A a true statement of fact

   B a story he has been told by his mother

   C something he remembers with pain

   D a deliberate exaggeration for effect.

24. Mr Bounderby's statement 'and nobody to thank for my being here but myself' (1. 61) reinforces the earlier impression that he is

   A a good business man

   B an old man

   C a self-made man

   D a commanding man.

25. When the writer says Mrs Gradgrind 'gave it up' (1. 66), he means she

   A gave up any effort to comprehend a world entirely alien to her

   B wanted to know what the real facts were

   C asked Mr Bounderby what 'bolted' meant

   D lost consciousness.

Now study the suggested answers given below and compare them with your own.

1. A	2. C	3. D	4. B	5. A	6. D	7. C
8. B	9. A	10. C	11. B	12. A	13. D	14. C
15. B	16. C	17. D	18. C	19. B	20. A	21. A
22. B	23. D	24. C	25. A			

5. Instructions

Since multiple tests of this kind are marked by computers, very careful directions have to be given to candidates about how they should fill in their answers. Below is a typical example of the kind of instructions that are given. It is in itself a comprehension exercise. Study these directions carefully. They may not be exactly the same as those that will be issued when you yourself sit the examination, but at least they will give you an indication of the kind of thing to expect, and you will not be taken by surprise.

for the General Certificate of Education

SURNAME ....INITIALS............CENTRE NAME......................

June Examination, 1976—Ordinary Level

ENGLISH LANGUAGE (READING COMPREHENSION)

Paper 2   **069/2**

Tuesday, 8 June, 2.00 p.m. to 2.50 p.m.

50 minutes allowed

After reading the whole of this page ask the invigilator if you do not understand any point.

INSTRUCTIONS

1. Do not break the seal on this booklet until told to do so by the invigilator.
2. Your position must be clear of all materials except HB pencils, a ruler, and your statement of entry.
3. If working is necessary, use the blank pages or spaces in the question booklet not the answer sheet.
4. No booklet (including any blank pages) may be taken out of the examination room.
5. Print, in block letters, your Name and the Centre Name in the spaces provided at the top of this page.
6. Without breaking the seal, take out your answer sheet from inside the front cover of the booklet. Check that the columns headed Subject Number have 069 already entered in them.
7. Write, in pencil, your Names and the Subject Title in the spaces provided on the answer sheet.

8. Enter, in the blank boxes provided on the answer sheet:

   (i) Your six-digit Centre Number;
   (ii) Your four-digit Candidate's Number.

   In the columns below these mark the appropriate numbers with horizontal lines by joining the guide marks. Do not let the line extend into the next box. Make bold, not feint, marks.

   A completed **example** is shown here.

Centre No.
1 7 5 0 2 6
0 0 0 0 0 0
1 1 1 1 1 1
2 2 2 2 2 2
3 3 3 3 3 3
4 4 4 4 4 4
5 5 5 5 5 5
6 6 6 6 6 6
7 7 7 7 7 7
8 8 8 8 8 8
9 9 9 9 9 9

Candidate's No.
0 0 9 5
0 0 0 0
1 1 1 1
2 2 2 2
3 3 3 3
4 4 4 4
5 5 5 5
6 6 6 6
7 7 7 7
8 8 8 8
E 9 0 9

ANSWERING THE QUESTIONS

9. Attempt all items. Each correct answer will score 1 mark. No deduction will be made for wrong answers.
10. Each item has 4 possible answers lettered A to D. Select your answer and indicate it on the answer sheet by drawing a bold horizontal line through the appropriate letter; e.g. if the answer to item 8 is thought to be C it should appear as:

8. | A   B   C   D |

Only one answer must be indicated. Any other form of answering is incorrect and will not score.

11. If you change your mind shade in the bottom half of the square you have marked and draw a line through the letter you now think correct; e.g. to cancel C and enter A instead it should appear as:

8 | A   B   C   D |

12. If you are not sure of the answer to an item do not linger over it, but pass on to the next item. If time permits you can return later to re-consider omitted items.
13. All answer sheets have provision for 90 items. Start at 1 and use only the spaces required for the test.

SPECIAL INSTRUCTION—The passage printed on a separate sheet is to be
read before answering the questions

© 1976 AEB

Appendix II

SPOKEN ENGLISH

It is likely that your examination will include a test on spoken English. However, this test can take a number of different forms, and examining boards vary in their requirements. It is therefore important that you check with your teacher or tutor to make sure you know what will be expected of you in the examination you will be taking.

Any test in spoken English will require you to be able to speak in a way that is audible, intelligible and appropriate to the situation being examined. The best preparation for this kind of test is to listen to good examples of the use of the spoken word (as in radio programmes like *Today, Woman's Hour, PM, Any Questions*) and of course to practise. It is a good idea to get someone to listen to you and to comment. Alternatively, you could record yourself, listen critically to the replay and record again.

Different oral tests require different skills, so it is useful to be aware of the various forms the test can take, the kinds of skill needed, and the kinds of audience aimed at.

1. Reading Aloud

In this test you will be given a passage lasting about three minutes which you will be expected to read aloud. You will be given ten minutes or so to read over the passage and prepare the reading.

The examiner will be looking for the following:

(a) clear diction, a reasonable speed and accurate observance of the punctuation;
(b) a pitch of voice that is audible and appropriate, together with variations as required by the text;
(c) the ability to interpret the text and make it dramatically interesting;
(d) a clear indication that the reader has understood the text.

The ten minutes allowed for preparation of the passage are clearly important. In that time, you must read the passage several times to really understand what it is about and also to decide to what extent it needs to be dramatised (for instance, the use of different voices or different tones if dialogue is involved, though this should not be overdone or exaggerated). Should the passage all be read at one pace, or should certain sections or sentences be faster or slower than others? Are there places where dramatic pauses would be appropriate? Is the basic tone serious or light? Emotional or ironic? Factual or intended to persuade?

If while practising you are unable to read aloud, then at least try to hear the words sounding in your head as you go through them.

When it comes to the actual test, remember that the purpose of reading aloud is to get your listener interested in what you are reading. Looking up from the passage every now and then and making eye-contact with your listener is a good idea so long as this does not disrupt the reading. Nothing is more boring for a listener than a constant image of the top of the reader's head.

Take your time. Don't rush at it and read too fast.

Try to let your eye take in the words ahead as you speak so that you can prepare the voice for what is coming and can modulate it appropriately.

It is possible that you will be allowed to choose your own passage for reading aloud. You may be expected to introduce it by setting it in its context if it is an extract from a novel or a longer piece, or by explaining why you have chosen this particular passage. A clear confident account that shows enthusiasm is what is wanted here, with good eye-contact with the listener, not an apologetic mumbling and squinting at notes.

You may be asked questions on the passage you have read. This is another reason why it is important to make sure you have understood the passage. The comprehension exercises in *A New English Course* should give you an idea of the kind of question that may be asked and the kind of answer required.

For practice, prepare several of the following passages for reading aloud. Practise actually reading aloud. Or record them on a cassette recorder. Ask someone to comment on your reading. Try it again.

Extract from *Room at the Top*—page 5
Extract from *Three Fingers are Plenty*—page 13
Extract from *The History of Mr Polly*—page 30
Extract from *Shane*—page 33
Article by Michael Frayn—page 44
Article from *The Listener*—page 55
'Witches' Loaves' by O. Henry—page 69
'Fur' by Saki—page 73
'Salvatore' by Somerset Maugham—page 78
'The Linesman' by Janet Frame—page 80
Extract from *English Journey*—page 110
Extract from *Pride and Prejudice*—page 133
'Dulce et Decorum Est' by Wilfred Owen—page 151
'My Last Duchess' by Robert Browning—page 161
Extract from *Three Men in a Boat*—page 186

Listen to how stories and novels are read on such radio programmes as *Morning Story, Woman's Hour, Story Time, A Book at Bedtime* and *Schools Broadcasts*.

2. Conversation/Discussion

In this test you, either alone or as one of four or five other candidates, will be required to talk about a subject chosen with the examiner or in the presence of the examiner. The discussion would last about fifteen minutes. You will be expected to put ideas clearly and convincingly, to give examples and instances to support views, to consider the arguments presented by other speakers. You must show your awareness of the full implications of the subject under discussion.

Here are some points to remember:

Say something! If you sit silent, you will get no marks.

Be polite—don't interrupt other speakers or make rude comments about what they say.

Don't make your contribution and then sit back and take no further part in the discussion.

Listen to what others have to say. Try to use their comments as a launching pad for your own ideas. Agree and add, or oppose and explain why.

Take the lead and steer the discussion in a new direction where you can contribute.

Avoid tiresome mannerisms of speech such as beginning every sentence with 'Well'.

Choosing a subject is important. It must be one that you know something about, and it must be one on which there is plenty to say. Having chosen your subject or subjects, start collecting notes on it, in the way you would for an argumentative essay (see pages 49–51). Read the newspapers regularly. Watch opinion and research programmes on television such as *Panorama*, *World in Action*, *TV Eye*, *Question Time* and listen to radio's *Any Questions* and *You the Jury*. Compare how events are reported in newspapers and on television. Keep adding new ideas to your notes so that you build up a supply of information and ideas about your subject. Raise the subject with family and friends. See what they think. Try out some of your ideas. Try to convince other people that your ideas are the right ones or listen to what they have to say and modify your opinions.

Here are some subjects you may care to consider:

space exploration
football hooliganism
racial prejudice
the police
strikes
crime
nationalisation and privatisation
marriage
divorce
abortion
old age
animal experimentation
public schools
the supernatural
unemployment
television
capital punishment
fashion
violence
equal opportunity
advertising
pollution.

214

Choose two or three of these subjects and make notes on different arguments or aspects you might develop. Write a talk you might give on one of them or write an essay. If possible, form a group with three or four other people and discuss the subject.

Use each of the following as the basis for a class or group discussion:

the extract from *The Times Educational Supplement*—page 41
the article by Michael Frayn—page 44
'Pros and Cons of Advertising'—page 55
'Arms and the Policeman'—page 112
'No Old-School Ties'—page 136
'Other Lives at Risk'—page 137
'Whose Responsibility?'—page 137
'Talking Suburban Posh'—page 138
'Wild Over the West'—page 148
'Latin Lovers: For and Against'—page 177.

3. Prepared Talk

The oral test may take the form of a prepared talk. It could be a speech presenting a point of view as in a debate, or it could be a talk about something you know well such as a hobby or a special interest.

In some ways, a prepared talk combines the skills needed for reading aloud and for discussion. The talker must engage the interest of the audience by his or her presence and presentation. You must speak clearly and give variety to your manner of speaking. You should look at the audience. But a prepared talk is *not* a written speech that is read out. You may refer to notes, but must not simply read out an essay. You must keep your eyes on your audience.

Above all, as a speaker you must have an enthusiasm for your subject and be able to communicate that enthusiasm.

As in discussion, you should have gathered together a number of ideas and arguments to present and know how to present them. But much more careful preparation and organisation are needed in a prepared talk. You will be entirely alone and cannot rely on other people to help with ideas.

The talk must have an interesting introduction which catches the attention of the audience. It must be clearly and logically developed so that the audience is involved and can feel that it is learning something. It must have a firm and definite conclusion and not just fade away as though the talker has run out of things to say.

Where possible, visual material should be used which you can refer to and which can illustrate the talk. For instance, maps, diagrams, models, pictures, photographs. These are likely to arouse a greater interest in the audience and provide you with something to hang your talk on. But it must always be remembered that it is the spoken word that is being tested and the fluency of the speaker. Too many visual aids could become a distraction from this.

The speaker will also be required to show skill in answering questions from the audience about the talk. This is another reason why you must choose a subject that you are something of an expert in. It is vital that you have enough confidence in your own knowledge to be able to answer any question that may arise.

Choose a subject for a prepared talk. It could be a hobby, a special interest, a subject on which you have done research, a subject about which you feel strongly, one of the subjects listed under 'Conversation/Discussion'. Make notes on your subject. Arrange your notes in order. Find visual material for your talk. Give your talk. Listen to any comments that could help you to improve the content or presentation of your talk.

4. Drama

A fourth type of oral test is drama, scripted or improvised. In scripted drama the same kind of skills needed in reading aloud are required. This is normally a group activity, and the candidate has to respond to the words and reactions of other members of the group, but what is being tested is the same—the ability to use spoken language clearly and appropriately to the situation. As with prepared talks, 'visual material' can be used to enhance the presentation—things like costume, make-up, gesture—but the emphasis is still on the spoken word. No amount of 'dressing up' will compensate for inarticulate speech or inappropriate delivery. It should be remembered too that you are not being judged on whether or not you can *act*. It is verbal communication that matters in this context. Do you understand the distinction?

Similarly, in improvised drama, it is the effectiveness of the words that counts and the way they are conveyed. Through speech, the candidate must show an understanding of the role being played and develop it convincingly and expressively.

Find a suitable scene from one of the following plays for presentation:

An Inspector Calls: J. B. Priestley
Spring and Port Wine: Bill Naughton
A Taste of Honey: Shelagh Delaney
The Long and the Short and the Tall: Willis Hall
Hobson's Choice: Harold Brighouse
Saint Joan: G. B. Shaw
A Man for All Seasons: Robert Bolt

Look Back in Anger: John Osborne
The Winslow Boy: Terence Rattigan
The Caretaker: Harold Pinter
Roots: Arnold Wesker
Under Milk Wood: Dylan Thomas
The Crucible: Arthur Miller

Choose one of the following situations to develop as an improvised scene:

1. The family reaction when one of the children arrives home late.
2. A row between two neighbouring families.
3. The leader of a gang has a rival for leadership.
4. A team that has lost carries out a post mortem.
5. A family discusses where to go on holiday.
6. A school council meeting discusses school dinners.
7. A group of children at play when there is an accident.
8. A group of people trapped underground by an explosion.

5. Aural

As well as a test in spoken English, some examinations may include an aural test. This is in a sense the opposite of speaking. It is an exercise in listening. Find out from your teacher or tutor whether your examination includes an aural test.

What usually happens is this. A recording is played containing material that is informative or argumentative. The subject matter will be of topical or general interest. It could be in the form of a conversation. The recording is played twice, first for listening and secondly to allow you to take notes. You will then be asked to use your notes to answer questions in writing. The questions are designed to test your recall of what is said and how it is said. You may be asked to use your notes to write a letter or a report or a summary or a speech.

Study the advice given on pages 138 to 140 on writing summaries. The process you would use in an aural test of this type is similar.

For practice, listen to a five-minute news summary on radio or television. Make notes on the various items reported. Write a letter to the radio or television station, approving or disapproving of the importance given to each item, judging from the sequence in which they are broadcast and the amount of time devoted to each.

Appendix III

COURSE WORK

Part of the assessment of your final mark in your examination will be based on course work, unless you are an external candidate. The requirements of the various examining boards differ, so check with your teacher or tutor whether or not course work is a component or an option of the particular examination you are taking.

Course work is work produced by the candidate in the course of the two years leading up to the examination. Some of the work may have to be produced in the classroom under examination conditions. But if course work is part of the examination you are studying for, then it means that not everything depends on the final papers you sit when you are probably taking other subjects as well. It is a way of spreading the load, of compensating for possible examination nerves, and perhaps allowing you to give a fairer and truer impression of your abilities.

Details are likely to vary from board to board so it is important that you study the syllabus or seek guidance from your teacher or tutor. You may be asked to provide a folder of eight to ten pieces of work produced in the two years leading up to the examination. This should be representative of your best work. The pieces should show a variety of different kinds of writing, for instance, imaginative writing, poetry, writing about literature, letters, argumentative essays. A piece of imaginative writing would normally be expected to be about 600 words long. A poem might be 12 or 15 lines, though it would not be essential to include a poem. All pieces must be submitted in their original form—in other words, they must not be fair copies of corrected work. Any candidate who produces fewer than the specified number of pieces would be in danger of getting no marks.

Work steadily at producing pieces for your folder. There should be no problem about writing the pieces in two years, but the idea is to select *your best work*. Clearly, the more you have produced, the greater choice you have when it comes to your final selection. Don't leave it all until the last two weeks and then expect to be able to come up with enough pieces of good work. You won't do it!

Advice on how to approach the different kinds of writing required for course work is given in *A New English Course* as follows:

> imaginative writing—pages 8–9, 16–21, 29–32, 38–41, 57–59, 66–68, 76–81, 155–157, 163–165, 179–181
> argumentative writing—pages 49–51
> response to literature—pages 96–98, 151–152
> letters—pages 119–120, 125–127, 135–138.

Acknowledgements

The author and publishers wish to thank the following for permission to reprint copyright material:

The Bodley Head for the extract from *Fur* by Saki; W. H. Allen and Co for the extract from *The Loneliness of the Long Distance Runner* by Alan Sillitoe; J. M. Dent and Sons Ltd for the extract from *The Railway Game* by Clifford Dyment and the extract from *Three Men in a Boat* by J. K. Jerome; Macdonald and Jane's for the extract from *The Polyglots* by William Gerhardie; Peter Davies Ltd for the extract from *The Daughters of Time* by Josephine Tey, the extract from *Below Stairs* by Margaret Powell and the extract from *It Isn't all Greek to Me* by Peter Bull; Jonathan Cape Ltd for the extract from *Roots* by Arnold Wesker from *The Wesker Trilogy*; Rupert Hart-Davis Ltd for the extract from *The Other Foot* by Ray Bradbury and the extract from *All Men are Islands* by Ronald Duncan; Valentine Mitchell for the extract from *Ash on a Young Man's Sleeve* by Dannie Abse, London 1971; Eyre Methuen for the extract from *Room at the Top* by John Braine; Thames and Hudson Ltd for the extract from *A Cack-handed War* by Edward Blishen; Martin Secker and Warburg Ltd for the extract from *The Last Grain Race* by Eric Newby and the extract from *A Little Companion* by Angus Wilson from *Such Darling Dodos*; William Heinemann Ltd for the extract from *English Journey* by J. B. Priestley; Associated Book Publishers Ltd for the extract from *Request Stop* by Harold Pinter from *A Slight Ache and Other Plays*; André Deutsch Ltd for the extract from *Shane* by Jack Shaefer; Faber and Faber Ltd for the extract from *A Voice through a Cloud* by Denton Welch; Weidenfeld Ltd for the extract from *Jerusalem the Golden* by Margaret Drabble; the Estate of W. Somerset Maugham and William Heinemann Ltd for the extract from *Salvatore* by Somerset Maugham;

Radio Times for the article 'Lost and Found'; Secker & Warburg Ltd and Laurence Lerner for 'Sledging' from *Selected Poems* (1984); Hilary Brocklehurst and *The Guardian* for 'Why the Arguments for Uniform are Wearing Rather Thin'; letters from *Education Guardian* are reprinted with permission of *The Guardian*; Abbey National Building Society (for Interest Rates summary used on p. 16).

It has not been possible in all cases to trace copyright holders; the publishers would be glad to hear from any such unacknowledged copyright holders.

List of Illustrations

Index of Authors and Titles Used

Index of Topics

(The main references only are given)